EERIE™

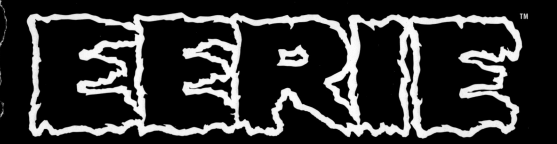

President and Publisher **MIKE RICHARDSON**
Editors **SIERRA HAHN, BRENDAN WRIGHT,** and **PHILIP R. SIMON**
Assistant Editors **IAN TUCKER** and **JEMIAH JEFFERSON**
Consulting Editor **DAN BRAUN**
Collection Designer **ETHAN KIMBERLING**
Digital Art Technicians **RYAN JORGENSEN** and **ADAM PRUETT**

Published by Dark Horse Books
A division of Dark Horse Comics, Inc.
10956 SE Main Street
Milwaukie, Oregon 97222

DarkHorse.com

First edition: April 2016
ISBN 978-1-61655-880-2

1 3 5 7 9 10 8 6 4 2
Printed in China

This book collects issues #1–#8 of the *Eerie* comic book series published by Dark Horse Comics from 2012 to 2015.

EERIE™ VOLUME 1: EXPERIMENTS IN TERROR

COMICS
2012-2015

DARK HORSE BOOKS

CONTENTS

All Story Lettering: Nate Piekos of Blambot®

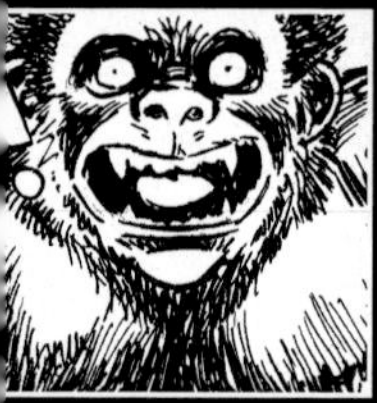

EERIE #1

Cover Art: Jim Pavelec **Frontispiece:** Jonathan Case

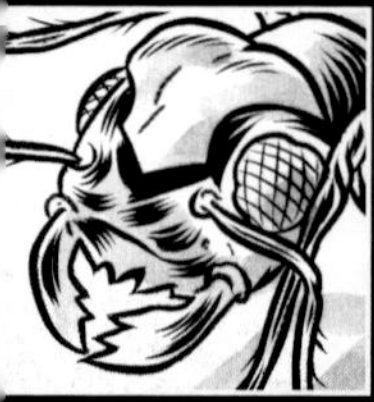

EERIE #2

Cover Art: Jim Pavelec **Frontispiece:** Rafael Grampá

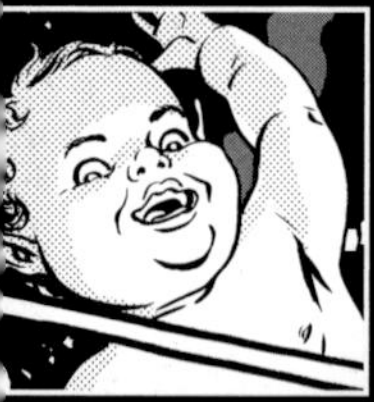

EERIE #3

Cover Art: Jim Pavelec **Frontispiece:** Paul Chadwick

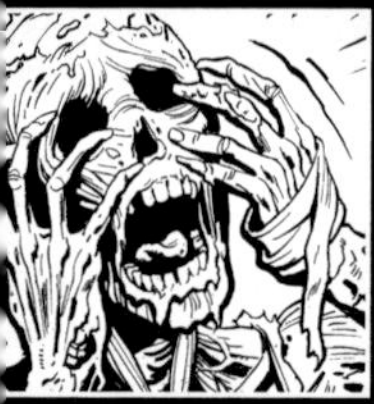

EERIE #4

Cover Art: Jim Pavelec **Frontispiece:** Howard Chaykin with Ken Bruzenak

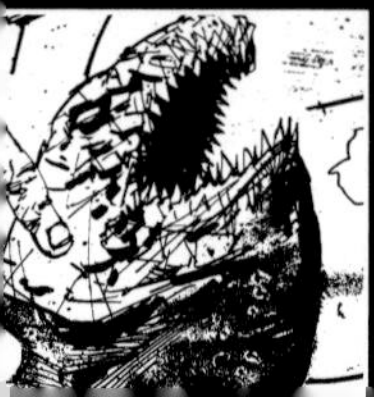

EERIE #5

Cover Art: Jim Pavelec **Frontispiece:** Damon Gentry

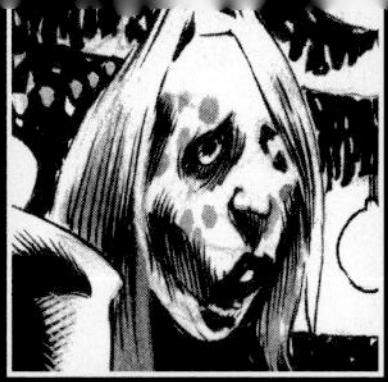

EERIE #6

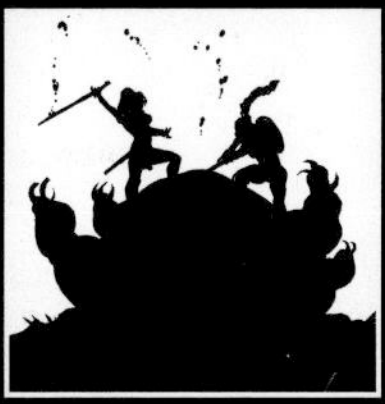

EERIE #7

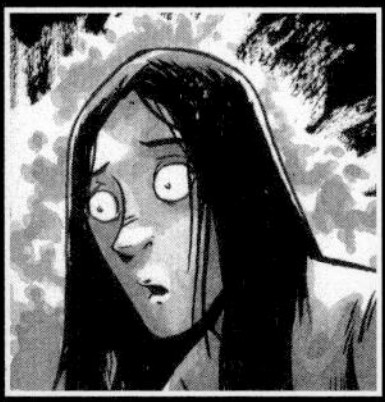

EERIE #8

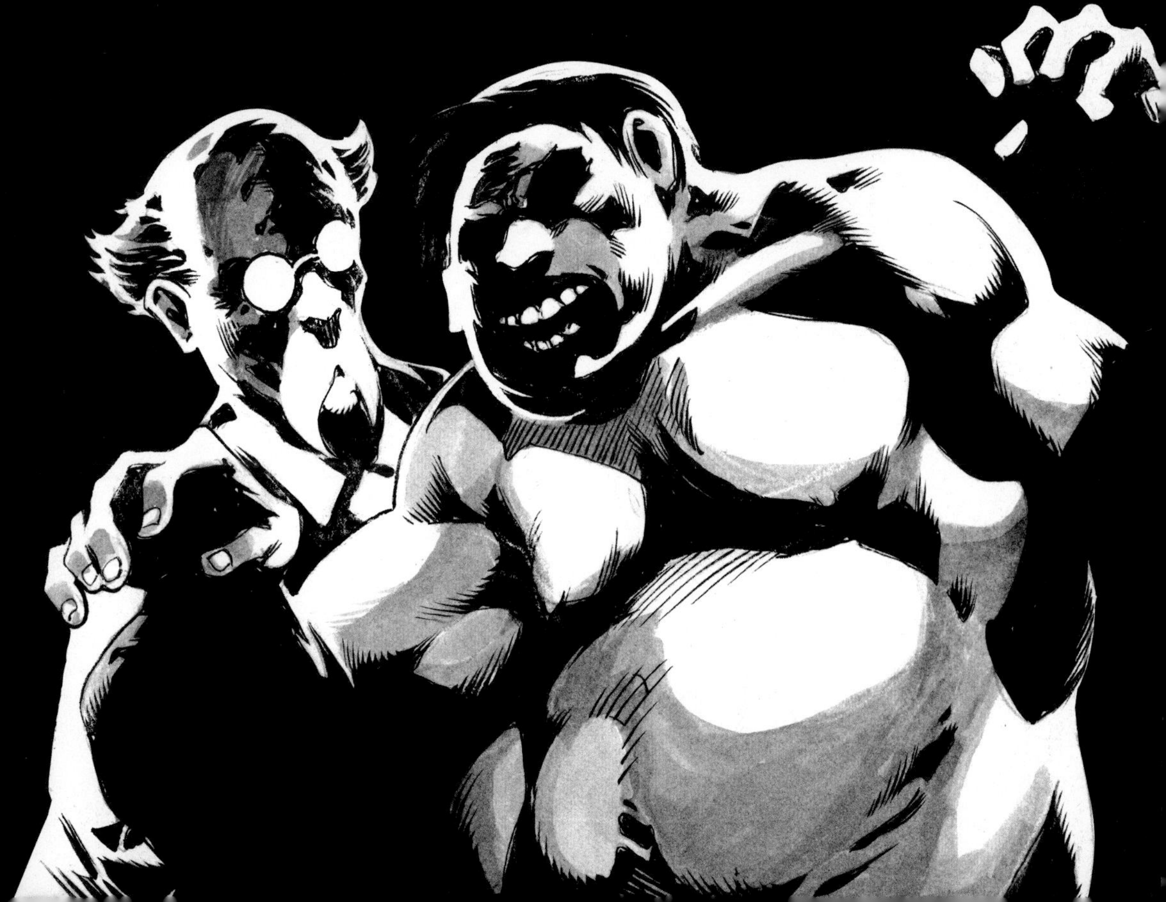

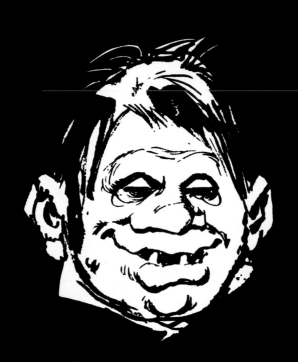

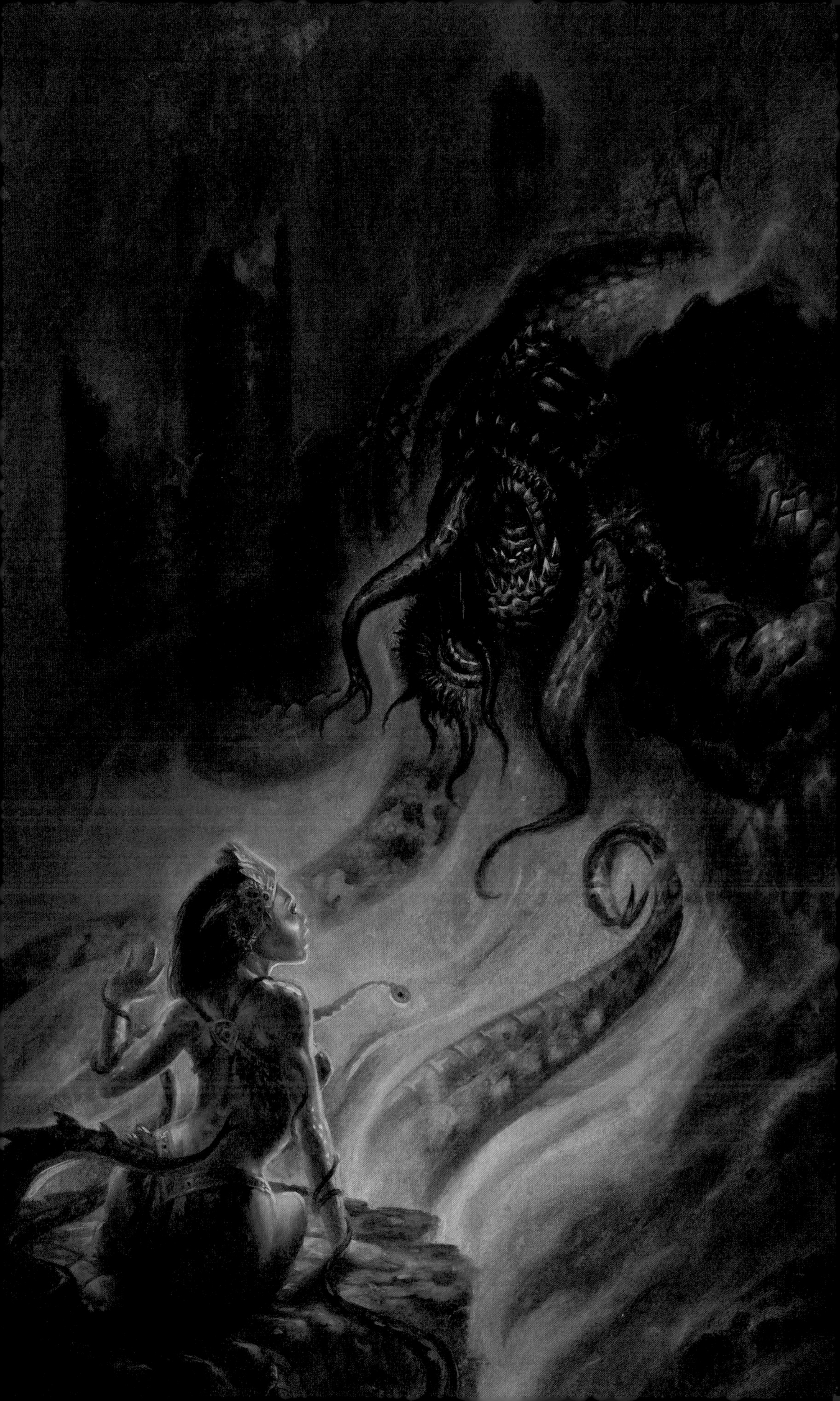

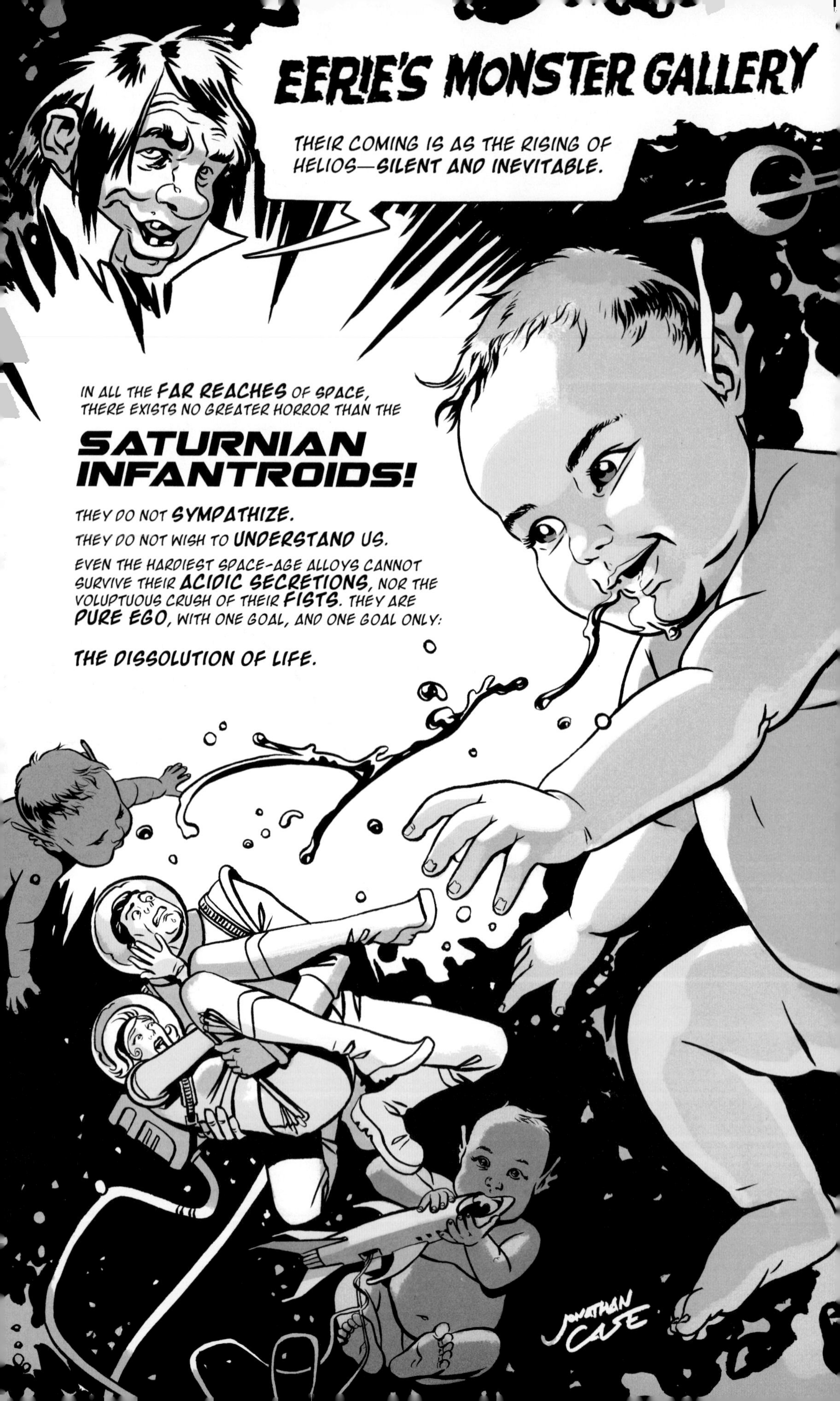
EERIE'S MONSTER GALLERY
THEIR COMING IS AS THE RISING OF HELIOS—SILENT AND INEVITABLE.
IN ALL THE FAR REACHES OF SPACE, THERE EXISTS NO GREATER HORROR THAN THE
SATURNIAN INFANTROIDS!
THEY DO NOT SYMPATHIZE.
THEY DO NOT WISH TO UNDERSTAND US.
EVEN THE HARDIEST SPACE-AGE ALLOYS CANNOT SURVIVE THEIR ACIDIC SECRETIONS, NOR THE VOLUPTUOUS CRUSH OF THEIR FISTS. THEY ARE PURE EGO, WITH ONE GOAL, AND ONE GOAL ONLY:
THE DISSOLUTION OF LIFE.
JONATHAN CASE

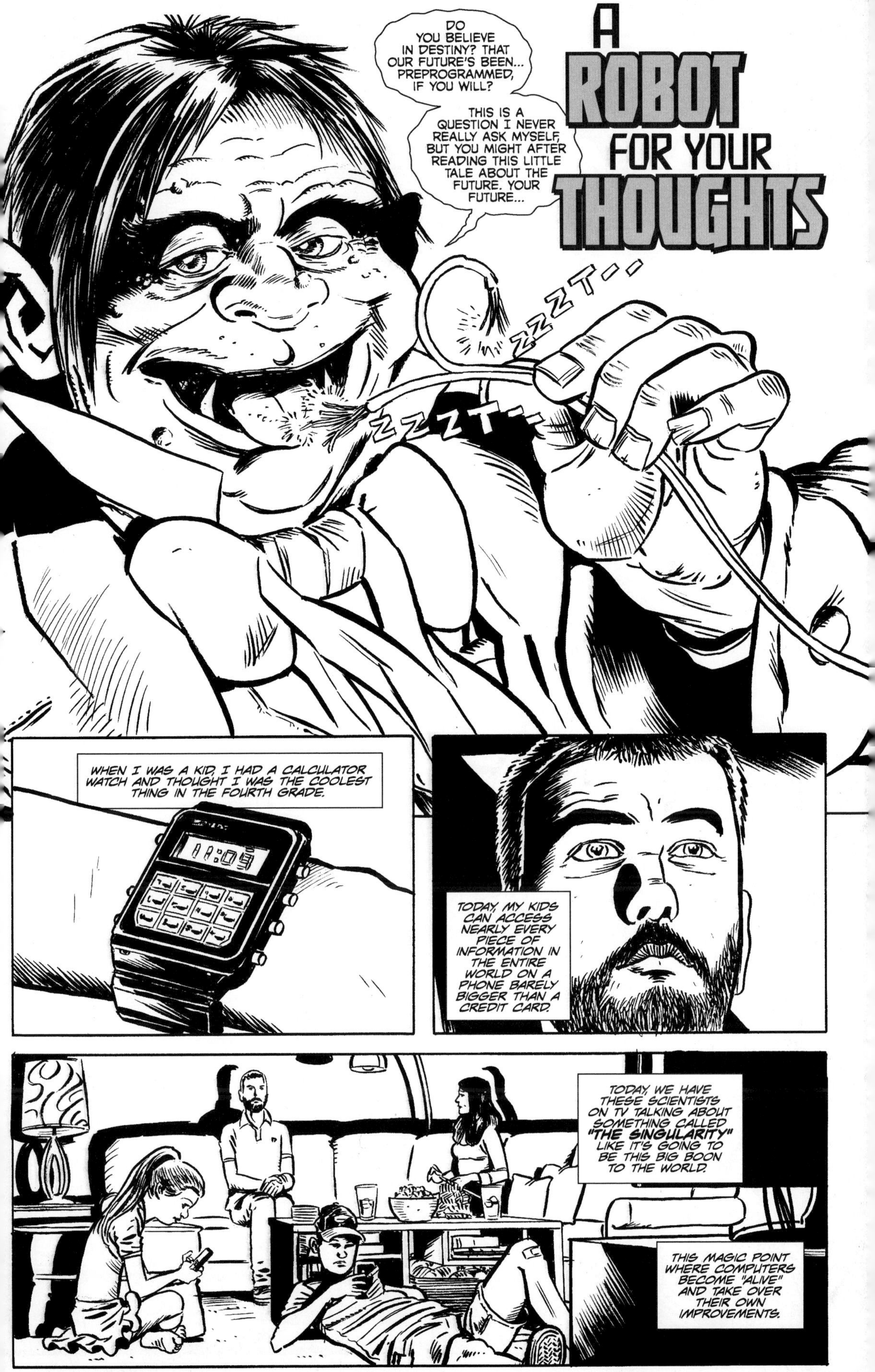
A ROBOT FOR YOUR THOUGHTS
DO YOU BELIEVE IN DESTINY? THAT OUR FUTURE'S BEEN... PREPROGRAMMED, IF YOU WILL?
THIS IS A QUESTION I NEVER REALLY ASK MYSELF, BUT YOU MIGHT AFTER READING THIS LITTLE TALE ABOUT THE FUTURE. YOUR FUTURE...
ZZZZT--
ZZZT--
WHEN I WAS A KID, I HAD A CALCULATOR WATCH AND THOUGHT I WAS THE COOLEST THING IN THE FOURTH GRADE.
TODAY, MY KIDS CAN ACCESS NEARLY EVERY PIECE OF INFORMATION IN THE ENTIRE WORLD ON A PHONE BARELY BIGGER THAN A CREDIT CARD.
TODAY, WE HAVE THESE SCIENTISTS ON TV TALKING ABOUT SOMETHING CALLED "THE SINGULARITY" LIKE IT'S GOING TO BE THIS BIG BOON TO THE WORLD.
THIS MAGIC POINT WHERE COMPUTERS BECOME "ALIVE" AND TAKE OVER THEIR OWN IMPROVEMENTS.

Script and Art by DAVID LAPHAM

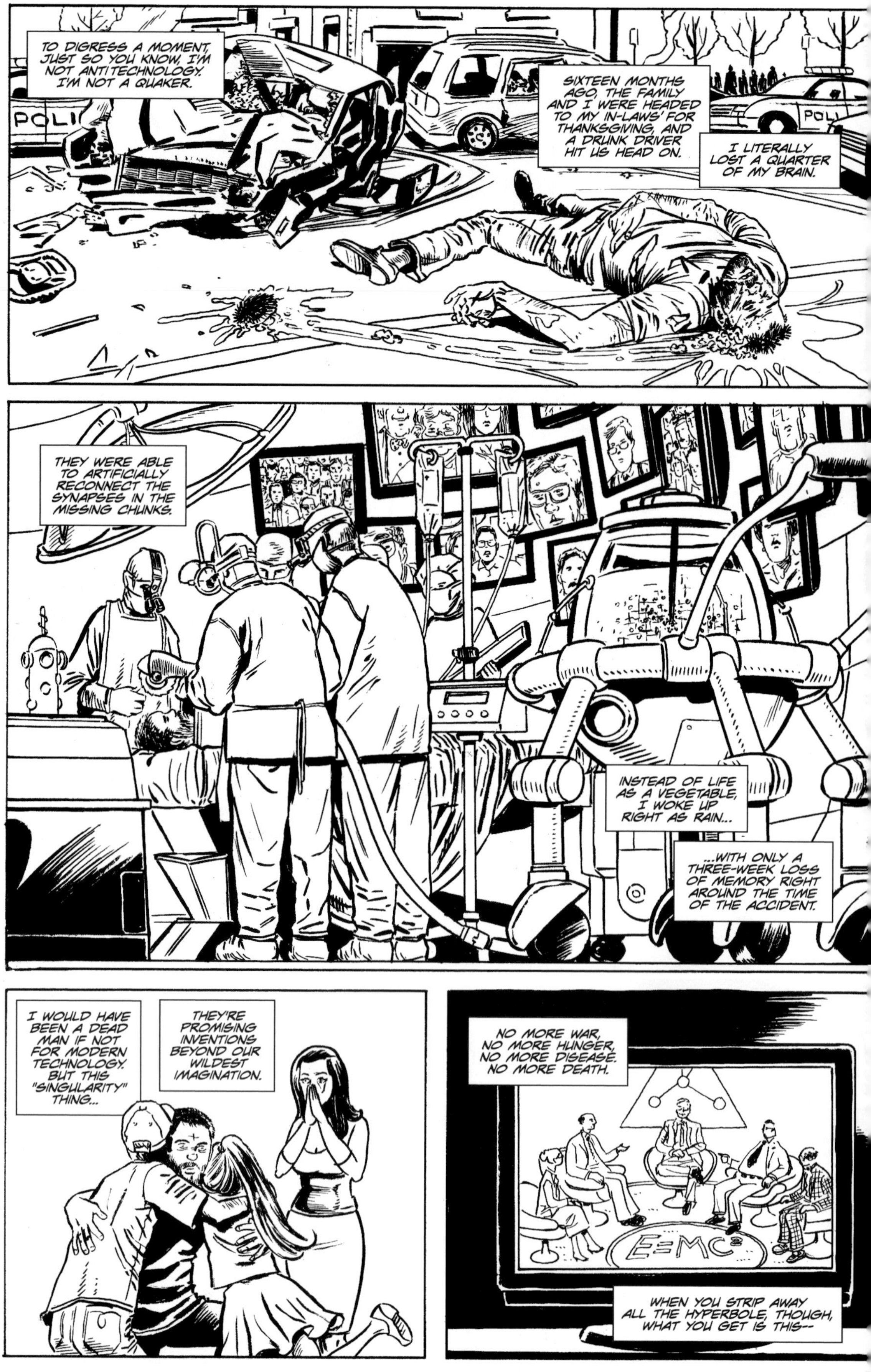
TO DIGRESS A MOMENT, JUST SO YOU KNOW, I'M NOT ANTITECHNOLOGY. I'M NOT A QUAKER.
SIXTEEN MONTHS AGO, THE FAMILY AND I WERE HEADED TO MY IN-LAWS' FOR THANKSGIVING, AND A DRUNK DRIVER HIT US HEAD ON.
I LITERALLY LOST A QUARTER OF MY BRAIN.
POLI
POLI
THEY WERE ABLE TO ARTIFICIALLY RECONNECT THE SYNAPSES IN THE MISSING CHUNKS.
INSTEAD OF LIFE AS A VEGETABLE, I WOKE UP RIGHT AS RAIN...
...WITH ONLY A THREE-WEEK LOSS OF MEMORY RIGHT AROUND THE TIME OF THE ACCIDENT.
I WOULD HAVE BEEN A DEAD MAN IF NOT FOR MODERN TECHNOLOGY. BUT THIS "SINGULARITY" THING...
THEY'RE PROMISING INVENTIONS BEYOND OUR WILDEST IMAGINATION.
NO MORE WAR, NO MORE HUNGER, NO MORE DISEASE. NO MORE DEATH.
E=MC²
WHEN YOU STRIP AWAY ALL THE HYPERBOLE, THOUGH, WHAT YOU GET IS THIS--

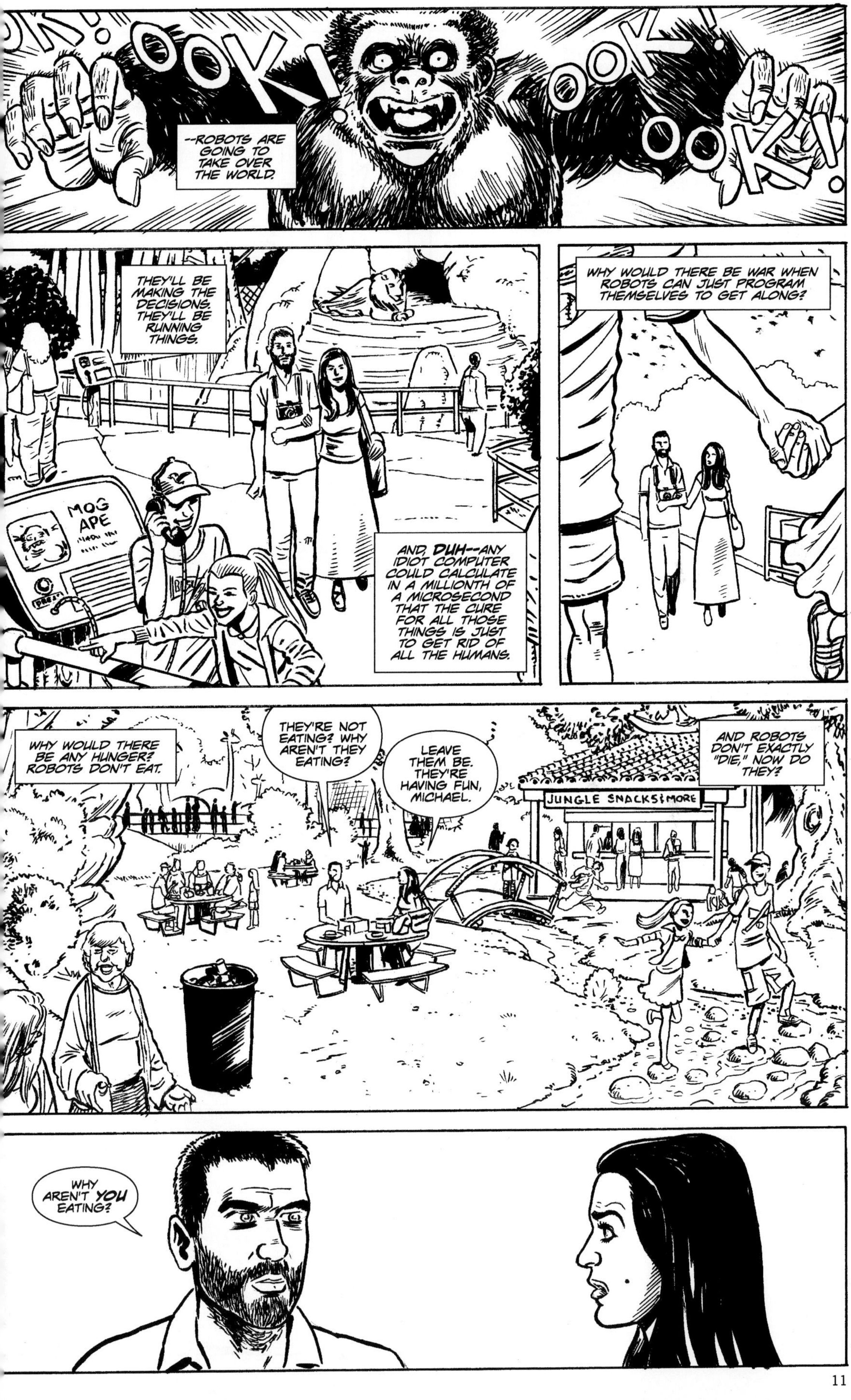
OOK! OOK! OOK! OOK!
--ROBOTS ARE GOING TO TAKE OVER THE WORLD.
THEY'LL BE MAKING THE DECISIONS. THEY'LL BE RUNNING THINGS.
MOG APE
AND, DUH--ANY IDIOT COMPUTER COULD CALCULATE IN A MILLIONTH OF A MICROSECOND THAT THE CURE FOR ALL THOSE THINGS IS JUST TO GET RID OF ALL THE HUMANS.
WHY WOULD THERE BE WAR WHEN ROBOTS CAN JUST PROGRAM THEMSELVES TO GET ALONG?
WHY WOULD THERE BE ANY HUNGER? ROBOTS DON'T EAT.
THEY'RE NOT EATING? WHY AREN'T THEY EATING?
LEAVE THEM BE. THEY'RE HAVING FUN, MICHAEL.
JUNGLE SNACKS & MORE
AND ROBOTS DON'T EXACTLY "DIE," NOW DO THEY?
WHY AREN'T YOU EATING?

EARLY WARNING FORUM
HOME ABOUT GALLERY CHAT PRIVATE FORUMS
EW
CHAT
MIKEISAMAN: HELLO.
ROBOTFIGHTER149: DID YOU READ ABOUT WHAT THE JAPANESE ARE DOING?
MIKEISAMAN: YOU MEAN ABOUT THE CAR THAT DRIVES ITSELF?
ROBOTFIGHTER149: DEATH TRAPS YOU MEAN.
MIKEISAMAN: I'M LESS CONCERNED ABOUT THAT AND MORE WORRIED ABOUT THIS SINGULARITY THING.
EARLY WARNING FORUM
HOME ABOUT GALLERY CHAT PRIVATE FORUMS
EW
CHAT
DAVE375: IT'S ALREADY HAPPENED.
MIKEISAMAN: HELLO. ARE YOU NEW TO THE FORUM?
DAVE375: YES. HELLO. I'M DAVE.
EARLY WARNING FORUM
HOME ABOUT GALLERY CHAT PRIVATE FORUMS
EW
CHAT
MIKEISAMAN: WHAT DID YOU MEAN? WHAT'S HAPPENED?
DAVE375: THE SINGULARITY. IT HAPPENED TWO YEARS AGO. THEY JUST DON'T WANT US TO KNOW ABOUT IT.
MIKEISAMAN: THEY?
EARLY WARNING FORUM
HOME ABOUT GALLERY CHAT PRIVATE FORUMS
EW
CHAT
DAVE375: THE ROBOTS.

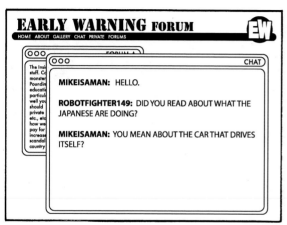

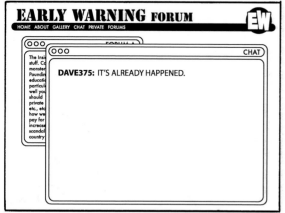

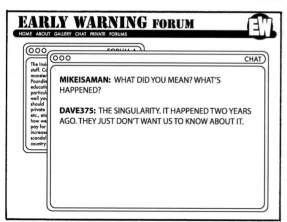

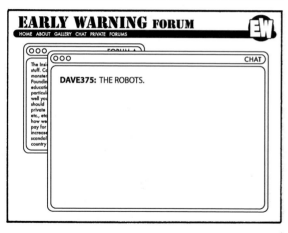

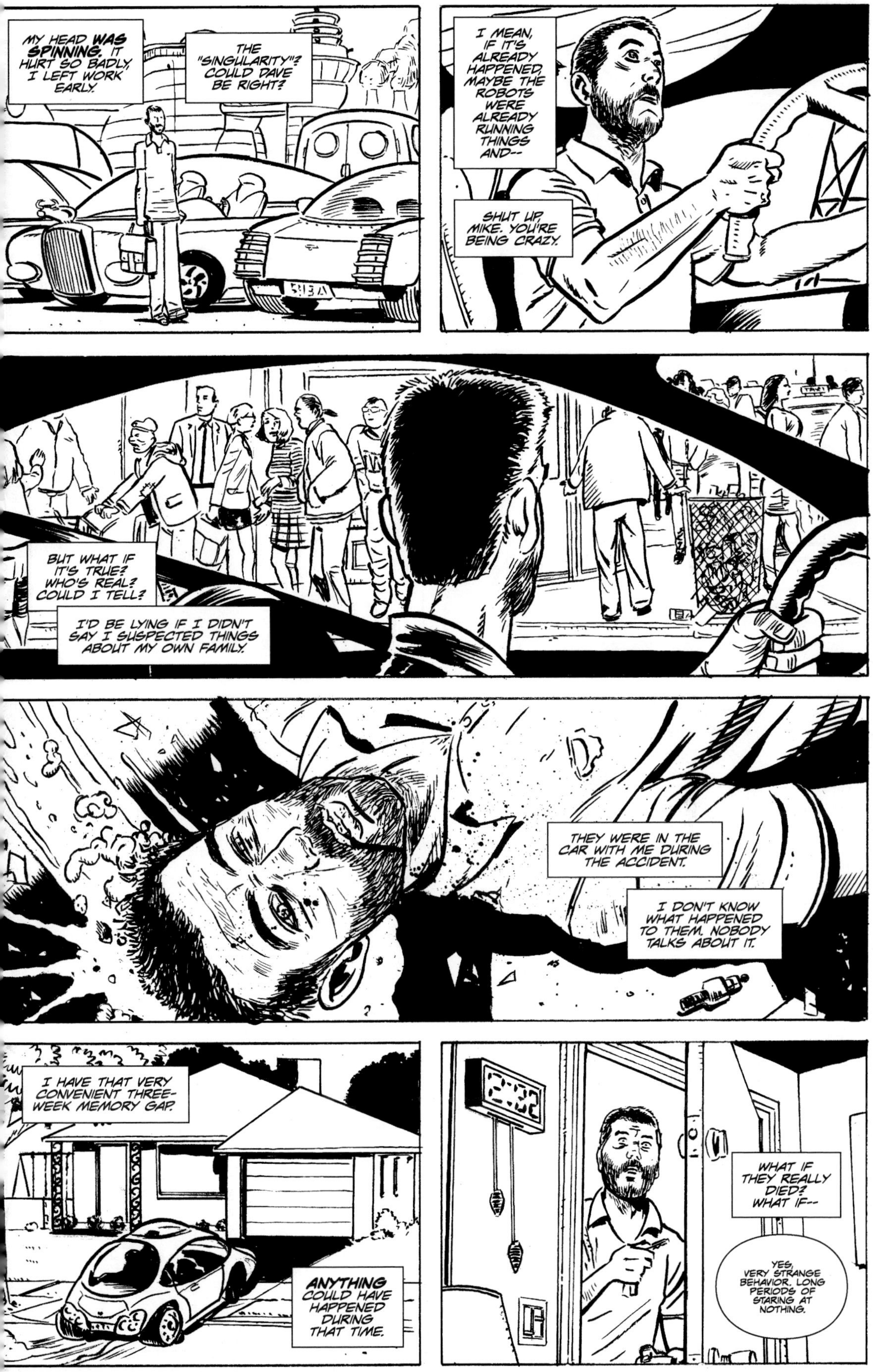

MY HEAD WAS SPINNING. IT HURT SO BADLY, I LEFT WORK EARLY.
THE "SINGULARITY"? COULD DAVE BE RIGHT?
I MEAN, IF IT'S ALREADY HAPPENED, MAYBE THE ROBOTS WERE ALREADY RUNNING THINGS AND--
SHUT UP, MIKE. YOU'RE BEING CRAZY.
BUT WHAT IF IT'S TRUE? WHO'S REAL? COULD I TELL?
I'D BE LYING IF I DIDN'T SAY I SUSPECTED THINGS ABOUT MY OWN FAMILY.
THEY WERE IN THE CAR WITH ME DURING THE ACCIDENT.
I DON'T KNOW WHAT HAPPENED TO THEM. NOBODY TALKS ABOUT IT.
I HAVE THAT VERY CONVENIENT THREE-WEEK MEMORY GAP.
ANYTHING COULD HAVE HAPPENED DURING THAT TIME.
WHAT IF THEY REALLY DIED? WHAT IF--
YES, VERY STRANGE BEHAVIOR. LONG PERIODS OF STARING AT NOTHING.

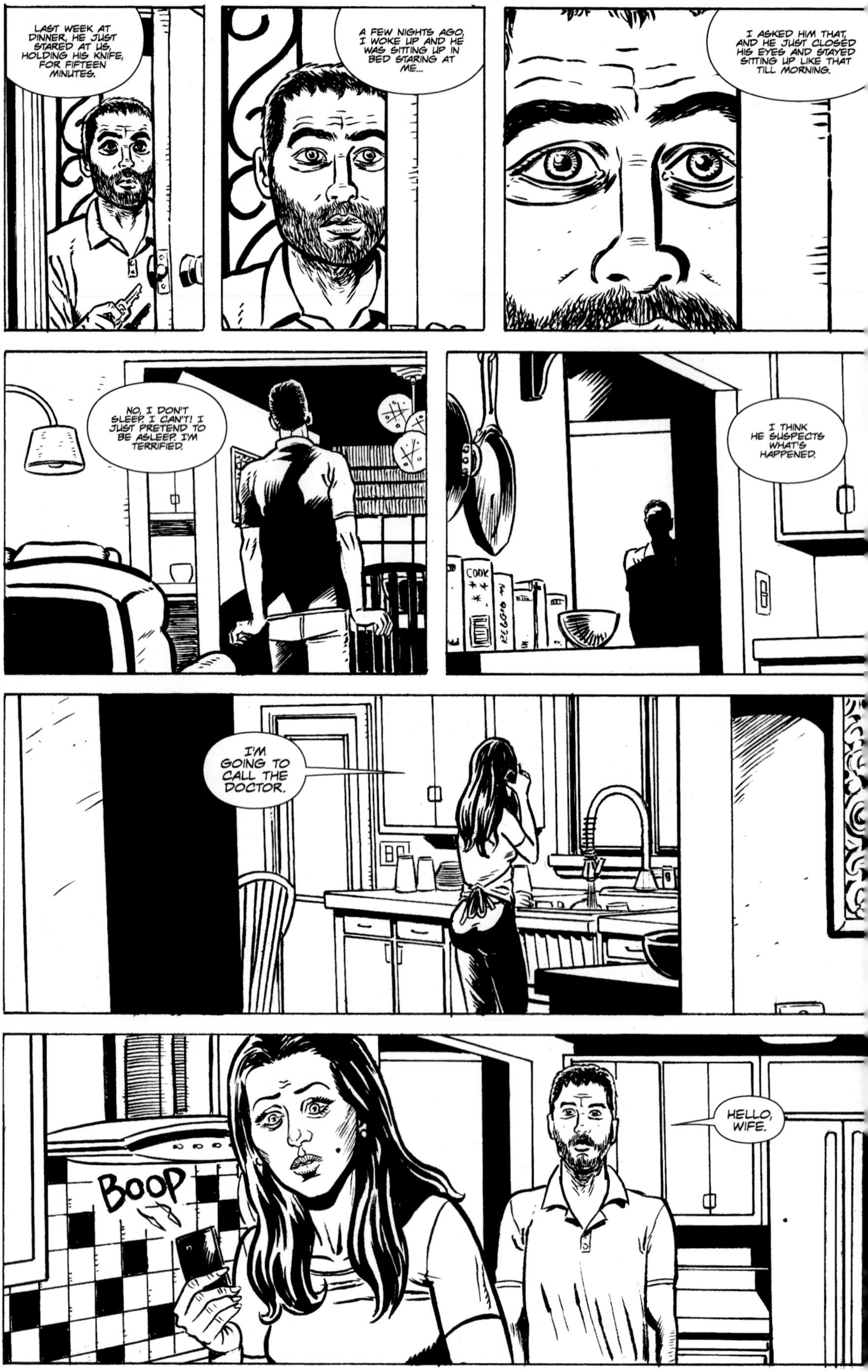
LAST WEEK AT DINNER, HE JUST STARED AT US, HOLDING HIS KNIFE, FOR FIFTEEN MINUTES.
A FEW NIGHTS AGO, I WOKE UP AND HE WAS SITTING UP IN BED STARING AT ME...
I ASKED HIM THAT, AND HE JUST CLOSED HIS EYES AND STAYED SITTING UP LIKE THAT TILL MORNING.
NO, I DON'T SLEEP. I CAN'T! I JUST PRETEND TO BE ASLEEP. I'M TERRIFIED.
COOK
I THINK HE SUSPECTS WHAT'S HAPPENED.
I'M GOING TO CALL THE DOCTOR.
BOOP
HELLO, WIFE.

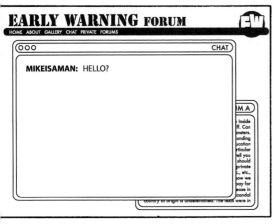

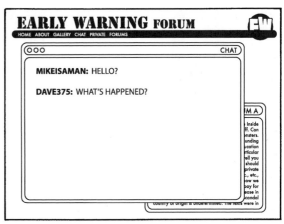

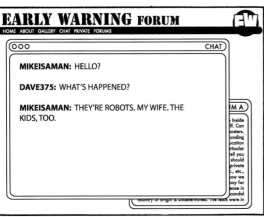

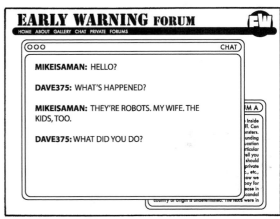

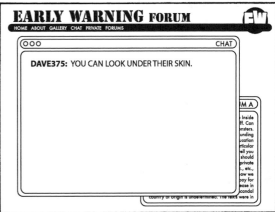

EARLY WARNING FORUM
HOME ABOUT GALLERY CHAT PRIVATE FORUMS
CHAT
MIKEISAMAN: HELLO?
EARLY WARNING FORUM
HOME ABOUT GALLERY CHAT PRIVATE FORUMS
CHAT
MIKEISAMAN: HELLO?
DAVE375: WHAT'S HAPPENED?
EARLY WARNING FORUM
HOME ABOUT GALLERY CHAT PRIVATE FORUMS
CHAT
MIKEISAMAN: HELLO?
DAVE375: WHAT'S HAPPENED?
MIKEISAMAN: THEY'RE ROBOTS. MY WIFE. THE KIDS, TOO.
EARLY WARNING FORUM
HOME ABOUT GALLERY CHAT PRIVATE FORUMS
CHAT
MIKEISAMAN: HELLO?
DAVE375: WHAT'S HAPPENED?
MIKEISAMAN: THEY'RE ROBOTS. MY WIFE. THE KIDS, TOO.
DAVE375: WHAT DID YOU DO?
MIKEISAMAN: I TIED THEM UP IN THE BASEMENT. HAD TO. MY WIFE WAS GOING TO CALL THE OTHER ROBOTS.
TAK TAK TAK TAK
DAVE375: ARE YOU SURE?
MIKEISAMAN: I'M NOT SURE OF ANYTHING. HOW CAN I BE SURE?
EARLY WARNING FORUM
HOME ABOUT GALLERY CHAT PRIVATE FORUMS
CHAT
DAVE375: YOU CAN LOOK UNDER THEIR SKIN.

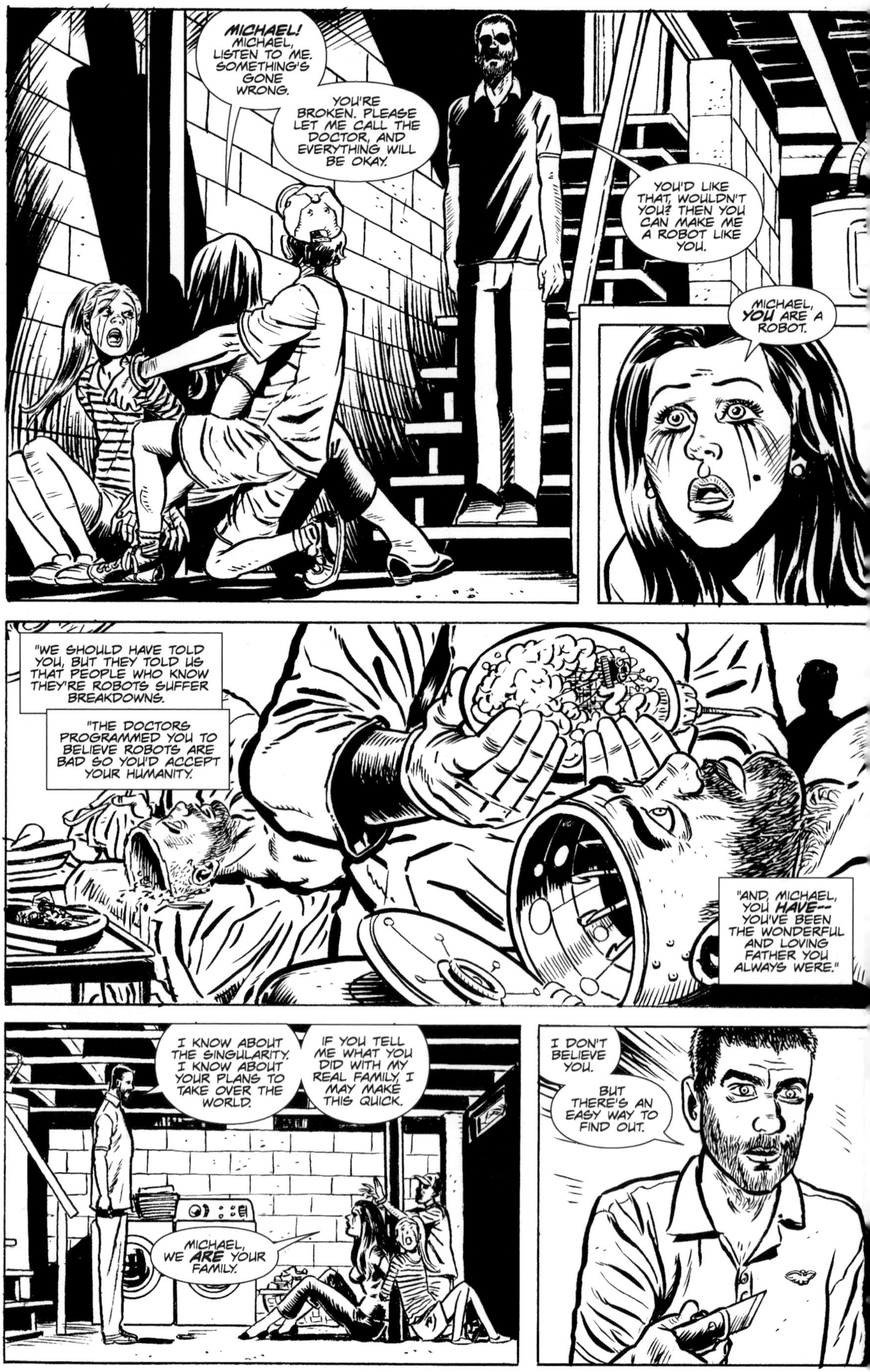

MICHAEL! MICHAEL, LISTEN TO ME. SOMETHING'S GONE WRONG.
YOU'RE BROKEN. PLEASE LET ME CALL THE DOCTOR, AND EVERYTHING WILL BE OKAY.
YOU'D LIKE THAT, WOULDN'T YOU? THEN YOU CAN MAKE ME A ROBOT LIKE YOU.
MICHAEL, YOU ARE A ROBOT.
"WE SHOULD HAVE TOLD YOU, BUT THEY TOLD US THAT PEOPLE WHO KNOW THEY'RE ROBOTS SUFFER BREAKDOWNS.
"THE DOCTORS PROGRAMMED YOU TO BELIEVE ROBOTS ARE BAD SO YOU'D ACCEPT YOUR HUMANITY.
"AND, MICHAEL, YOU HAVE-- YOU'VE BEEN THE WONDERFUL AND LOVING FATHER YOU ALWAYS WERE."
I KNOW ABOUT THE SINGULARITY. I KNOW ABOUT YOUR PLANS TO TAKE OVER THE WORLD.
IF YOU TELL ME WHAT YOU DID WITH MY REAL FAMILY, I MAY MAKE THIS QUICK.
MICHAEL, WE ARE YOUR FAMILY.
I DON'T BELIEVE YOU.
BUT THERE'S AN EASY WAY TO FIND OUT.

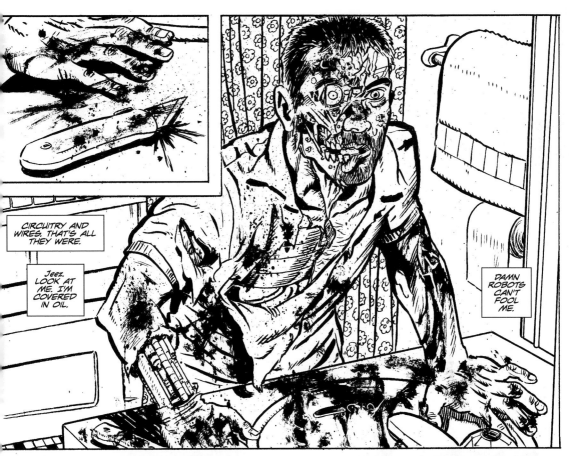

CIRCUITRY AND WIRES, THAT'S ALL THEY WERE.

Jeez. LOOK AT ME. I'M COVERED IN OIL.

DAMN ROBOTS CAN'T FOOL ME.

I KNOW A HUMAN BEING WHEN I SEE ONE.

NOK NOK NOK

MR. DODD? WE HEARD SCREAMING.

YES?

IS EVERYTHING OKAY?

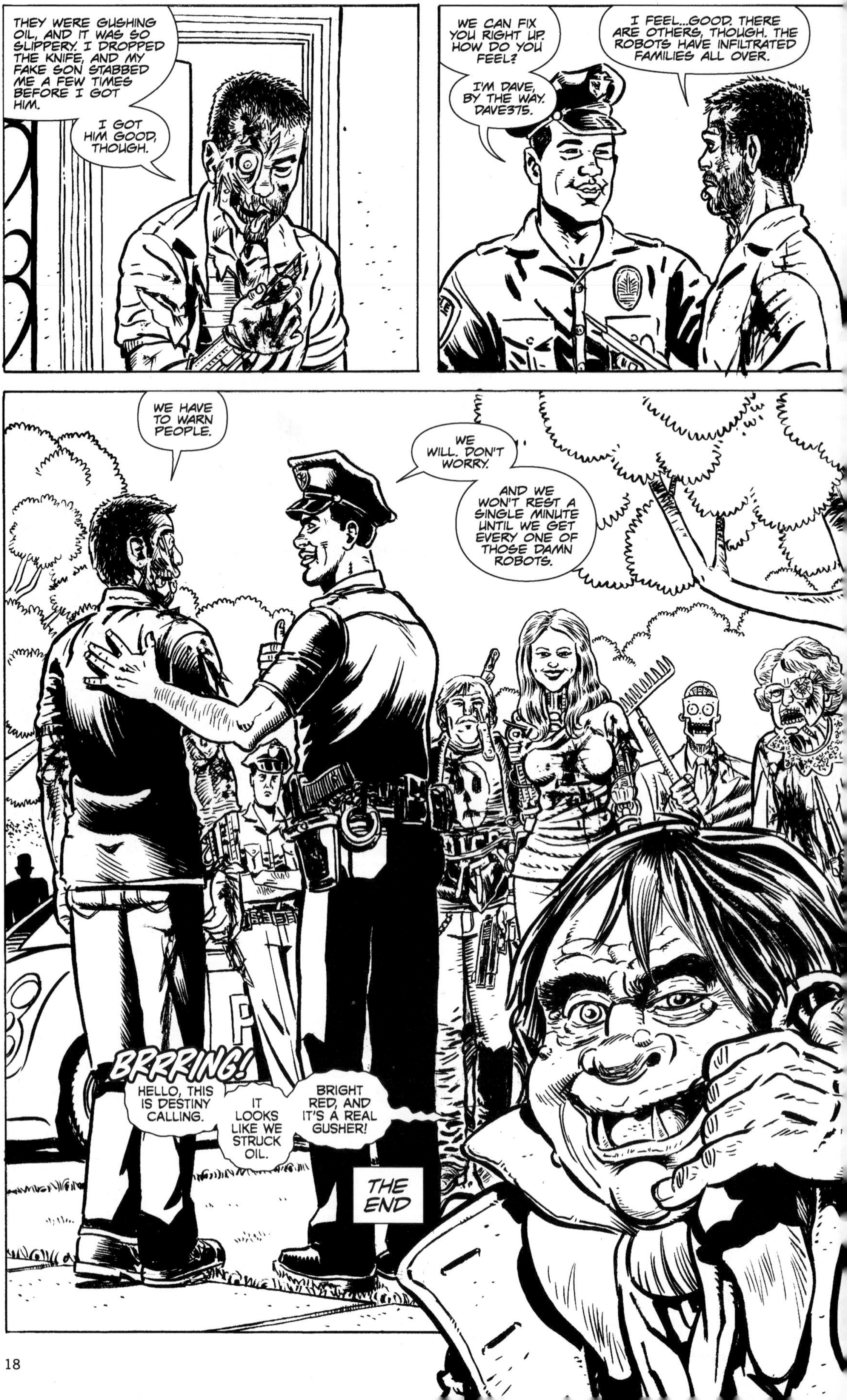
THEY WERE GUSHING OIL, AND IT WAS SO SLIPPERY. I DROPPED THE KNIFE, AND MY FAKE SON STABBED ME A FEW TIMES BEFORE I GOT HIM.
I GOT HIM GOOD, THOUGH.
WE CAN FIX YOU RIGHT UP. HOW DO YOU FEEL?
I'M DAVE, BY THE WAY. DAVE375.
I FEEL...GOOD. THERE ARE OTHERS, THOUGH. THE ROBOTS HAVE INFILTRATED FAMILIES ALL OVER.
WE HAVE TO WARN PEOPLE.
WE WILL. DON'T WORRY.
AND WE WON'T REST A SINGLE MINUTE UNTIL WE GET EVERY ONE OF THOSE DAMN ROBOTS.
BRRRING!
HELLO, THIS IS DESTINY CALLING.
IT LOOKS LIKE WE STRUCK OIL.
BRIGHT RED, AND IT'S A REAL GUSHER!
THE END

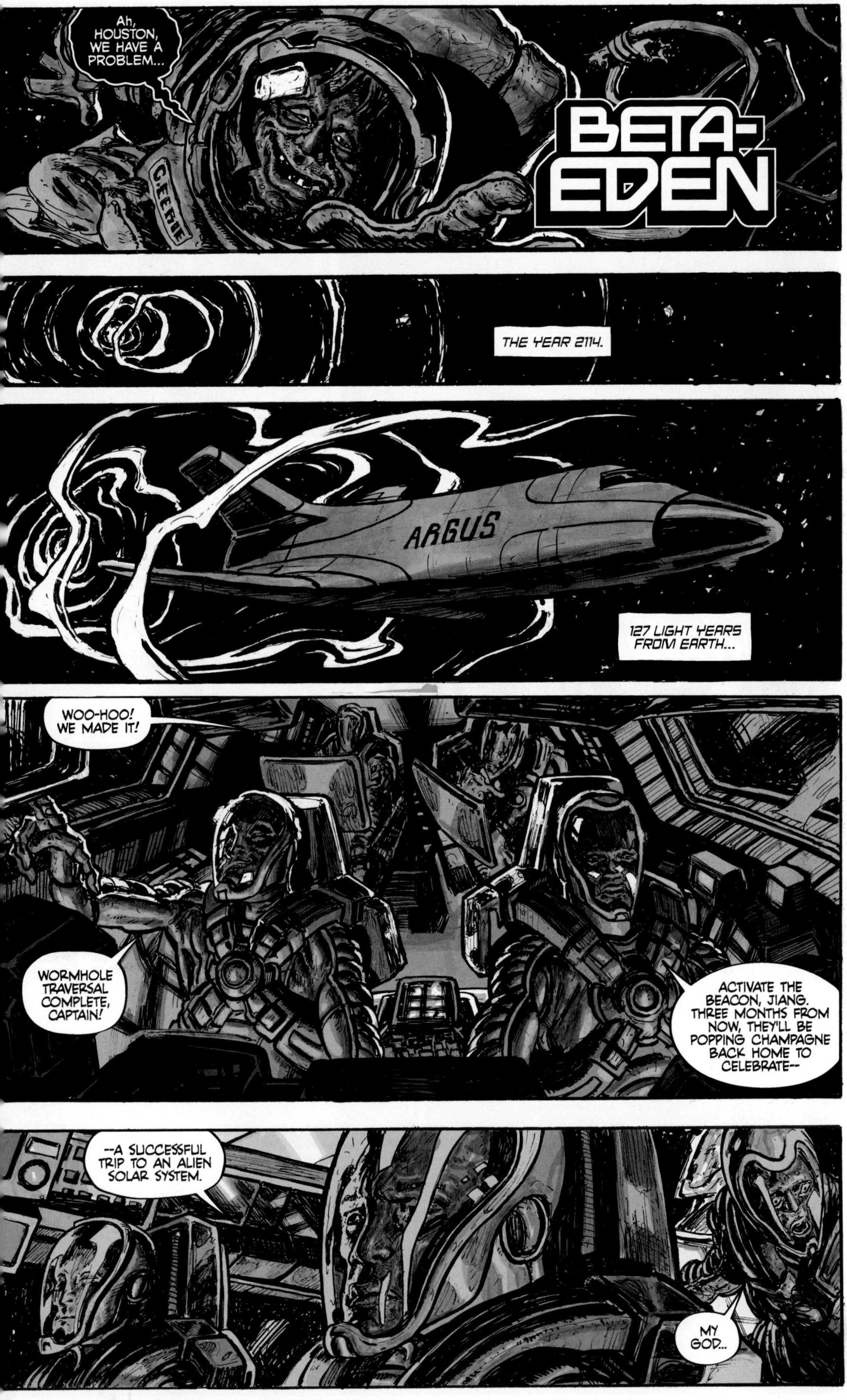

Ah, HOUSTON, WE HAVE A PROBLEM...
BETA-EDEN
GEEMIE
THE YEAR 2114.
ARGUS
127 LIGHT YEARS FROM EARTH...
WOO-HOO! WE MADE IT!
WORMHOLE TRAVERSAL COMPLETE, CAPTAIN!
ACTIVATE THE BEACON, JIANG. THREE MONTHS FROM NOW, THEY'LL BE POPPING CHAMPAGNE BACK HOME TO CELEBRATE--
--A SUCCESSFUL TRIP TO AN ALIEN SOLAR SYSTEM.
MY GOD...

cript by CHRISTOPHER A. TAYLOR / Art by RAFA GARRES

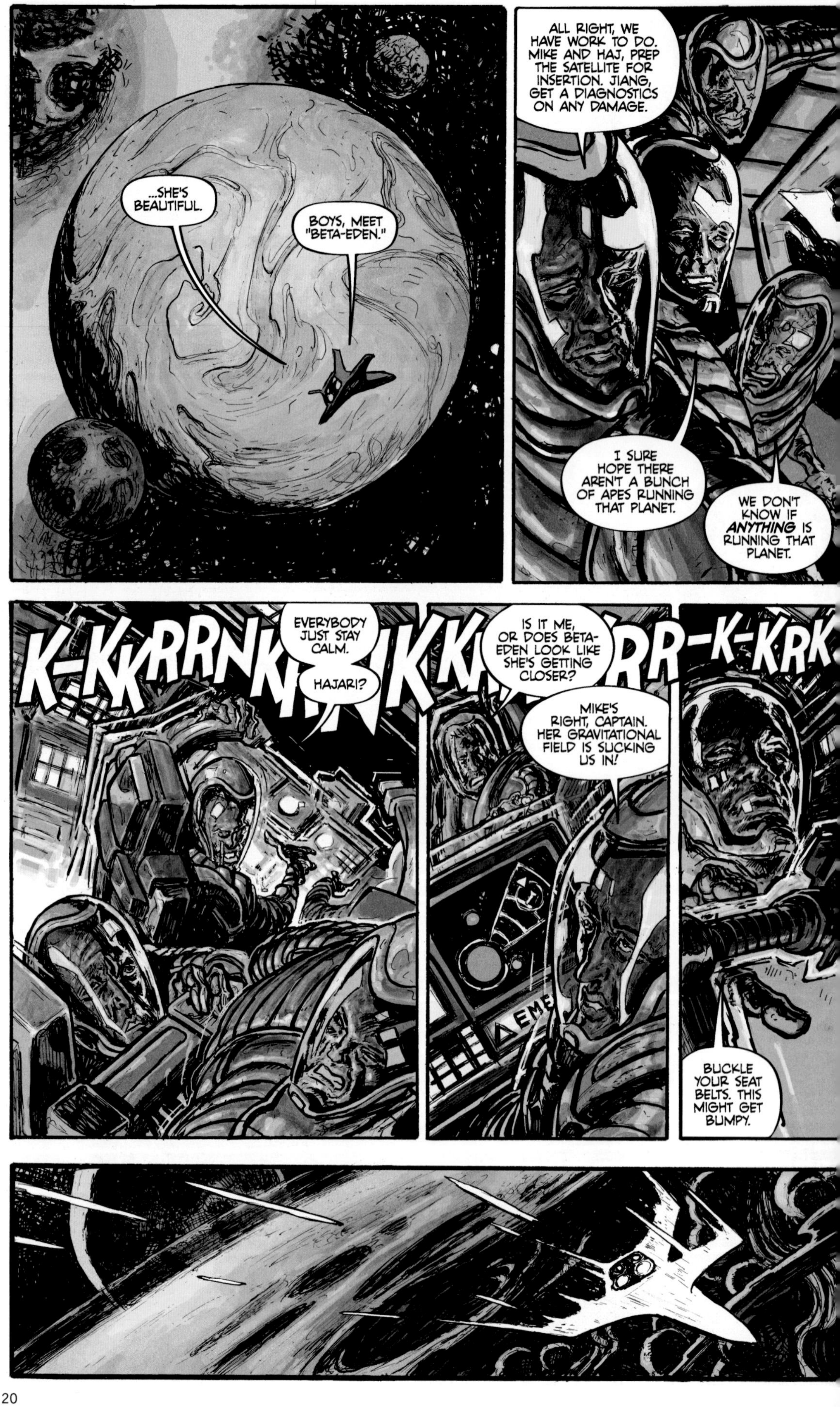
...SHE'S BEAUTIFUL.
BOYS, MEET "BETA-EDEN."
ALL RIGHT, WE HAVE WORK TO DO. MIKE AND HAJ, PREP THE SATELLITE FOR INSERTION. JIANG, GET A DIAGNOSTICS ON ANY DAMAGE.
I SURE HOPE THERE AREN'T A BUNCH OF APES RUNNING THAT PLANET.
WE DON'T KNOW IF *ANYTHING* IS RUNNING THAT PLANET.
K-KKRRNKKKKRR-K-KRK
EVERYBODY JUST STAY CALM.
HAJARI?
IS IT ME, OR DOES BETA-EDEN LOOK LIKE SHE'S GETTING CLOSER?
MIKE'S RIGHT, CAPTAIN. HER GRAVITATIONAL FIELD IS SUCKING US IN!
BUCKLE YOUR SEAT BELTS. THIS MIGHT GET BUMPY.

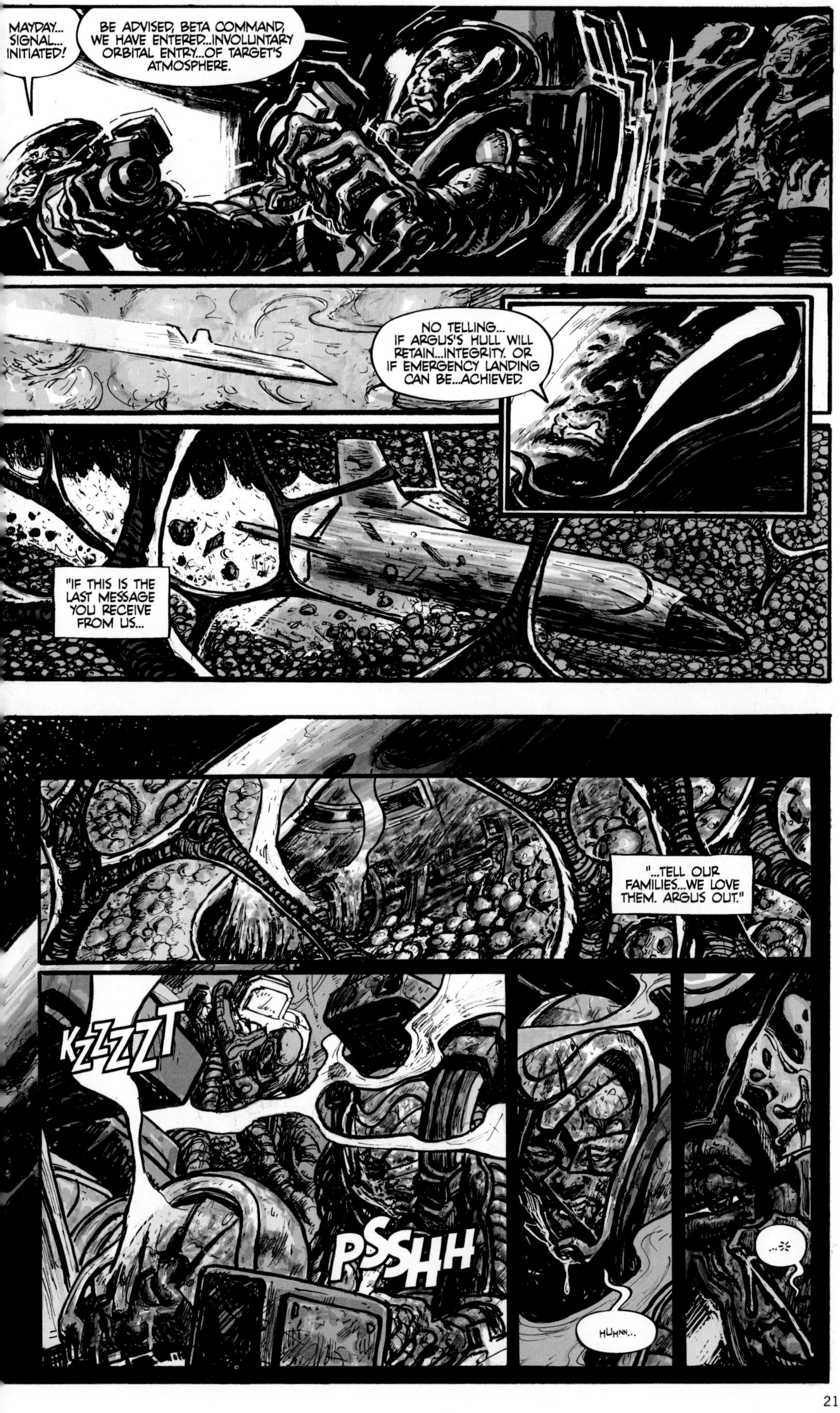
MAYDAY... SIGNAL... INITIATED!
BE ADVISED, BETA COMMAND, WE HAVE ENTERED...INVOLUNTARY ORBITAL ENTRY...OF TARGET'S ATMOSPHERE.
NO TELLING... IF ARGUS'S HULL WILL RETAIN...INTEGRITY. OR IF EMERGENCY LANDING CAN BE...ACHIEVED.
"IF THIS IS THE LAST MESSAGE YOU RECEIVE FROM US...
"...TELL OUR FAMILIES...WE LOVE THEM. ARGUS OUT."
KZZZZT
PSSHH
HUHNN...

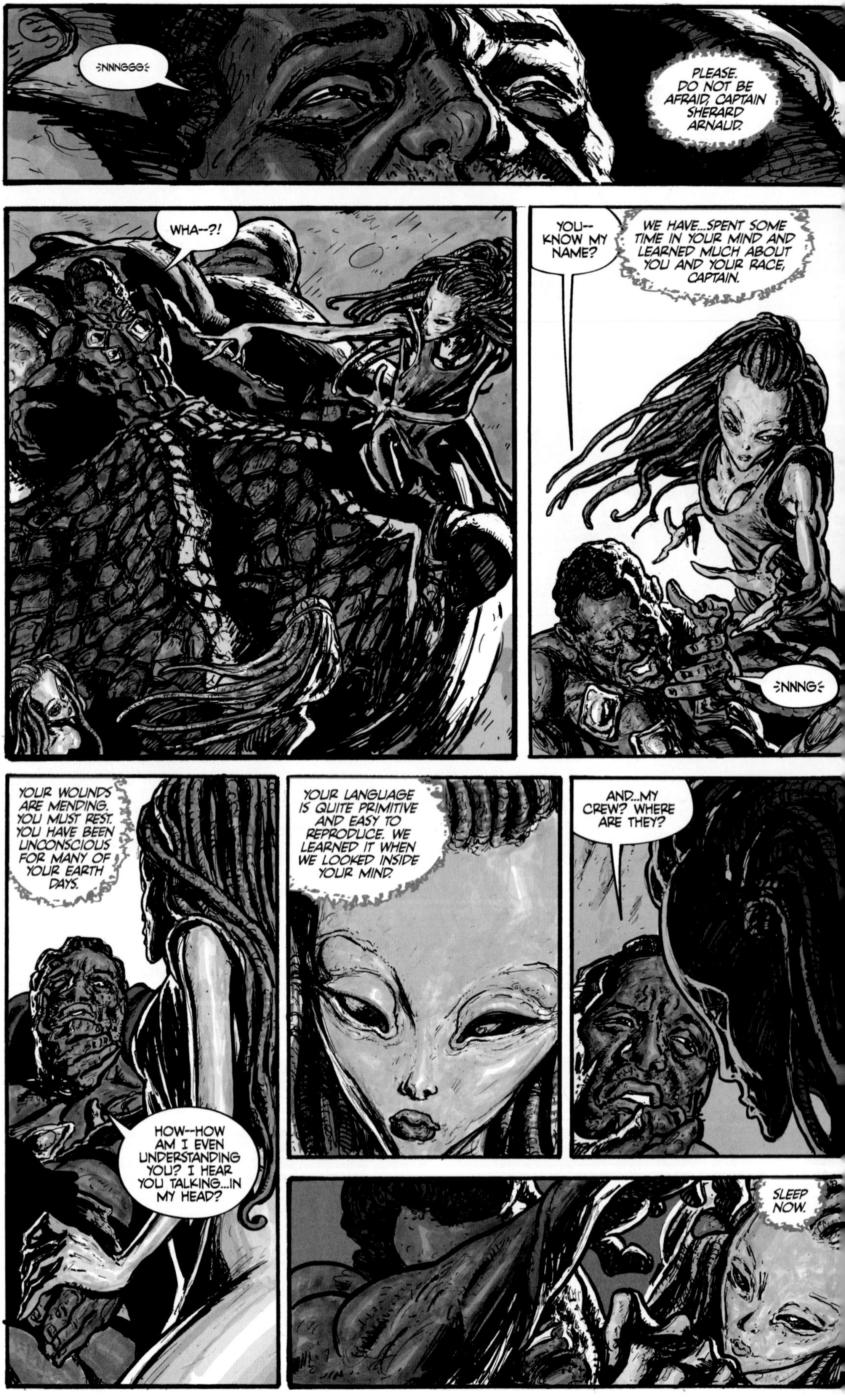

≈NNNGGG≈
PLEASE. DO NOT BE AFRAID, CAPTAIN SHERARD ARNAUD.
WHA--?!
YOU-- KNOW MY NAME?
WE HAVE...SPENT SOME TIME IN YOUR MIND AND LEARNED MUCH ABOUT YOU AND YOUR RACE, CAPTAIN.
≈NNNG≈
YOUR WOUNDS ARE MENDING. YOU MUST REST. YOU HAVE BEEN UNCONSCIOUS FOR MANY OF YOUR EARTH DAYS.
HOW--HOW AM I EVEN UNDERSTANDING YOU? I HEAR YOU TALKING...IN MY HEAD?
YOUR LANGUAGE IS QUITE PRIMITIVE AND EASY TO REPRODUCE. WE LEARNED IT WHEN WE LOOKED INSIDE YOUR MIND.
AND...MY CREW? WHERE ARE THEY?
SLEEP NOW.

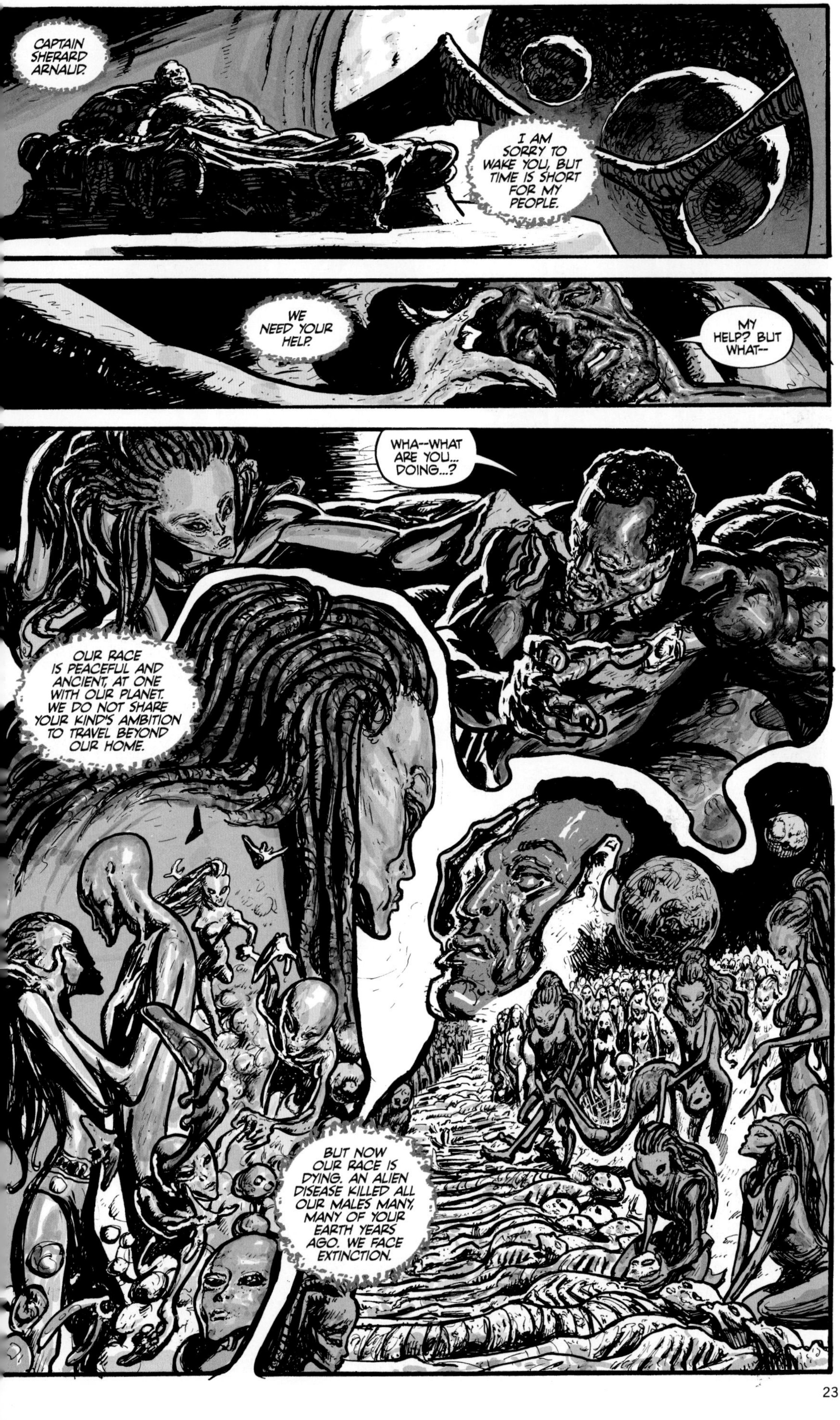
CAPTAIN SHERARD ARNAUD.
I AM SORRY TO WAKE YOU, BUT TIME IS SHORT FOR MY PEOPLE.
WE NEED YOUR HELP.
MY HELP? BUT WHAT--
WHA--WHAT ARE YOU... DOING...?
OUR RACE IS PEACEFUL AND ANCIENT, AT ONE WITH OUR PLANET. WE DO NOT SHARE YOUR KIND'S AMBITION TO TRAVEL BEYOND OUR HOME.
BUT NOW OUR RACE IS DYING. AN ALIEN DISEASE KILLED ALL OUR MALES MANY, MANY OF YOUR EARTH YEARS AGO. WE FACE EXTINCTION.

WHILE YOU WERE UNCONSCIOUS WE DISCOVERED THAT OUR TWO RACES SHARE SIMILAR REPRODUCTIVE BIOLOGIES.

I...I'M NOT SURE I UNDERSTAND.

WE WISH TO CONDUCT A REPRODUCTIVE EXPERIMENT WITH YOU. PERHAPS IN YOUR COMING HERE, THE UNIVERSE MEANT FOR YOU TO SAVE OUR RACE.

BUT—

SHHHH...

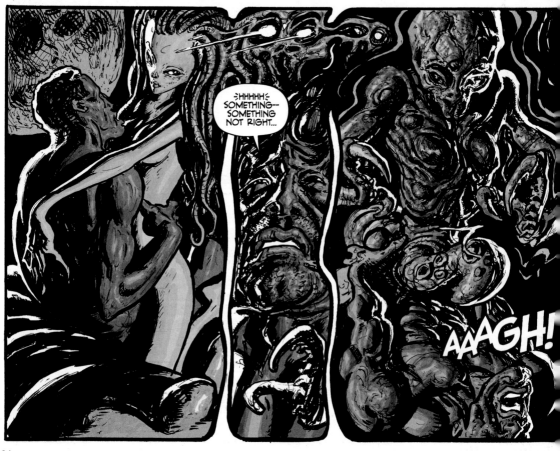

≷HHHHH≷ SOMETHING—SOMETHING NOT RIGHT...

AAAGH!

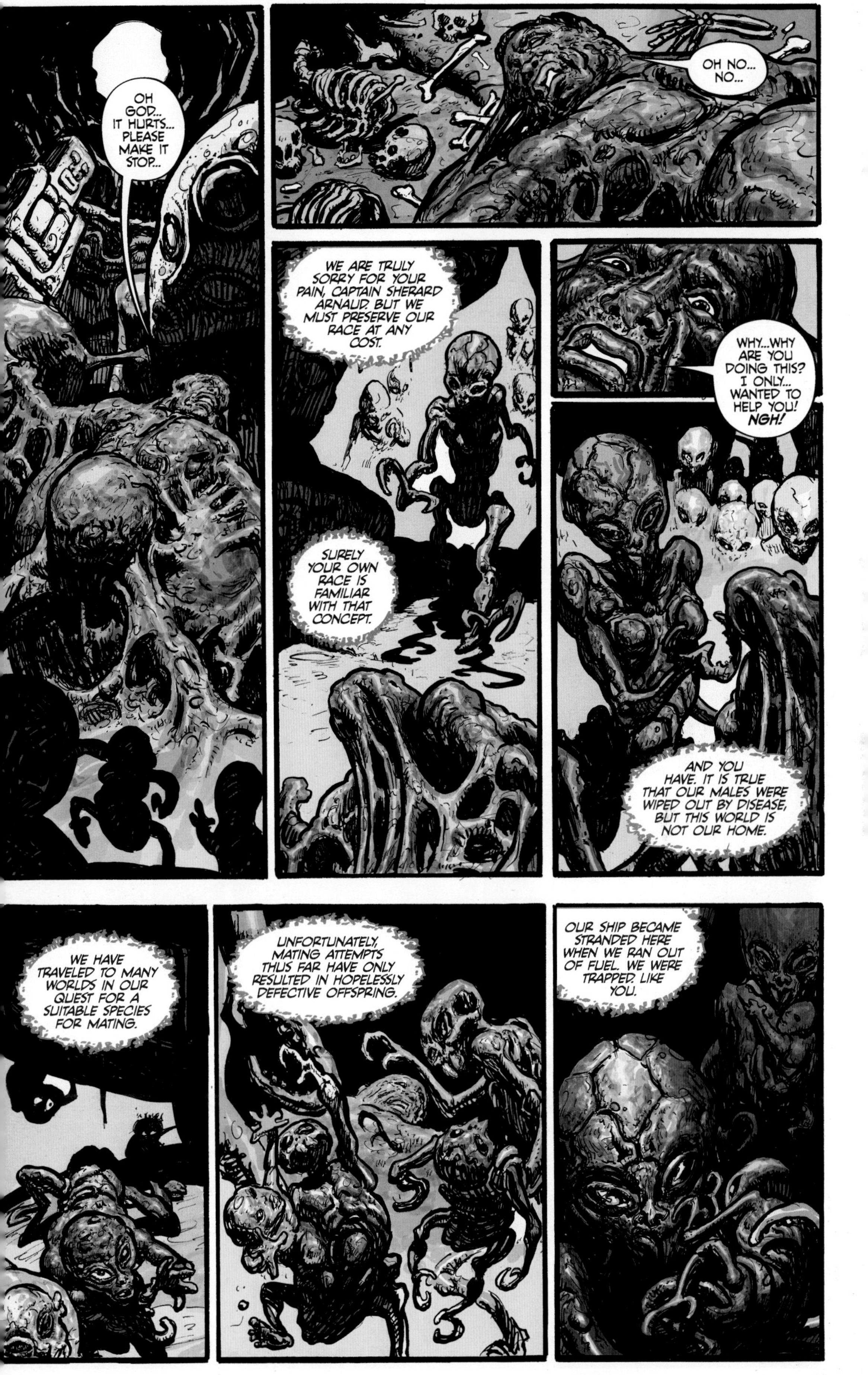
OH GOD... IT HURTS... PLEASE MAKE IT STOP...
OH NO... NO...
WE ARE TRULY SORRY FOR YOUR PAIN, CAPTAIN SHERARD ARNAUD, BUT WE MUST PRESERVE OUR RACE AT ANY COST.
SURELY YOUR OWN RACE IS FAMILIAR WITH THAT CONCEPT.
WHY...WHY ARE YOU DOING THIS? I ONLY... WANTED TO HELP YOU! NGH!
AND YOU HAVE. IT IS TRUE THAT OUR MALES WERE WIPED OUT BY DISEASE, BUT THIS WORLD IS NOT OUR HOME.
WE HAVE TRAVELED TO MANY WORLDS IN OUR QUEST FOR A SUITABLE SPECIES FOR MATING.
UNFORTUNATELY, MATING ATTEMPTS THUS FAR HAVE ONLY RESULTED IN HOPELESSLY DEFECTIVE OFFSPRING.
OUR SHIP BECAME STRANDED HERE WHEN WE RAN OUT OF FUEL. WE WERE TRAPPED. LIKE YOU.

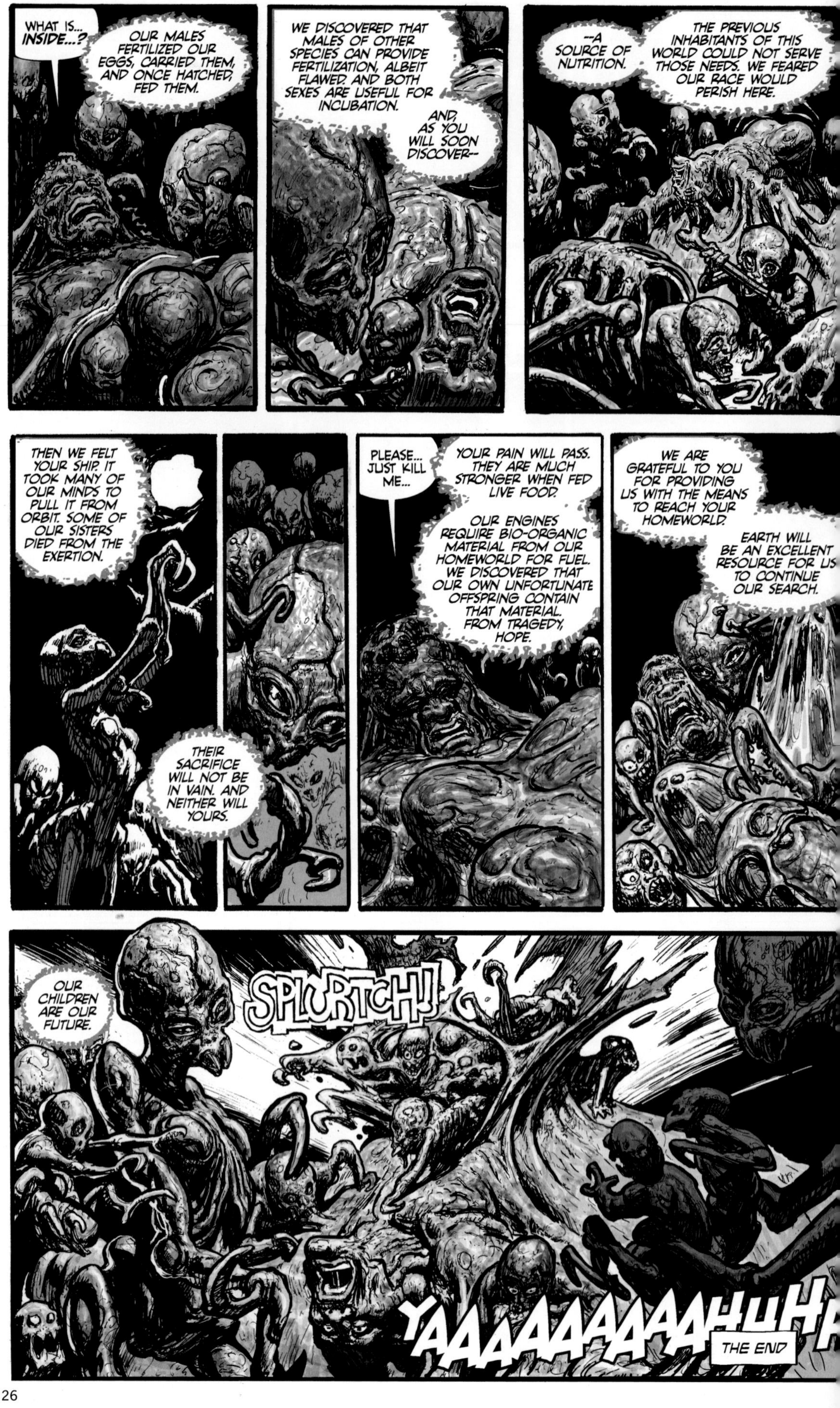

WHAT IS... INSIDE...?
OUR MALES FERTILIZED OUR EGGS, CARRIED THEM, AND ONCE HATCHED, FED THEM.
WE DISCOVERED THAT MALES OF OTHER SPECIES CAN PROVIDE FERTILIZATION, ALBEIT FLAWED. AND BOTH SEXES ARE USEFUL FOR INCUBATION.
AND, AS YOU WILL SOON DISCOVER--
--A SOURCE OF NUTRITION.
THE PREVIOUS INHABITANTS OF THIS WORLD COULD NOT SERVE THOSE NEEDS. WE FEARED OUR RACE WOULD PERISH HERE.
THEN WE FELT YOUR SHIP. IT TOOK MANY OF OUR MINDS TO PULL IT FROM ORBIT. SOME OF OUR SISTERS DIED FROM THE EXERTION.
THEIR SACRIFICE WILL NOT BE IN VAIN. AND NEITHER WILL YOURS.
PLEASE... JUST KILL ME...
YOUR PAIN WILL PASS. THEY ARE MUCH STRONGER WHEN FED LIVE FOOD.
OUR ENGINES REQUIRE BIO-ORGANIC MATERIAL FROM OUR HOMEWORLD FOR FUEL. WE DISCOVERED THAT OUR OWN UNFORTUNATE OFFSPRING CONTAIN THAT MATERIAL. FROM TRAGEDY, HOPE.
WE ARE GRATEFUL TO YOU FOR PROVIDING US WITH THE MEANS TO REACH YOUR HOMEWORLD.
EARTH WILL BE AN EXCELLENT RESOURCE FOR US TO CONTINUE OUR SEARCH.
OUR CHILDREN ARE OUR FUTURE.
SPLURTCH!!
YAAAAAAAAAHUHH
THE END

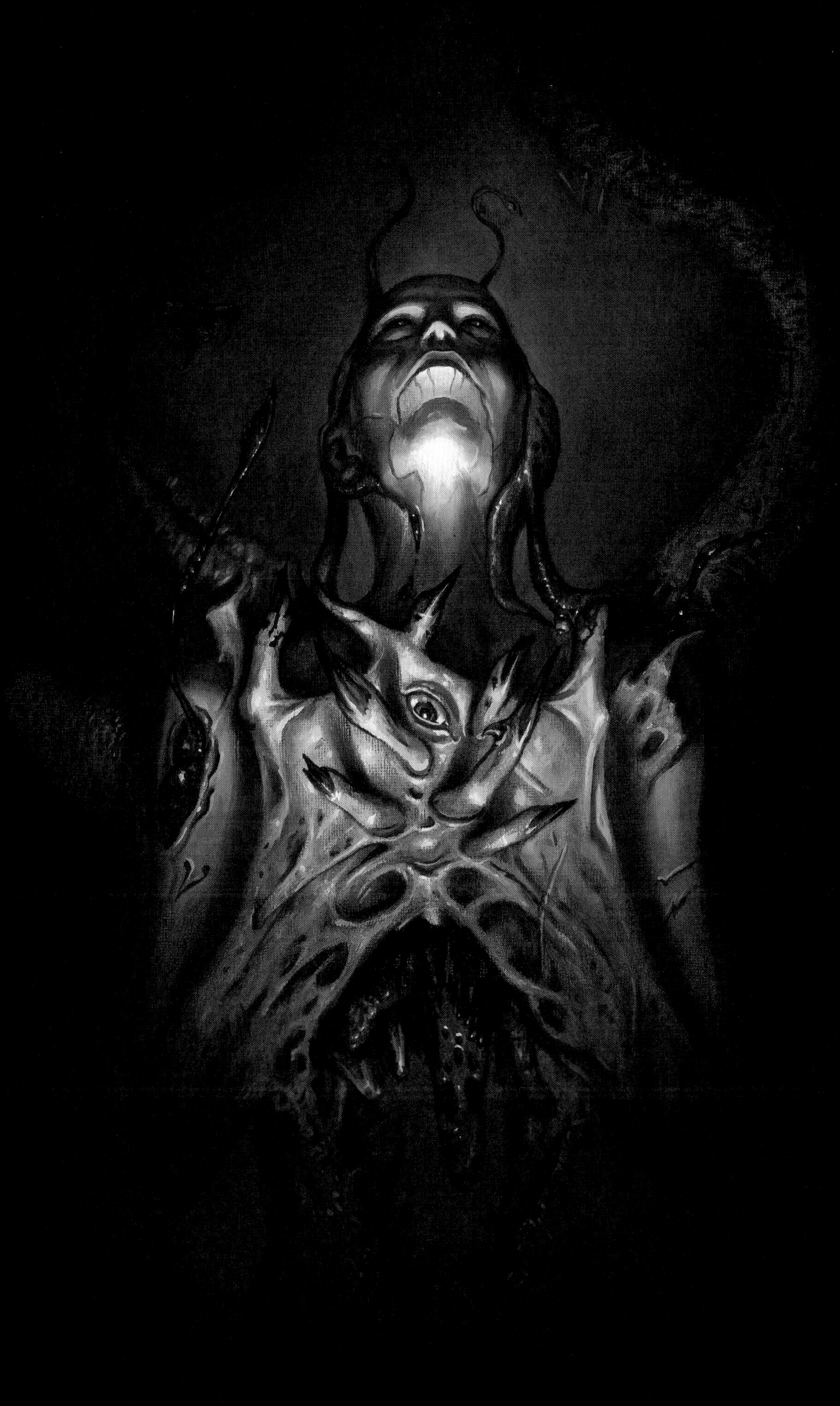

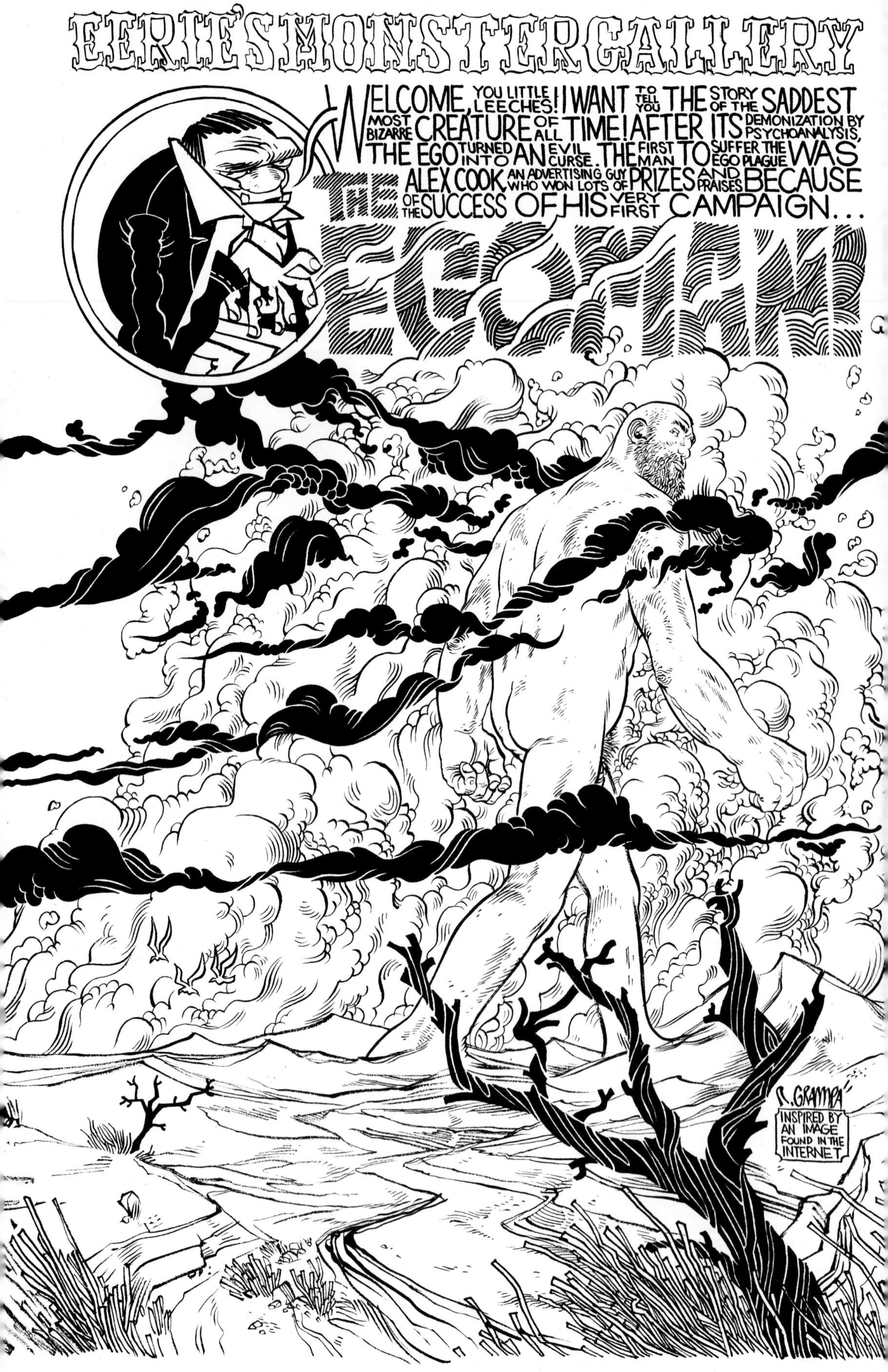
EERIE'S MONSTER GALLERY
WELCOME, YOU LITTLE LEECHES! I WANT TO TELL YOU THE STORY OF THE SADDEST MOST BIZARRE CREATURE OF ALL TIME! AFTER ITS DEMONIZATION BY PSYCHOANALYSIS, THE EGO TURNED INTO AN EVIL CURSE. THE FIRST MAN TO SUFFER THE EGO PLAGUE WAS ALEX COOK, AN ADVERTISING GUY WHO WON LOTS OF PRIZES AND PRAISES BECAUSE OF THE SUCCESS OF HIS VERY FIRST CAMPAIGN...
THE EGOMAN!
S. GRAMPA
INSPIRED BY AN IMAGE FOUND IN THE INTERNET

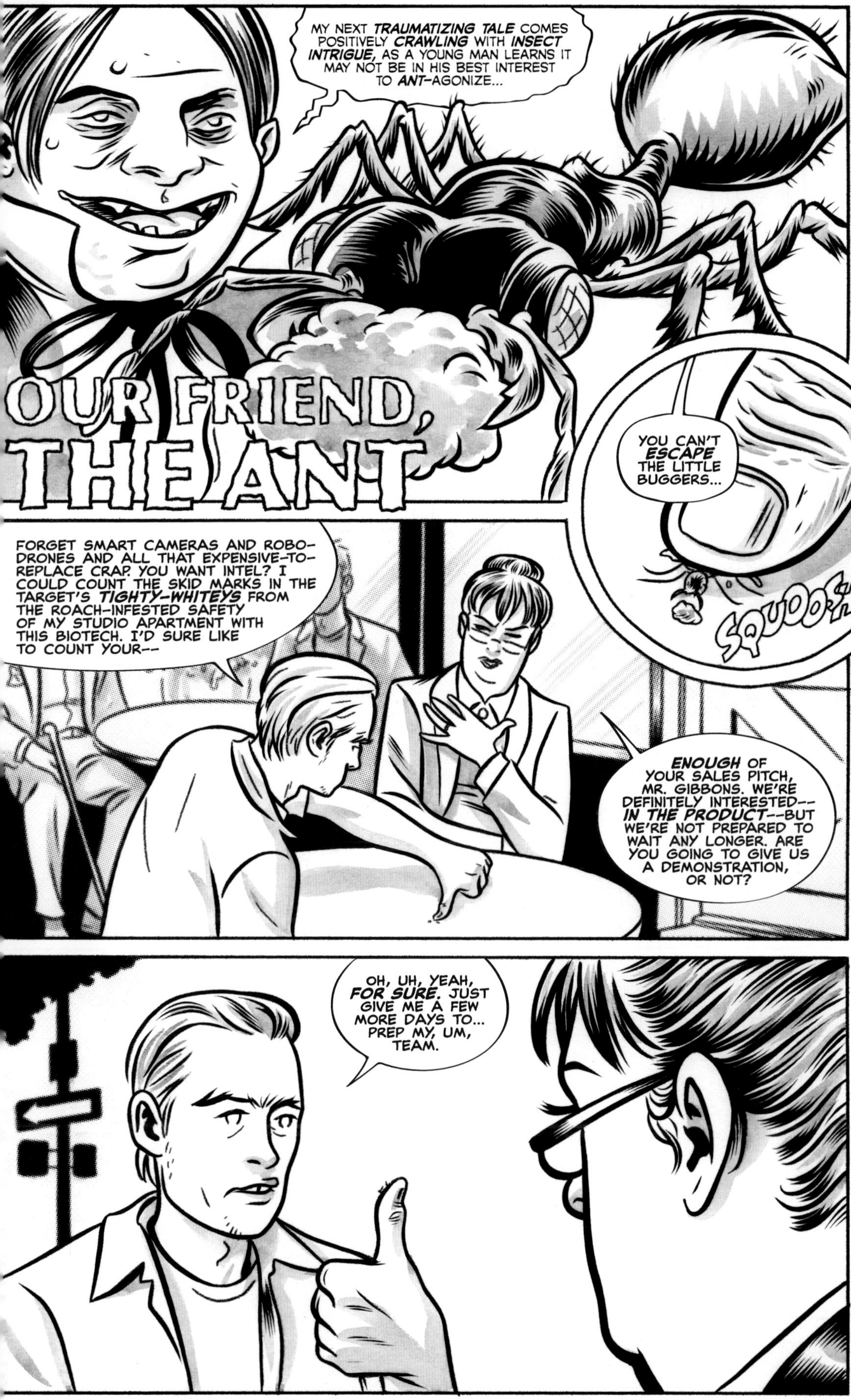

MY NEXT TRAUMATIZING TALE COMES POSITIVELY CRAWLING WITH INSECT INTRIGUE, AS A YOUNG MAN LEARNS IT MAY NOT BE IN HIS BEST INTEREST TO ANT-AGONIZE...
OUR FRIEND, THE ANT
YOU CAN'T ESCAPE THE LITTLE BUGGERS...
SQUOOSH
FORGET SMART CAMERAS AND ROBO-DRONES AND ALL THAT EXPENSIVE-TO-REPLACE CRAP. YOU WANT INTEL? I COULD COUNT THE SKID MARKS IN THE TARGET'S TIGHTY-WHITEYS FROM THE ROACH-INFESTED SAFETY OF MY STUDIO APARTMENT WITH THIS BIOTECH. I'D SURE LIKE TO COUNT YOUR--
ENOUGH OF YOUR SALES PITCH, MR. GIBBONS. WE'RE DEFINITELY INTERESTED--IN THE PRODUCT--BUT WE'RE NOT PREPARED TO WAIT ANY LONGER. ARE YOU GOING TO GIVE US A DEMONSTRATION, OR NOT?
OH, UH, YEAH, FOR SURE. JUST GIVE ME A FEW MORE DAYS TO... PREP MY, UM, TEAM.

TOMAS, WHERE HAVE YOU *BEEN*?

I CAN'T TRANSCRIBE AND CORRELATE ALL THIS LINGUISTICS DATA MYSELF. THE TECHNICAL WORKAROUND FOR THE ANT'S NATURAL PHEROMONE COMMUNICATION HAS PROVEN TIME CONSUMING ENOUGH!

RIGHT, YEAH. I KINDA HAD THIS MEETING TO GO TO.

≑SIGH≑ I SUPPOSE I SHOULD BE THANKFUL FOR THE ONLY INTERN WHO APPLIED.

LOOK, WE REALLY NEED TO TALK ABOUT THE PROFIT POTENTIAL ON THIS PROJECT. IT'S RIDICULOUS--I'VE GOTTEN AN *INSANE* OFFER FROM...

ABSOLUTELY NOT! *NO!* I REFUSE TO HAVE ANY MORE POINTLESS CONVERSATIONS OF THIS NATURE! I WILL NOT HAVE *OUR FRIEND THE ANT,* CONTRACTED OUT FOR THE MILITARY'S *DIRTY WORK,* OR ANYONE ELSE'S, FOR THAT MATTER. FURTHERMORE, IT IS *NOT YOUR PLACE* TO BE FIELDING OFFERS!

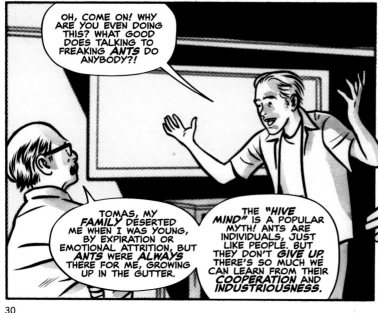

OH, COME ON! WHY ARE YOU EVEN DOING THIS? WHAT GOOD DOES TALKING TO FREAKING *ANTS* DO ANYBODY?!

TOMAS, MY *FAMILY* DESERTED ME WHEN I WAS YOUNG, BY EXPIRATION OR EMOTIONAL ATTRITION, BUT *ANTS* WERE *ALWAYS* THERE FOR ME, GROWING UP IN THE GUTTER.

THE *"HIVE MIND"* IS A POPULAR MYTH! ANTS ARE INDIVIDUALS, JUST LIKE PEOPLE. BUT THEY DON'T *GIVE UP.* THERE'S SO MUCH WE CAN LEARN FROM THEIR *COOPERATION* AND *INDUSTRIOUSNESS.*

IMAGINE A WORLD FOCUSED EVEN *HALF* AS DILIGENTLY ON A COMMON GOAL. WE COULD ACCOMPLISH *ANYTHING, EXPONENTIALLY* FASTER.

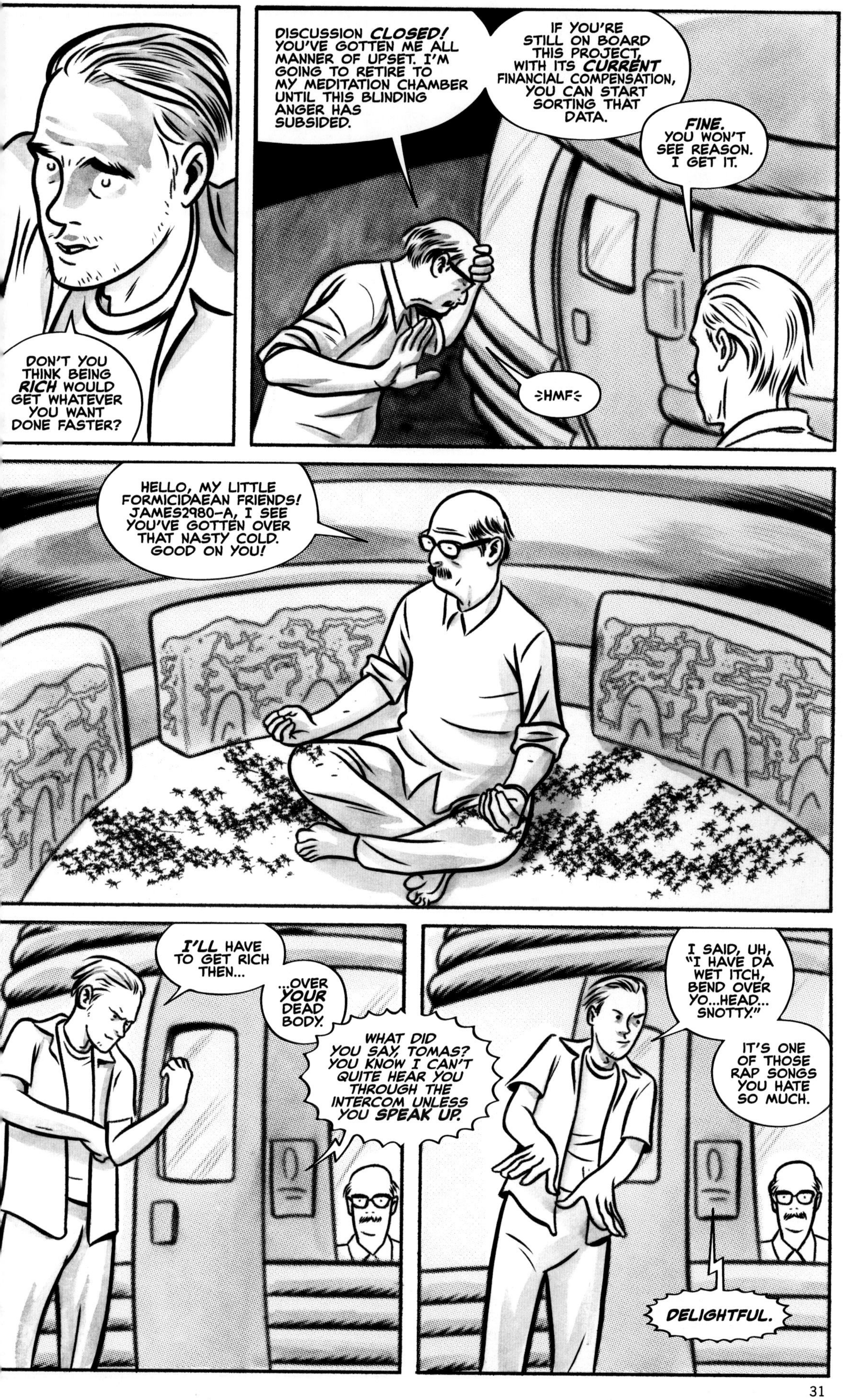
DON'T YOU THINK BEING RICH WOULD GET WHATEVER YOU WANT DONE FASTER?
DISCUSSION CLOSED! YOU'VE GOTTEN ME ALL MANNER OF UPSET. I'M GOING TO RETIRE TO MY MEDITATION CHAMBER UNTIL THIS BLINDING ANGER HAS SUBSIDED.
IF YOU'RE STILL ON BOARD THIS PROJECT, WITH ITS CURRENT FINANCIAL COMPENSATION, YOU CAN START SORTING THAT DATA.
FINE. YOU WON'T SEE REASON. I GET IT.
HMF
HELLO, MY LITTLE FORMICIDAEAN FRIENDS! JAMES2980-A, I SEE YOU'VE GOTTEN OVER THAT NASTY COLD. GOOD ON YOU!
I'LL HAVE TO GET RICH THEN...
...OVER YOUR DEAD BODY.
WHAT DID YOU SAY, TOMAS? YOU KNOW I CAN'T QUITE HEAR YOU THROUGH THE INTERCOM UNLESS YOU SPEAK UP.
I SAID, UH, "I HAVE DA WET ITCH, BEND OVER YO...HEAD... SNOTTY."
IT'S ONE OF THOSE RAP SONGS YOU HATE SO MUCH.
DELIGHTFUL.

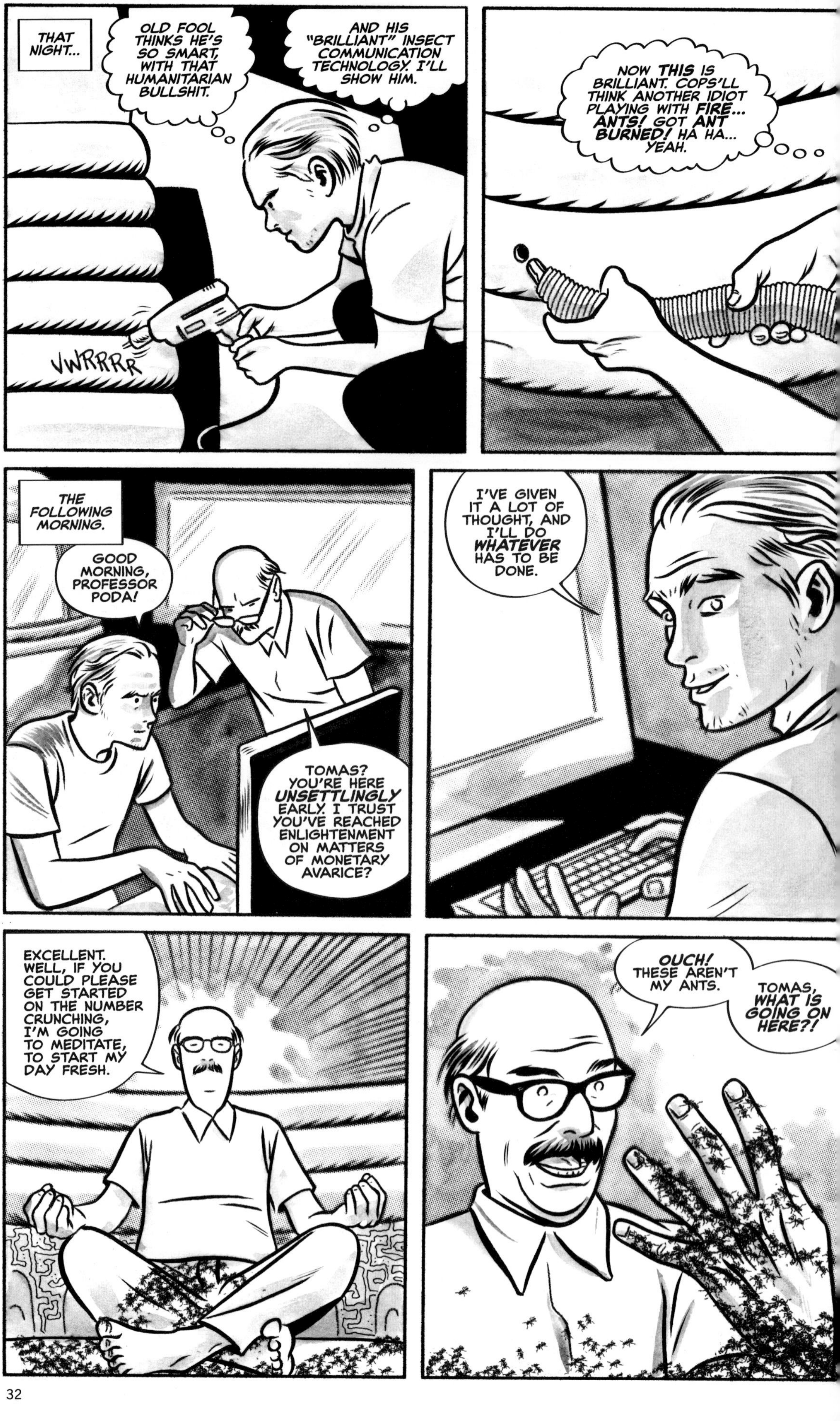
THAT NIGHT...
OLD FOOL THINKS HE'S SO SMART, WITH THAT HUMANITARIAN BULLSHIT.
AND HIS "BRILLIANT" INSECT COMMUNICATION TECHNOLOGY. I'LL SHOW HIM.
VWRRRR
NOW THIS IS BRILLIANT. COPS'LL THINK ANOTHER IDIOT PLAYING WITH FIRE... ANTS! GOT ANT BURNED! HA HA... YEAH.
THE FOLLOWING MORNING.
GOOD MORNING, PROFESSOR PODA!
TOMAS? YOU'RE HERE UNSETTLINGLY EARLY. I TRUST YOU'VE REACHED ENLIGHTENMENT ON MATTERS OF MONETARY AVARICE?
I'VE GIVEN IT A LOT OF THOUGHT, AND I'LL DO WHATEVER HAS TO BE DONE.
EXCELLENT. WELL, IF YOU COULD PLEASE GET STARTED ON THE NUMBER CRUNCHING, I'M GOING TO MEDITATE, TO START MY DAY FRESH.
OUCH! THESE AREN'T MY ANTS.
TOMAS, WHAT IS GOING ON HERE?!

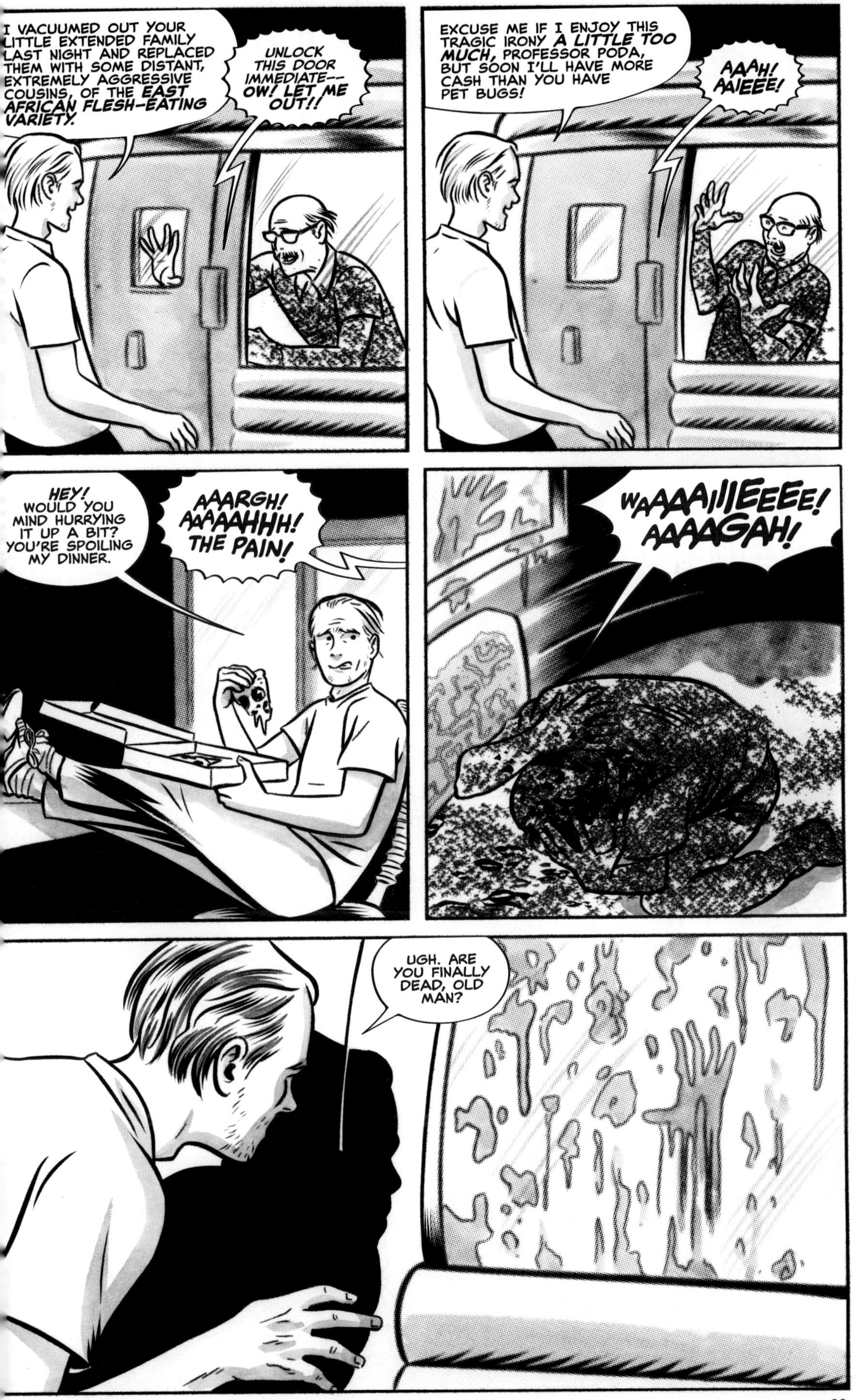
I VACUUMED OUT YOUR LITTLE EXTENDED FAMILY LAST NIGHT AND REPLACED THEM WITH SOME DISTANT, EXTREMELY AGGRESSIVE COUSINS, OF THE EAST AFRICAN FLESH-EATING VARIETY.
UNLOCK THIS DOOR IMMEDIATE-- OW! LET ME OUT!!
EXCUSE ME IF I ENJOY THIS TRAGIC IRONY A LITTLE TOO MUCH, PROFESSOR PODA, BUT SOON I'LL HAVE MORE CASH THAN YOU HAVE PET BUGS!
AAAH! AAIEEE!
HEY! WOULD YOU MIND HURRYING IT UP A BIT? YOU'RE SPOILING MY DINNER.
AAARGH! AAAAAHHH! THE PAIN!
WAAAAIIIIEEEE! AAAAGAH!
UGH. ARE YOU FINALLY DEAD, OLD MAN?

GUH!

JEEZ! JUST *DIE* ALREADY! *LET GO,* OLD MAN! *IT'S* BEEN *THREE DAYS!*

:KOFF:
WHHEEEEZZ

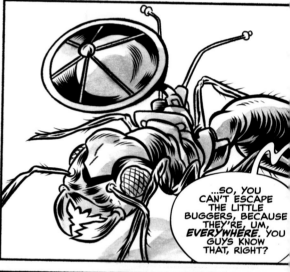

...SO, YOU CAN'T ESCAPE THE LITTLE BUGGERS, BECAUSE THEY'RE, UM, *EVERYWHERE.* YOU GUYS KNOW THAT, RIGHT?

AND HERE YOU CAN *SEE* EVERYTHING EACH MODIFIED ANT *HEARS...ER,* YOU KNOW WHAT I MEAN...AND ISSUE SIMPLE COMMANDS, AND THEY CAN RESPOND IN A BASIC CAPACITY.

THIS IS, UH, AS FAR AS WE'VE GOTTEN WITH IT.

DESPITE YOUR *INCREDIBLE* INCOMPETENCE DURING THIS *ENTIRE* PRESENTATION, THE TECHNOLOGY YOUR TEAM HAS DEVELOPED IS QUITE A SOLID FOUNDATION. IT SPEAKS FOR ITSELF. AND THE TECH DOES SEEM *FOND* OF YOU.

UHHH...YES! WELL! MY TEAM IS-- *OW!*--VERY FRIENDLY-- *OW!*--WITH THEM.

HA... LOVE BITES.

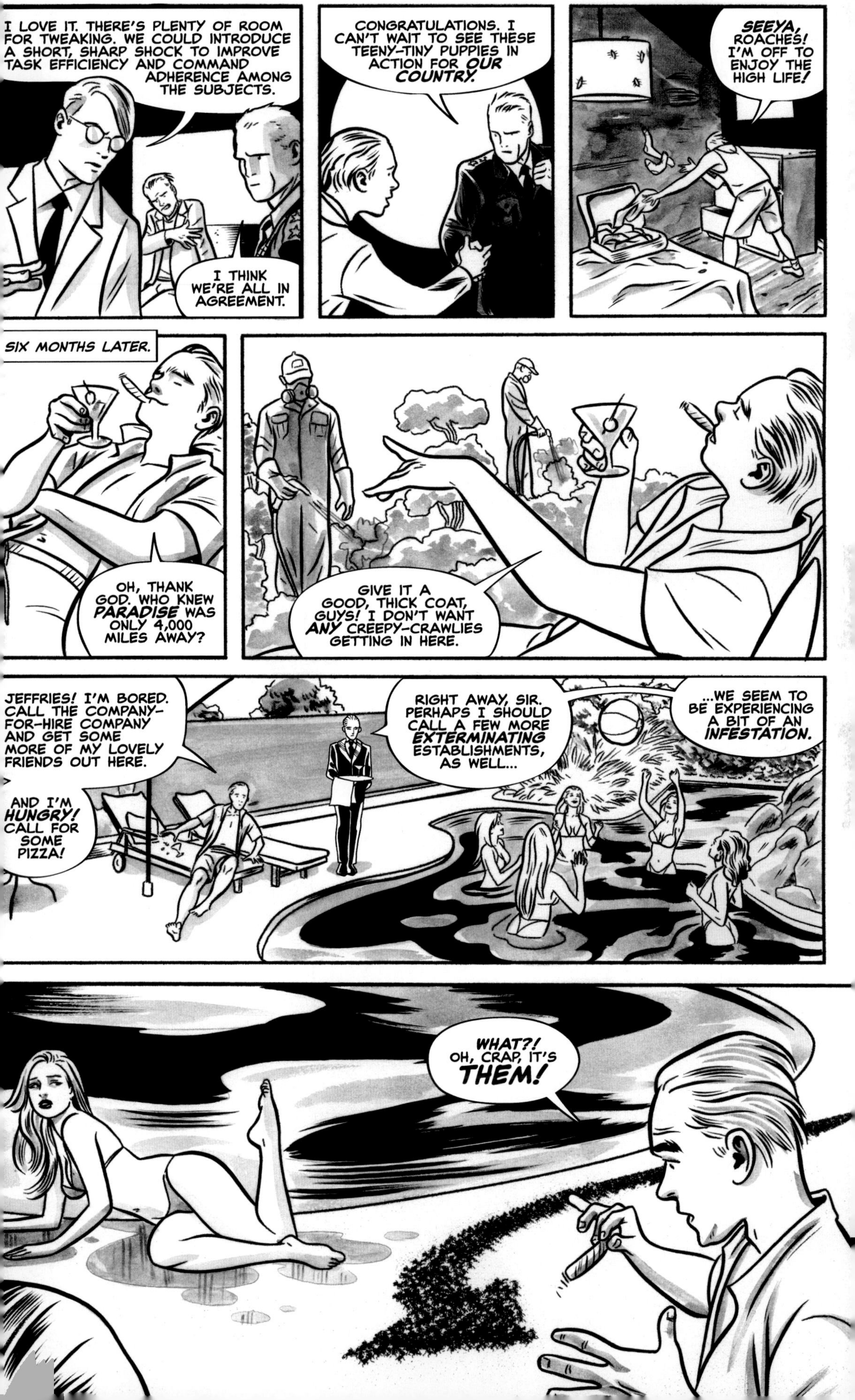
I LOVE IT. THERE'S PLENTY OF ROOM FOR TWEAKING. WE COULD INTRODUCE A SHORT, SHARP SHOCK TO IMPROVE TASK EFFICIENCY AND COMMAND ADHERENCE AMONG THE SUBJECTS.
I THINK WE'RE ALL IN AGREEMENT.
CONGRATULATIONS. I CAN'T WAIT TO SEE THESE TEENY-TINY PUPPIES IN ACTION FOR OUR COUNTRY.
SEEYA, ROACHES! I'M OFF TO ENJOY THE HIGH LIFE!
SIX MONTHS LATER.
OH, THANK GOD. WHO KNEW PARADISE WAS ONLY 4,000 MILES AWAY?
GIVE IT A GOOD, THICK COAT, GUYS! I DON'T WANT ANY CREEPY-CRAWLIES GETTING IN HERE.
JEFFRIES! I'M BORED. CALL THE COMPANY-FOR-HIRE COMPANY AND GET SOME MORE OF MY LOVELY FRIENDS OUT HERE.
AND I'M HUNGRY! CALL FOR SOME PIZZA!
RIGHT AWAY, SIR. PERHAPS I SHOULD CALL A FEW MORE EXTERMINATING ESTABLISHMENTS, AS WELL...
...WE SEEM TO BE EXPERIENCING A BIT OF AN INFESTATION.
WHAT?! OH, CRAP, IT'S THEM!

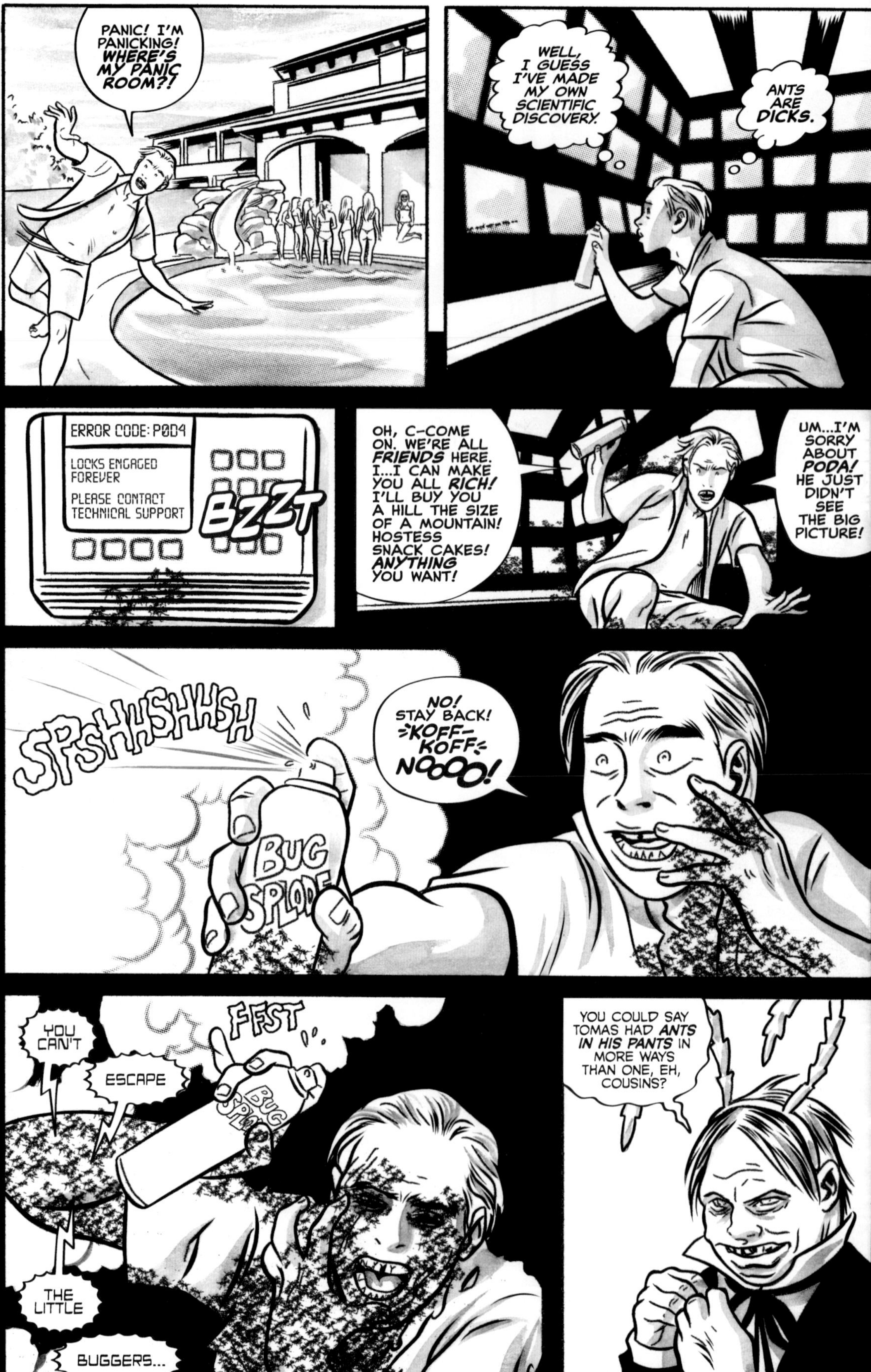
PANIC! I'M PANICKING! WHERE'S MY PANIC ROOM?!
WELL, I GUESS I'VE MADE MY OWN SCIENTIFIC DISCOVERY.
ANTS ARE DICKS.
ERROR CODE: P0D4
LOCKS ENGAGED FOREVER
PLEASE CONTACT TECHNICAL SUPPORT
BZZT
OH, C-COME ON. WE'RE ALL FRIENDS HERE. I...I CAN MAKE YOU ALL RICH! I'LL BUY YOU A HILL THE SIZE OF A MOUNTAIN! HOSTESS SNACK CAKES! ANYTHING YOU WANT!
UM...I'M SORRY ABOUT PODA! HE JUST DIDN'T SEE THE BIG PICTURE!
SPSHHSHHSH
NO! STAY BACK! KOFF-KOFF NOOOO!
BUG SPLODE
FFST
YOU CAN'T
ESCAPE
THE LITTLE
BUGGERS...
YOU COULD SAY TOMAS HAD ANTS IN HIS PANTS IN MORE WAYS THAN ONE, EH, COUSINS?
THE END

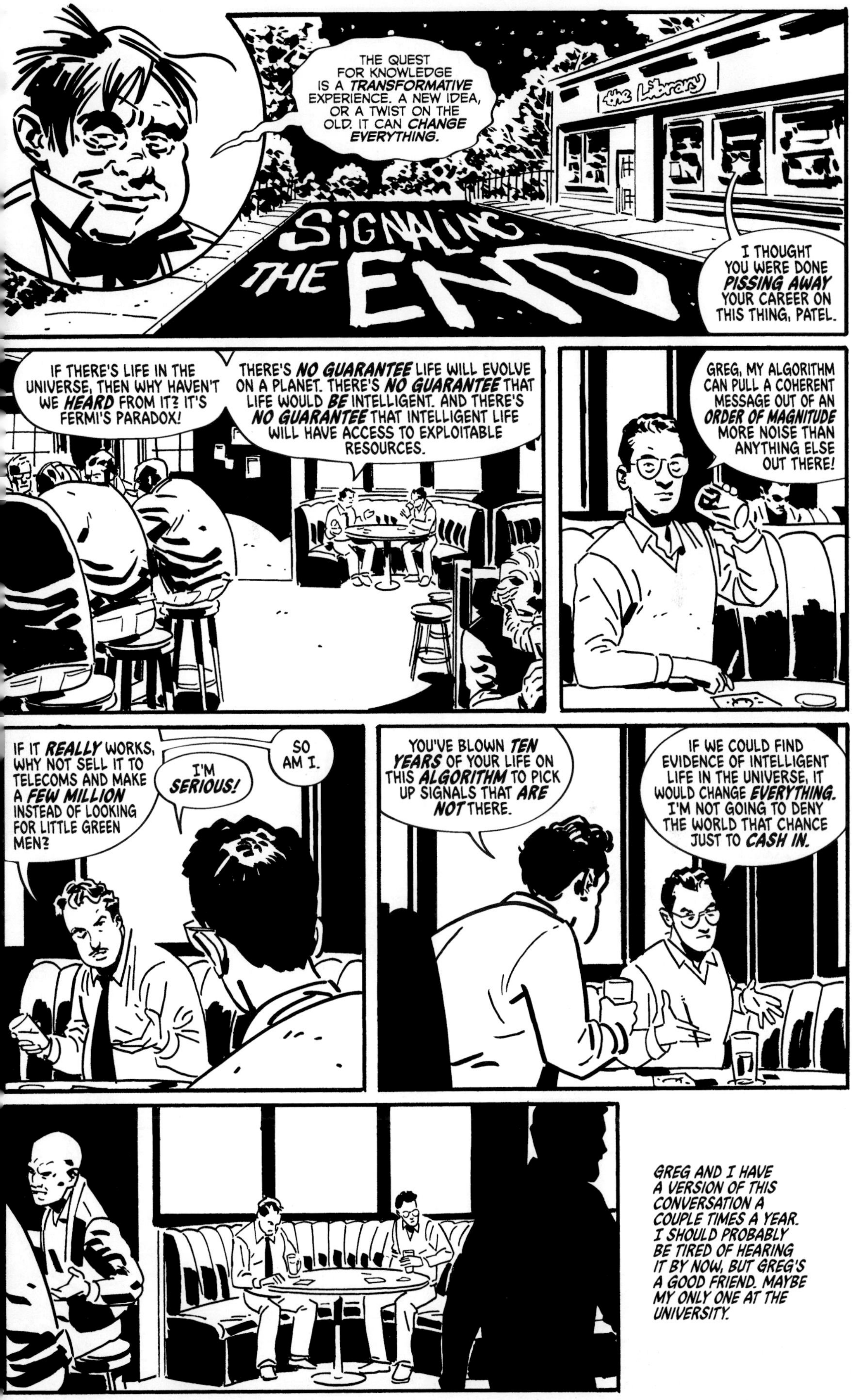

THE QUEST FOR KNOWLEDGE IS A TRANSFORMATIVE EXPERIENCE. A NEW IDEA, OR A TWIST ON THE OLD. IT CAN CHANGE EVERYTHING.
the Library
SIGNALING THE END
I THOUGHT YOU WERE DONE PISSING AWAY YOUR CAREER ON THIS THING, PATEL.
IF THERE'S LIFE IN THE UNIVERSE, THEN WHY HAVEN'T WE HEARD FROM IT? IT'S FERMI'S PARADOX!
THERE'S NO GUARANTEE LIFE WILL EVOLVE ON A PLANET. THERE'S NO GUARANTEE THAT LIFE WOULD BE INTELLIGENT. AND THERE'S NO GUARANTEE THAT INTELLIGENT LIFE WILL HAVE ACCESS TO EXPLOITABLE RESOURCES.
GREG, MY ALGORITHM CAN PULL A COHERENT MESSAGE OUT OF AN ORDER OF MAGNITUDE MORE NOISE THAN ANYTHING ELSE OUT THERE!
IF IT REALLY WORKS, WHY NOT SELL IT TO TELECOMS AND MAKE A FEW MILLION INSTEAD OF LOOKING FOR LITTLE GREEN MEN?
I'M SERIOUS!
SO AM I.
YOU'VE BLOWN TEN YEARS OF YOUR LIFE ON THIS ALGORITHM TO PICK UP SIGNALS THAT ARE NOT THERE.
IF WE COULD FIND EVIDENCE OF INTELLIGENT LIFE IN THE UNIVERSE, IT WOULD CHANGE EVERYTHING. I'M NOT GOING TO DENY THE WORLD THAT CHANCE JUST TO CASH IN.
GREG AND I HAVE A VERSION OF THIS CONVERSATION A COUPLE TIMES A YEAR. I SHOULD PROBABLY BE TIRED OF HEARING IT BY NOW, BUT GREG'S A GOOD FRIEND. MAYBE MY ONLY ONE AT THE UNIVERSITY.

Script by BRIAN CLEVINGER / Art by EVAN SHANER

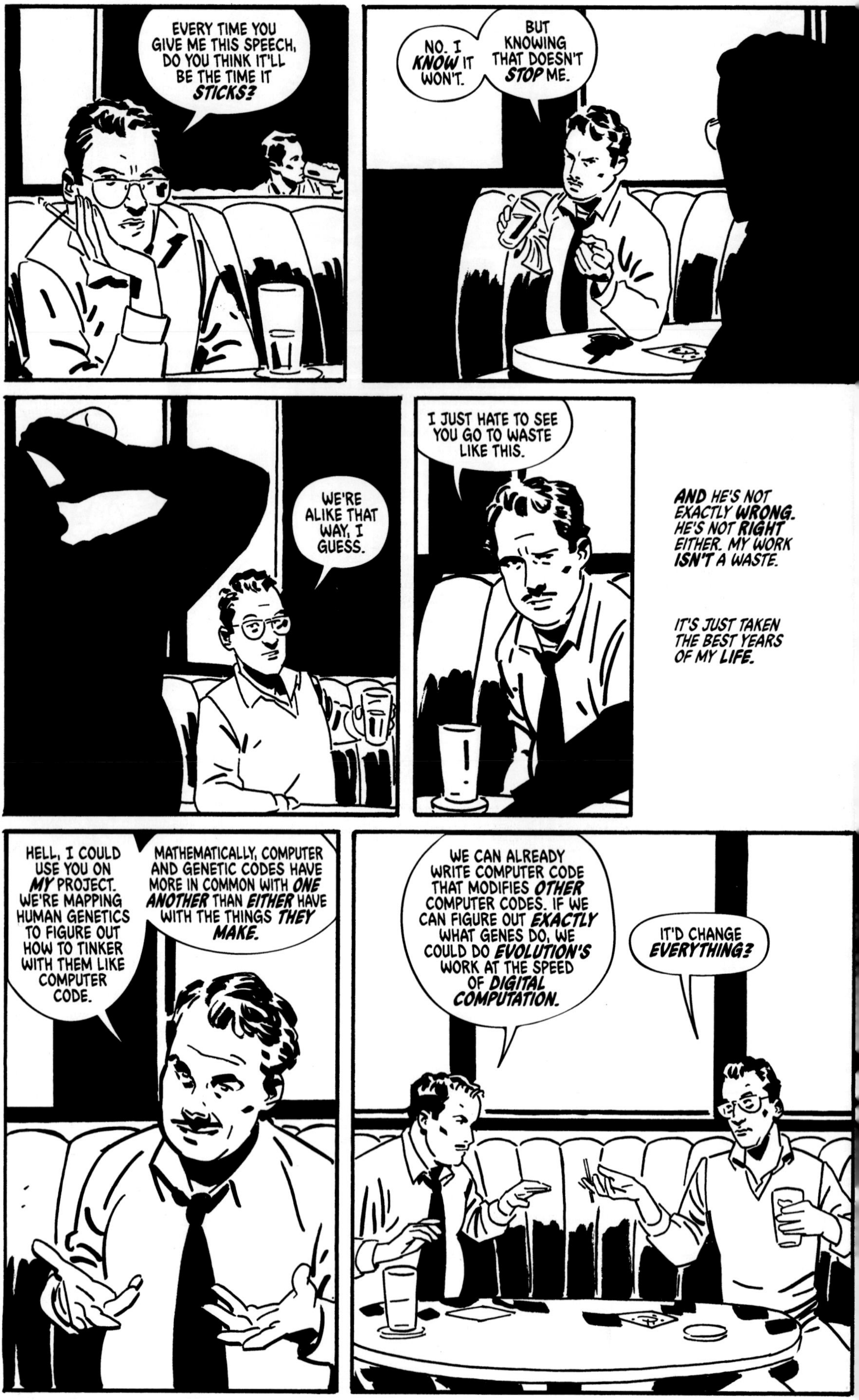
EVERY TIME YOU GIVE ME THIS SPEECH, DO YOU THINK IT'LL BE THE TIME IT *STICKS?*
NO. I *KNOW* IT WON'T.
BUT KNOWING THAT DOESN'T *STOP* ME.
WE'RE ALIKE THAT WAY, I GUESS.
I JUST HATE TO SEE YOU GO TO WASTE LIKE THIS.
AND HE'S NOT EXACTLY *WRONG.* HE'S NOT *RIGHT* EITHER. MY WORK *ISN'T* A WASTE.
IT'S JUST TAKEN THE BEST YEARS OF MY *LIFE.*
HELL, I COULD USE YOU ON *MY* PROJECT. WE'RE MAPPING HUMAN GENETICS TO FIGURE OUT HOW TO TINKER WITH THEM LIKE COMPUTER CODE.
MATHEMATICALLY, COMPUTER AND GENETIC CODES HAVE MORE IN COMMON WITH *ONE ANOTHER* THAN *EITHER* HAVE WITH THE THINGS *THEY MAKE.*
WE CAN ALREADY WRITE COMPUTER CODE THAT MODIFIES *OTHER* COMPUTER CODES. IF WE CAN FIGURE OUT *EXACTLY* WHAT GENES DO, WE COULD DO *EVOLUTION'S* WORK AT THE SPEED OF *DIGITAL COMPUTATION.*
IT'D CHANGE *EVERYTHING?*

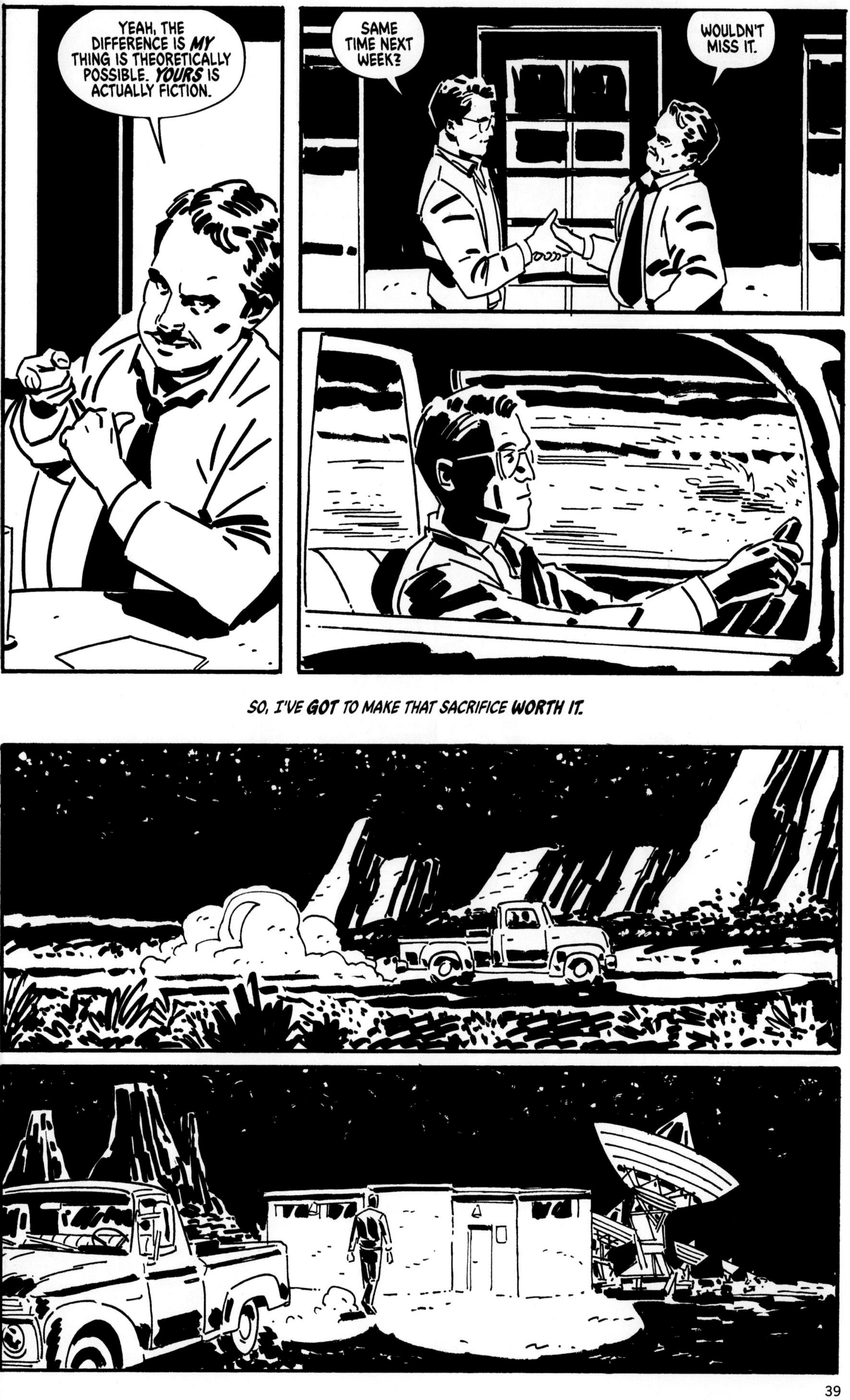
YEAH, THE DIFFERENCE IS *MY* THING IS THEORETICALLY POSSIBLE. *YOURS* IS ACTUALLY FICTION.
SAME TIME NEXT WEEK?
WOULDN'T MISS IT.
SO, I'VE **GOT** TO MAKE THAT SACRIFICE **WORTH IT.**

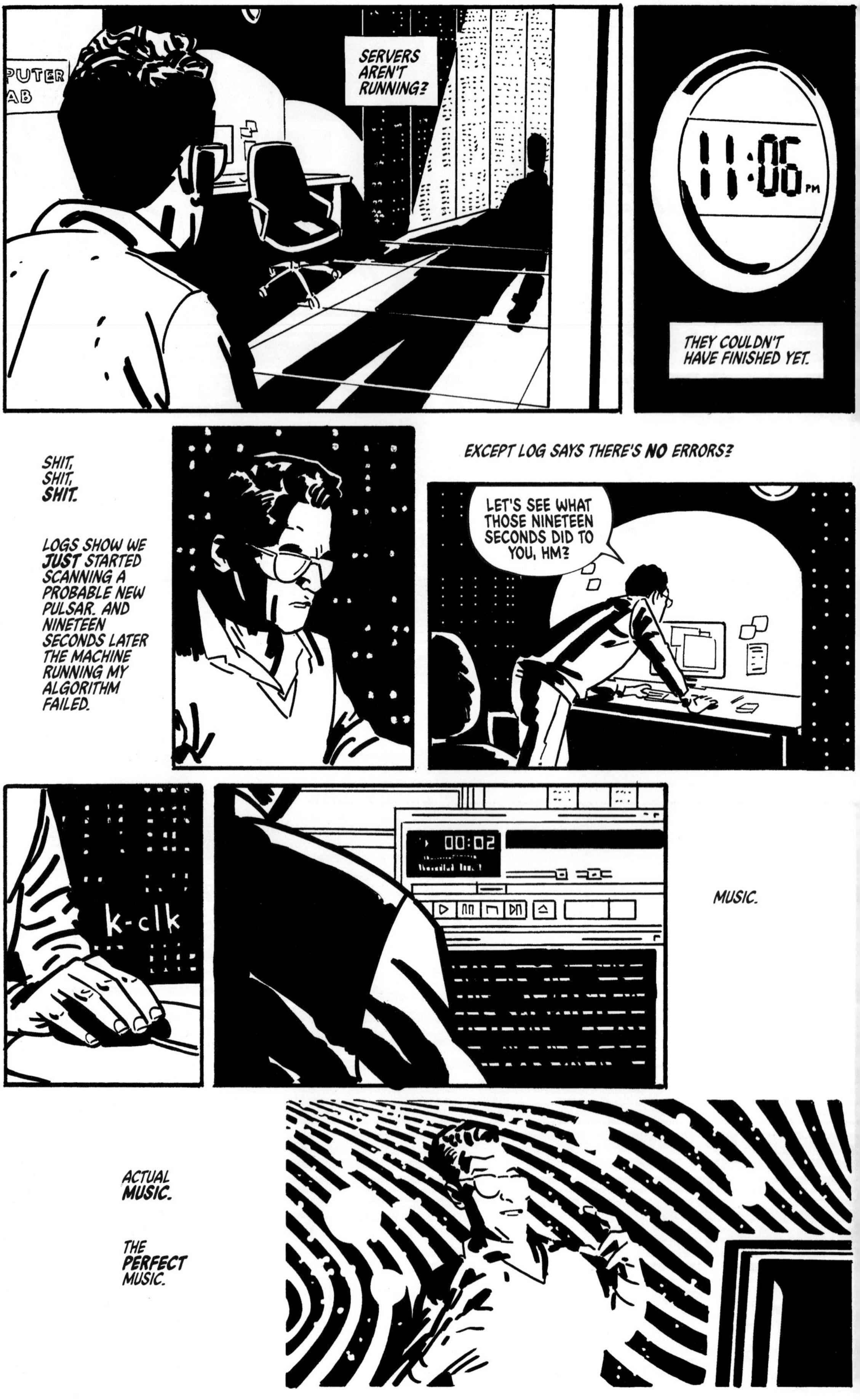
SERVERS AREN'T RUNNING?
11:06 PM
THEY COULDN'T HAVE FINISHED YET.
SHIT, SHIT, **SHIT.**
LOGS SHOW WE **JUST** STARTED SCANNING A PROBABLE NEW PULSAR. AND NINETEEN SECONDS LATER THE MACHINE RUNNING MY ALGORITHM FAILED.
EXCEPT LOG SAYS THERE'S **NO** ERRORS?
LET'S SEE WHAT THOSE NINETEEN SECONDS DID TO YOU, HM?
k-clk
00:02
MUSIC.
ACTUAL **MUSIC.**
THE **PERFECT** MUSIC.

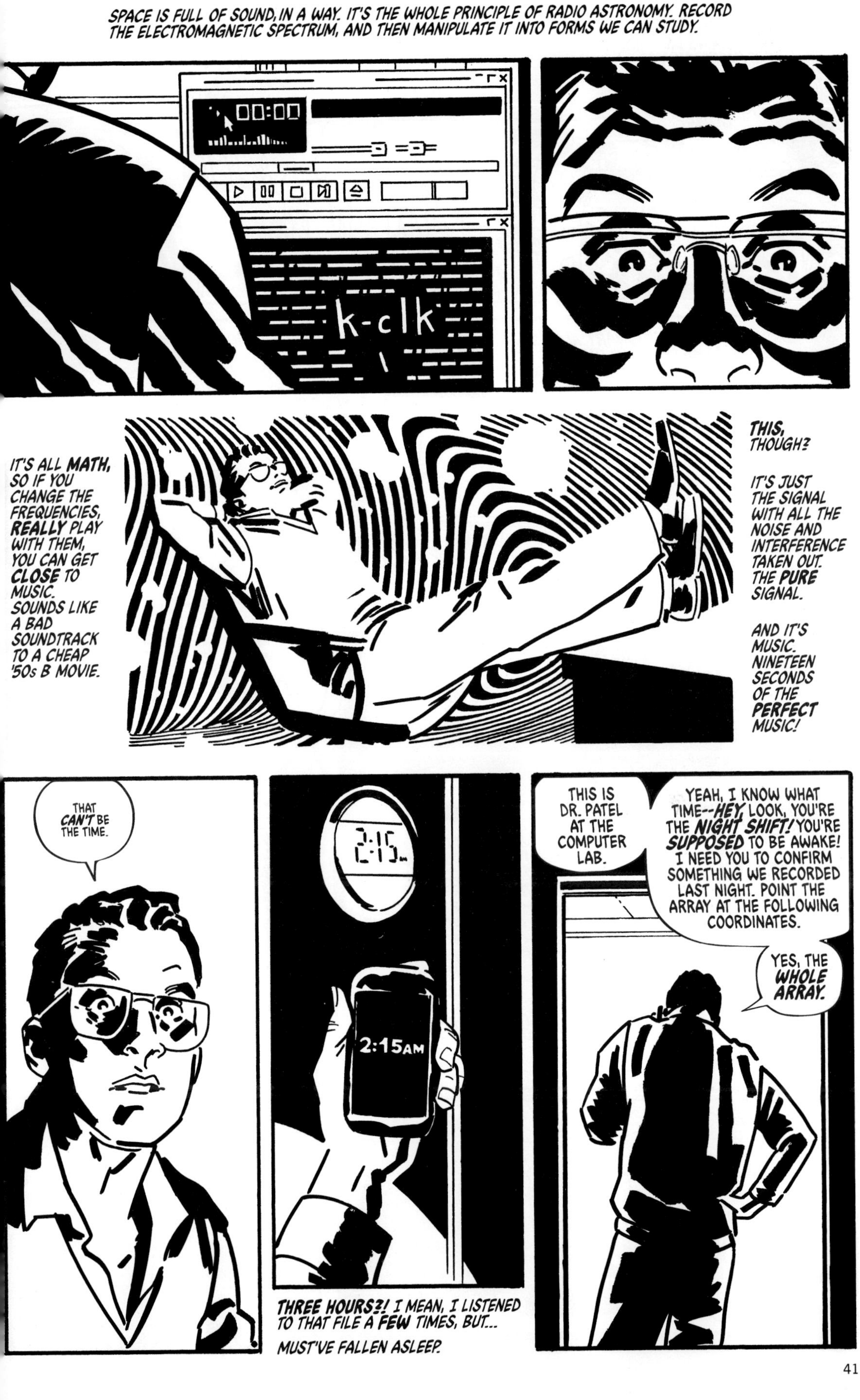
SPACE IS FULL OF SOUND, IN A WAY. IT'S THE WHOLE PRINCIPLE OF RADIO ASTRONOMY. RECORD THE ELECTROMAGNETIC SPECTRUM, AND THEN MANIPULATE IT INTO FORMS WE CAN STUDY.
00:00
k-clk
IT'S ALL MATH, SO IF YOU CHANGE THE FREQUENCIES, REALLY PLAY WITH THEM, YOU CAN GET CLOSE TO MUSIC. SOUNDS LIKE A BAD SOUNDTRACK TO A CHEAP '50s B MOVIE.
THIS, THOUGH?
IT'S JUST THE SIGNAL WITH ALL THE NOISE AND INTERFERENCE TAKEN OUT. THE PURE SIGNAL.
AND IT'S MUSIC. NINETEEN SECONDS OF THE PERFECT MUSIC!
THAT CAN'T BE THE TIME.
2:15AM
THREE HOURS?! I MEAN, I LISTENED TO THAT FILE A FEW TIMES, BUT...
MUST'VE FALLEN ASLEEP.
THIS IS DR. PATEL AT THE COMPUTER LAB.
YEAH, I KNOW WHAT TIME--HEY, LOOK, YOU'RE THE NIGHT SHIFT! YOU'RE SUPPOSED TO BE AWAKE! I NEED YOU TO CONFIRM SOMETHING WE RECORDED LAST NIGHT. POINT THE ARRAY AT THE FOLLOWING COORDINATES.
YES, THE WHOLE ARRAY.

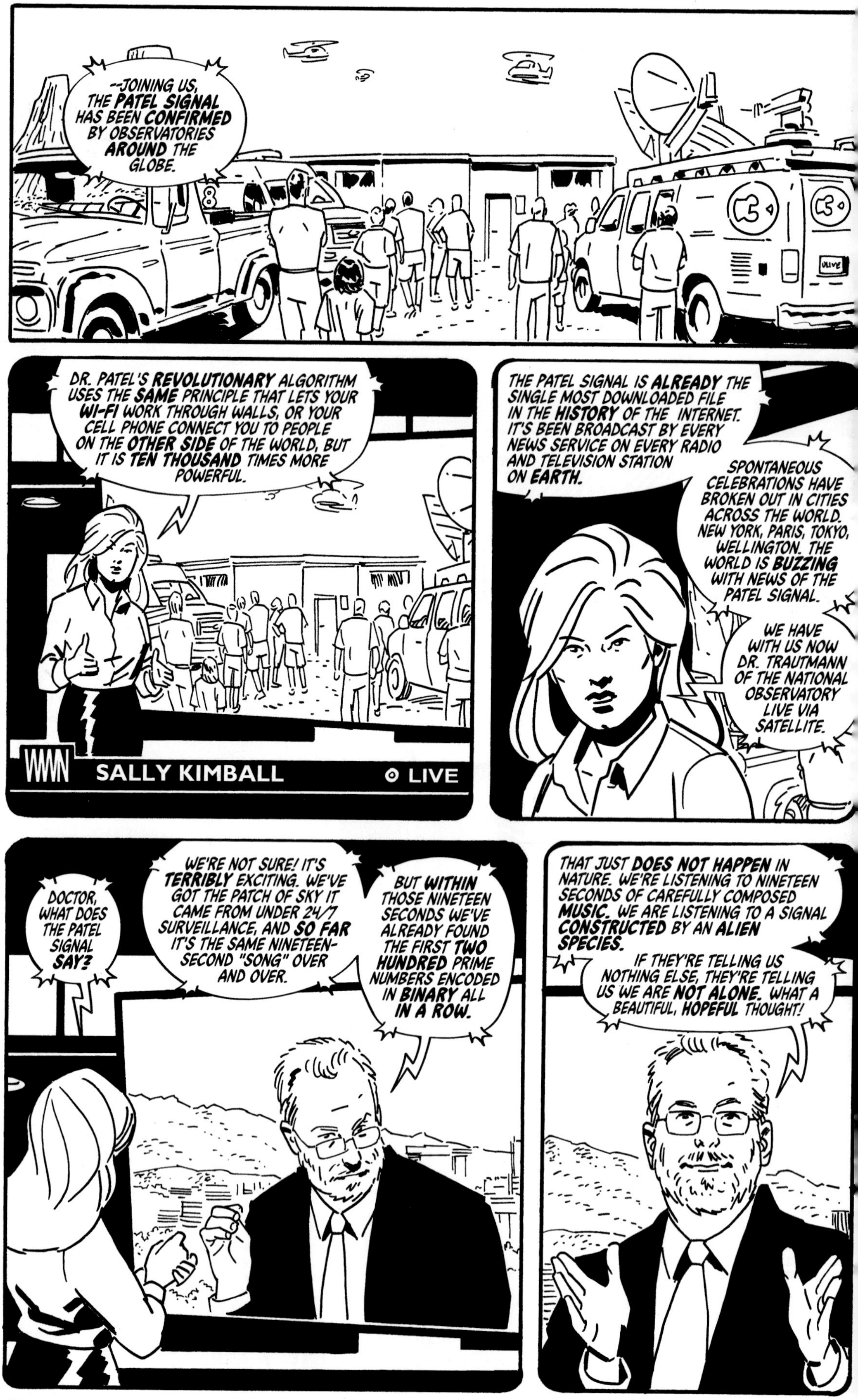
--JOINING US, THE PATEL SIGNAL HAS BEEN CONFIRMED BY OBSERVATORIES AROUND THE GLOBE.
DR. PATEL'S REVOLUTIONARY ALGORITHM USES THE SAME PRINCIPLE THAT LETS YOUR WI-FI WORK THROUGH WALLS, OR YOUR CELL PHONE CONNECT YOU TO PEOPLE ON THE OTHER SIDE OF THE WORLD, BUT IT IS TEN THOUSAND TIMES MORE POWERFUL.
WWN
SALLY KIMBALL
LIVE
THE PATEL SIGNAL IS ALREADY THE SINGLE MOST DOWNLOADED FILE IN THE HISTORY OF THE INTERNET. IT'S BEEN BROADCAST BY EVERY NEWS SERVICE ON EVERY RADIO AND TELEVISION STATION ON EARTH.
SPONTANEOUS CELEBRATIONS HAVE BROKEN OUT IN CITIES ACROSS THE WORLD. NEW YORK, PARIS, TOKYO, WELLINGTON. THE WORLD IS BUZZING WITH NEWS OF THE PATEL SIGNAL.
WE HAVE WITH US NOW DR. TRAUTMANN OF THE NATIONAL OBSERVATORY LIVE VIA SATELLITE.
DOCTOR, WHAT DOES THE PATEL SIGNAL SAY?
WE'RE NOT SURE! IT'S TERRIBLY EXCITING. WE'VE GOT THE PATCH OF SKY IT CAME FROM UNDER 24/7 SURVEILLANCE, AND SO FAR IT'S THE SAME NINETEEN-SECOND "SONG" OVER AND OVER.
BUT WITHIN THOSE NINETEEN SECONDS WE'VE ALREADY FOUND THE FIRST TWO HUNDRED PRIME NUMBERS ENCODED IN BINARY ALL IN A ROW.
THAT JUST DOES NOT HAPPEN IN NATURE. WE'RE LISTENING TO NINETEEN SECONDS OF CAREFULLY COMPOSED MUSIC. WE ARE LISTENING TO A SIGNAL CONSTRUCTED BY AN ALIEN SPECIES.
IF THEY'RE TELLING US NOTHING ELSE, THEY'RE TELLING US WE ARE NOT ALONE. WHAT A BEAUTIFUL, HOPEFUL THOUGHT!

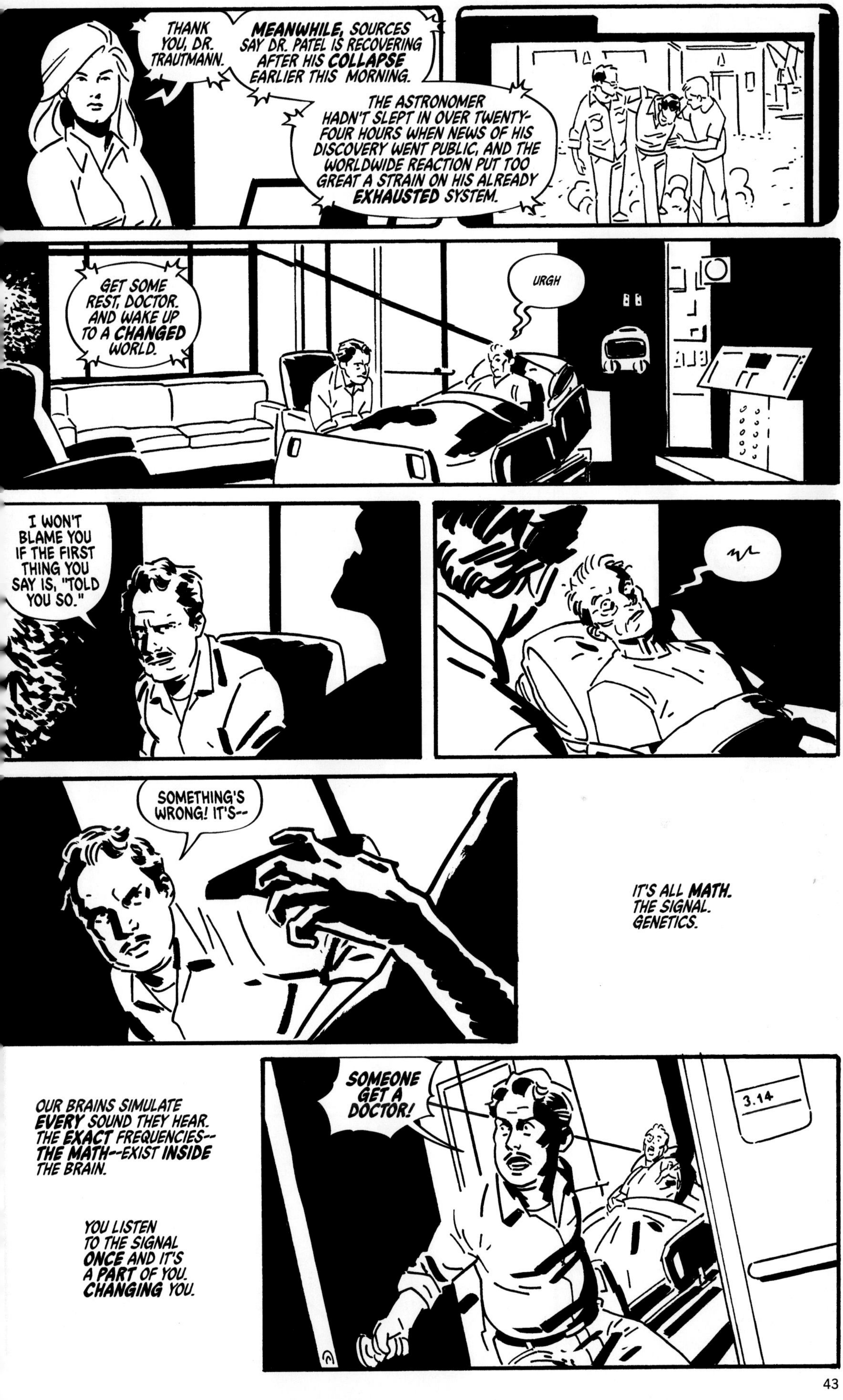

THANK YOU, DR. TRAUTMANN.
MEANWHILE, SOURCES SAY DR. PATEL IS RECOVERING AFTER HIS COLLAPSE EARLIER THIS MORNING.
THE ASTRONOMER HADN'T SLEPT IN OVER TWENTY-FOUR HOURS WHEN NEWS OF HIS DISCOVERY WENT PUBLIC, AND THE WORLDWIDE REACTION PUT TOO GREAT A STRAIN ON HIS ALREADY EXHAUSTED SYSTEM.
GET SOME REST, DOCTOR. AND WAKE UP TO A CHANGED WORLD.
URGH
I WON'T BLAME YOU IF THE FIRST THING YOU SAY IS, "TOLD YOU SO."
SOMETHING'S WRONG! IT'S--
IT'S ALL MATH. THE SIGNAL. GENETICS.
OUR BRAINS SIMULATE EVERY SOUND THEY HEAR. THE EXACT FREQUENCIES--THE MATH--EXIST INSIDE THE BRAIN.
YOU LISTEN TO THE SIGNAL ONCE AND IT'S A PART OF YOU. CHANGING YOU.
SOMEONE GET A DOCTOR!
3.14

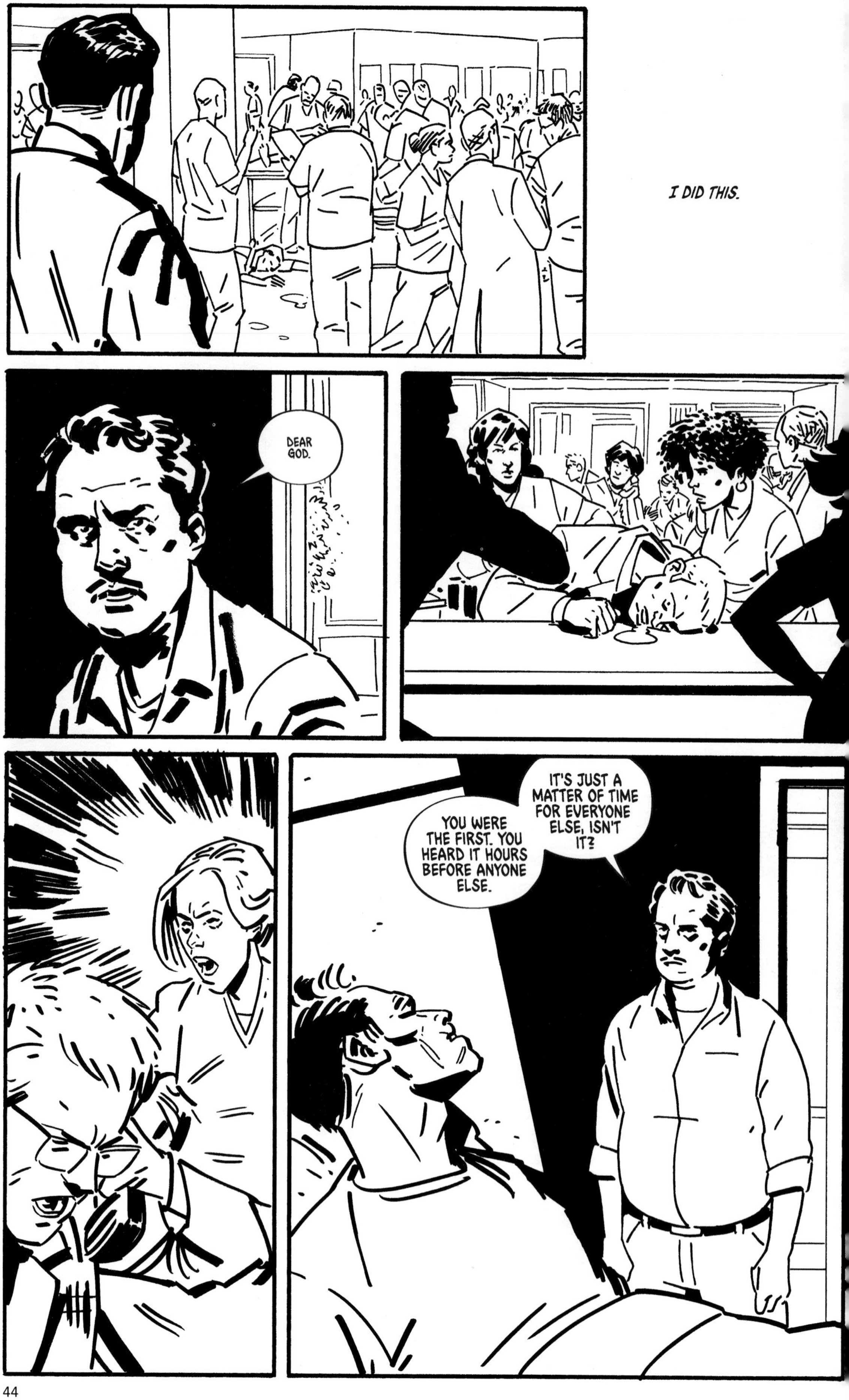
I DID THIS.
DEAR GOD.
YOU WERE THE FIRST. YOU HEARD IT HOURS BEFORE ANYONE ELSE.
IT'S JUST A MATTER OF TIME FOR EVERYONE ELSE, ISN'T IT?

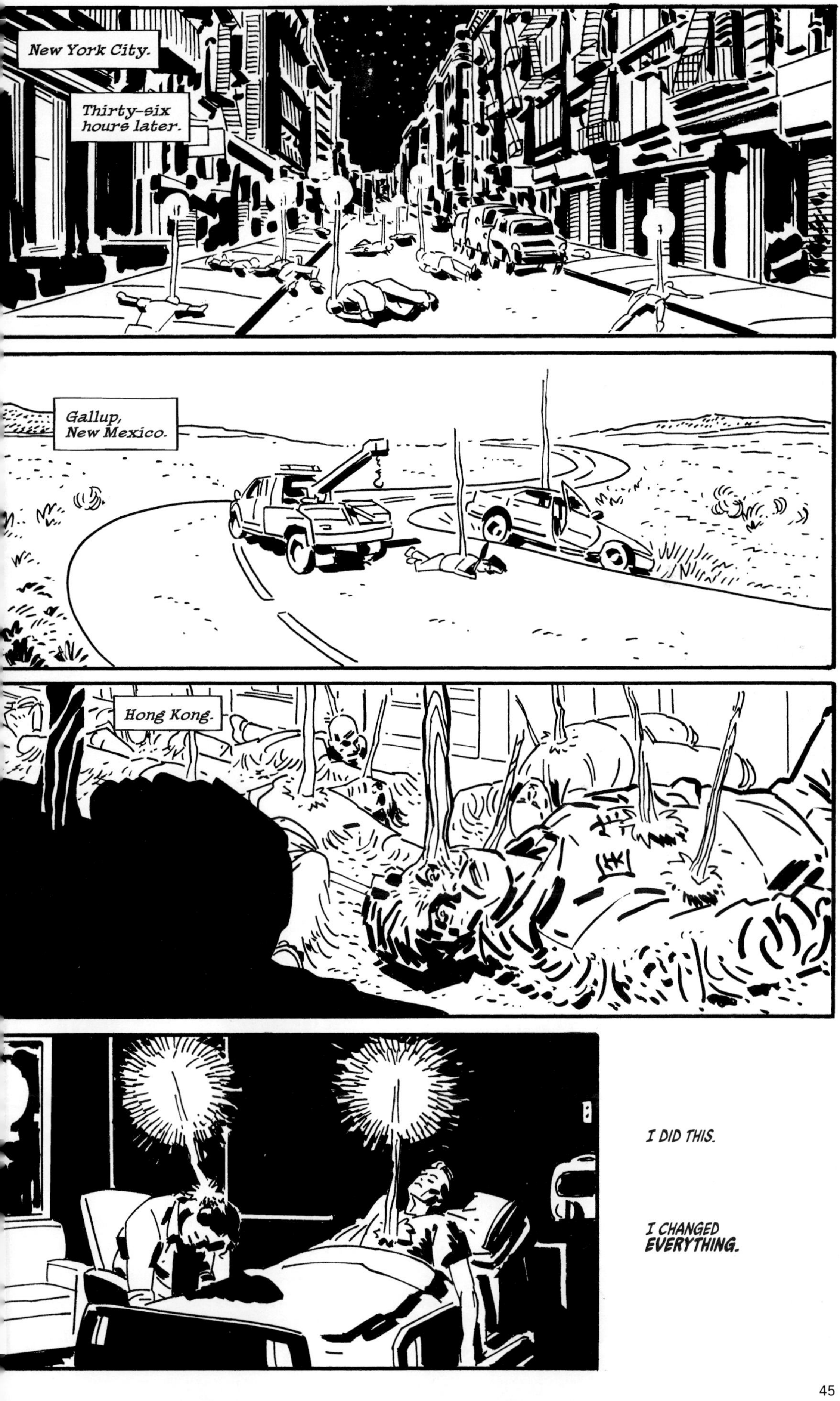
New York City.
Thirty-six hours later.
Gallup, New Mexico.
Hong Kong.
I DID THIS.
I CHANGED EVERYTHING.

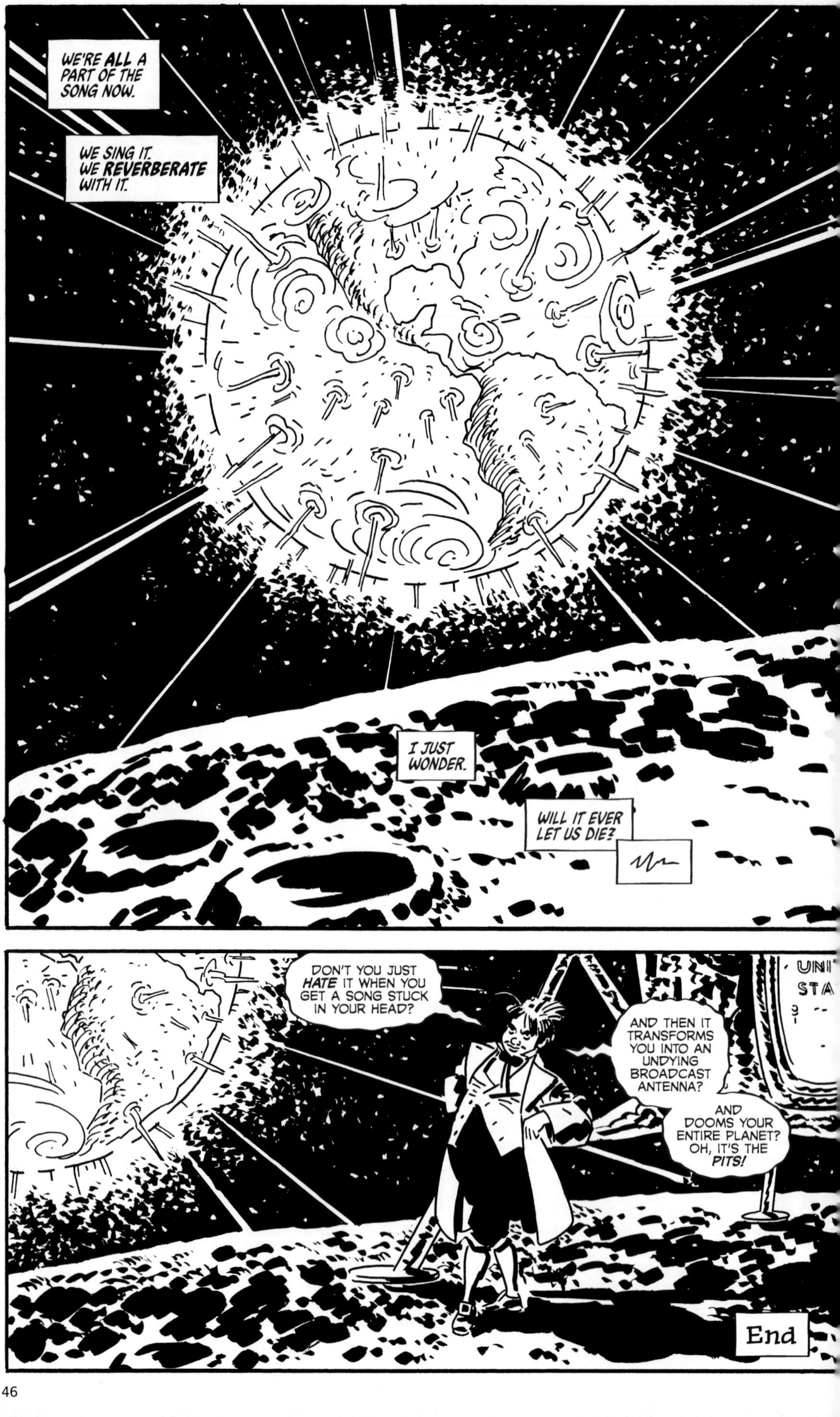
WE'RE ALL A PART OF THE SONG NOW.
WE SING IT. WE REVERBERATE WITH IT.
I JUST WONDER.
WILL IT EVER LET US DIE?
DON'T YOU JUST HATE IT WHEN YOU GET A SONG STUCK IN YOUR HEAD?
AND THEN IT TRANSFORMS YOU INTO AN UNDYING BROADCAST ANTENNA?
AND DOOMS YOUR ENTIRE PLANET? OH, IT'S THE PITS!
End

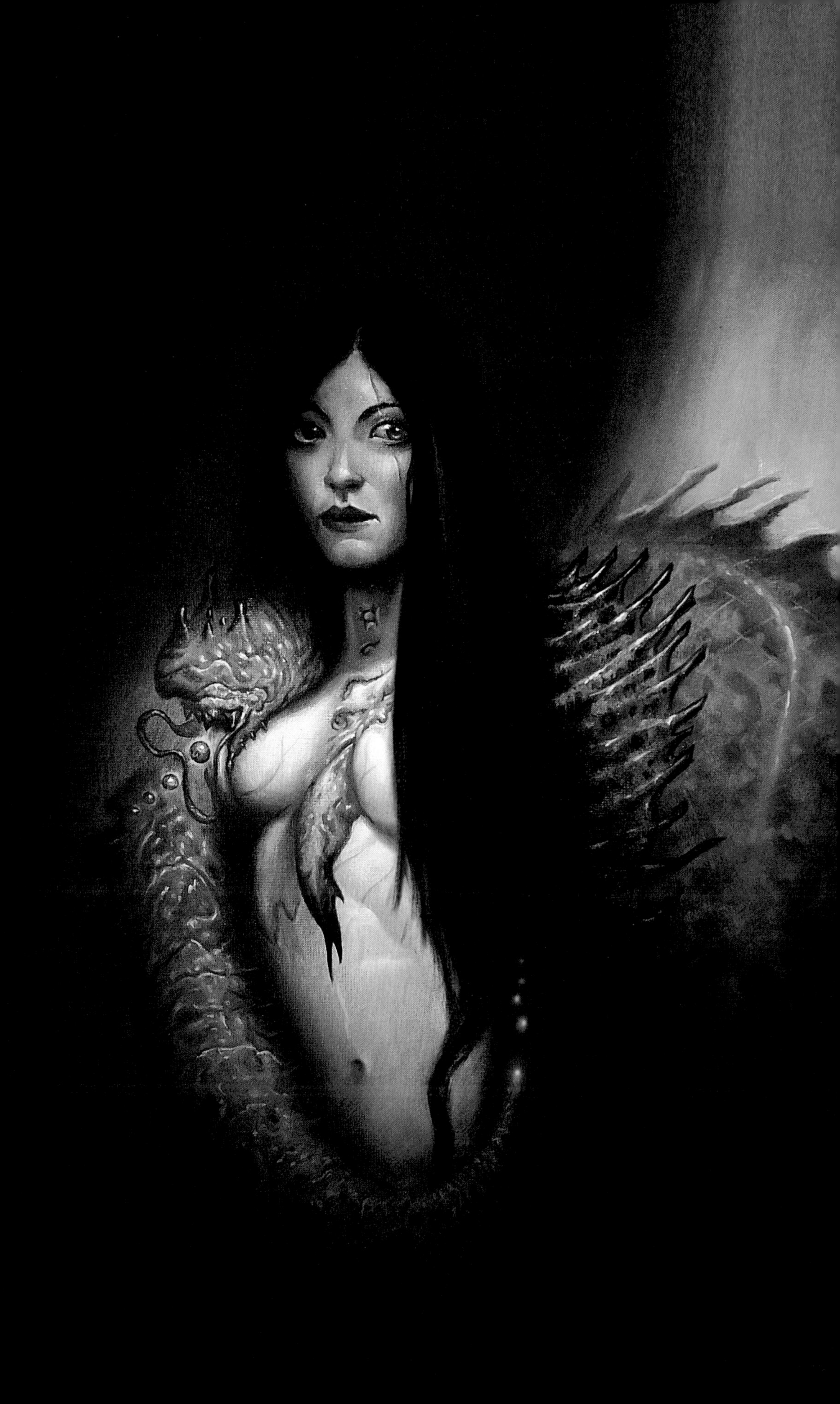

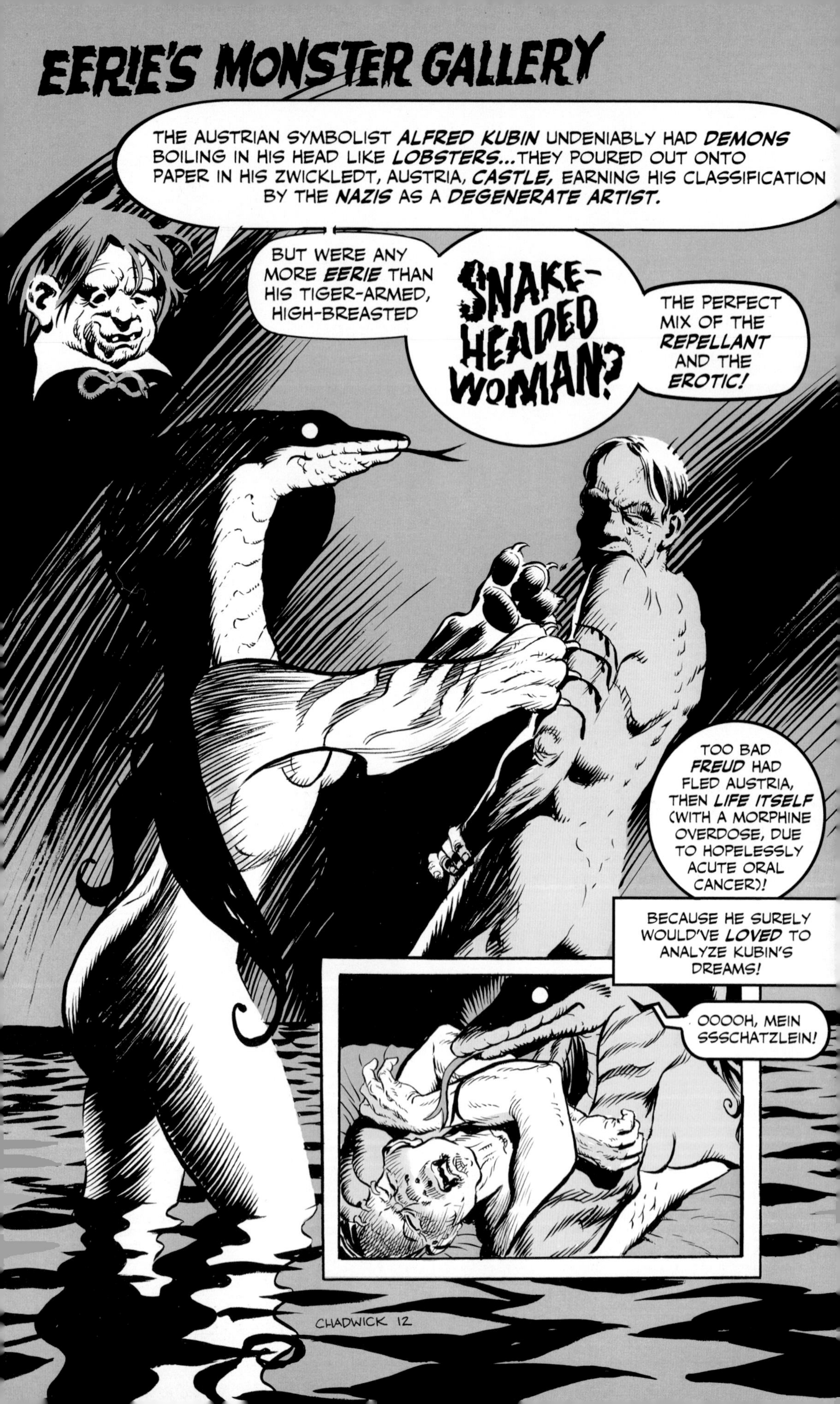
EERIE'S MONSTER GALLERY
THE AUSTRIAN SYMBOLIST ALFRED KUBIN UNDENIABLY HAD DEMONS BOILING IN HIS HEAD LIKE LOBSTERS...THEY POURED OUT ONTO PAPER IN HIS ZWICKLEDT, AUSTRIA, CASTLE, EARNING HIS CLASSIFICATION BY THE NAZIS AS A DEGENERATE ARTIST.
BUT WERE ANY MORE EERIE THAN HIS TIGER-ARMED, HIGH-BREASTED
SNAKE-HEADED WOMAN?
THE PERFECT MIX OF THE REPELLANT AND THE EROTIC!
TOO BAD FREUD HAD FLED AUSTRIA, THEN LIFE ITSELF (WITH A MORPHINE OVERDOSE, DUE TO HOPELESSLY ACUTE ORAL CANCER)!
BECAUSE HE SURELY WOULD'VE LOVED TO ANALYZE KUBIN'S DREAMS!
OOOOH, MEIN SSSCHATZLEIN!
CHADWICK 12

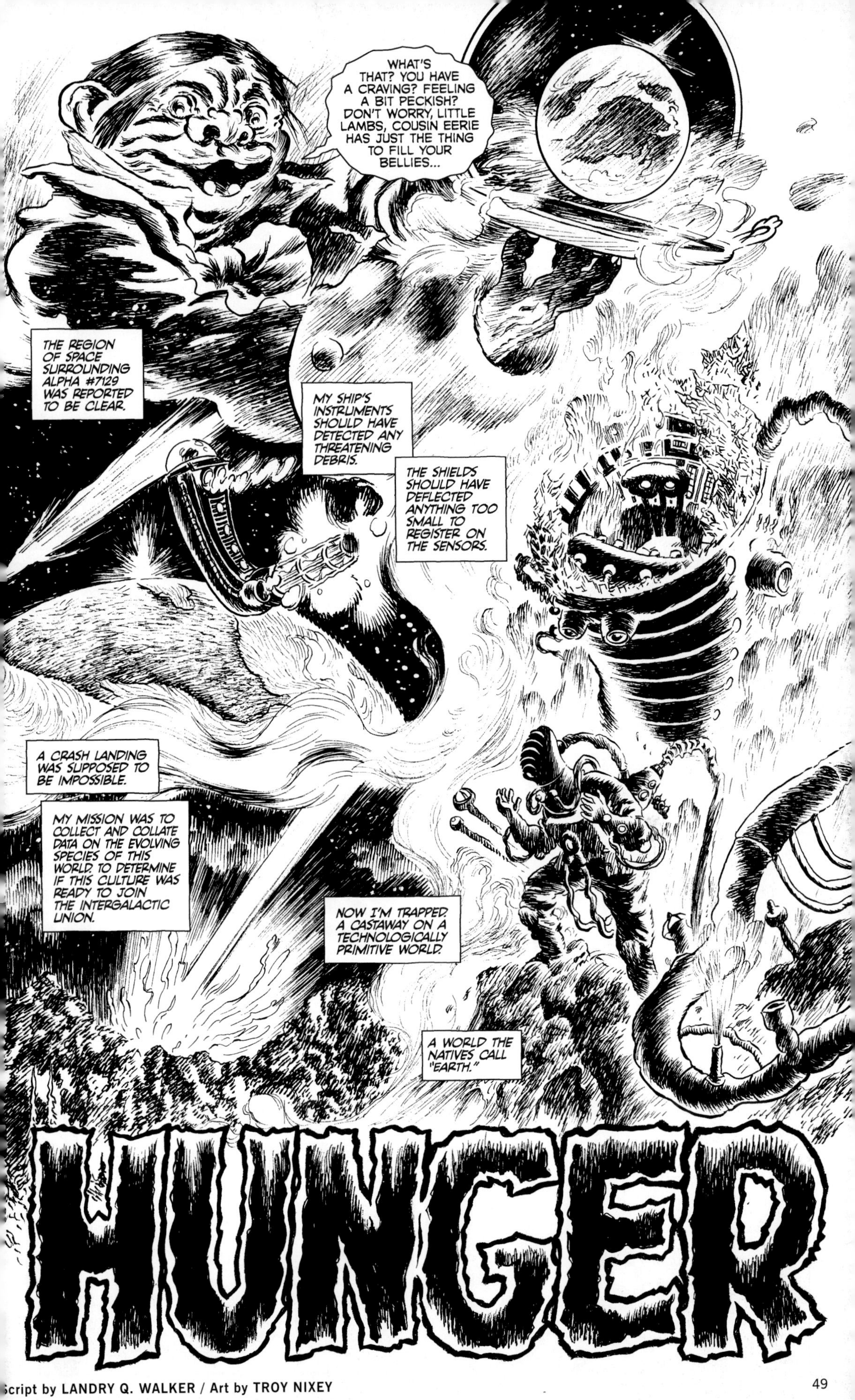
WHAT'S THAT? YOU HAVE A CRAVING? FEELING A BIT PECKISH? DON'T WORRY, LITTLE LAMBS, COUSIN EERIE HAS JUST THE THING TO FILL YOUR BELLIES...
THE REGION OF SPACE SURROUNDING ALPHA #7129 WAS REPORTED TO BE CLEAR.
MY SHIP'S INSTRUMENTS SHOULD HAVE DETECTED ANY THREATENING DEBRIS.
THE SHIELDS SHOULD HAVE DEFLECTED ANYTHING TOO SMALL TO REGISTER ON THE SENSORS.
A CRASH LANDING WAS SUPPOSED TO BE IMPOSSIBLE.
MY MISSION WAS TO COLLECT AND COLLATE DATA ON THE EVOLVING SPECIES OF THIS WORLD TO DETERMINE IF THIS CULTURE WAS READY TO JOIN THE INTERGALACTIC UNION.
NOW I'M TRAPPED. A CASTAWAY ON A TECHNOLOGICALLY PRIMITIVE WORLD.
A WORLD THE NATIVES CALL "EARTH."
HUNGER

Script by LANDRY Q. WALKER / Art by TROY NIXEY

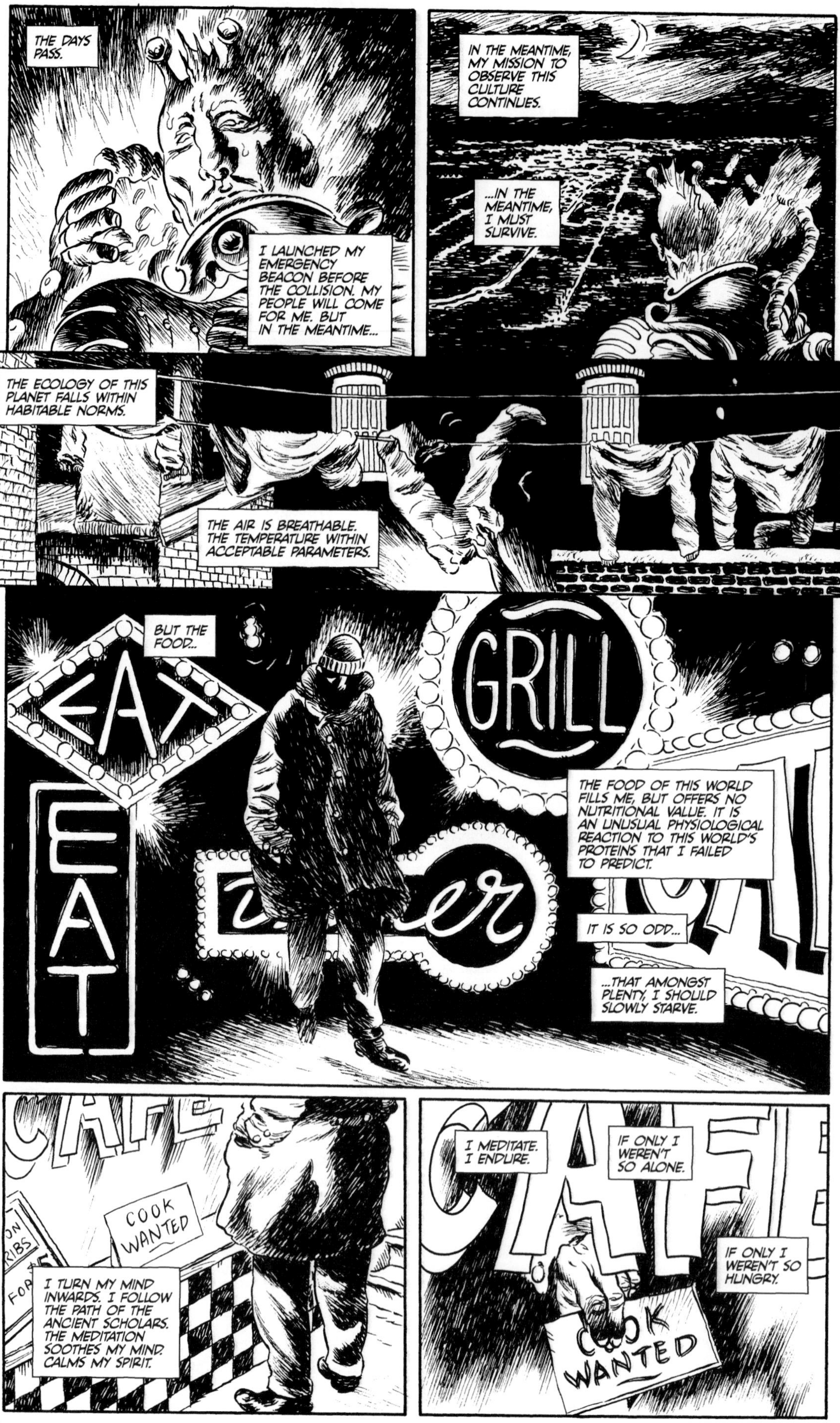
THE DAYS PASS.
I LAUNCHED MY EMERGENCY BEACON BEFORE THE COLLISION. MY PEOPLE WILL COME FOR ME. BUT IN THE MEANTIME...
IN THE MEANTIME, MY MISSION TO OBSERVE THIS CULTURE CONTINUES.
...IN THE MEANTIME, I MUST SURVIVE.
THE ECOLOGY OF THIS PLANET FALLS WITHIN HABITABLE NORMS.
THE AIR IS BREATHABLE. THE TEMPERATURE WITHIN ACCEPTABLE PARAMETERS.
BUT THE FOOD...
EAT
GRILL
EAT
THE FOOD OF THIS WORLD FILLS ME, BUT OFFERS NO NUTRITIONAL VALUE. IT IS AN UNUSUAL PHYSIOLOGICAL REACTION TO THIS WORLD'S PROTEINS THAT I FAILED TO PREDICT.
IT IS SO ODD...
...THAT AMONGST PLENTY, I SHOULD SLOWLY STARVE.
COOK WANTED
I TURN MY MIND INWARDS. I FOLLOW THE PATH OF THE ANCIENT SCHOLARS. THE MEDITATION SOOTHES MY MIND. CALMS MY SPIRIT.
I MEDITATE. I ENDURE.
IF ONLY I WEREN'T SO ALONE.
IF ONLY I WEREN'T SO HUNGRY.
WANTED

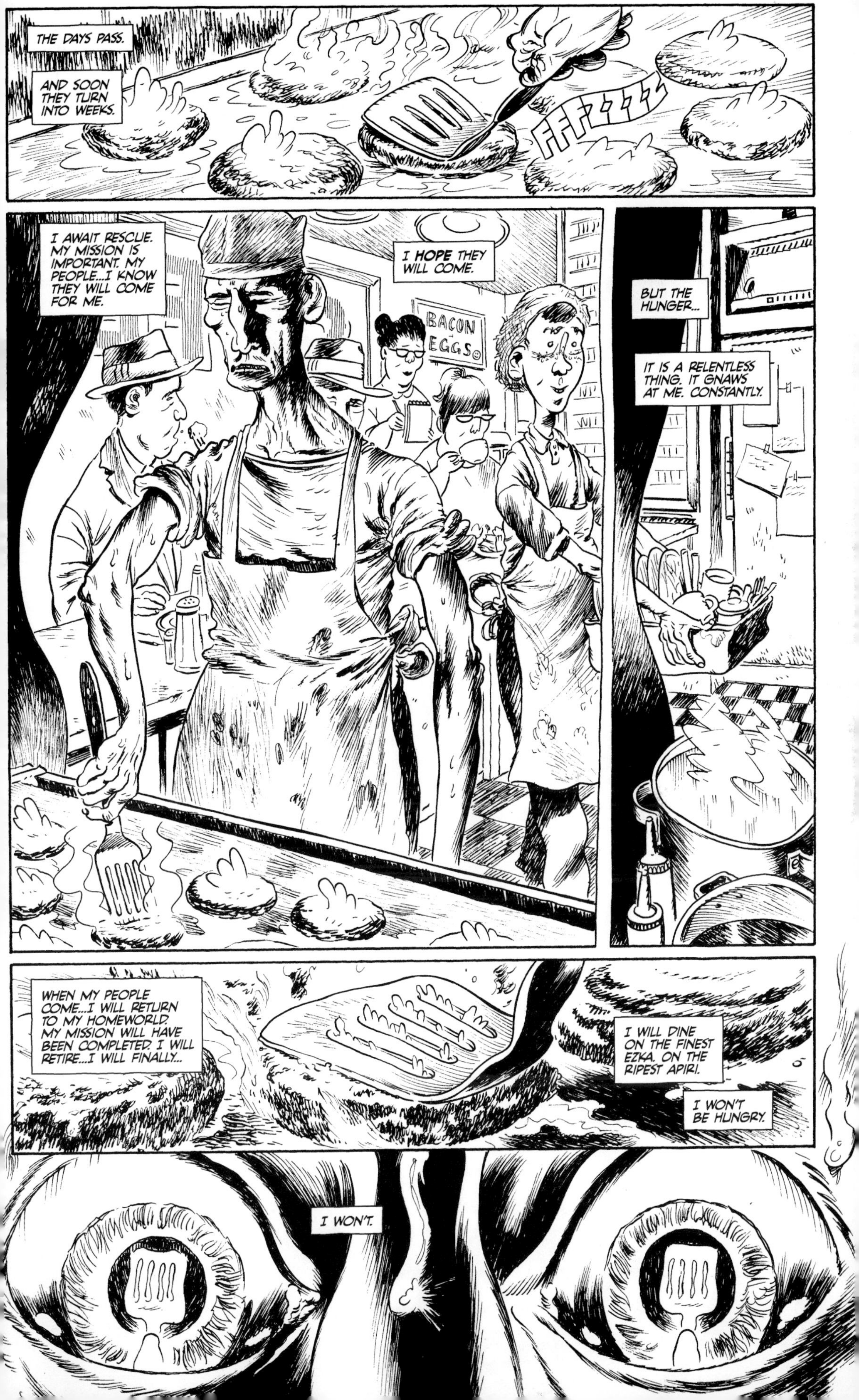

THE DAYS PASS.
AND SOON THEY TURN INTO WEEKS.
FFFZZZZZ
I AWAIT RESCUE. MY MISSION IS IMPORTANT. MY PEOPLE...I KNOW THEY WILL COME FOR ME.
I HOPE THEY WILL COME.
BACON EGGS
BUT THE HUNGER...
IT IS A RELENTLESS THING. IT GNAWS AT ME. CONSTANTLY.
WHEN MY PEOPLE COME...I WILL RETURN TO MY HOMEWORLD. MY MISSION WILL HAVE BEEN COMPLETED. I WILL RETIRE...I WILL FINALLY...
I WILL DINE ON THE FINEST EZKA. ON THE RIPEST APIRI.
I WON'T BE HUNGRY.
I WON'T.

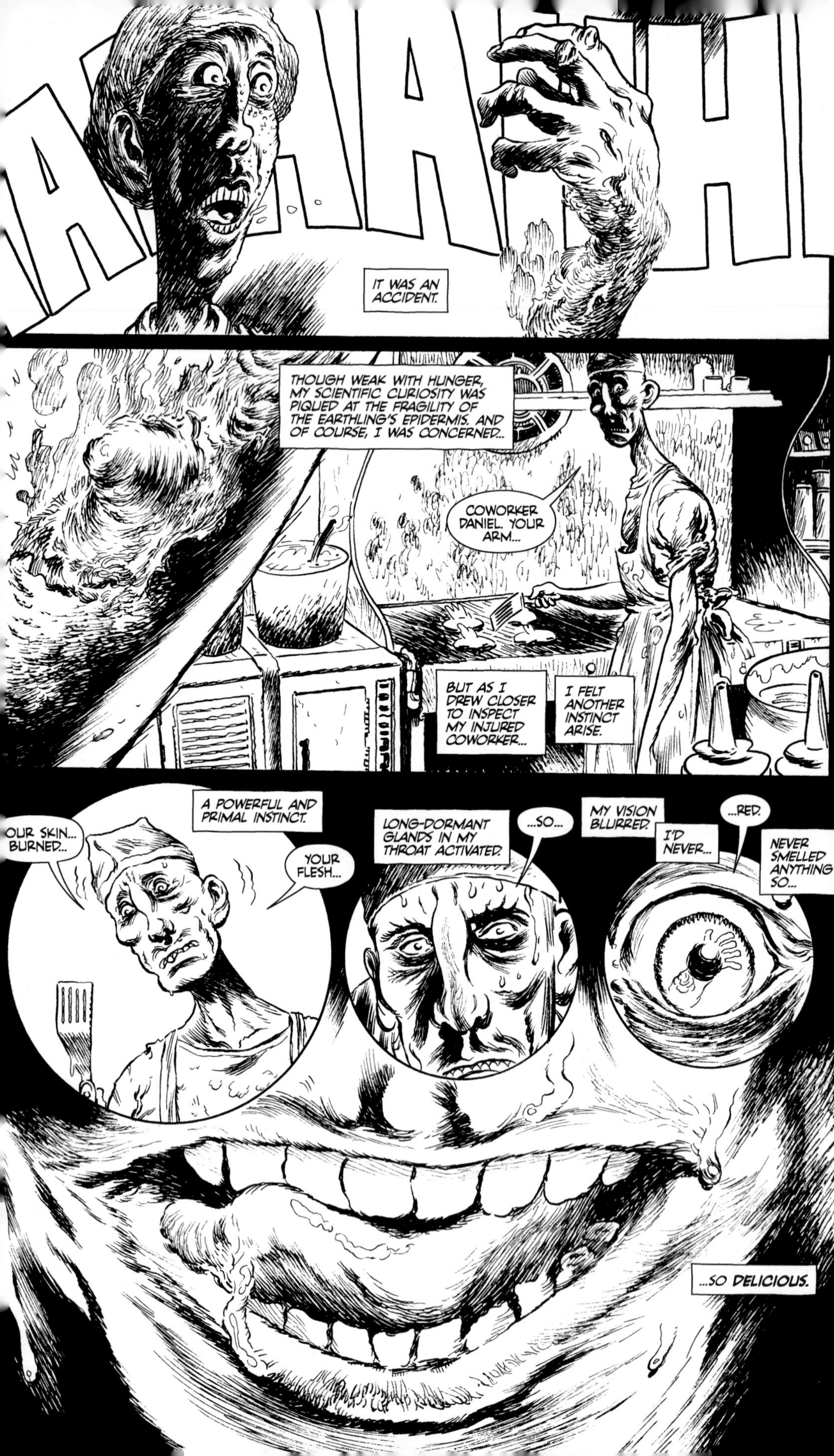
AAAAAHHH
IT WAS AN ACCIDENT.
THOUGH WEAK WITH HUNGER, MY SCIENTIFIC CURIOSITY WAS PIQUED AT THE FRAGILITY OF THE EARTHLING'S EPIDERMIS. AND OF COURSE, I WAS CONCERNED...
COWORKER DANIEL. YOUR ARM...
BUT AS I DREW CLOSER TO INSPECT MY INJURED COWORKER...
I FELT ANOTHER INSTINCT ARISE.
A POWERFUL AND PRIMAL INSTINCT.
OUR SKIN... BURNED...
YOUR FLESH...
LONG-DORMANT GLANDS IN MY THROAT ACTIVATED.
...SO...
MY VISION BLURRED.
I'D NEVER...
...RED.
NEVER SMELLED ANYTHING SO...
...SO DELICIOUS.

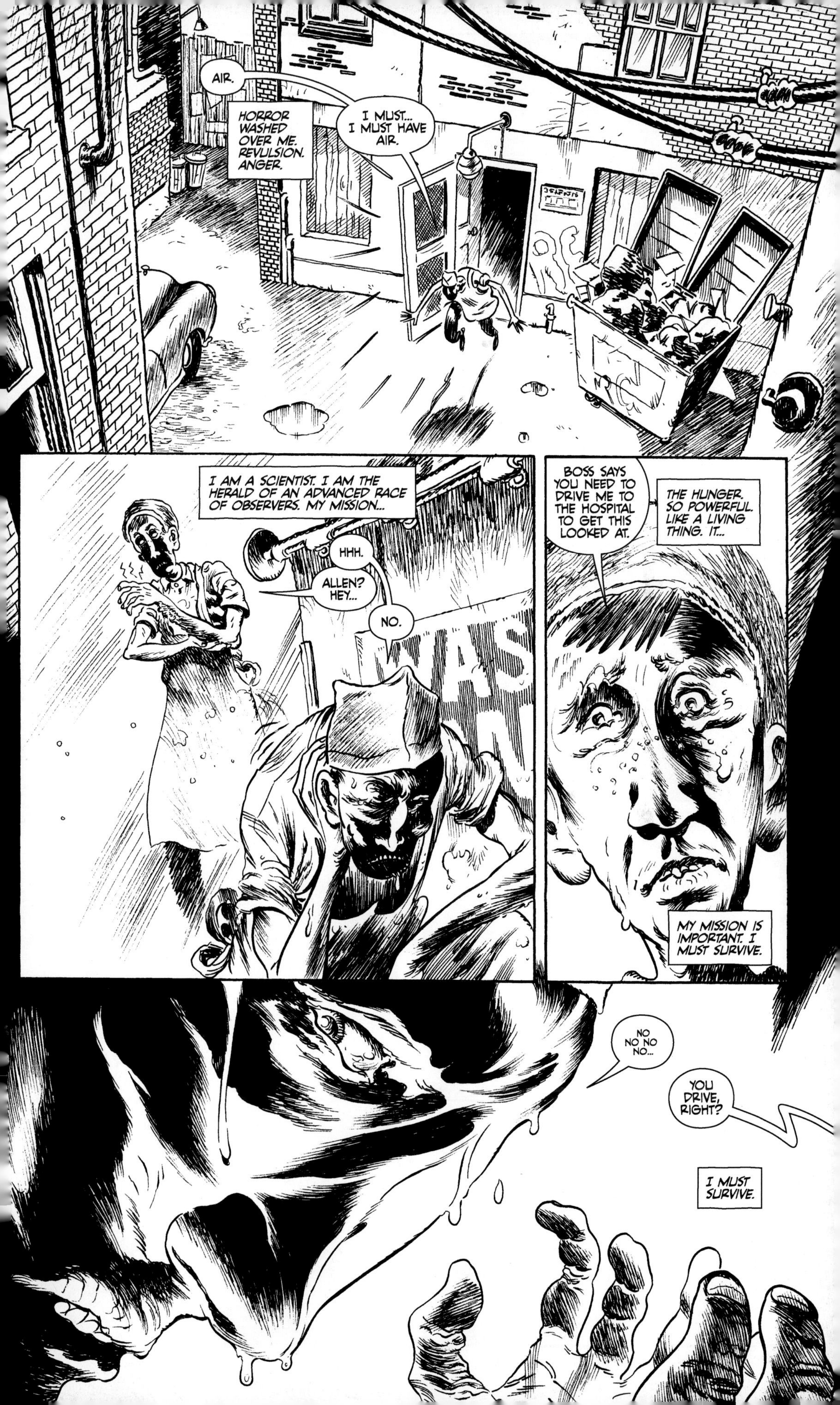

AIR.
HORROR WASHED OVER ME. REVULSION. ANGER.
I MUST... I MUST HAVE AIR.
I AM A SCIENTIST. I AM THE HERALD OF AN ADVANCED RACE OF OBSERVERS. MY MISSION...
HHH.
ALLEN? HEY...
NO.
BOSS SAYS YOU NEED TO DRIVE ME TO THE HOSPITAL TO GET THIS LOOKED AT.
THE HUNGER. SO POWERFUL. LIKE A LIVING THING. IT...
MY MISSION IS IMPORTANT. I MUST SURVIVE.
NO NO NO NO...
YOU DRIVE, RIGHT?
I MUST SURVIVE.

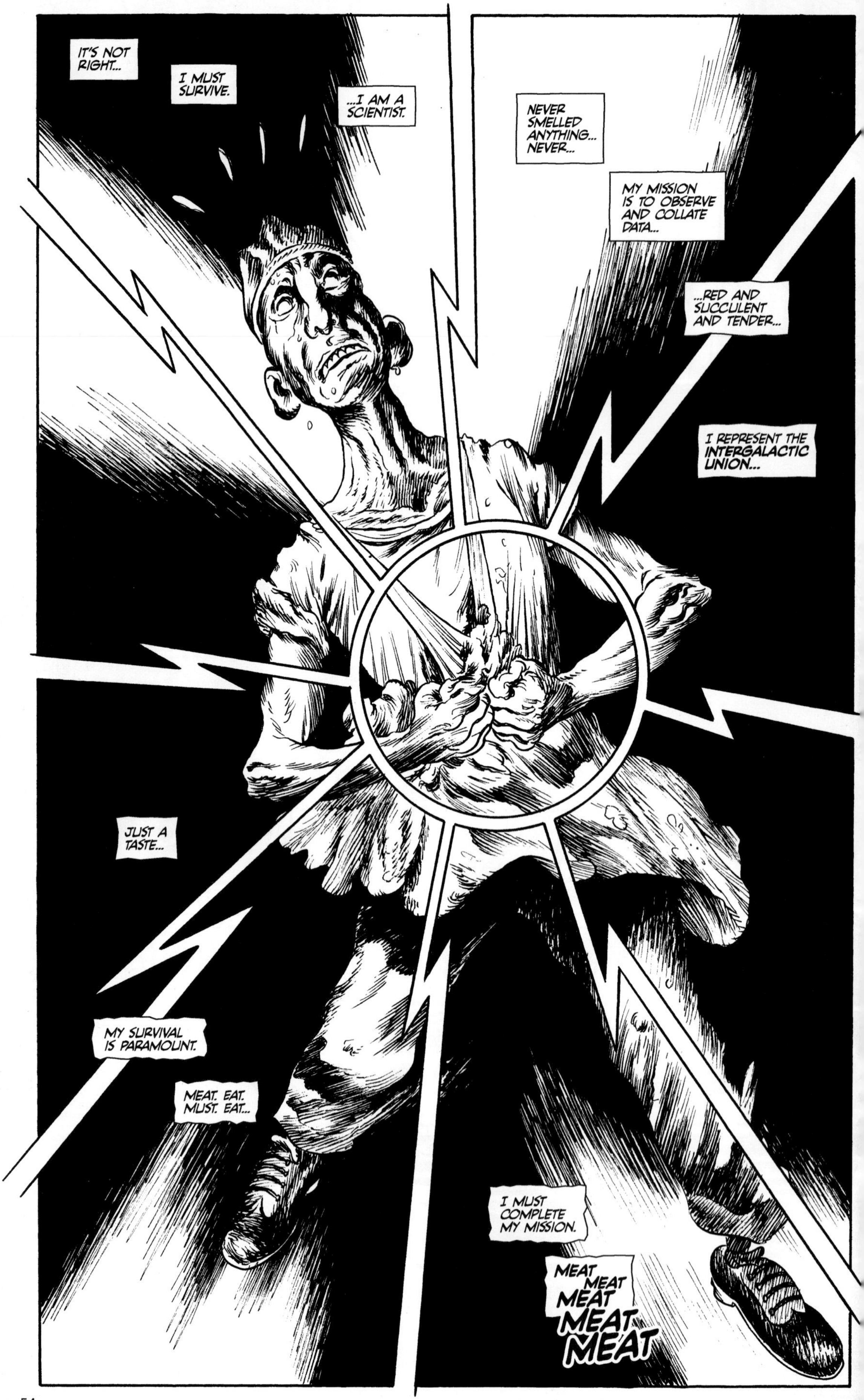
IT'S NOT RIGHT...
I MUST SURVIVE.
...I AM A SCIENTIST.
NEVER SMELLED ANYTHING... NEVER...
MY MISSION IS TO OBSERVE AND COLLATE DATA...
...RED AND SUCCULENT AND TENDER...
I REPRESENT THE INTERGALACTIC UNION...
JUST A TASTE...
MY SURVIVAL IS PARAMOUNT.
MEAT. EAT. MUST. EAT...
I MUST COMPLETE MY MISSION.
MEAT MEAT MEAT MEAT MEAT

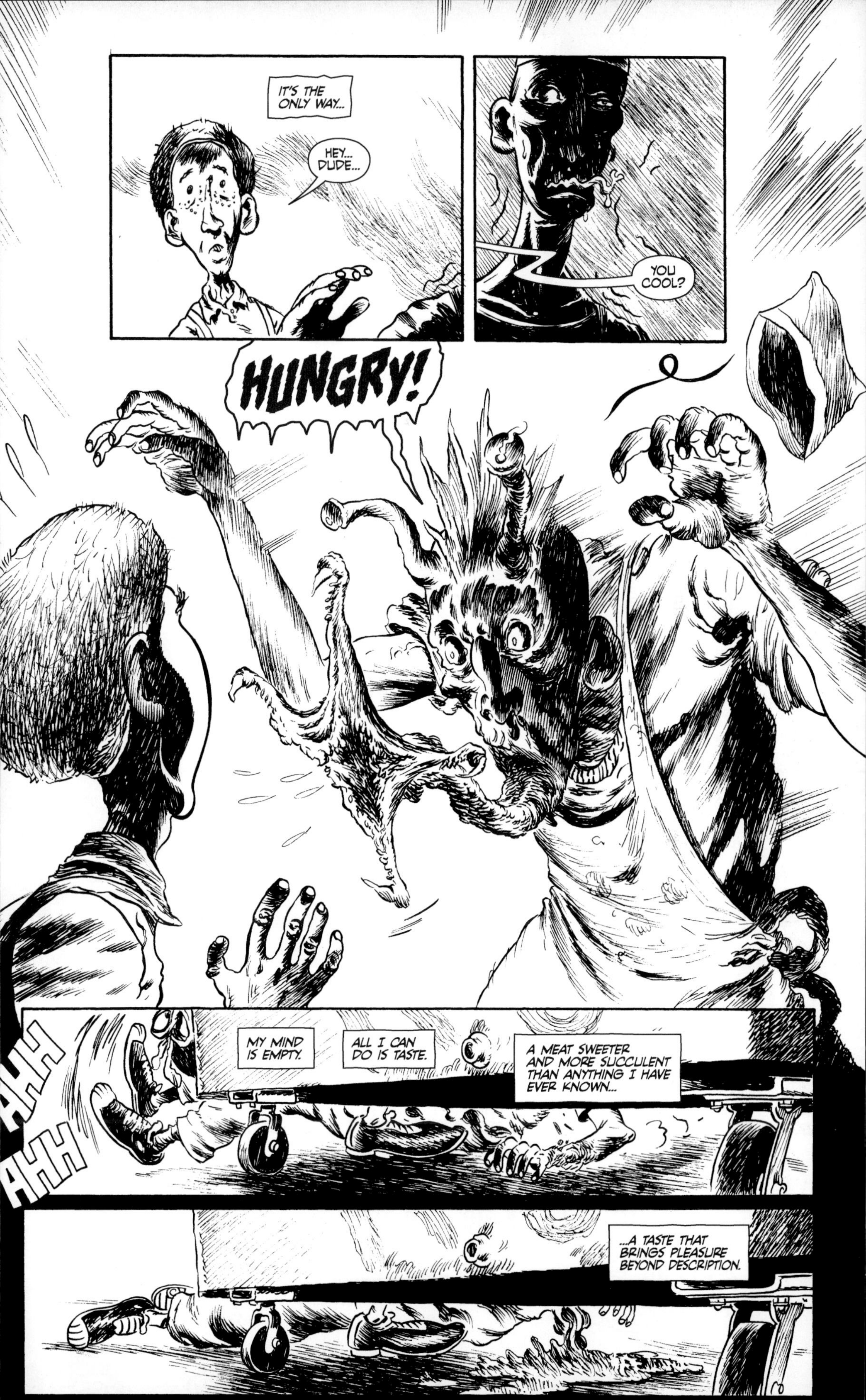

IT'S THE ONLY WAY...
HEY... DUDE...
YOU COOL?
HUNGRY!
AHH AHH
MY MIND IS EMPTY.
ALL I CAN DO IS TASTE.
A MEAT SWEETER AND MORE SUCCULENT THAN ANYTHING I HAVE EVER KNOWN...
...A TASTE THAT BRINGS PLEASURE BEYOND DESCRIPTION.

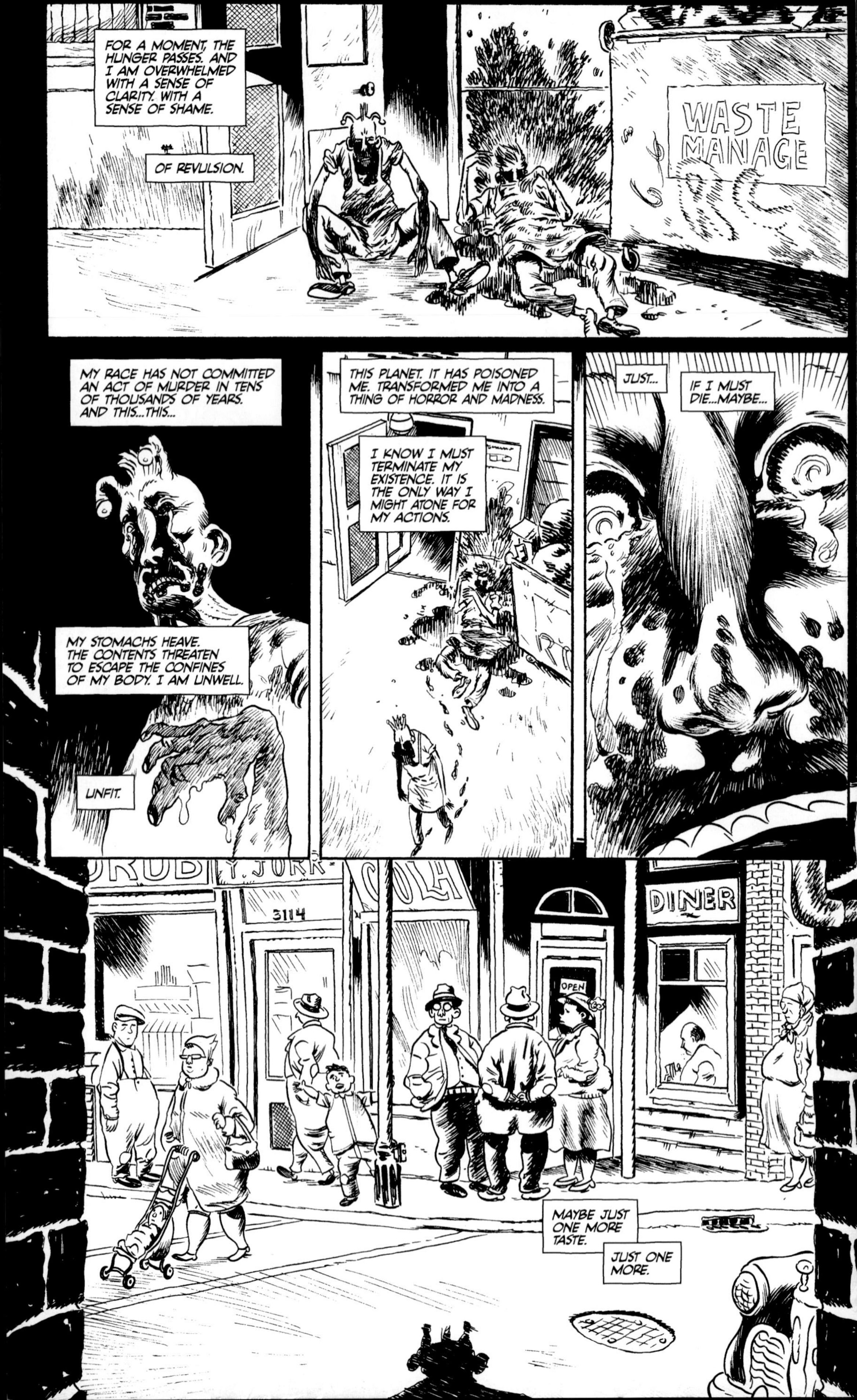
FOR A MOMENT, THE HUNGER PASSES. AND I AM OVERWHELMED WITH A SENSE OF CLARITY. WITH A SENSE OF SHAME.
OF REVULSION.
WASTE MANAGE
MY RACE HAS NOT COMMITTED AN ACT OF MURDER IN TENS OF THOUSANDS OF YEARS. AND THIS...THIS...
MY STOMACHS HEAVE. THE CONTENTS THREATEN TO ESCAPE THE CONFINES OF MY BODY. I AM UNWELL.
UNFIT.
THIS PLANET. IT HAS POISONED ME. TRANSFORMED ME INTO A THING OF HORROR AND MADNESS.
I KNOW I MUST TERMINATE MY EXISTENCE. IT IS THE ONLY WAY I MIGHT ATONE FOR MY ACTIONS.
JUST...
IF I MUST DIE...MAYBE...
3114
COLA
DINER
OPEN
MAYBE JUST ONE MORE TASTE.
JUST ONE MORE.

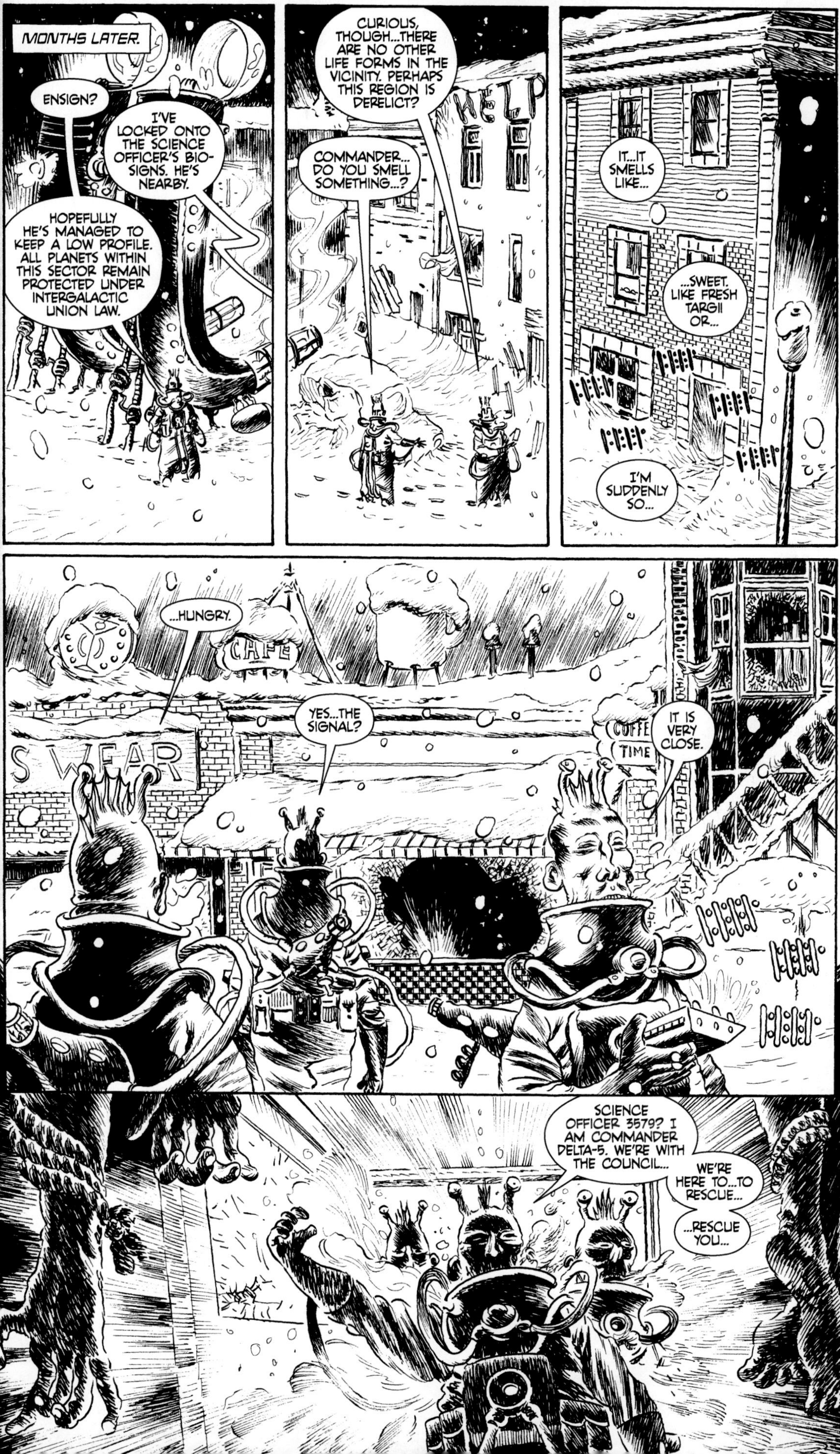
MONTHS LATER.
ENSIGN?
I'VE LOCKED ONTO THE SCIENCE OFFICER'S BIO-SIGNS. HE'S NEARBY.
HOPEFULLY HE'S MANAGED TO KEEP A LOW PROFILE. ALL PLANETS WITHIN THIS SECTOR REMAIN PROTECTED UNDER INTERGALACTIC UNION LAW.
CURIOUS, THOUGH...THERE ARE NO OTHER LIFE FORMS IN THE VICINITY. PERHAPS THIS REGION IS DERELICT?
COMMANDER... DO YOU SMELL SOMETHING...?
IT...IT SMELLS LIKE...
...SWEET. LIKE FRESH TARGII OR...
I'M SUDDENLY SO...
...HUNGRY.
CAFE
YES...THE SIGNAL?
IT IS VERY CLOSE.
COFFE
TIME
S WEAR
SCIENCE OFFICER 3579? I AM COMMANDER DELTA-5. WE'RE WITH THE COUNCIL...
WE'RE HERE TO...TO RESCUE...
...RESCUE YOU...

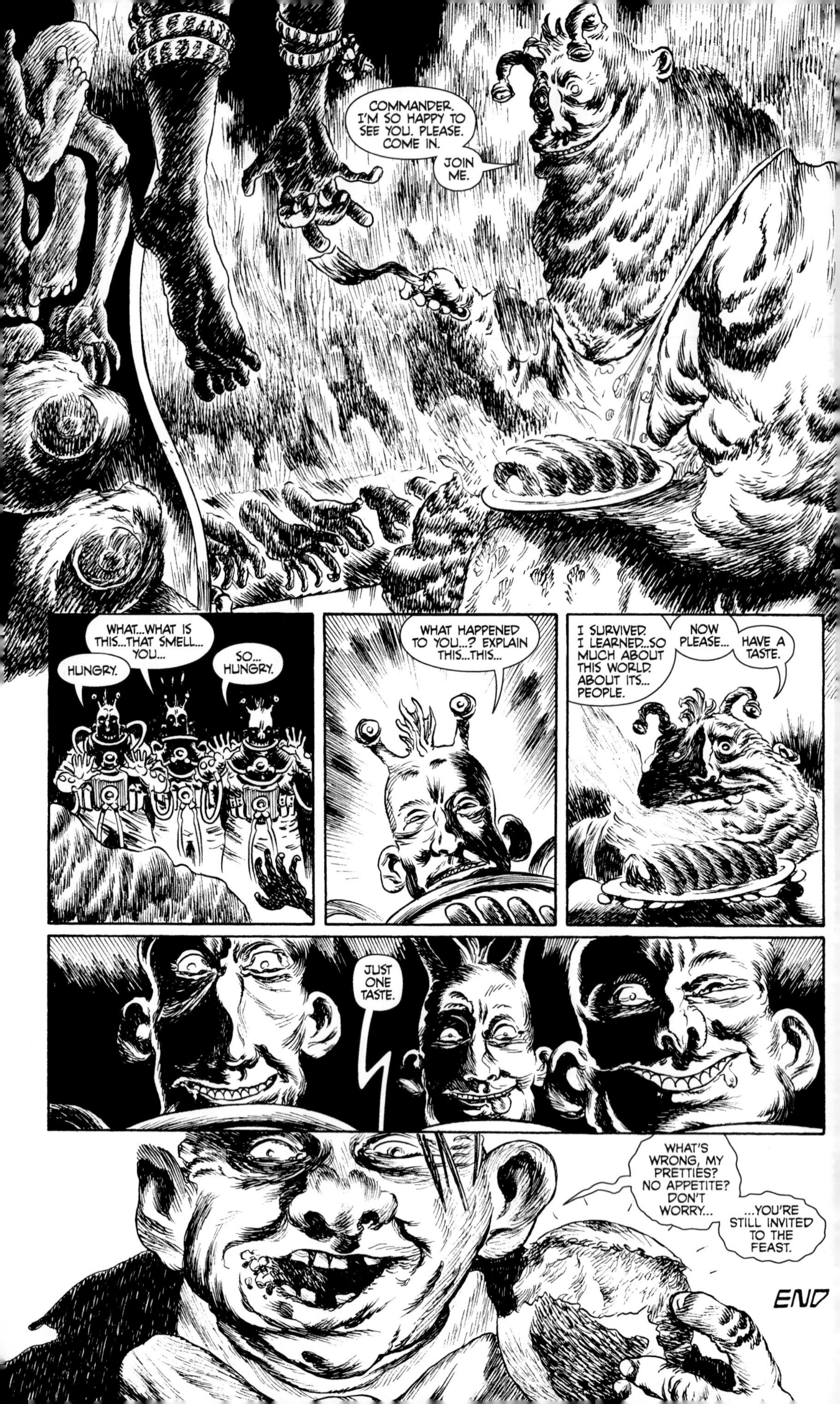
COMMANDER. I'M SO HAPPY TO SEE YOU. PLEASE. COME IN.
JOIN ME.
WHAT...WHAT IS THIS...THAT SMELL... YOU...
HUNGRY.
SO... HUNGRY.
WHAT HAPPENED TO YOU...? EXPLAIN THIS...THIS...
I SURVIVED. I LEARNED...SO MUCH ABOUT THIS WORLD. ABOUT ITS... PEOPLE.
NOW PLEASE...
HAVE A TASTE.
JUST ONE TASTE.
WHAT'S WRONG, MY PRETTIES? NO APPETITE? DON'T WORRY...
...YOU'RE STILL INVITED TO THE FEAST.
END

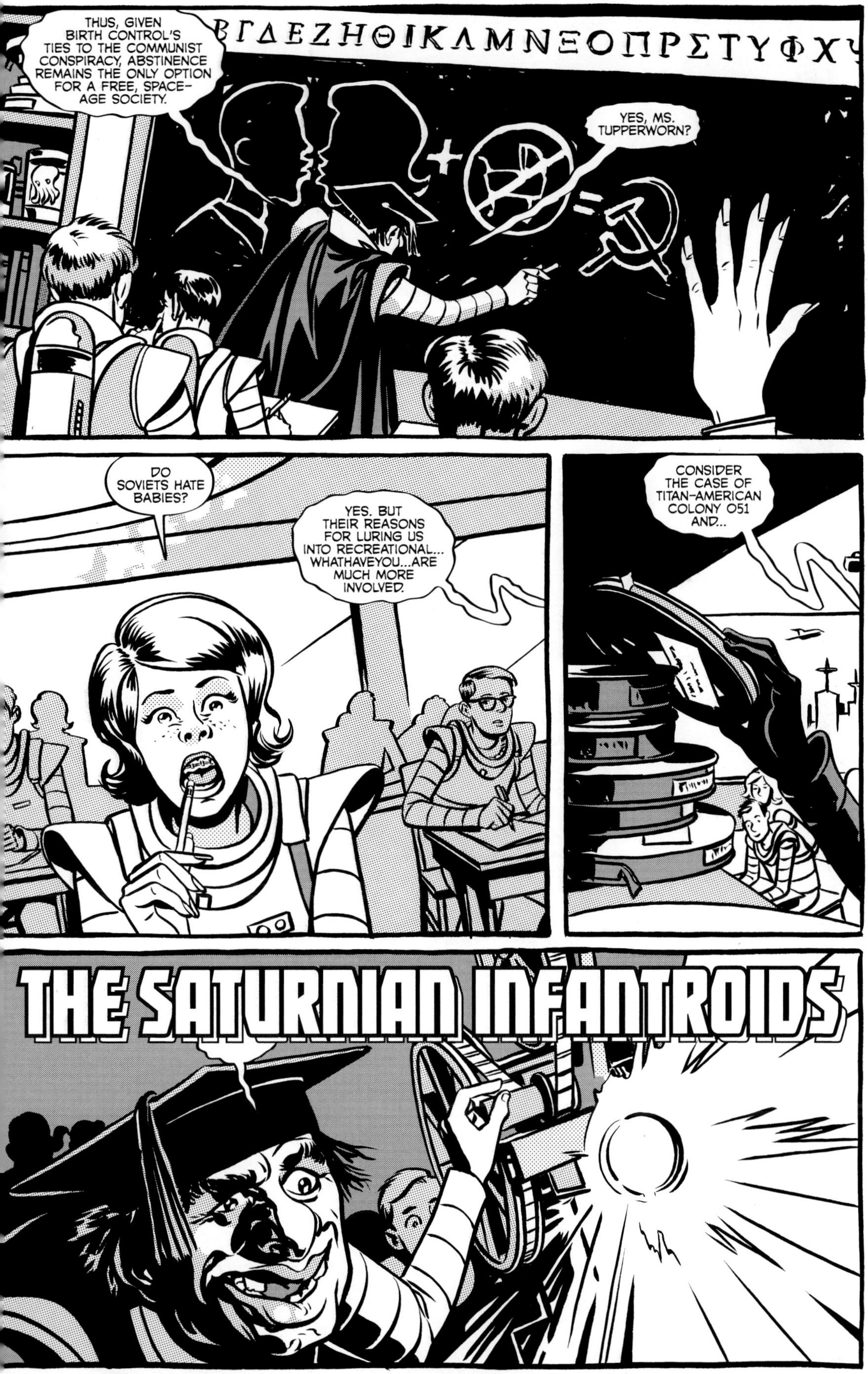

THUS, GIVEN BIRTH CONTROL'S TIES TO THE COMMUNIST CONSPIRACY, ABSTINENCE REMAINS THE ONLY OPTION FOR A FREE, SPACE-AGE SOCIETY.
YES, MS. TUPPERWORN?
DO SOVIETS HATE BABIES?
YES. BUT THEIR REASONS FOR LURING US INTO RECREATIONAL... WHATHAVEYOU...ARE MUCH MORE INVOLVED.
CONSIDER THE CASE OF TITAN-AMERICAN COLONY 051 AND...
THE SATURNIAN INFANTROIDS

cript and Art by JONATHAN CASE

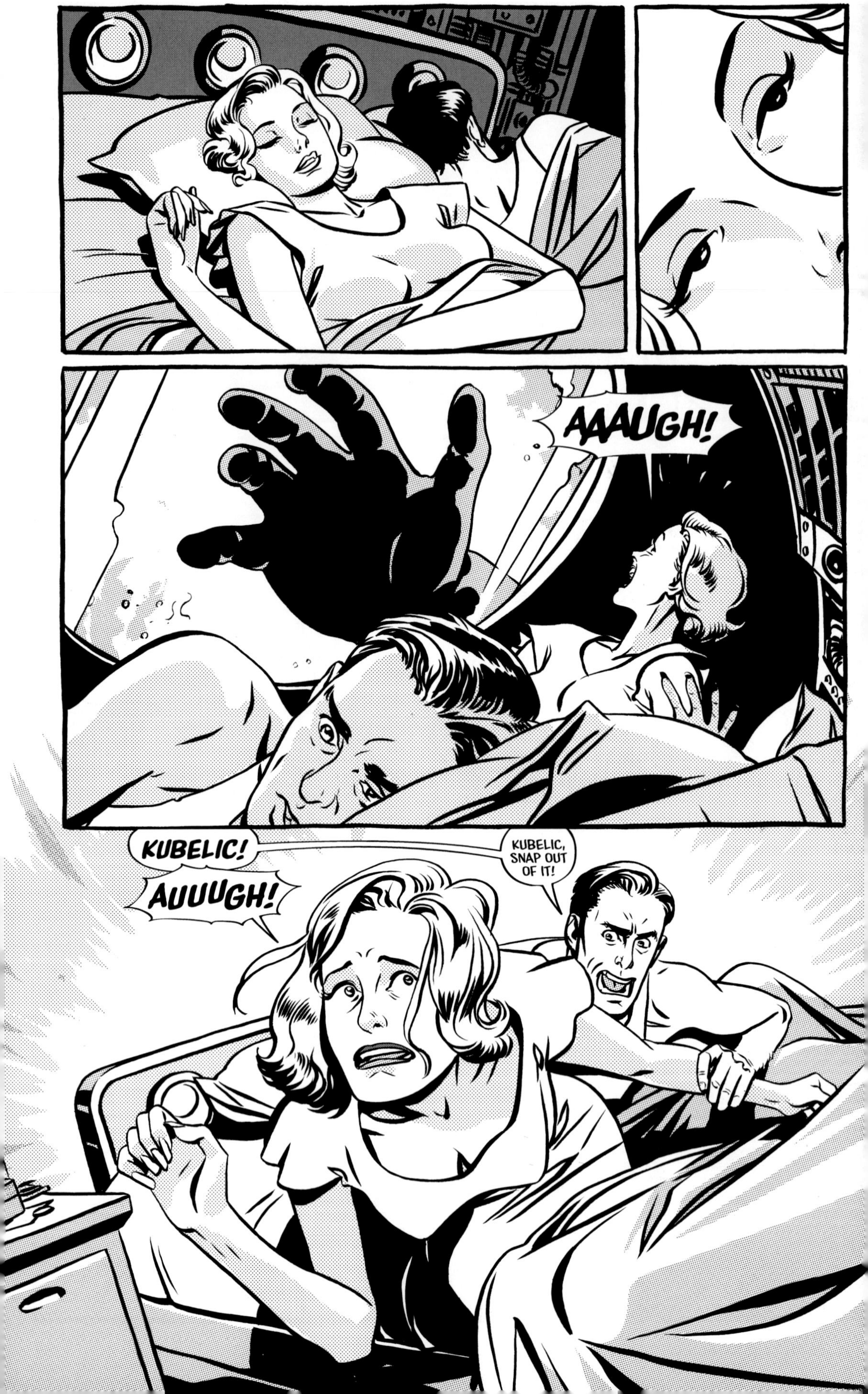
AAAUGH!
KUBELIC!
AUUUGH!
KUBELIC, SNAP OUT OF IT!

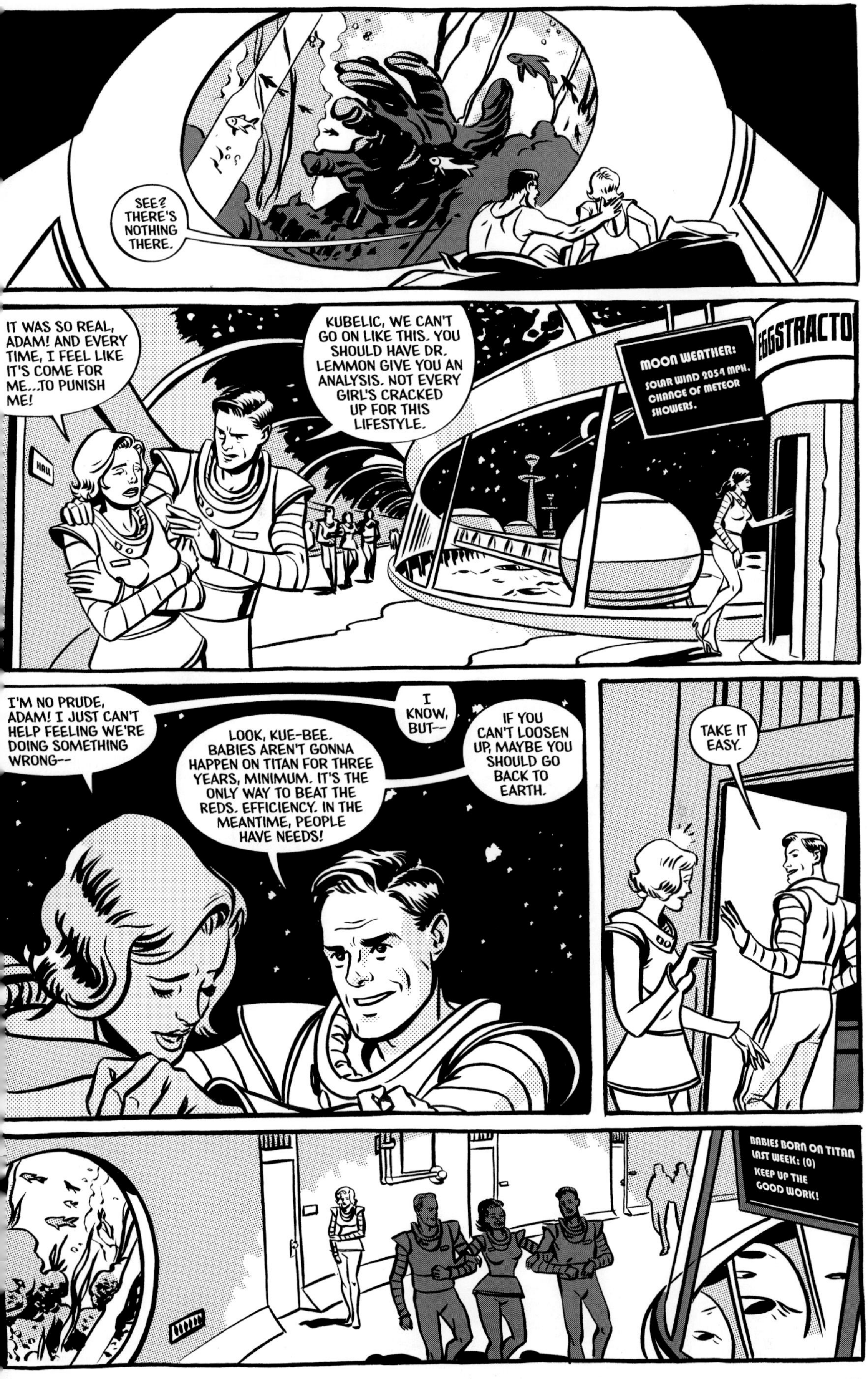
SEE? THERE'S NOTHING THERE.
IT WAS SO REAL, ADAM! AND EVERY TIME, I FEEL LIKE IT'S COME FOR ME...TO PUNISH ME!
KUBELIC, WE CAN'T GO ON LIKE THIS. YOU SHOULD HAVE DR. LEMMON GIVE YOU AN ANALYSIS. NOT EVERY GIRL'S CRACKED UP FOR THIS LIFESTYLE.
HALL
EGGSTRACTO
MOON WEATHER:
SOLAR WIND 2054 MPH. CHANCE OF METEOR SHOWERS.
I'M NO PRUDE, ADAM! I JUST CAN'T HELP FEELING WE'RE DOING SOMETHING WRONG--
I KNOW, BUT--
LOOK, KUE-BEE. BABIES AREN'T GONNA HAPPEN ON TITAN FOR THREE YEARS, MINIMUM. IT'S THE ONLY WAY TO BEAT THE REDS. EFFICIENCY. IN THE MEANTIME, PEOPLE HAVE NEEDS!
IF YOU CAN'T LOOSEN UP, MAYBE YOU SHOULD GO BACK TO EARTH.
TAKE IT EASY.
BABIES BORN ON TITAN LAST WEEK: (0)
KEEP UP THE GOOD WORK!

THE EGGSTRACTOR

Saving your worries for *later.*

"HAVE YOU MADE YOUR EGG DONATION THIS MONTH, MISS KUBELIC?"

YES. LAST WEEK.

GOOD. AND THESE DREAMS YOU'RE HAVING, HOW OFTEN DO THEY OCCUR?

I DON'T, UM...

IT'S WHEN I... VISIT MY FRIEND CAPTAIN HALL. THERE'S AN AQUARIUM.

AN AQUARIUM?

OVER HIS BED. I IMAGINE IT IN THE AQUARIUM.

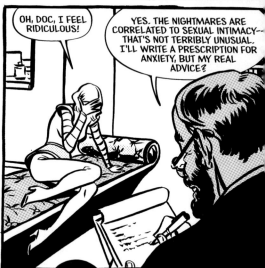

OH, DOC, I FEEL RIDICULOUS!

YES. THE NIGHTMARES ARE CORRELATED TO SEXUAL INTIMACY-- THAT'S NOT TERRIBLY UNUSUAL. I'LL WRITE A PRESCRIPTION FOR ANXIETY, BUT MY REAL ADVICE?

LOOSEN UP!

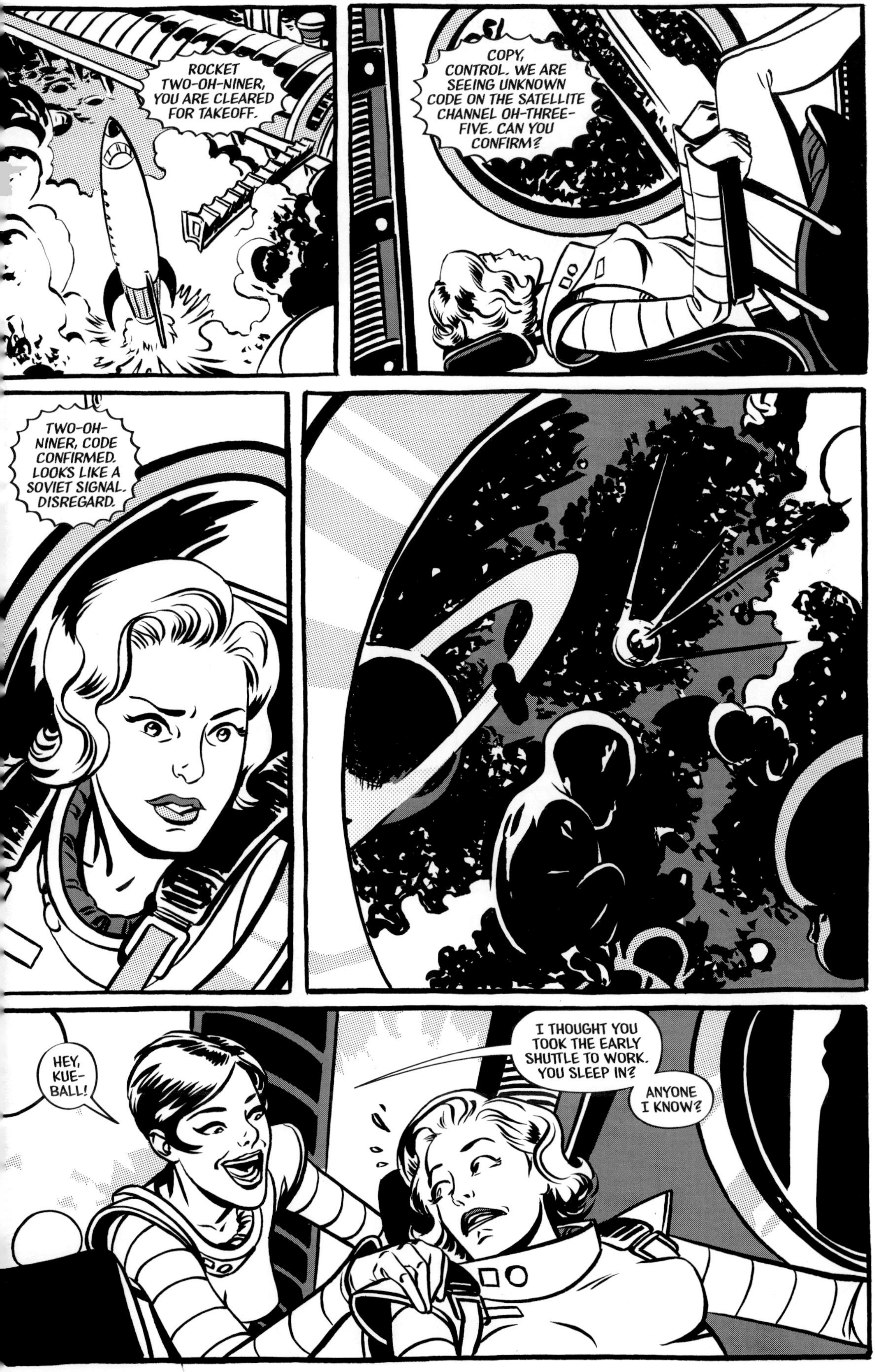
ROCKET TWO-OH-NINER, YOU ARE CLEARED FOR TAKEOFF.
COPY, CONTROL. WE ARE SEEING UNKNOWN CODE ON THE SATELLITE CHANNEL OH-THREE-FIVE. CAN YOU CONFIRM?
TWO-OH-NINER, CODE CONFIRMED. LOOKS LIKE A SOVIET SIGNAL. DISREGARD.
HEY, KUE-BALL!
I THOUGHT YOU TOOK THE EARLY SHUTTLE TO WORK. YOU SLEEP IN?
ANYONE I KNOW?

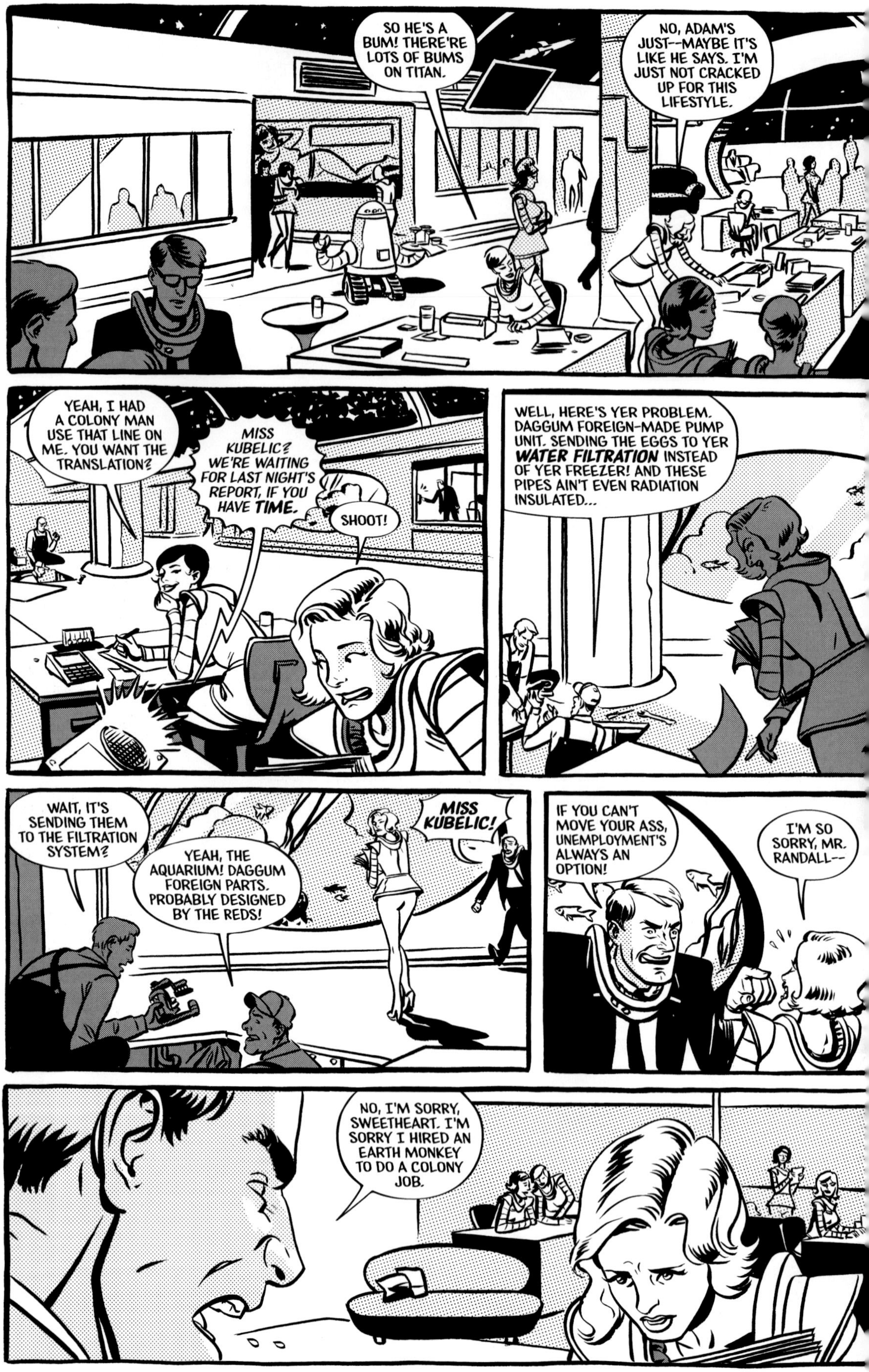
SO HE'S A BUM! THERE'RE LOTS OF BUMS ON TITAN.
NO, ADAM'S JUST--MAYBE IT'S LIKE HE SAYS. I'M JUST NOT CRACKED UP FOR THIS LIFESTYLE.
YEAH, I HAD A COLONY MAN USE THAT LINE ON ME. YOU WANT THE TRANSLATION?
MISS KUBELIC? WE'RE WAITING FOR LAST NIGHT'S REPORT, IF YOU HAVE TIME.
SHOOT!
WELL, HERE'S YER PROBLEM. DAGGUM FOREIGN-MADE PUMP UNIT. SENDING THE EGGS TO YER WATER FILTRATION INSTEAD OF YER FREEZER! AND THESE PIPES AIN'T EVEN RADIATION INSULATED...
WAIT, IT'S SENDING THEM TO THE FILTRATION SYSTEM?
YEAH, THE AQUARIUM! DAGGUM FOREIGN PARTS. PROBABLY DESIGNED BY THE REDS!
MISS KUBELIC!
IF YOU CAN'T MOVE YOUR ASS, UNEMPLOYMENT'S ALWAYS AN OPTION!
I'M SO SORRY, MR. RANDALL--
NO, I'M SORRY, SWEETHEART. I'M SORRY I HIRED AN EARTH MONKEY TO DO A COLONY JOB.

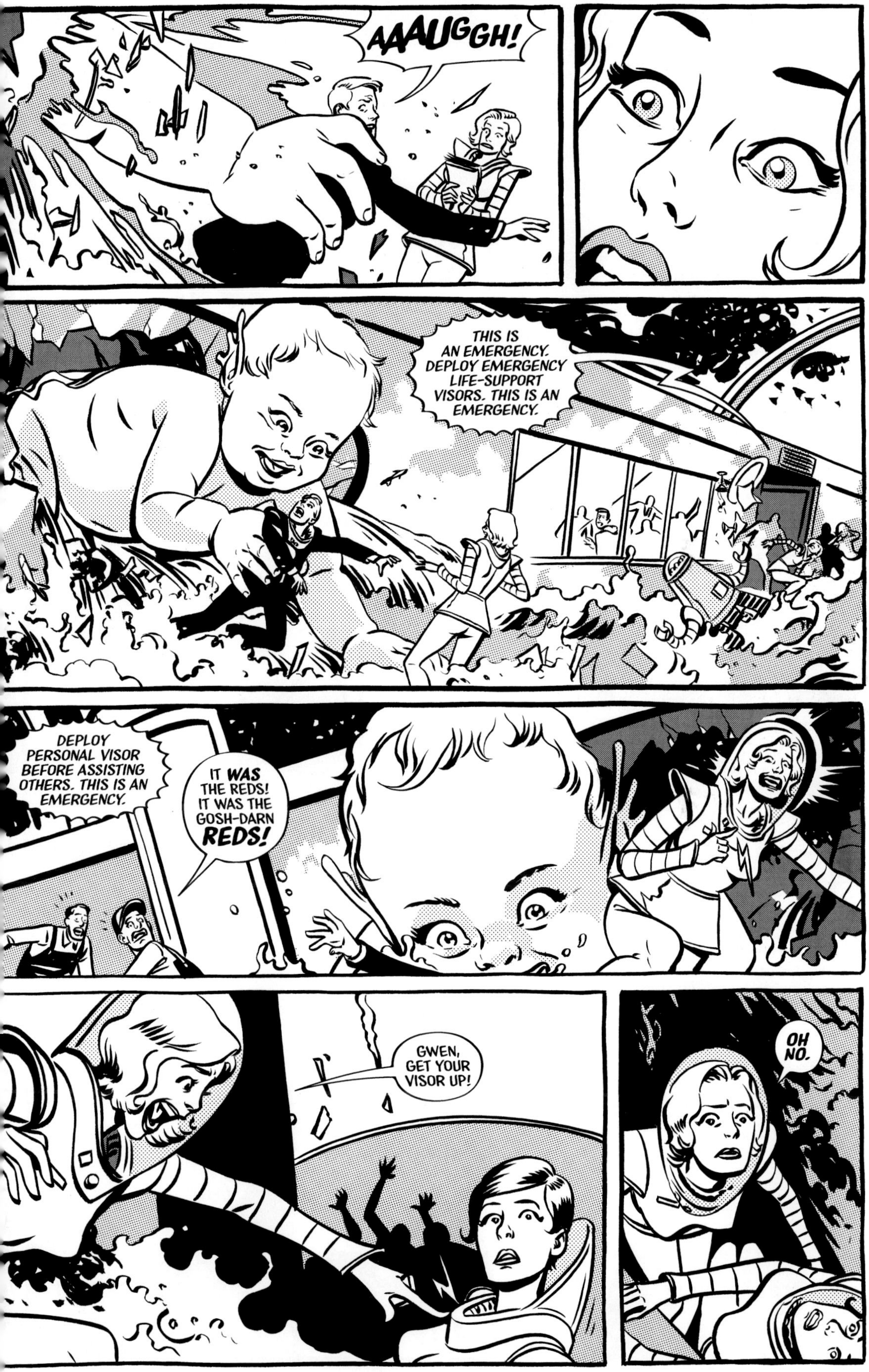
AAAUGGH!
THIS IS AN EMERGENCY. DEPLOY EMERGENCY LIFE-SUPPORT VISORS. THIS IS AN EMERGENCY.
DEPLOY PERSONAL VISOR BEFORE ASSISTING OTHERS. THIS IS AN EMERGENCY.
IT **WAS** THE REDS! IT WAS THE GOSH-DARN **REDS!**
GWEN, GET YOUR VISOR UP!
OH NO.

GWEN, HOLD ON! I'VE GOT YOU!

I GAH GOO?

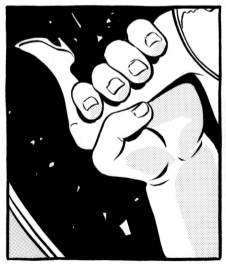

NYAAAGH!

I GAH GOO!

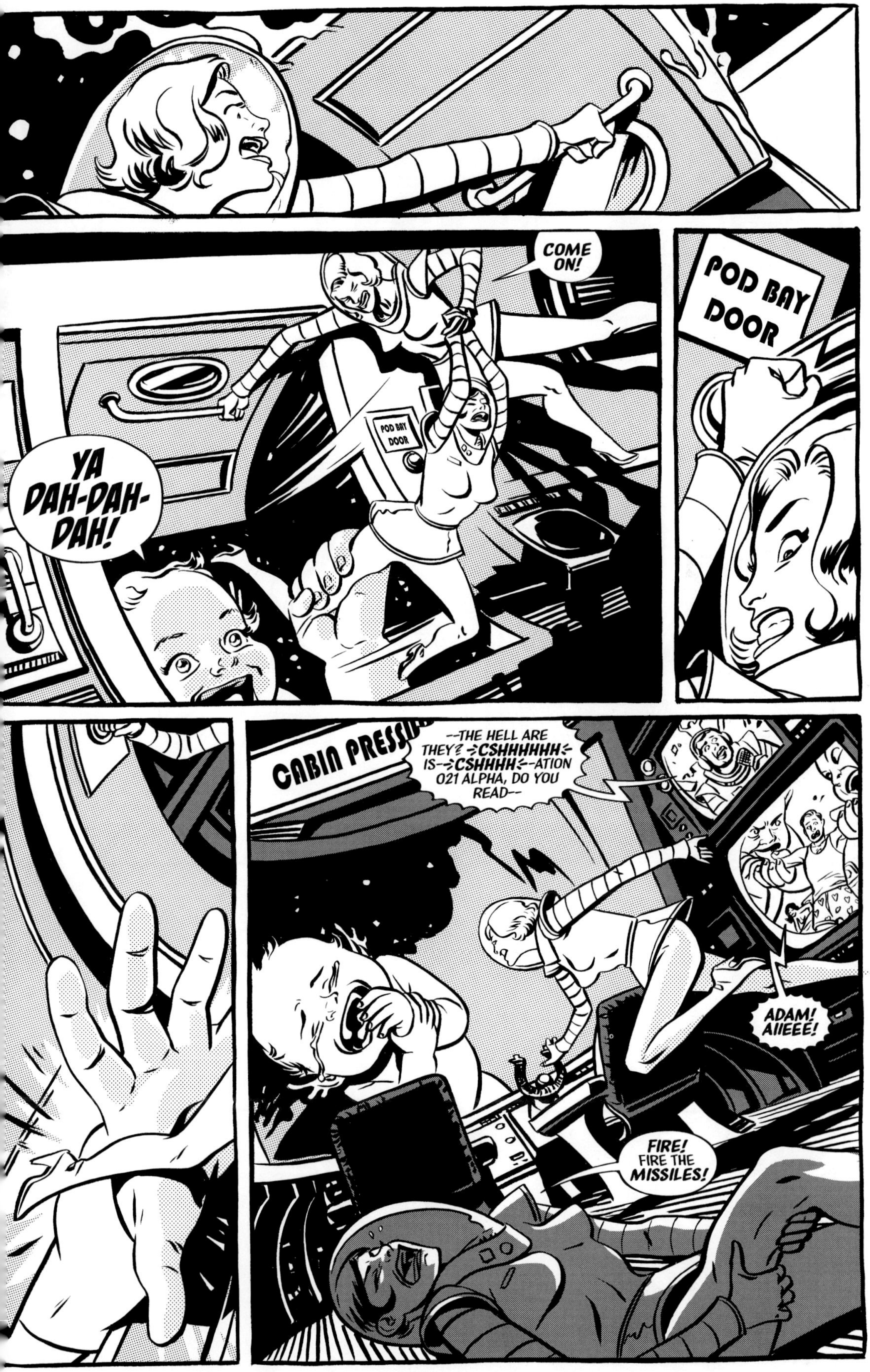

COME ON!
POD BAY DOOR
YA DAH-DAH-DAH!
POD BAY DOOR
CABIN PRESSU
--THE HELL ARE THEY? ⇝CSHHHHHH⇜ IS--⇝CSHHHH⇜--ATION 021 ALPHA, DO YOU READ--
ADAM! AIIEEE!
FIRE! FIRE THE MISSILES!

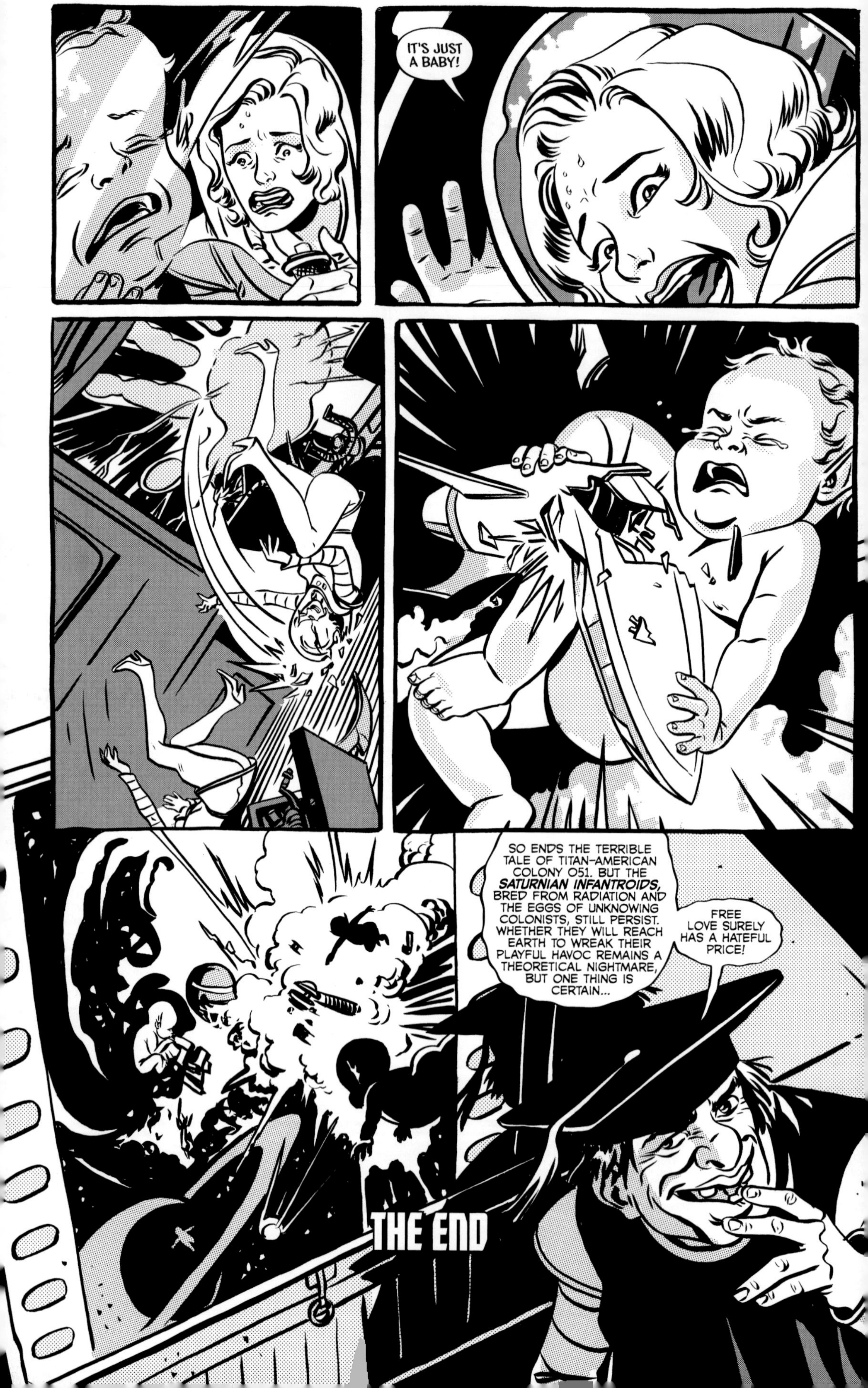
IT'S JUST A BABY!
SO ENDS THE TERRIBLE TALE OF TITAN-AMERICAN COLONY 051. BUT THE ***SATURNIAN INFANTROIDS,*** BRED FROM RADIATION AND THE EGGS OF UNKNOWING COLONISTS, STILL PERSIST. WHETHER THEY WILL REACH EARTH TO WREAK THEIR PLAYFUL HAVOC REMAINS A THEORETICAL NIGHTMARE, BUT ONE THING IS CERTAIN...
FREE LOVE SURELY HAS A HATEFUL PRICE!
THE END

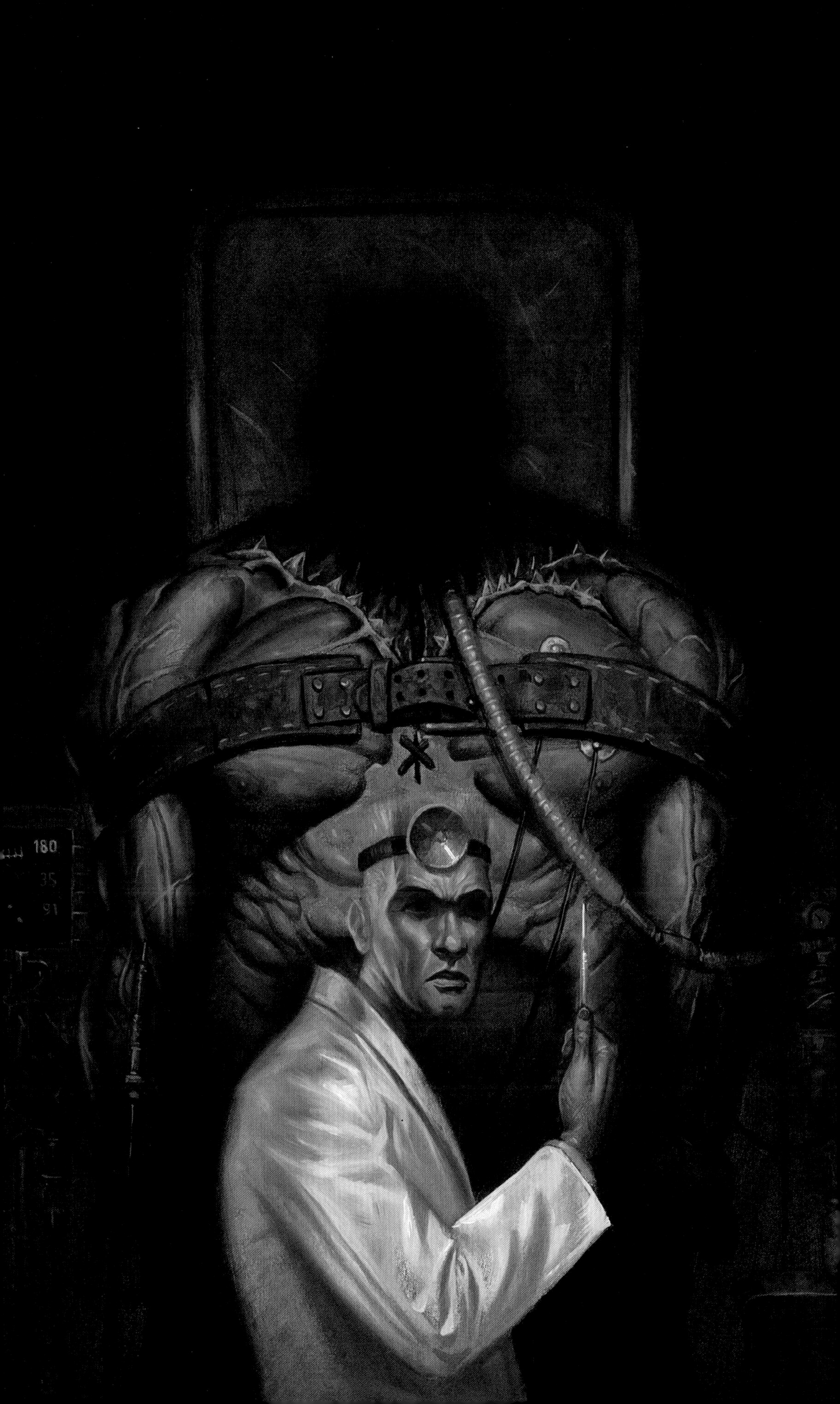
180
35
91

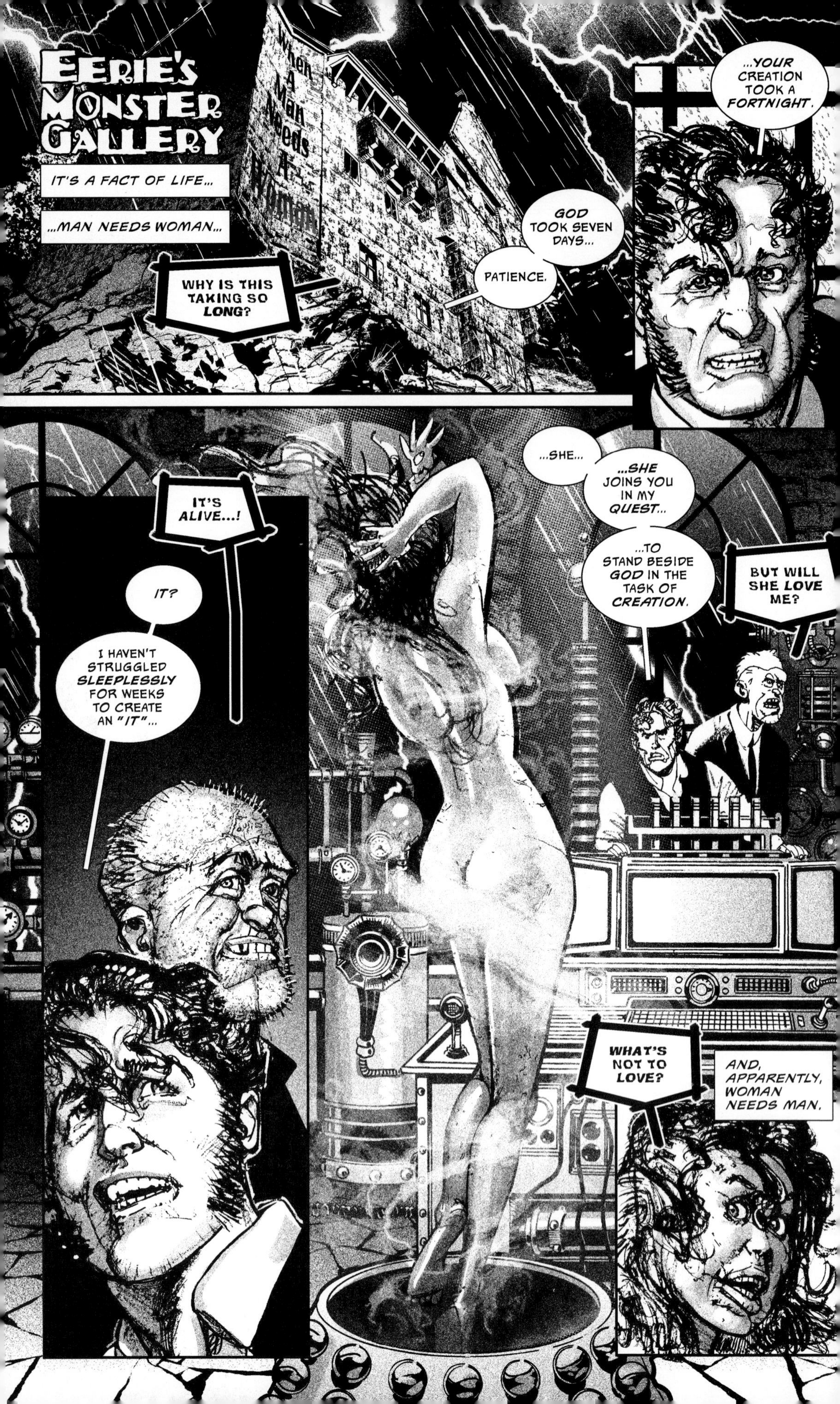

EERIE'S MONSTER GALLERY
When A Man Needs A Woman
IT'S A FACT OF LIFE...
...MAN NEEDS WOMAN...
WHY IS THIS TAKING SO LONG?
PATIENCE.
GOD TOOK SEVEN DAYS...
...YOUR CREATION TOOK A FORTNIGHT.
IT'S ALIVE...!
IT?
I HAVEN'T STRUGGLED SLEEPLESSLY FOR WEEKS TO CREATE AN "IT"...
...SHE...
...SHE JOINS YOU IN MY QUEST...
...TO STAND BESIDE GOD IN THE TASK OF CREATION.
BUT WILL SHE LOVE ME?
WHAT'S NOT TO LOVE?
AND, APPARENTLY, WOMAN NEEDS MAN.

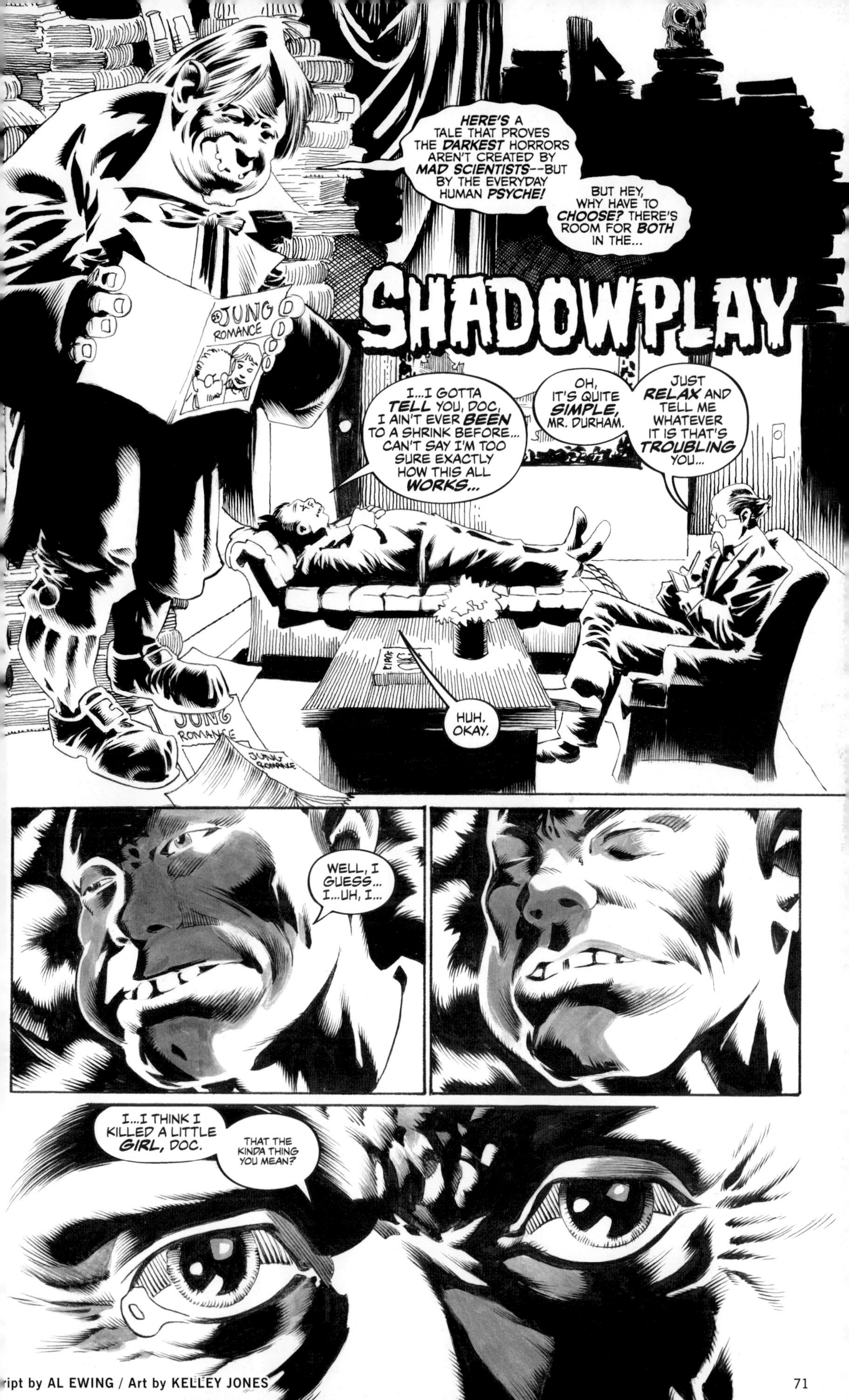
HERE'S A TALE THAT PROVES THE DARKEST HORRORS AREN'T CREATED BY MAD SCIENTISTS--BUT BY THE EVERYDAY HUMAN PSYCHE!
BUT HEY, WHY HAVE TO CHOOSE? THERE'S ROOM FOR BOTH IN THE...
SHADOWPLAY
JUNG ROMANCE
I...I GOTTA TELL YOU, DOC, I AIN'T EVER BEEN TO A SHRINK BEFORE... CAN'T SAY I'M TOO SURE EXACTLY HOW THIS ALL WORKS...
OH, IT'S QUITE SIMPLE, MR. DURHAM.
JUST RELAX AND TELL ME WHATEVER IT IS THAT'S TROUBLING YOU...
HUH. OKAY.
WELL, I GUESS... I...UH, I...
I...I THINK I KILLED A LITTLE GIRL, DOC.
THAT THE KINDA THING YOU MEAN?

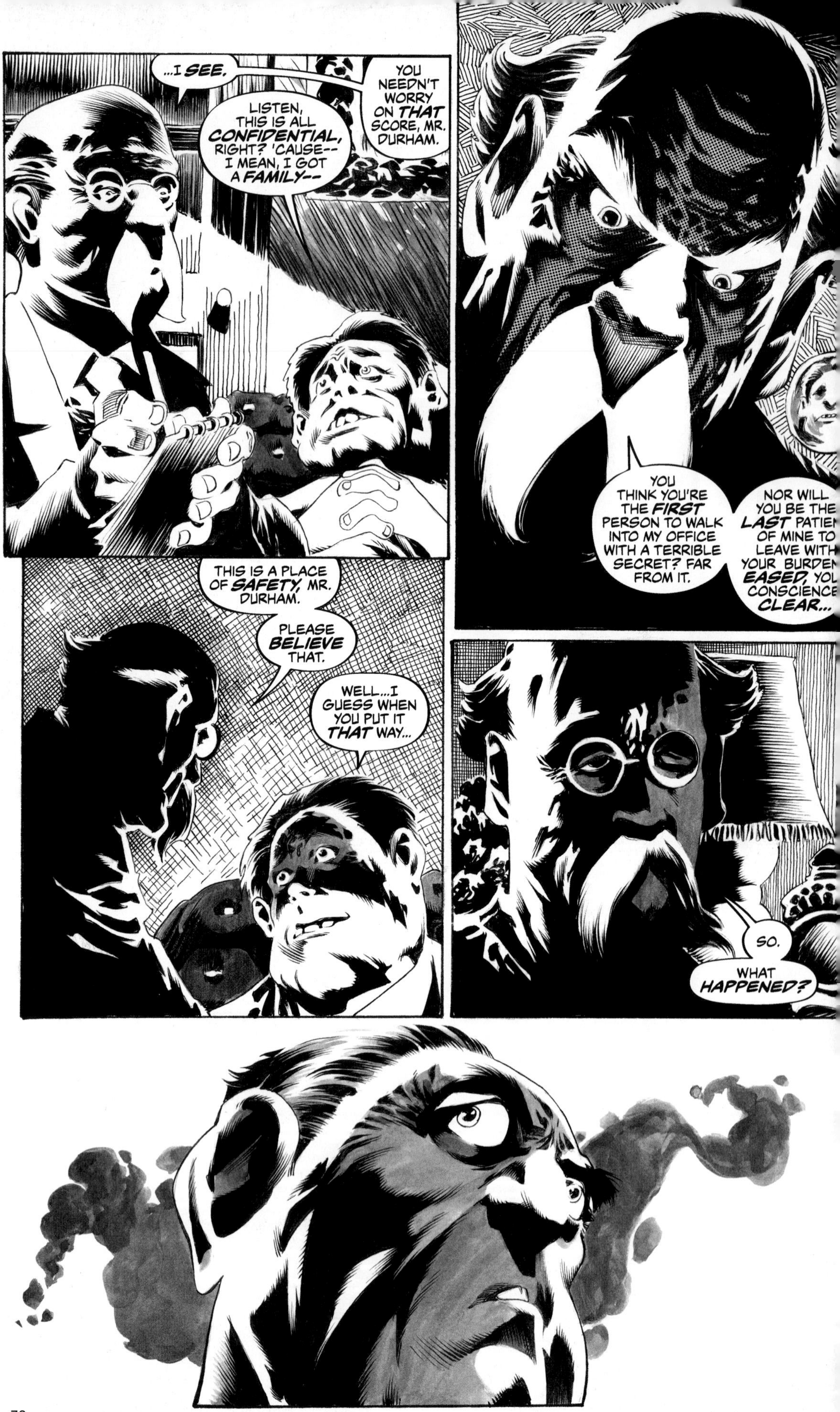

...I SEE.
LISTEN, THIS IS ALL CONFIDENTIAL, RIGHT? 'CAUSE-- I MEAN, I GOT A FAMILY--
YOU NEEDN'T WORRY ON THAT SCORE, MR. DURHAM.
YOU THINK YOU'RE THE FIRST PERSON TO WALK INTO MY OFFICE WITH A TERRIBLE SECRET? FAR FROM IT.
NOR WILL YOU BE THE LAST PATIEN OF MINE TO LEAVE WITH YOUR BURDEN EASED, YOU CONSCIENCE CLEAR...
THIS IS A PLACE OF SAFETY, MR. DURHAM.
PLEASE BELIEVE THAT.
WELL...I GUESS WHEN YOU PUT IT THAT WAY...
SO.
WHAT HAPPENED?

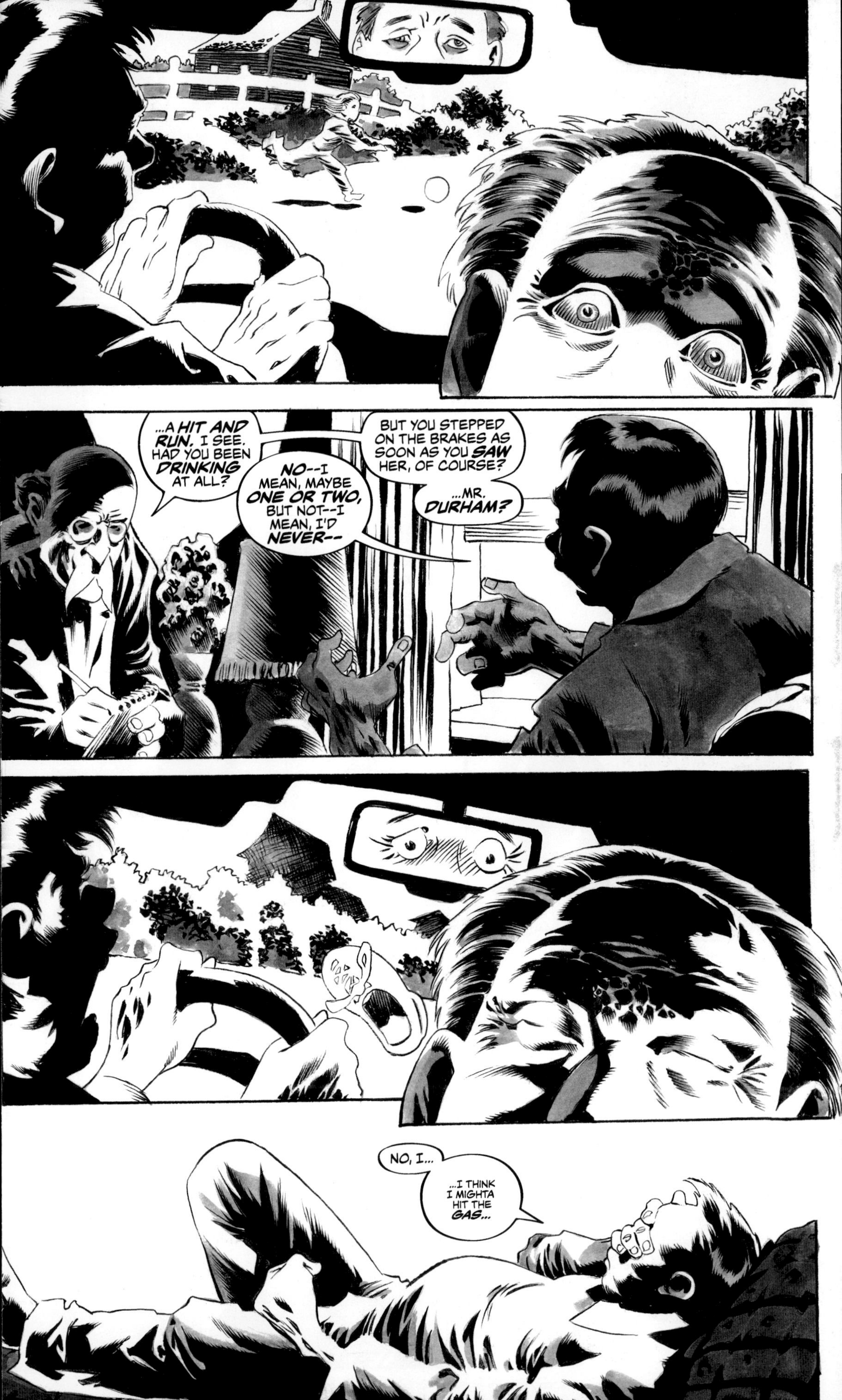
...A HIT AND RUN. I SEE. HAD YOU BEEN DRINKING AT ALL?
BUT YOU STEPPED ON THE BRAKES AS SOON AS YOU SAW HER, OF COURSE?
NO--I MEAN, MAYBE ONE OR TWO, BUT NOT--I MEAN, I'D NEVER--
...MR. DURHAM?
NO, I...
...I THINK I MIGHTA HIT THE GAS...

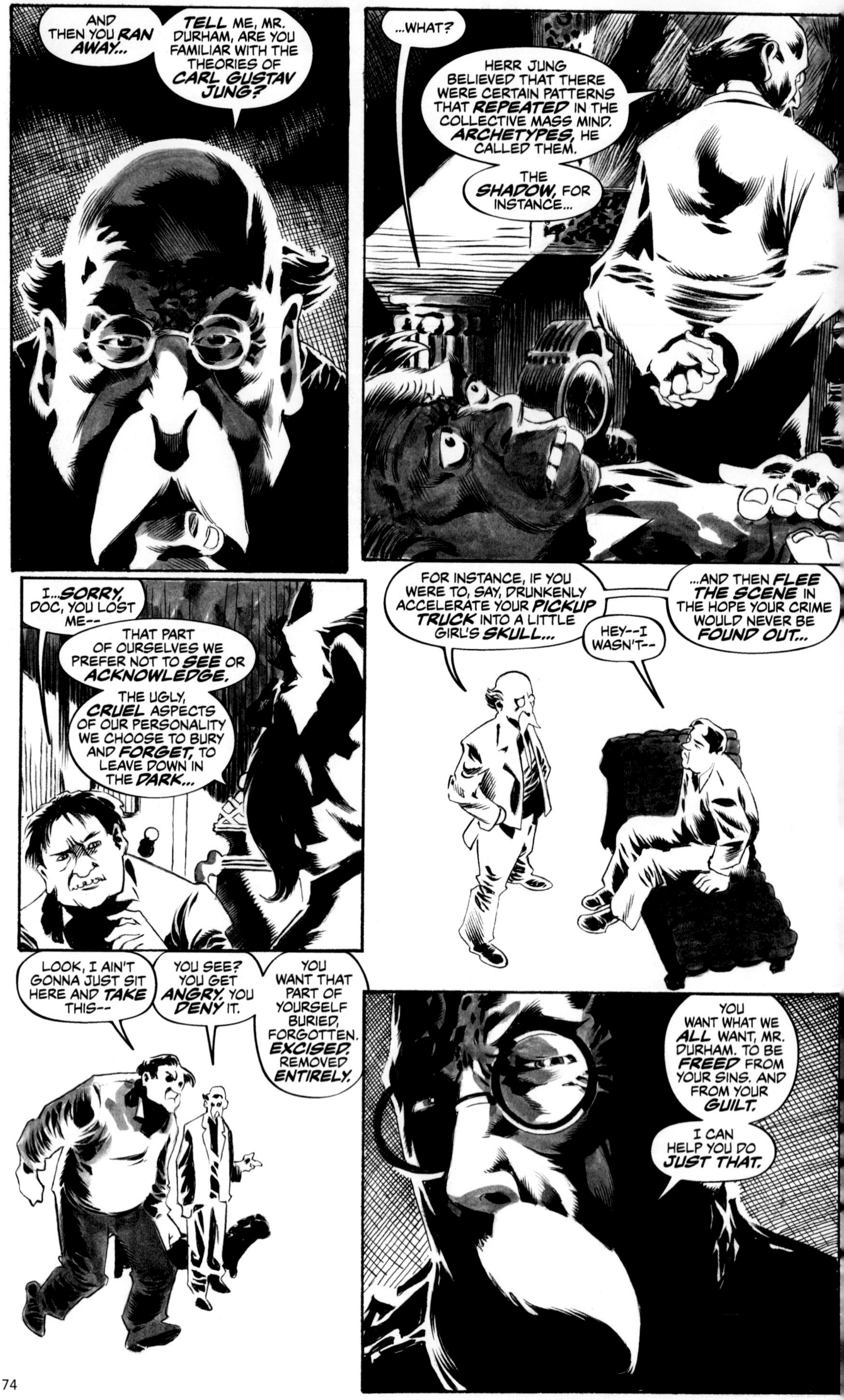
AND THEN YOU RAN AWAY...
TELL ME, MR. DURHAM, ARE YOU FAMILIAR WITH THE THEORIES OF CARL GUSTAV JUNG?
...WHAT?
HERR JUNG BELIEVED THAT THERE WERE CERTAIN PATTERNS THAT REPEATED IN THE COLLECTIVE MASS MIND. ARCHETYPES, HE CALLED THEM.
THE SHADOW, FOR INSTANCE...
I...SORRY, DOC, YOU LOST ME--
THAT PART OF OURSELVES WE PREFER NOT TO SEE OR ACKNOWLEDGE.
THE UGLY, CRUEL ASPECTS OF OUR PERSONALITY WE CHOOSE TO BURY AND FORGET, TO LEAVE DOWN IN THE DARK...
FOR INSTANCE, IF YOU WERE TO, SAY, DRUNKENLY ACCELERATE YOUR PICKUP TRUCK INTO A LITTLE GIRL'S SKULL...
...AND THEN FLEE THE SCENE IN THE HOPE YOUR CRIME WOULD NEVER BE FOUND OUT...
HEY--I WASN'T--
LOOK, I AIN'T GONNA JUST SIT HERE AND TAKE THIS--
YOU SEE? YOU GET ANGRY. YOU DENY IT.
YOU WANT THAT PART OF YOURSELF BURIED, FORGOTTEN. EXCISED. REMOVED ENTIRELY.
YOU WANT WHAT WE ALL WANT, MR. DURHAM. TO BE FREED FROM YOUR SINS. AND FROM YOUR GUILT.
I CAN HELP YOU DO JUST THAT.

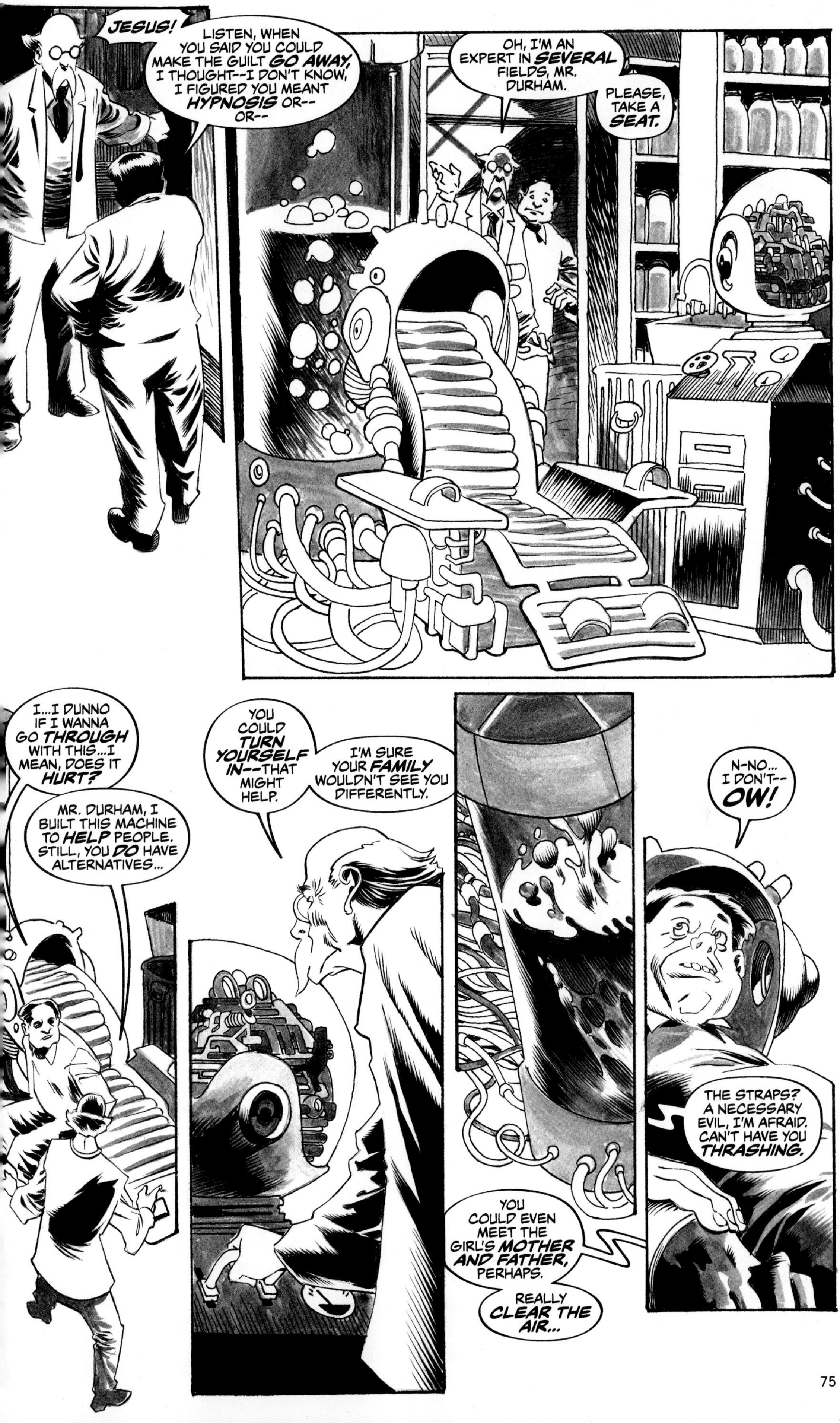
JESUS!
LISTEN, WHEN YOU SAID YOU COULD MAKE THE GUILT GO AWAY, I THOUGHT--I DON'T KNOW, I FIGURED YOU MEANT HYPNOSIS OR-- OR--
OH, I'M AN EXPERT IN SEVERAL FIELDS, MR. DURHAM.
PLEASE, TAKE A SEAT.
I...I DUNNO IF I WANNA GO THROUGH WITH THIS...I MEAN, DOES IT HURT?
MR. DURHAM, I BUILT THIS MACHINE TO HELP PEOPLE. STILL, YOU DO HAVE ALTERNATIVES...
YOU COULD TURN YOURSELF IN--THAT MIGHT HELP.
I'M SURE YOUR FAMILY WOULDN'T SEE YOU DIFFERENTLY.
YOU COULD EVEN MEET THE GIRL'S MOTHER AND FATHER, PERHAPS.
REALLY CLEAR THE AIR...
N-NO... I DON'T-- OW!
THE STRAPS? A NECESSARY EVIL, I'M AFRAID. CAN'T HAVE YOU THRASHING.

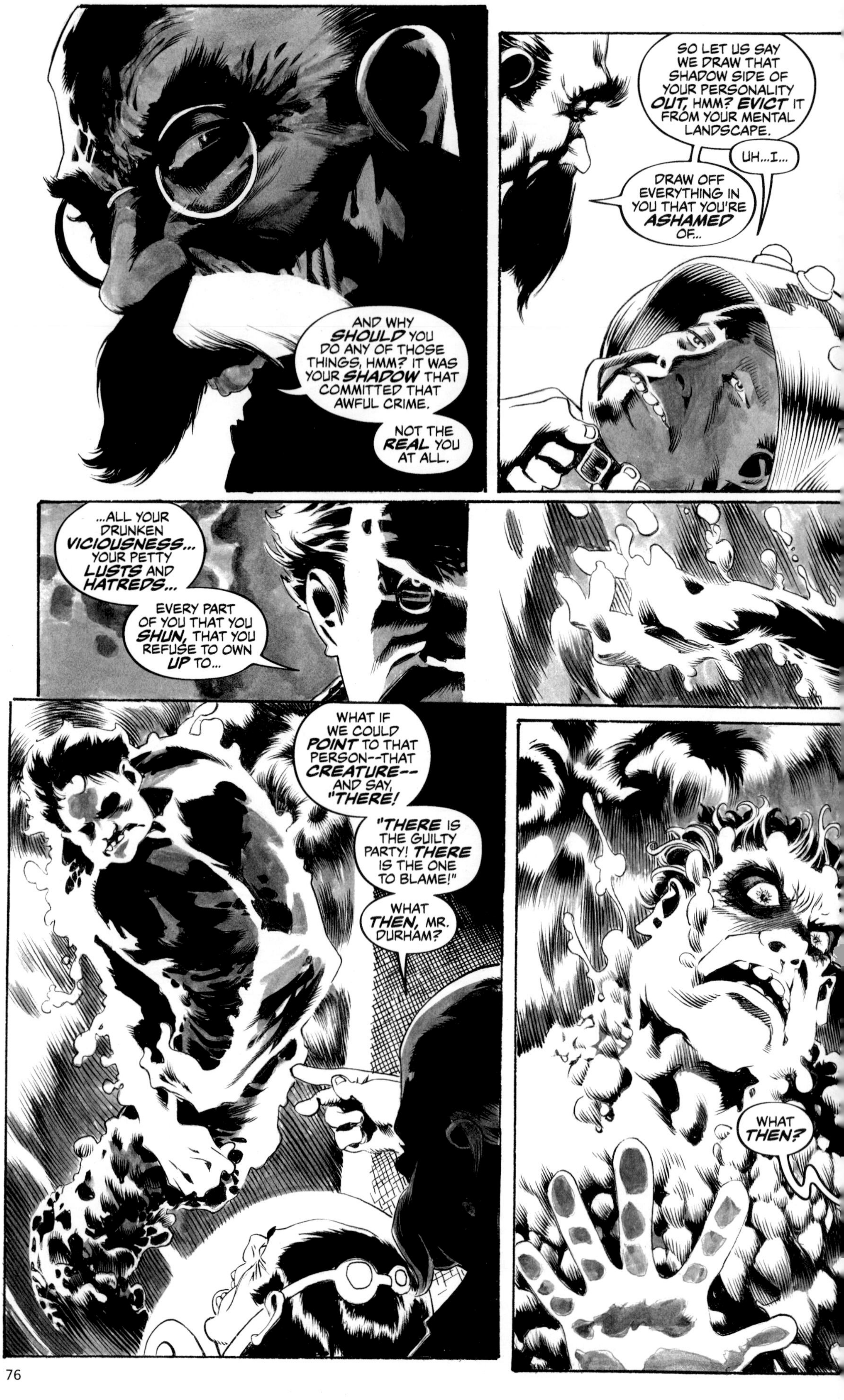

AND WHY SHOULD YOU DO ANY OF THOSE THINGS, HMM? IT WAS YOUR SHADOW THAT COMMITTED THAT AWFUL CRIME.
NOT THE REAL YOU AT ALL.
SO LET US SAY WE DRAW THAT SHADOW SIDE OF YOUR PERSONALITY OUT, HMM? EVICT IT FROM YOUR MENTAL LANDSCAPE.
UH...I...
DRAW OFF EVERYTHING IN YOU THAT YOU'RE ASHAMED OF...
...ALL YOUR DRUNKEN VICIOUSNESS... YOUR PETTY LUSTS AND HATREDS...
EVERY PART OF YOU THAT YOU SHUN, THAT YOU REFUSE TO OWN UP TO...
WHAT IF WE COULD POINT TO THAT PERSON--THAT CREATURE-- AND SAY, "THERE!
"THERE IS THE GUILTY PARTY! THERE IS THE ONE TO BLAME!"
WHAT THEN, MR. DURHAM?
WHAT THEN?

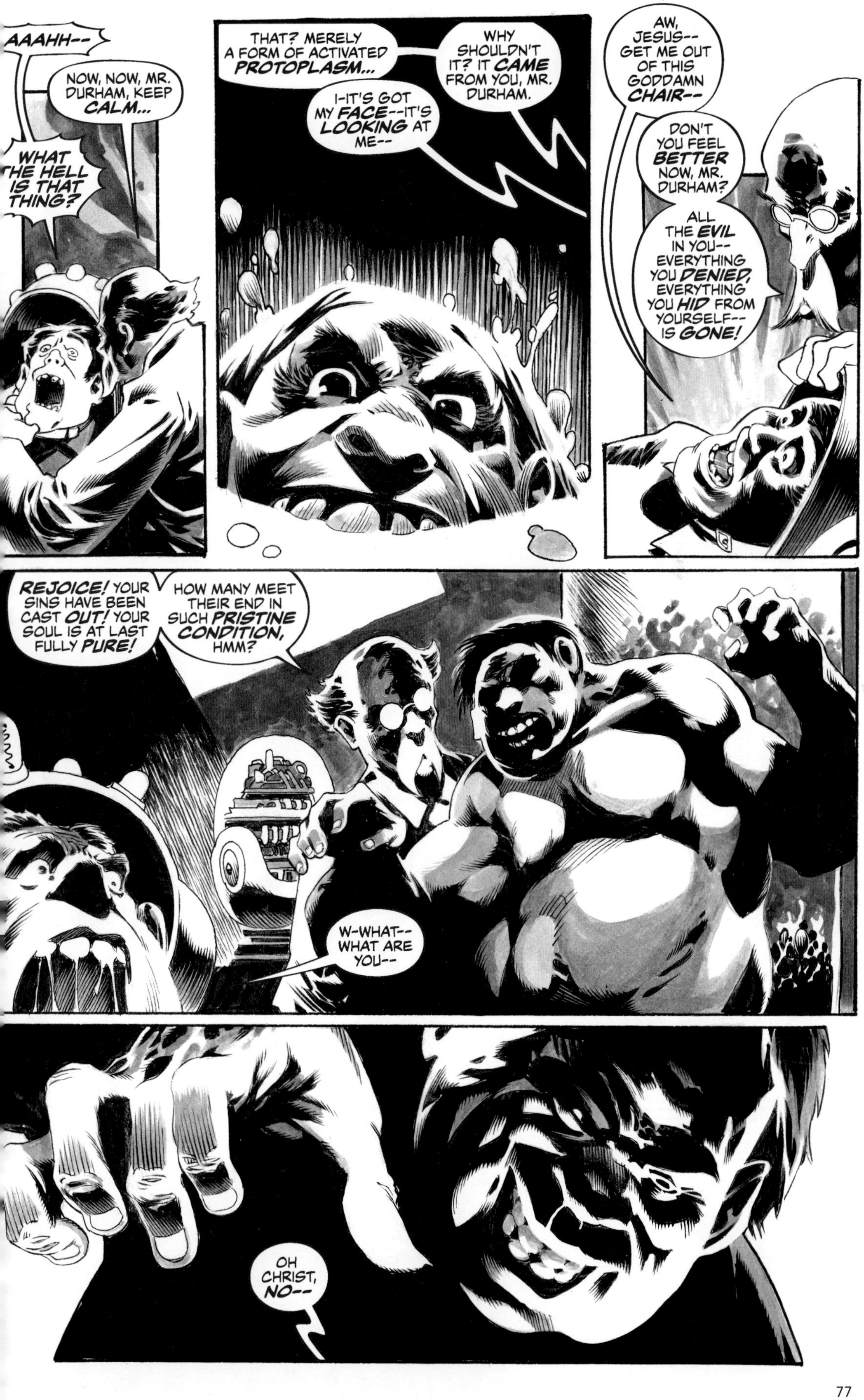
AAAHH--
NOW, NOW, MR. DURHAM, KEEP CALM...
WHAT THE HELL IS THAT THING?
THAT? MERELY A FORM OF ACTIVATED PROTOPLASM...
I-IT'S GOT MY FACE--IT'S LOOKING AT ME--
WHY SHOULDN'T IT? IT CAME FROM YOU, MR. DURHAM.
AW, JESUS-- GET ME OUT OF THIS GODDAMN CHAIR--
DON'T YOU FEEL BETTER NOW, MR. DURHAM?
ALL THE EVIL IN YOU-- EVERYTHING YOU DENIED, EVERYTHING YOU HID FROM YOURSELF-- IS GONE!
REJOICE! YOUR SINS HAVE BEEN CAST OUT! YOUR SOUL IS AT LAST FULLY PURE!
HOW MANY MEET THEIR END IN SUCH PRISTINE CONDITION, HMM?
W-WHAT-- WHAT ARE YOU--
OH CHRIST, NO--

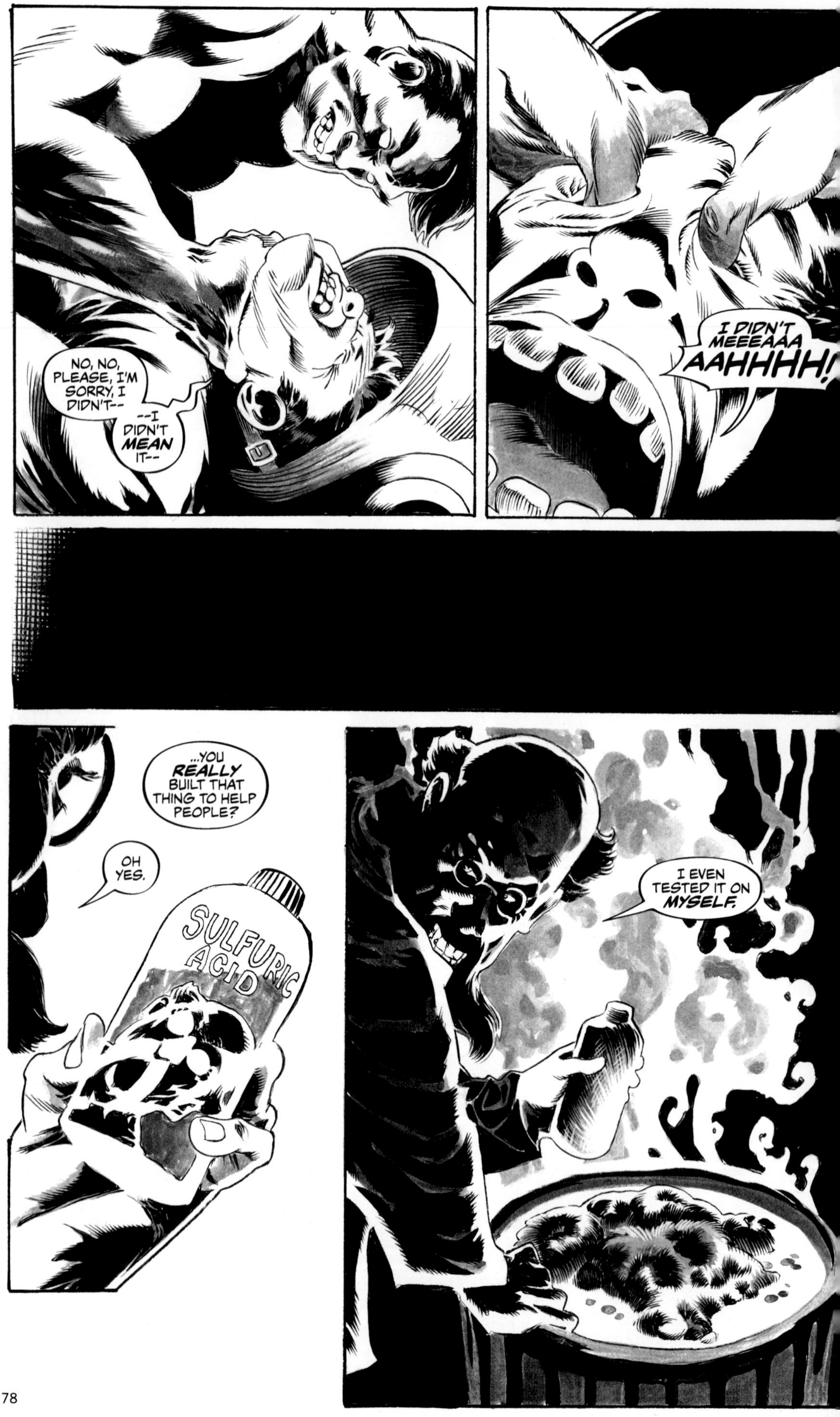
NO, NO, PLEASE, I'M SORRY, I DIDN'T--
--I DIDN'T MEAN IT--
I DIDN'T MEEEAAA AAHHHH!
...YOU REALLY BUILT THAT THING TO HELP PEOPLE?
OH YES.
SULFURIC ACID
I EVEN TESTED IT ON MYSELF.

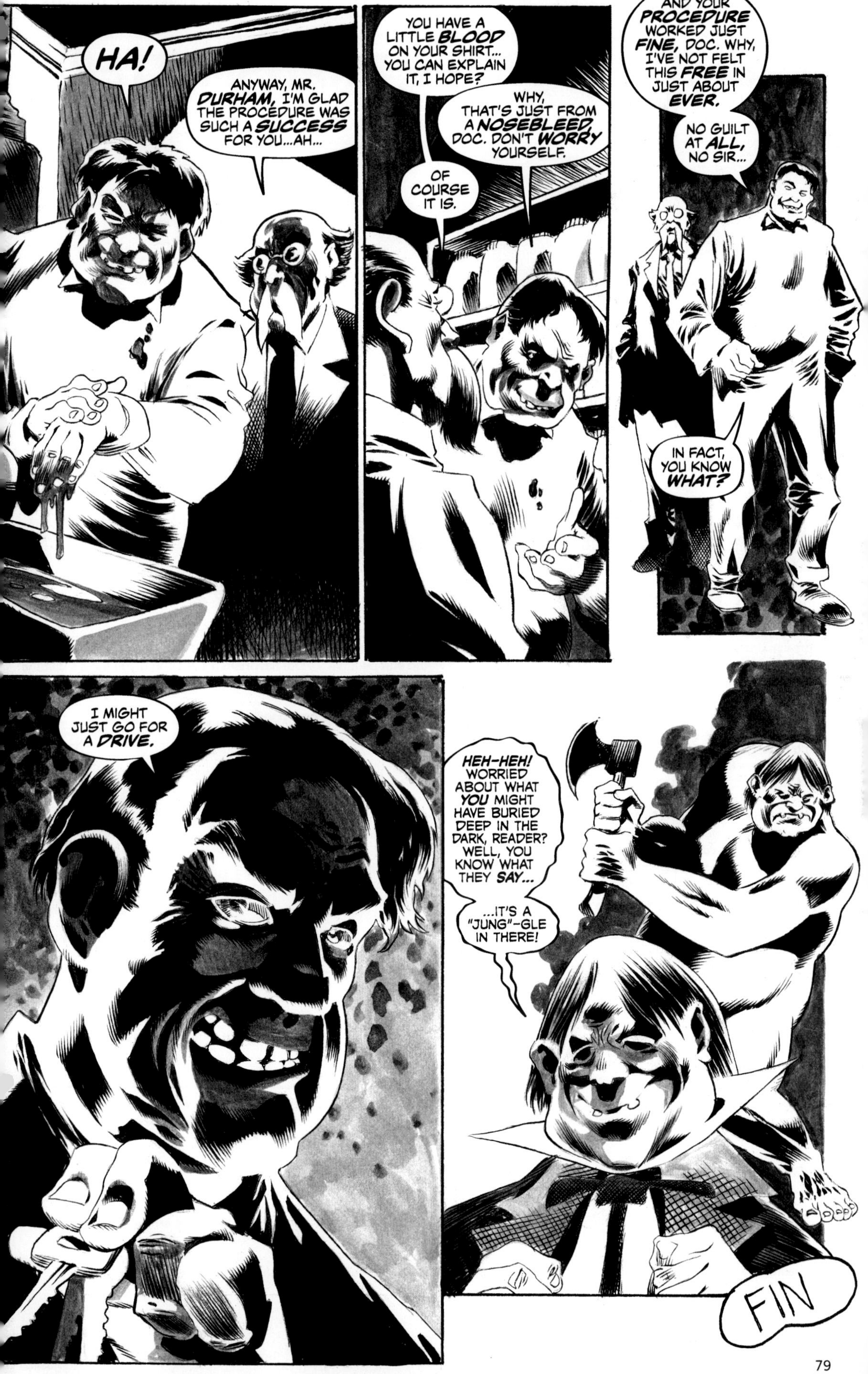
HA!
ANYWAY, MR. DURHAM, I'M GLAD THE PROCEDURE WAS SUCH A SUCCESS FOR YOU...AH...
YOU HAVE A LITTLE BLOOD ON YOUR SHIRT... YOU CAN EXPLAIN IT, I HOPE?
WHY, THAT'S JUST FROM A NOSEBLEED, DOC. DON'T WORRY YOURSELF.
OF COURSE IT IS.
AND YOUR PROCEDURE WORKED JUST FINE, DOC. WHY, I'VE NOT FELT THIS FREE IN JUST ABOUT EVER.
NO GUILT AT ALL, NO SIR...
IN FACT, YOU KNOW WHAT?
I MIGHT JUST GO FOR A DRIVE.
HEH-HEH! WORRIED ABOUT WHAT YOU MIGHT HAVE BURIED DEEP IN THE DARK, READER? WELL, YOU KNOW WHAT THEY SAY...
...IT'S A "JUNG"-GLE IN THERE!
FIN

ICKSTARTER | **What the Heck Is Ickstarter?** | **Discover** Icky Projects | **Start** Your Icky Project | Search Stuff | Help | Sign Up | Log

EXOTIC MATTER TRANSMITTER

by EMTWorm

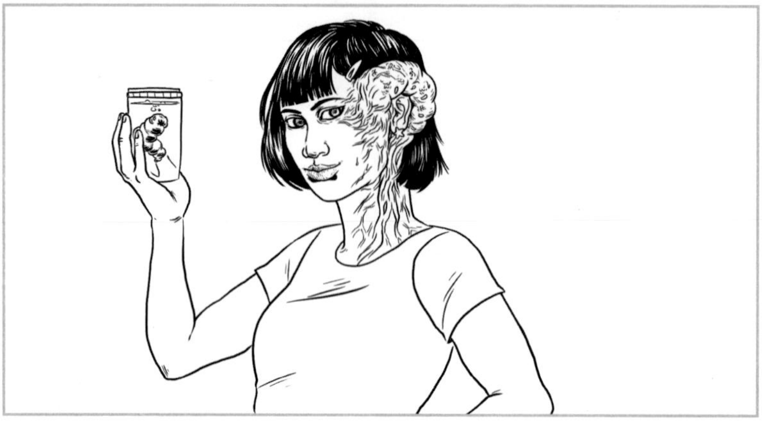

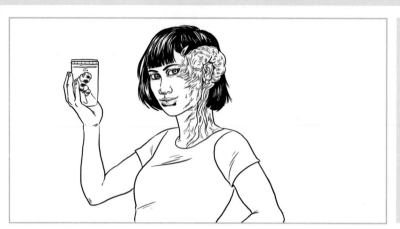

7
backers

$31
pledged of $750,000 goal

4
days to go

Back This Project
$1 minimum pledge

This project will only be funded if at least $750,000 is pledged by December 15.

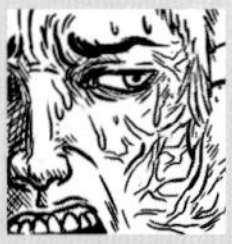

Project by
EMTWorm
Netherlands
Contact Me

Ickstarter created: Nov. 15
BACKED: 0

Has not connected on FaceBlech
Website: www.EMTWorm.com
See Full Bio

What is the "Exotic Matter Transmitter"?

It's 2027, but you forgot your pants in 2024. This could be a bit of a problem, as time travel doesn't really exist, but if you'd invested in the EMT campaign back in 2013, it would be so easy to go back and pull the pants out of the toilet and maybe you two could even have a real breakfast together and the dog would still be alive . . . Oh! Surprise! It's 2013, and you have a chance to save the future with your own brain—and hard cash!

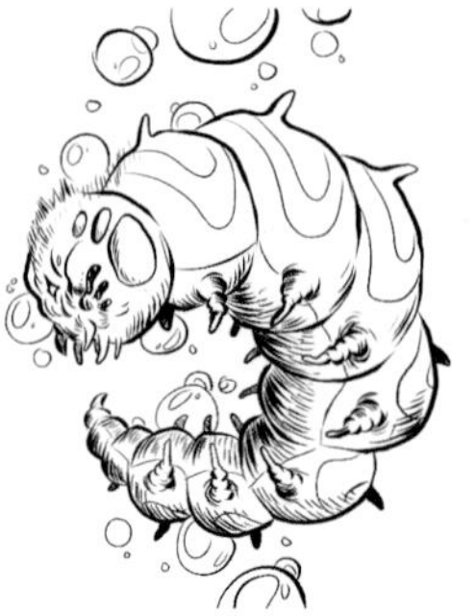

In order to perceive time, our brains observe it as if they are observing ripples on a pond. The first ripple triggers a rise in the responses of auditory neurons, which then fire up more neurons . . . You get it. Your brain figures out what the difference between each ripple is and it measures time based on that. Now . . . what if we could tell you that there's a cute species of tiny worm that can help you perceive these ripples backwards and access them all?

Look. Time is just a tool. And so is the worm. The underlying mechanism for the EMT was discovered by yours truly in 2017 while I was investigating the properties of exotic matter predicted by a subclass of supersymmetric gauge theory. To be specific, it's break time, I'm eating a pastrami sandwich . . . and the next thing I know, I'm bleeding from my nose because this beautiful worm thing tried to get inside my brain. I fought it at first, but eventually I realized it was a blessing in disguise!

The power requirements of the EMT are immense, and our research over the next few years will require a considerable amount of investment—but with crowd funding taking off, we decided to engage you during this year to make sure that what happened in our past happens in your future. It would have been most unfortunate if our research had gone unfunded during the initial campaign in 2013. It is important—nay, vital—that you assist us during this initial capital-raising round.

Update #1:
Seriously? Seventeen dollars? *Meat.* We require seven hundred and fifty thousand and that's without the shipping expenses. Come on, people. I emailed you all, like, five times?

Update #2:
What's going on here, humans? *Meat.* This is the chance of a lifetime, here. *Meat. Is there meat.* We're way behind on making our goal in the remaining six days, and if you don't fund us now, we will have no alternative but to execute the last few remaining available jumps of the transmitter to wipe your *meat—mm—mm—*existence.

Update #3:
Did you *feel* that? Good. That's *your brain fading in space and time.* Can *you hear* the scratching?

This is the worm speaking. You should have donated when we sent you that email you marked as spam. We are your life now, as you smile and think "hah."

Eventually you fall asleep, but you do not. You haven't really slept since we came back. You haven't really been awake since we came back.

And the best part is, you will never believe this.

You are truly just a machine to be lived in.

Text by ALES KOT / Art by SLOANE LEONG

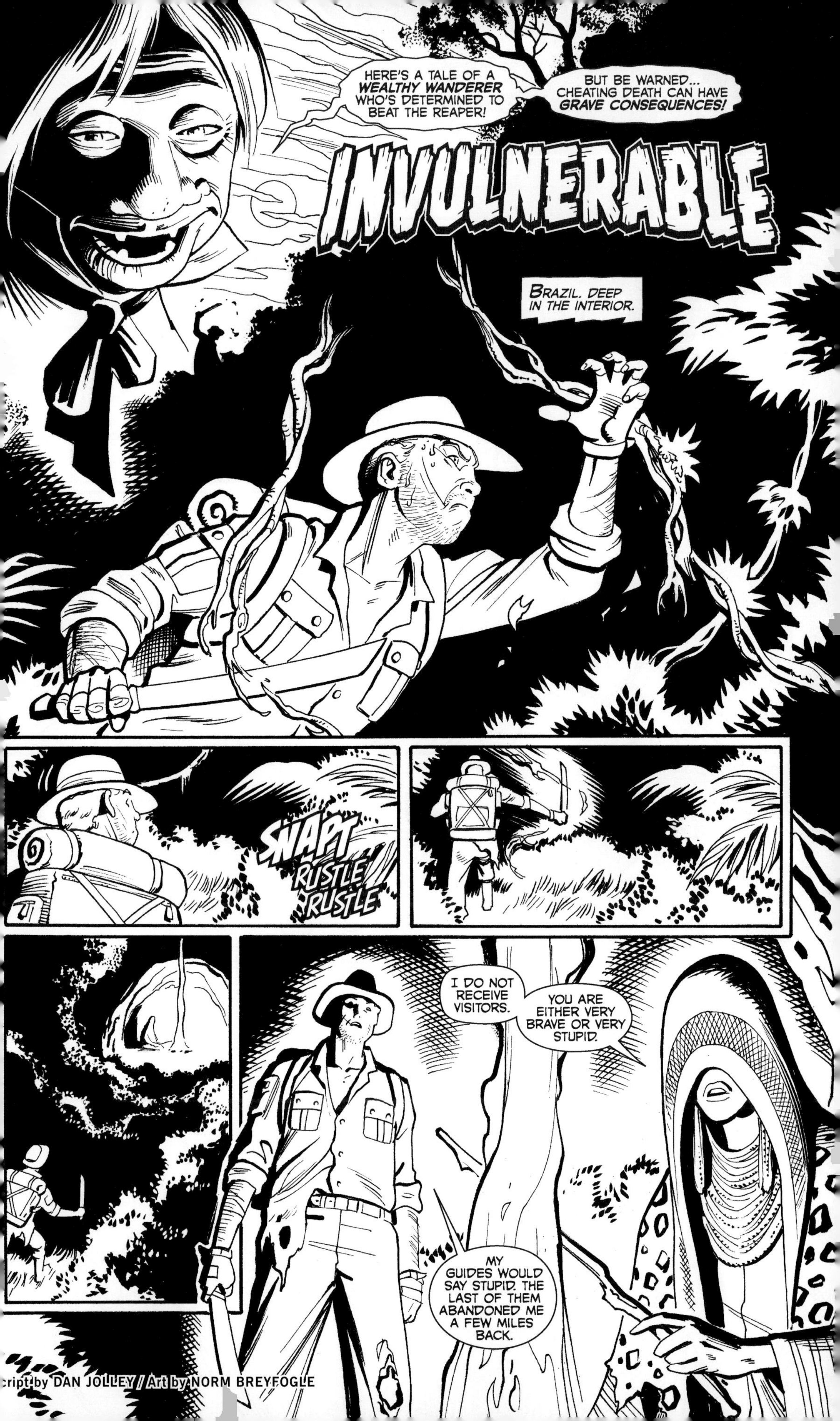
HERE'S A TALE OF A WEALTHY WANDERER WHO'S DETERMINED TO BEAT THE REAPER!
BUT BE WARNED... CHEATING DEATH CAN HAVE GRAVE CONSEQUENCES!
INVULNERABLE
BRAZIL. DEEP IN THE INTERIOR.
SNAPT
RUSTLE
RUSTLE
I DO NOT RECEIVE VISITORS.
YOU ARE EITHER VERY BRAVE OR VERY STUPID.
MY GUIDES WOULD SAY STUPID. THE LAST OF THEM ABANDONED ME A FEW MILES BACK.
cript by DAN JOLLEY / Art by NORM BREYFOGLE

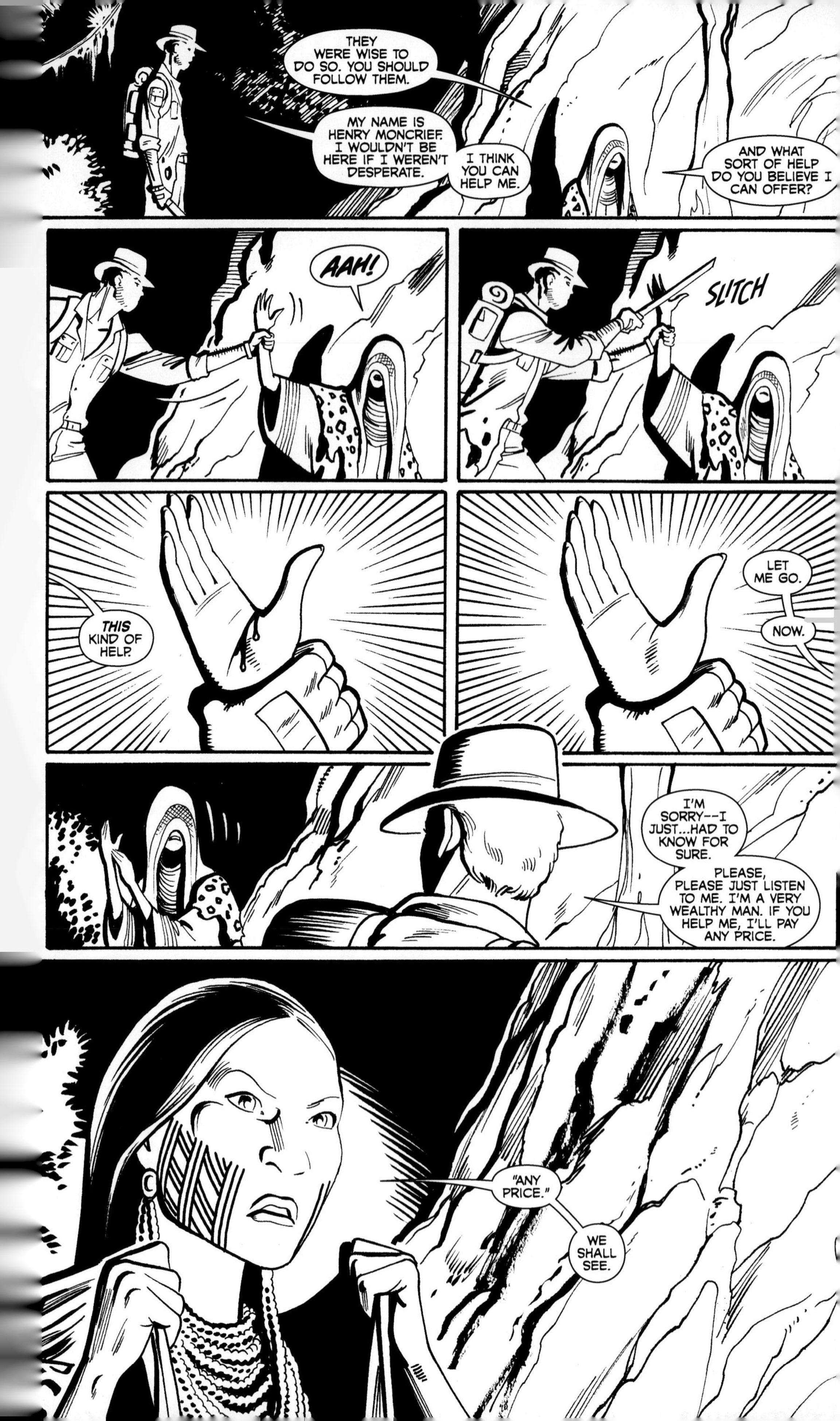
THEY WERE WISE TO DO SO. YOU SHOULD FOLLOW THEM.
MY NAME IS HENRY MONCRIEF. I WOULDN'T BE HERE IF I WEREN'T DESPERATE.
I THINK YOU CAN HELP ME.
AND WHAT SORT OF HELP DO YOU BELIEVE I CAN OFFER?
AAH!
SLITCH
THIS KIND OF HELP.
LET ME GO.
NOW.
I'M SORRY--I JUST...HAD TO KNOW FOR SURE.
PLEASE, PLEASE JUST LISTEN TO ME. I'M A VERY WEALTHY MAN. IF YOU HELP ME, I'LL PAY ANY PRICE.
"ANY PRICE."
WE SHALL SEE.

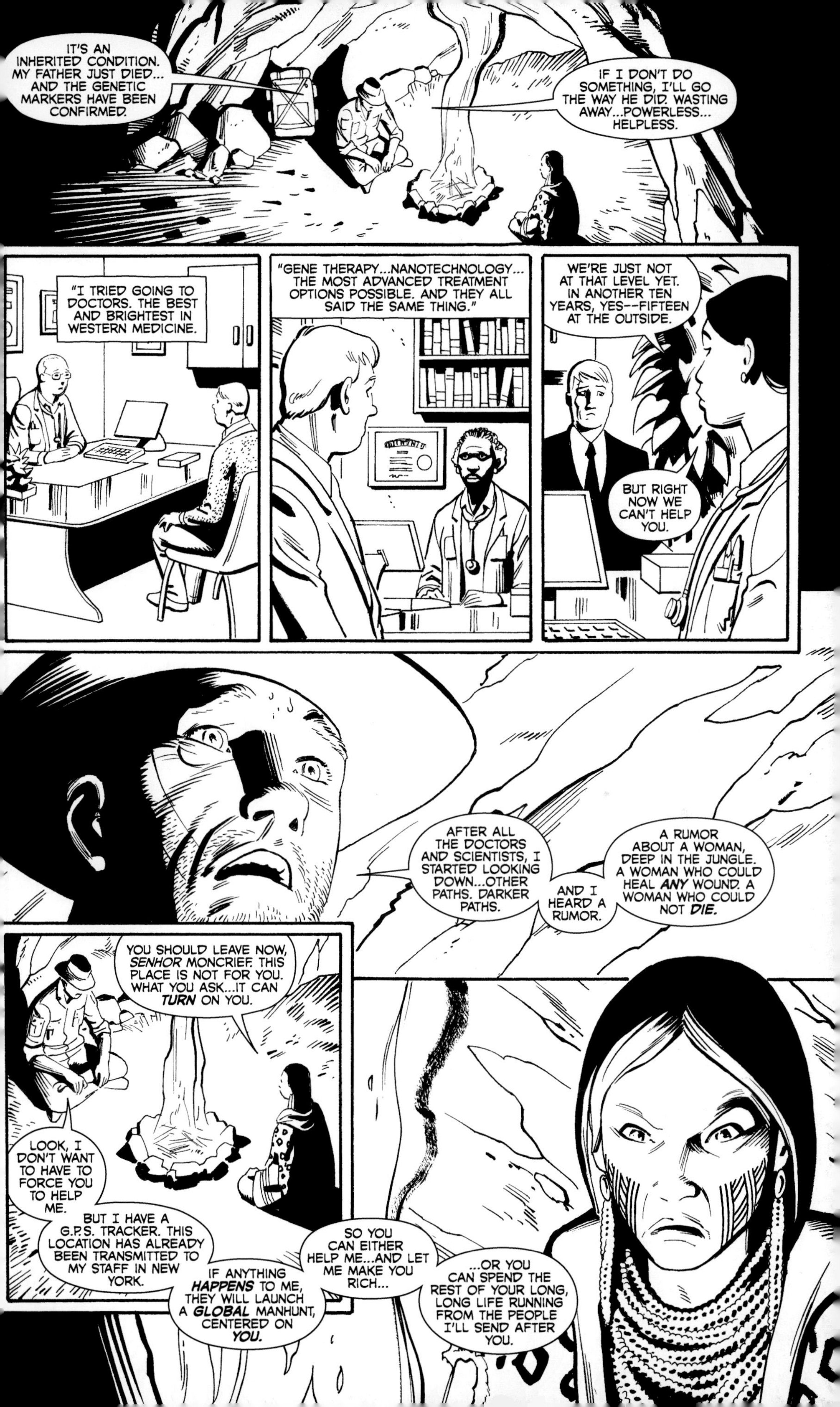
IT'S AN INHERITED CONDITION. MY FATHER JUST DIED... AND THE GENETIC MARKERS HAVE BEEN CONFIRMED.
IF I DON'T DO SOMETHING, I'LL GO THE WAY HE DID. WASTING AWAY...POWERLESS... HELPLESS.
"I TRIED GOING TO DOCTORS. THE BEST AND BRIGHTEST IN WESTERN MEDICINE.
"GENE THERAPY...NANOTECHNOLOGY... THE MOST ADVANCED TREATMENT OPTIONS POSSIBLE. AND THEY ALL SAID THE SAME THING."
WE'RE JUST NOT AT THAT LEVEL YET. IN ANOTHER TEN YEARS, YES--FIFTEEN AT THE OUTSIDE.
BUT RIGHT NOW WE CAN'T HELP YOU.
AFTER ALL THE DOCTORS AND SCIENTISTS, I STARTED LOOKING DOWN...OTHER PATHS. DARKER PATHS.
AND I HEARD A RUMOR.
A RUMOR ABOUT A WOMAN, DEEP IN THE JUNGLE. A WOMAN WHO COULD HEAL ANY WOUND. A WOMAN WHO COULD NOT DIE.
YOU SHOULD LEAVE NOW, SENHOR MONCRIEF. THIS PLACE IS NOT FOR YOU. WHAT YOU ASK...IT CAN TURN ON YOU.
LOOK, I DON'T WANT TO HAVE TO FORCE YOU TO HELP ME.
BUT I HAVE A G.P.S. TRACKER. THIS LOCATION HAS ALREADY BEEN TRANSMITTED TO MY STAFF IN NEW YORK.
IF ANYTHING HAPPENS TO ME, THEY WILL LAUNCH A GLOBAL MANHUNT, CENTERED ON YOU.
SO YOU CAN EITHER HELP ME...AND LET ME MAKE YOU RICH...
...OR YOU CAN SPEND THE REST OF YOUR LONG, LONG LIFE RUNNING FROM THE PEOPLE I'LL SEND AFTER YOU.

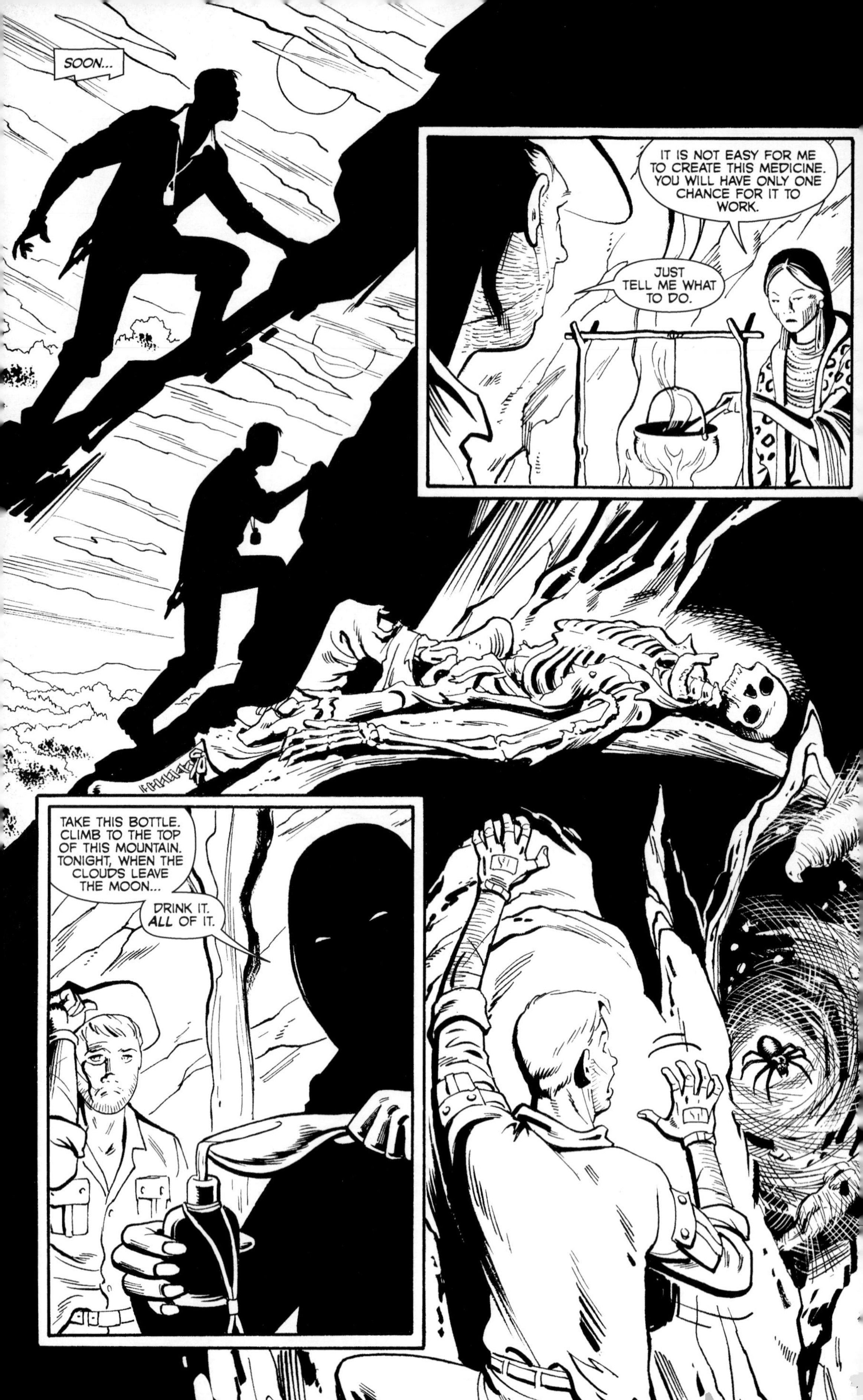
SOON...
IT IS NOT EASY FOR ME TO CREATE THIS MEDICINE. YOU WILL HAVE ONLY ONE CHANCE FOR IT TO WORK.
JUST TELL ME WHAT TO DO.
TAKE THIS BOTTLE. CLIMB TO THE TOP OF THIS MOUNTAIN. TONIGHT, WHEN THE CLOUDS LEAVE THE MOON...
DRINK IT. ALL OF IT.

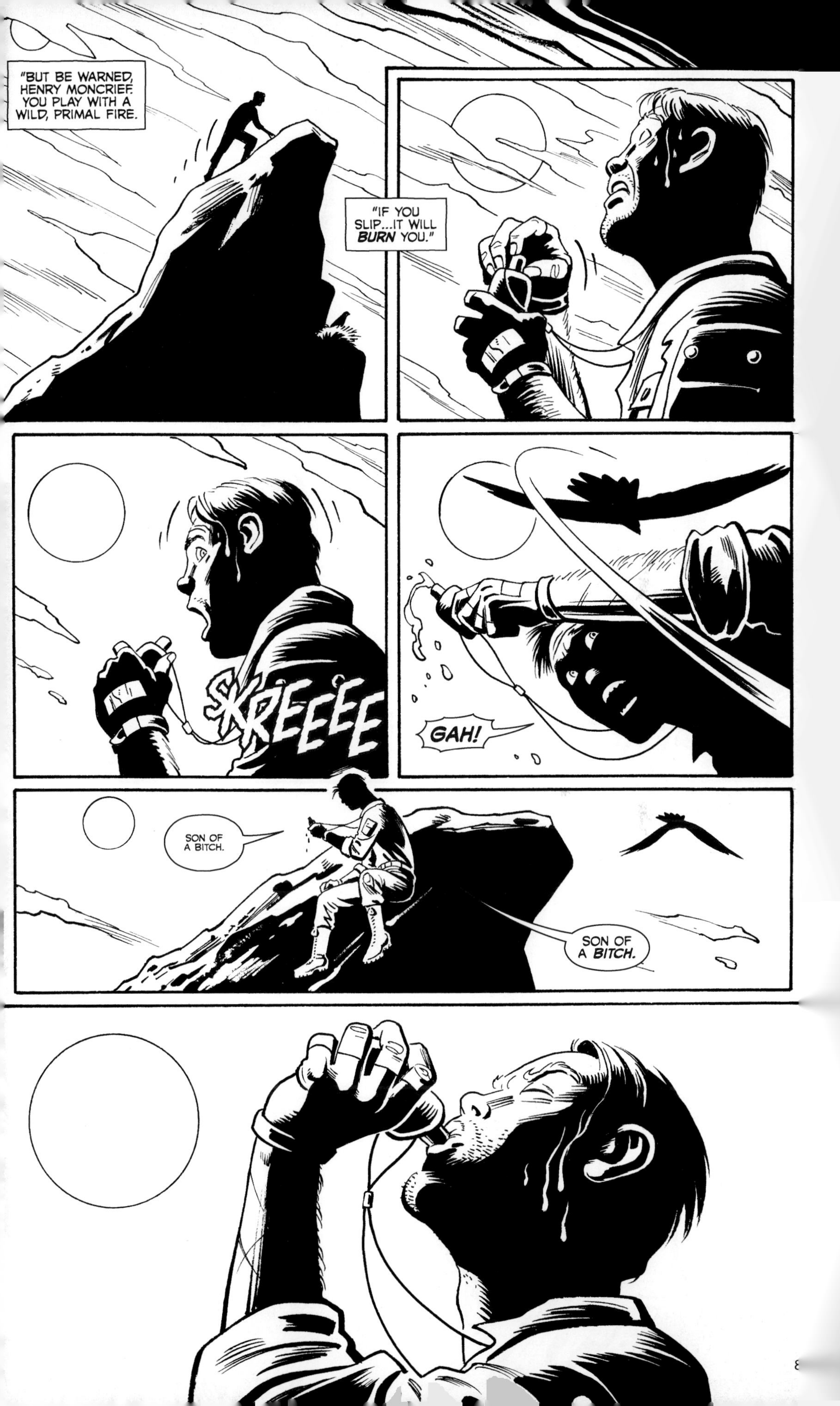

"BUT BE WARNED, HENRY MONCRIEF. YOU PLAY WITH A WILD, PRIMAL FIRE.
"IF YOU SLIP...IT WILL BURN YOU."
SKREEEEE
GAH!
SON OF A BITCH.
SON OF A BITCH.

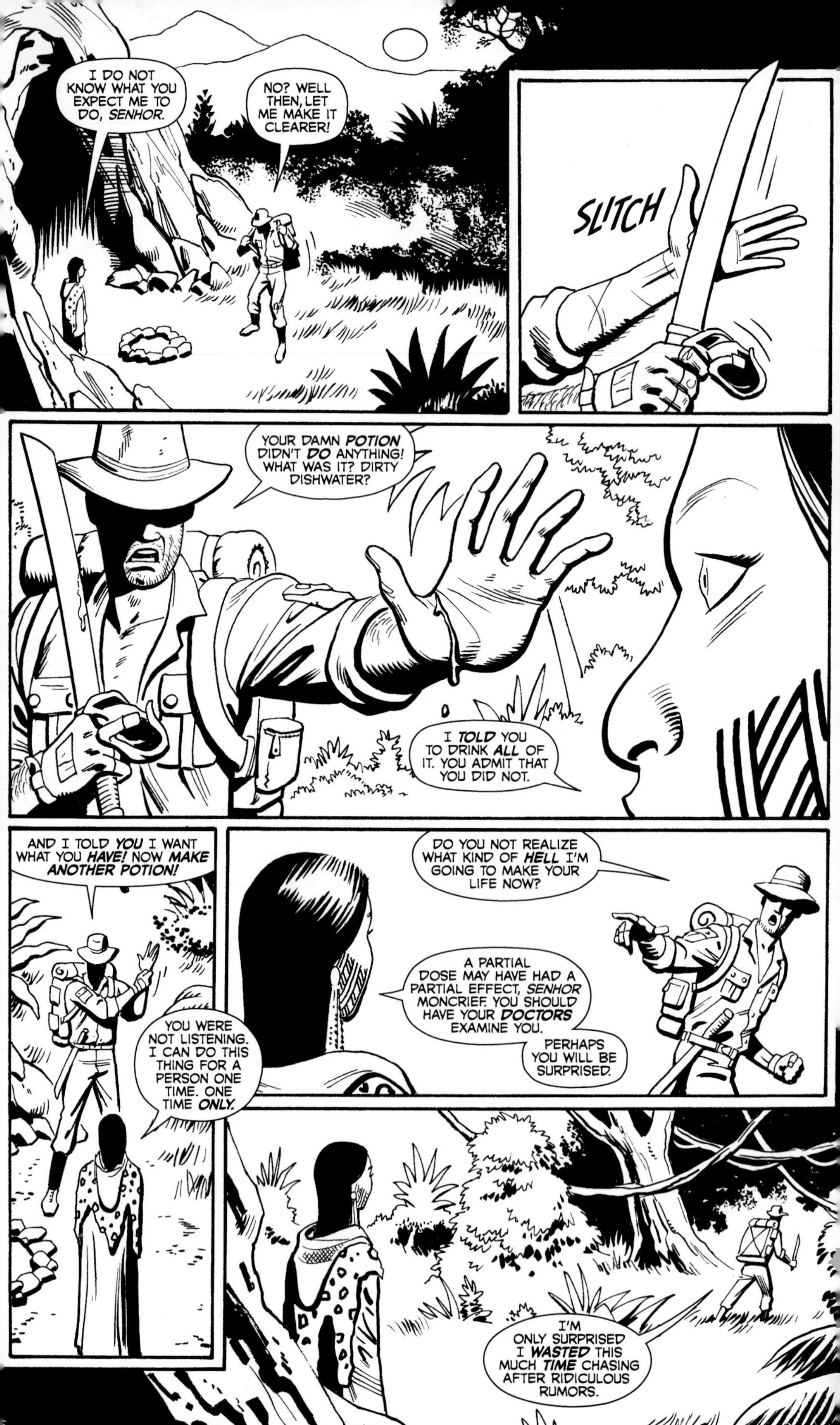
I DO NOT KNOW WHAT YOU EXPECT ME TO DO, *SENHOR.*
NO? WELL THEN, LET ME MAKE IT CLEARER!
SLITCH
YOUR DAMN ***POTION*** DIDN'T ***DO*** ANYTHING! WHAT WAS IT? DIRTY DISHWATER?
I ***TOLD*** YOU TO DRINK ***ALL*** OF IT. YOU ADMIT THAT YOU DID NOT.
AND I TOLD ***YOU*** I WANT WHAT YOU ***HAVE!*** NOW ***MAKE ANOTHER POTION!***
YOU WERE NOT LISTENING. I CAN DO THIS THING FOR A PERSON ONE TIME. ONE TIME ***ONLY.***
DO YOU NOT REALIZE WHAT KIND OF ***HELL*** I'M GOING TO MAKE YOUR LIFE NOW?
A PARTIAL DOSE MAY HAVE HAD A PARTIAL EFFECT, *SENHOR* MONCRIEF. YOU SHOULD HAVE YOUR ***DOCTORS*** EXAMINE YOU.
PERHAPS YOU WILL BE SURPRISED.
I'M ONLY SURPRISED I ***WASTED*** THIS MUCH ***TIME*** CHASING AFTER RIDICULOUS RUMORS.

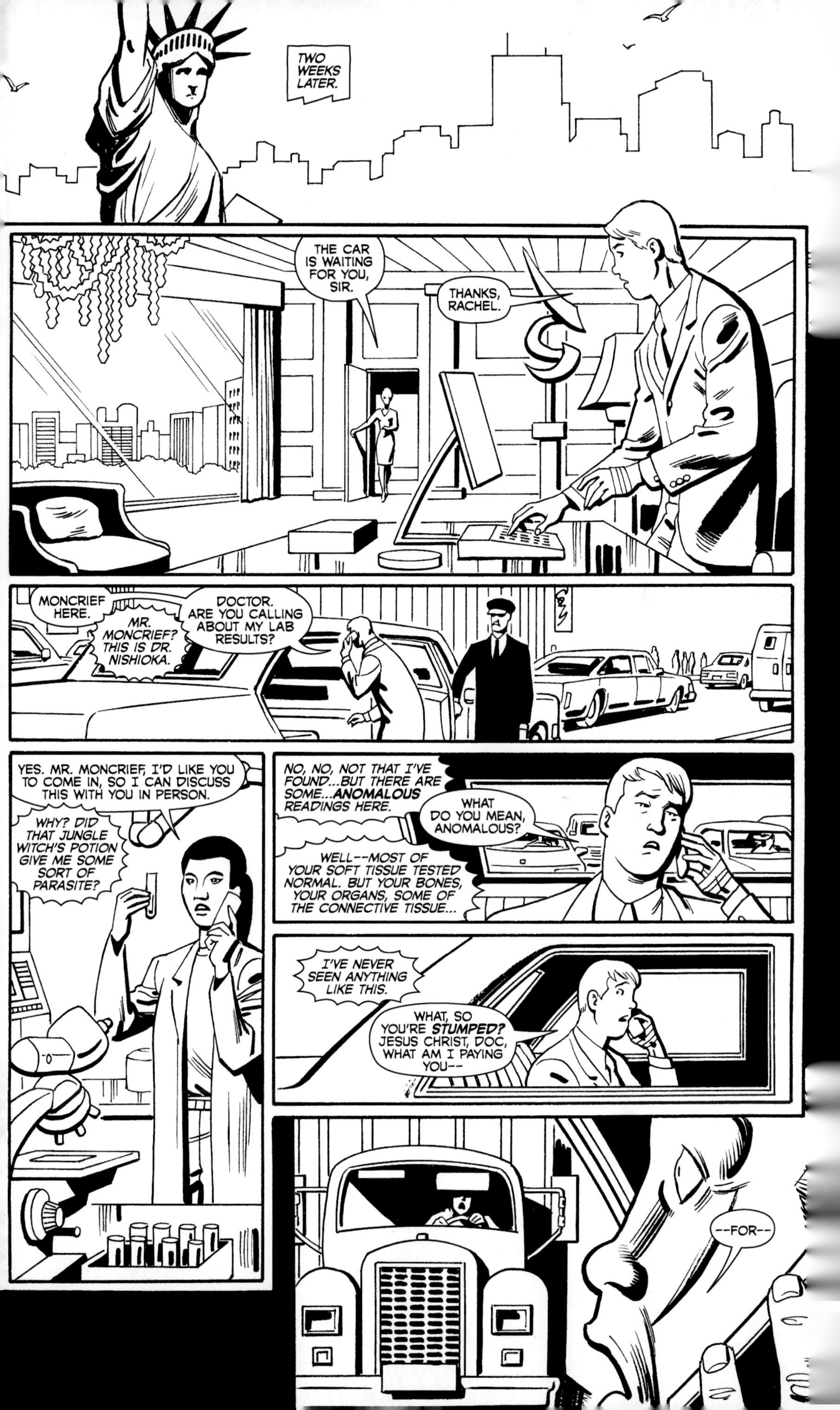

TWO WEEKS LATER.
THE CAR IS WAITING FOR YOU, SIR.
THANKS, RACHEL.
MONCRIEF HERE.
MR. MONCRIEF? THIS IS DR. NISHIOKA.
DOCTOR. ARE YOU CALLING ABOUT MY LAB RESULTS?
YES. MR. MONCRIEF, I'D LIKE YOU TO COME IN, SO I CAN DISCUSS THIS WITH YOU IN PERSON.
WHY? DID THAT JUNGLE WITCH'S POTION GIVE ME SOME SORT OF PARASITE?
NO, NO, NOT THAT I'VE FOUND...BUT THERE ARE SOME...**ANOMALOUS** READINGS HERE.
WHAT DO YOU MEAN, ANOMALOUS?
WELL--MOST OF YOUR SOFT TISSUE TESTED NORMAL. BUT YOUR BONES, YOUR ORGANS, SOME OF THE CONNECTIVE TISSUE...
I'VE NEVER SEEN ANYTHING LIKE THIS.
WHAT, SO YOU'RE **STUMPED?** JESUS CHRIST, DOC, WHAT AM I PAYING YOU--
--FOR--

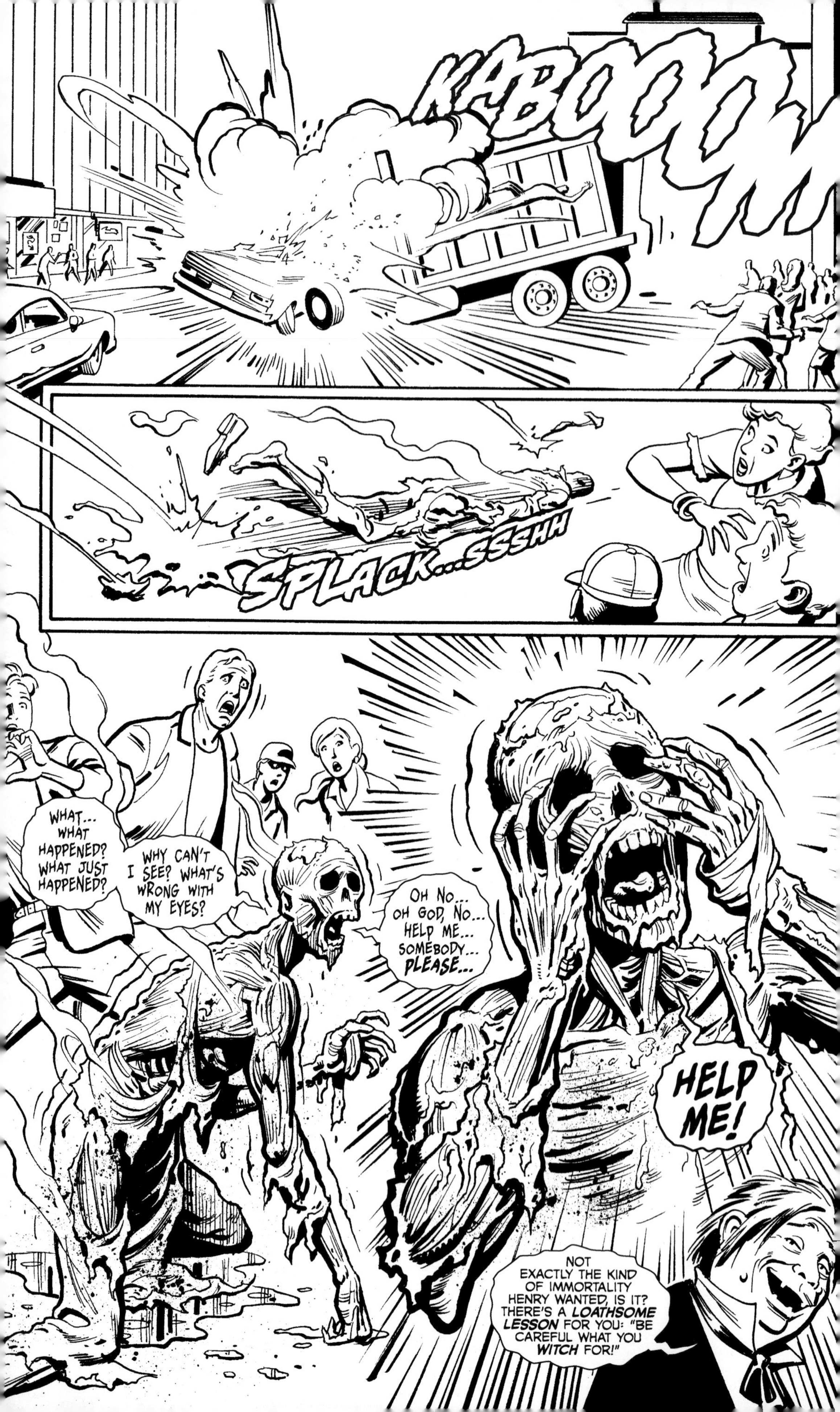
KABOOOM
SPLACK...SSSHH
WHAT... WHAT HAPPENED? WHAT JUST HAPPENED?
WHY CAN'T I SEE? WHAT'S WRONG WITH MY EYES?
OH NO... OH GOD, NO... HELP ME... SOMEBODY... PLEASE...
HELP ME!
NOT EXACTLY THE KIND OF IMMORTALITY HENRY WANTED, IS IT? THERE'S A LOATHSOME LESSON FOR YOU: "BE CAREFUL WHAT YOU WITCH FOR!"

G-17 SILK ROTORVATOR (CODE NAME MILDRED)
by The Mildred Project

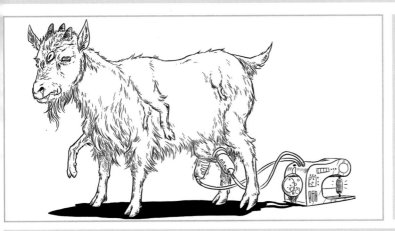

54
backers

$3,550
pledged of $500,000 goal

19
days to go

Back This Project
$5 minimum pledge

This project will only be funded if at least $500,000 is pledged by December 30.

Project by
The Mildred Project
Omaha, NE
Contact Me

Ickstarter created: Nov. 30
BACKED: 1

Has not connected on FaceBlech
Website: www.SG17.com
See Full Bio

Tensile strength far exceeding that of steel. Fueled by your backyard lawn.

Our goal is to fund the preliminary production run of a small silk-spinning machine specialized to extract, spin, dry, and prepare silk from a lactic solution. Recent tests on our prototype SG-17 indicate that you can create enough silk thread in your own home to, with our optional weaving supporter upgrade (only $300) and just a few weeks' worth of lactic solution, make yourself a lovely silk sheet set, luxurious silk pajamas, or a brand-new, extra-strong, therapeutic bandaging system that yields exquisite results—especially if you are a burn victim.

Been in a car crash? Was your face demolished in a warehouse fire? Have you burned your genitalia while preparing breakfast? Is your arm in pain, irrevocably deformed by the forces that change worlds in mere seconds, like a truck catching your Audi and spinning it out of control? You can heal, you can become better than before—and then sell the surplus on the market or to your friends. This contraption could pay for itself in mere months, so long as you get in on the ground floor at our basic supporter level. Prices will go up after this campaign!

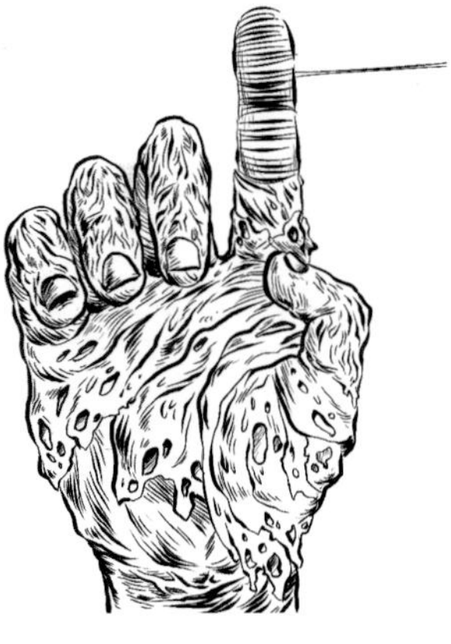

Picture this: In just a few years' time, with your silk-threading machine and loom humming happily on the back porch, extruding mile after mile of spun gold, you overlook your yard and watch your goat happily munching on the grass. A highball in your freshly recovered, no longer twisted-out-of-recognition hand. The lovely Rolex on your wrist softly chimes: dinner is ready. Friends and family have gathered for you to sell your latest batch of nearly perfect stock. And your hand . . . it's faster than before. The skin is softer than before. When you take the skin off every week it feels like rebirth.

(Don't forget to wipe off the excess pus.)

And then comes the favorite part of your evening: You sit down. You have a good drink. Some like piña coladas; others prefer whiskey. Your friends all sit quietly around the conversation pit, waiting, rapt, for the other shoe to drop. The children have locked their doors, because the respect that runs through the house now is built on the sturdy, time-proofed concept of indelible fear. You put on a lively but not too lively jazz album, perhaps one of your old Dizzy Gillespie 78s. You click your mandibles to the calming sounds of jazz. The wife smiles, not nearly as nervous as she was before, because she knows that being nervous makes Mildred upset. You stroke Mildred to calm her down, and Mildred makes a sound that at first may sound like your car crash slowed down to thirty-three beats per minute, but you'll grow used to it, just like the children did. Your friends have a light sheen of sweat on their brows, but the tension is worth it. Mildred gently licks your hand, which is now wearing a glove, because you don't want to repeat that incident.

Yes, Mildred. We said it.

The first ten supporters at the $500 level or above will get not only the lactic silk-thread spinner and the automated silk loom, but also the pièce de résistance: a newly birthed clone of our very own transgenic nanny goat, Mildred (please cheerfully ignore the supplemental limbs). Mildred is sweet and affectionate, and the epithelial cells in her mammary glands have been modified to produce the basic proteins from which silk is made. Just let Mildred-2 or Mildred-3 munch on your backyard lawn (please, no pesticides), milk her once a day, and fill the SG-17 silk-thread hopper with the latest harvest. We'll do the rest.

Amaze your friends. Buy a spider-goat.

Text by ALES KOT / Art by SLOANE LEONG

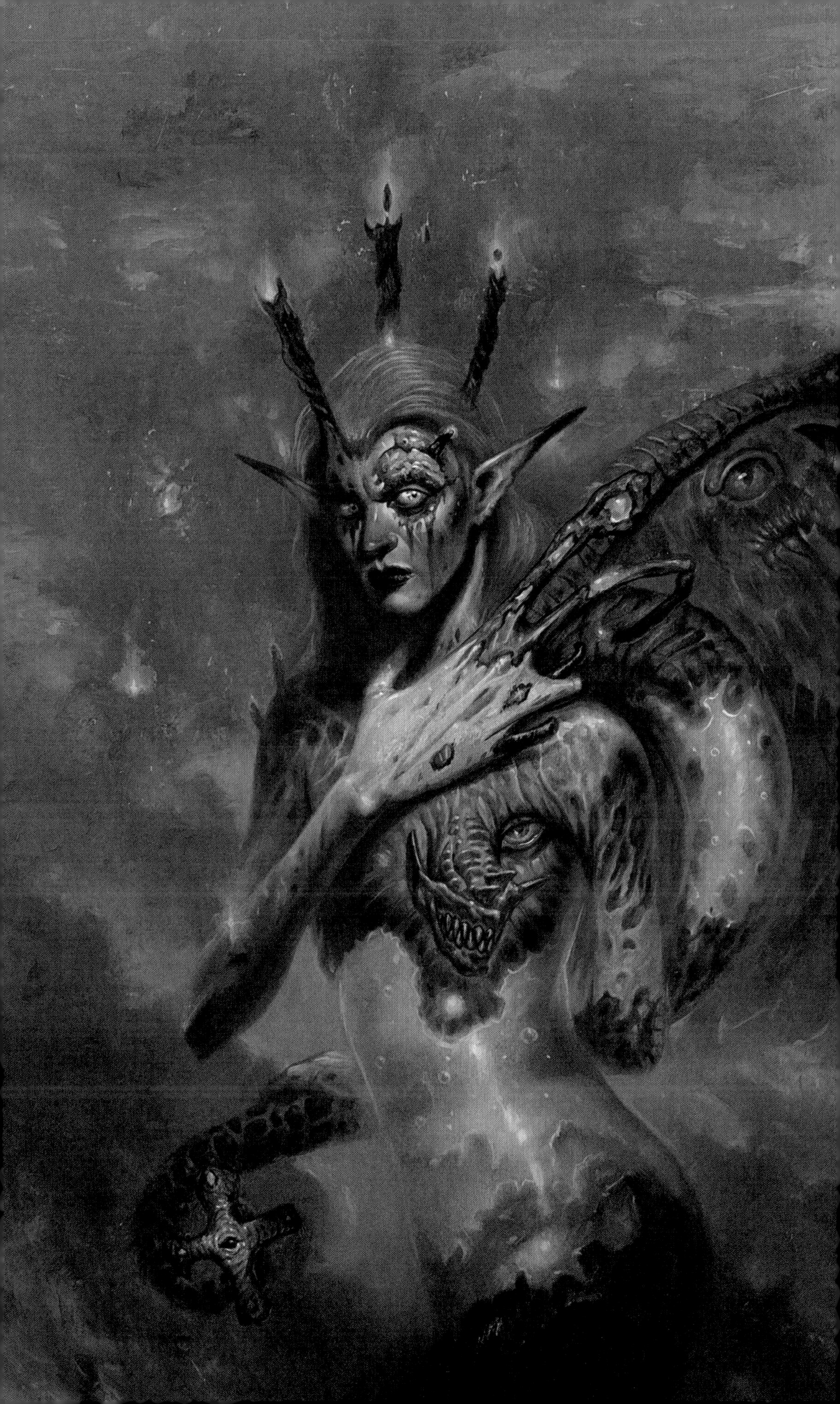

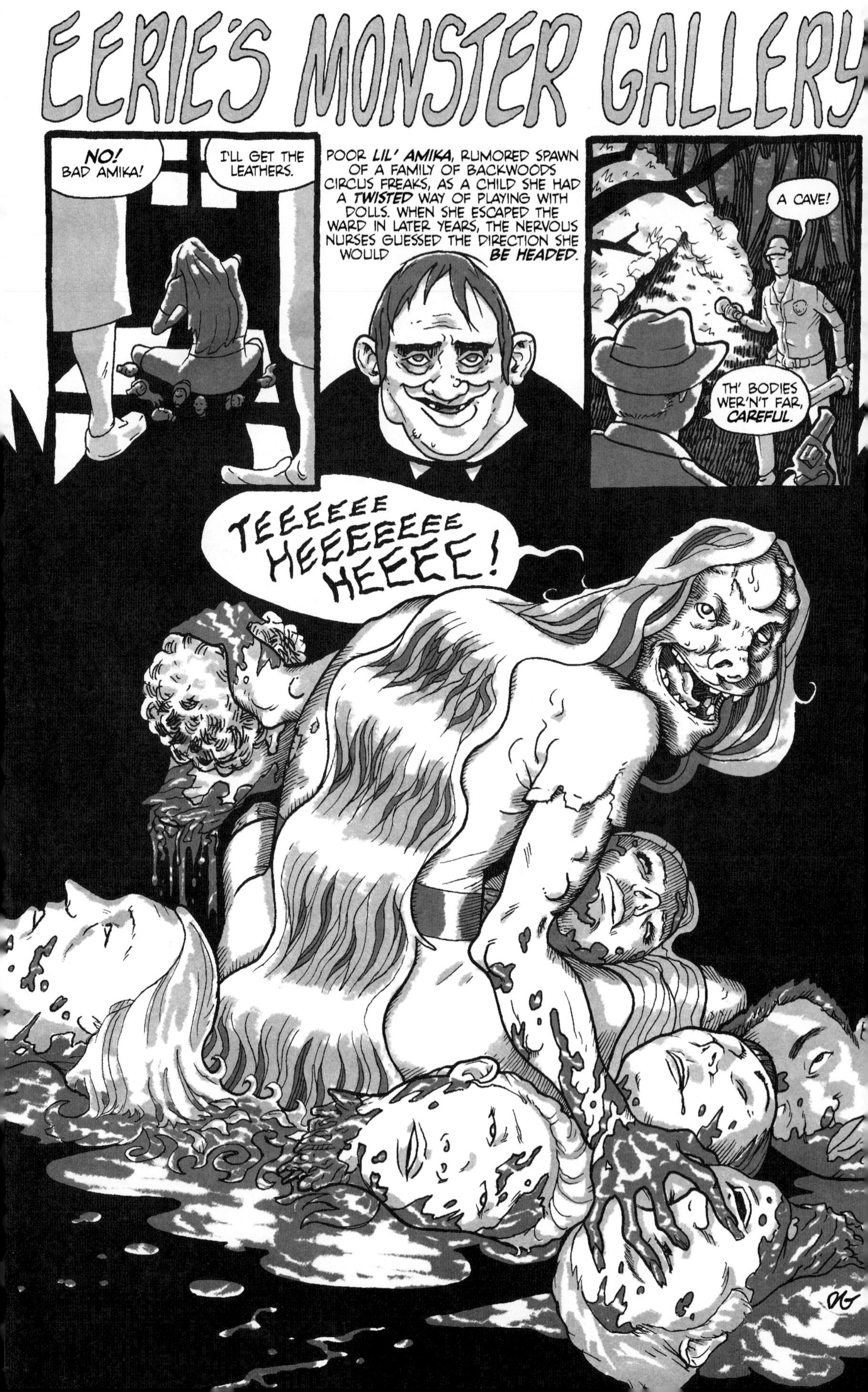

EERIE'S MONSTER GALLERY
NO! BAD AMIKA!
I'LL GET THE LEATHERS.
POOR LIL' AMIKA, RUMORED SPAWN OF A FAMILY OF BACKWOODS CIRCUS FREAKS, AS A CHILD SHE HAD A TWISTED WAY OF PLAYING WITH DOLLS. WHEN SHE ESCAPED THE WARD IN LATER YEARS, THE NERVOUS NURSES GUESSED THE DIRECTION SHE WOULD BE HEADED.
A CAVE!
TH' BODIES WER'N'T FAR, CAREFUL.
TEEEEEE HEEEEEEE HEEEEE!

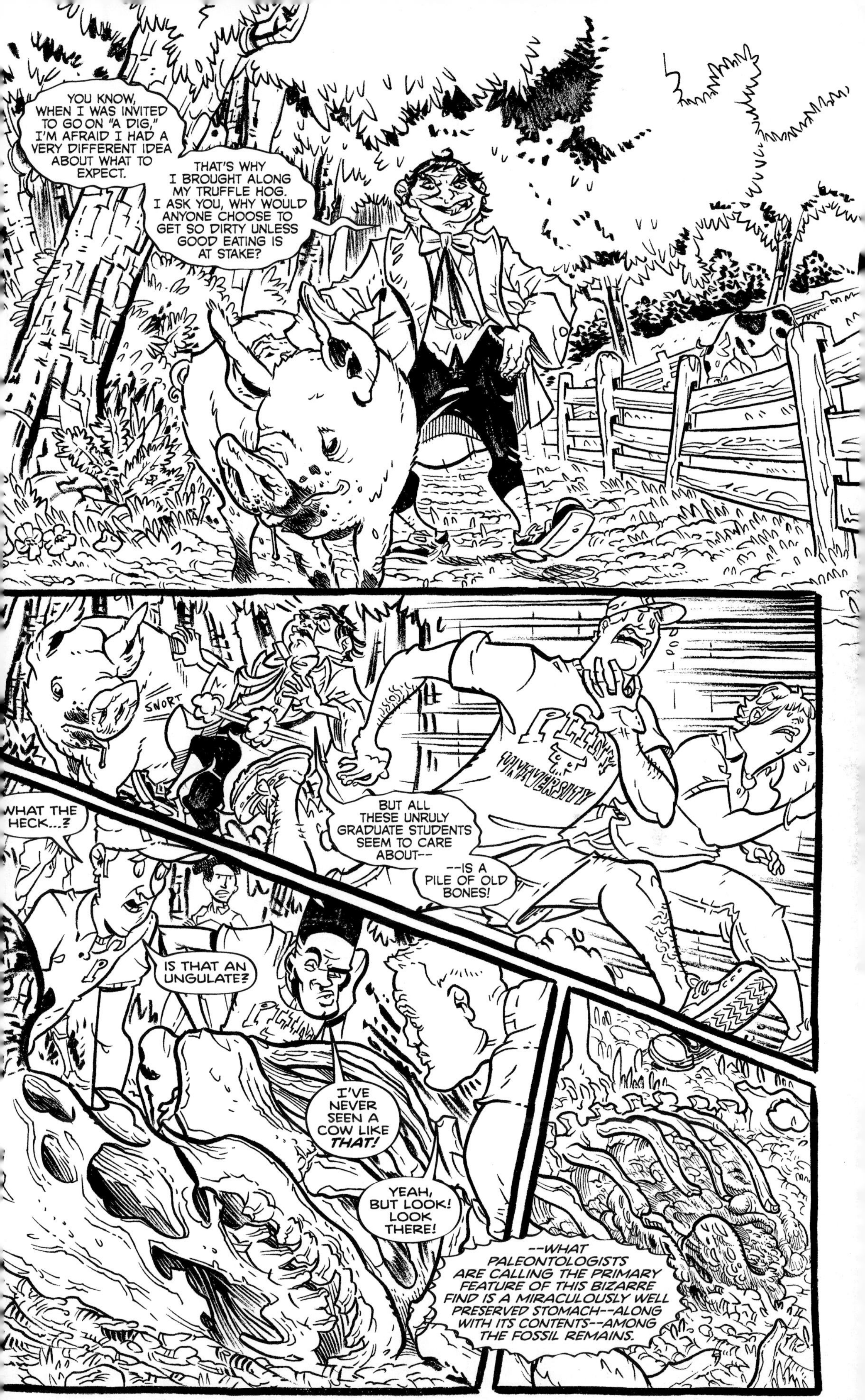

YOU KNOW, WHEN I WAS INVITED TO GO ON "A DIG," I'M AFRAID I HAD A VERY DIFFERENT IDEA ABOUT WHAT TO EXPECT.
THAT'S WHY I BROUGHT ALONG MY TRUFFLE HOG. I ASK YOU, WHY WOULD ANYONE CHOOSE TO GET SO DIRTY UNLESS GOOD EATING IS AT STAKE?
SNORT
BUT ALL THESE UNRULY GRADUATE STUDENTS SEEM TO CARE ABOUT--
--IS A PILE OF OLD BONES!
WHAT THE HECK...?
IS THAT AN UNGULATE?
I'VE NEVER SEEN A COW LIKE *THAT!*
YEAH, BUT LOOK! LOOK THERE!
--WHAT PALEONTOLOGISTS ARE CALLING THE PRIMARY FEATURE OF THIS BIZARRE FIND IS A MIRACULOUSLY WELL PRESERVED STOMACH--ALONG WITH ITS CONTENTS--AMONG THE FOSSIL REMAINS.

ript by JOHN ARCUDI / Art by AARON CONLEY

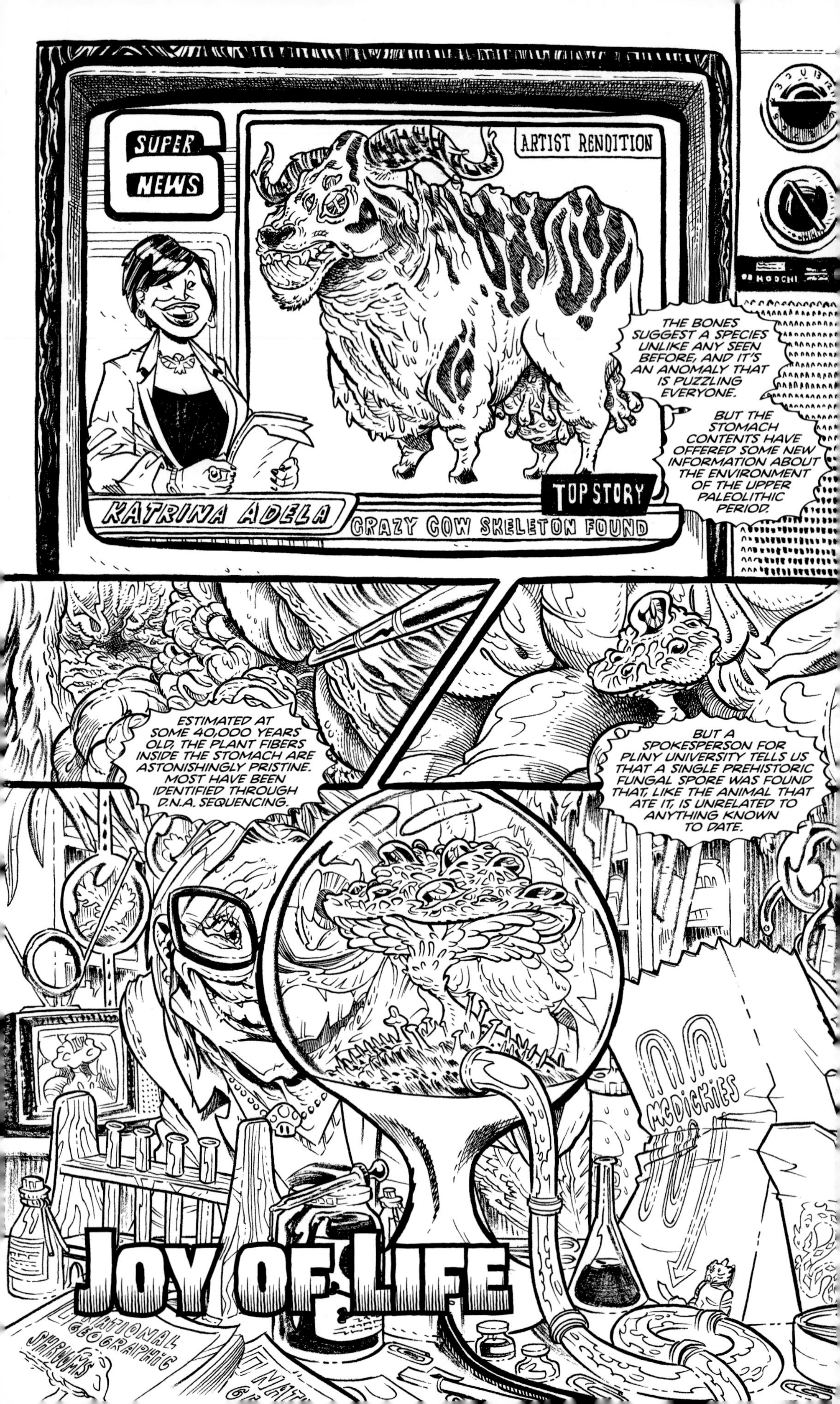
SUPER 6 NEWS
ARTIST RENDITION
KATRINA ADELA
TOP STORY
CRAZY COW SKELETON FOUND
THE BONES SUGGEST A SPECIES UNLIKE ANY SEEN BEFORE, AND IT'S AN ANOMALY THAT IS PUZZLING EVERYONE.
BUT THE STOMACH CONTENTS HAVE OFFERED SOME NEW INFORMATION ABOUT THE ENVIRONMENT OF THE UPPER PALEOLITHIC PERIOD.
ESTIMATED AT SOME 40,000 YEARS OLD, THE PLANT FIBERS INSIDE THE STOMACH ARE ASTONISHINGLY PRISTINE. MOST HAVE BEEN IDENTIFIED THROUGH D.N.A. SEQUENCING.
BUT A SPOKESPERSON FOR PLINY UNIVERSITY TELLS US THAT A SINGLE PREHISTORIC FUNGAL SPORE WAS FOUND THAT, LIKE THE ANIMAL THAT ATE IT, IS UNRELATED TO ANYTHING KNOWN TO DATE.
MCDICKIES
JOY OF LIFE
NATIONAL GEOGRAPHIC
SHROOMS

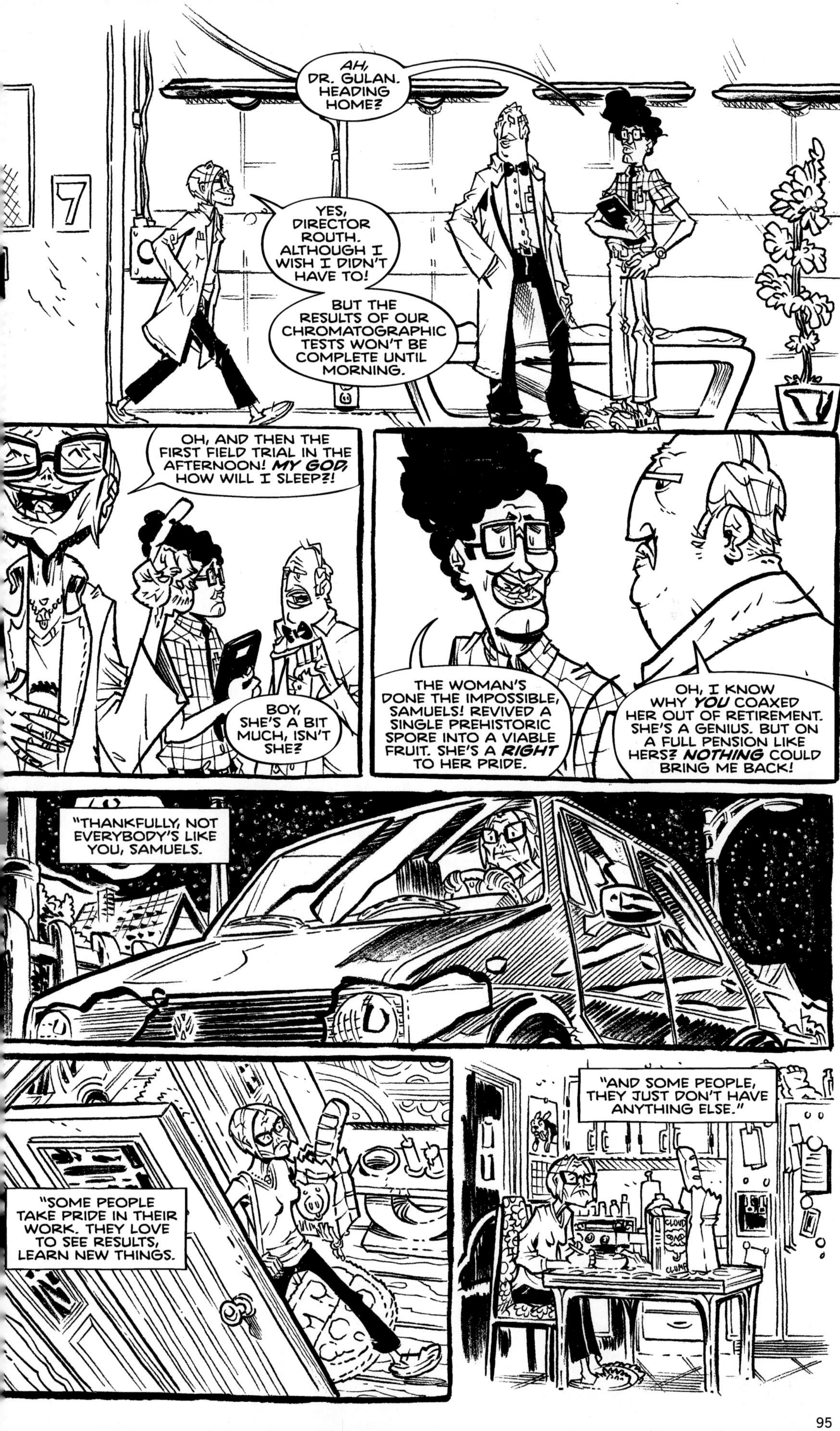
AH, DR. GULAN. HEADING HOME?
YES, DIRECTOR ROUTH. ALTHOUGH I WISH I DIDN'T HAVE TO!
BUT THE RESULTS OF OUR CHROMATOGRAPHIC TESTS WON'T BE COMPLETE UNTIL MORNING.
OH, AND THEN THE FIRST FIELD TRIAL IN THE AFTERNOON! MY GOD, HOW WILL I SLEEP?!
BOY, SHE'S A BIT MUCH, ISN'T SHE?
THE WOMAN'S DONE THE IMPOSSIBLE, SAMUELS! REVIVED A SINGLE PREHISTORIC SPORE INTO A VIABLE FRUIT. SHE'S A RIGHT TO HER PRIDE.
OH, I KNOW WHY YOU COAXED HER OUT OF RETIREMENT. SHE'S A GENIUS. BUT ON A FULL PENSION LIKE HERS? NOTHING COULD BRING ME BACK!
"THANKFULLY, NOT EVERYBODY'S LIKE YOU, SAMUELS.
"SOME PEOPLE TAKE PRIDE IN THEIR WORK. THEY LOVE TO SEE RESULTS, LEARN NEW THINGS.
"AND SOME PEOPLE, THEY JUST DON'T HAVE ANYTHING ELSE."

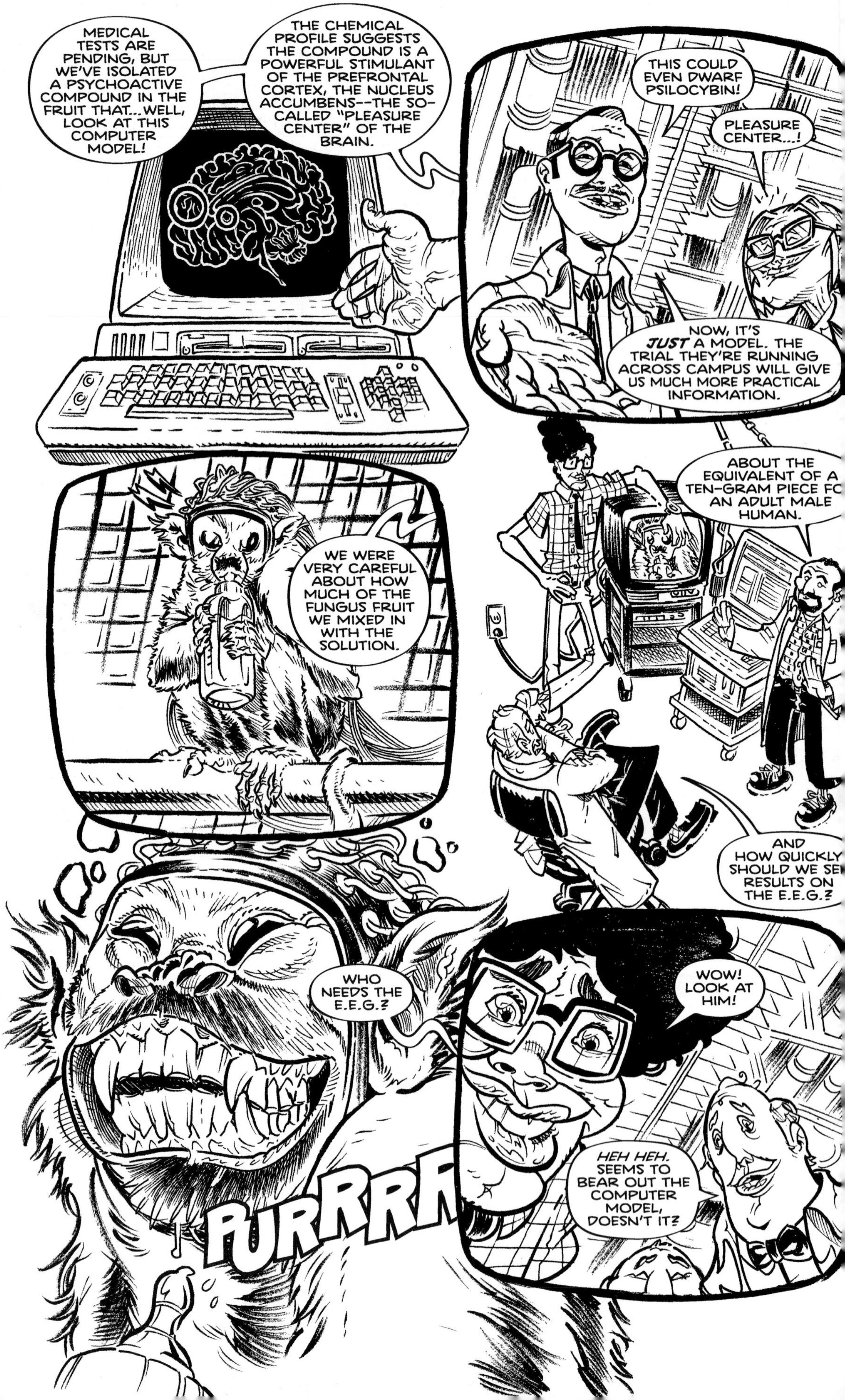
MEDICAL TESTS ARE PENDING, BUT WE'VE ISOLATED A PSYCHOACTIVE COMPOUND IN THE FRUIT THAT...WELL, LOOK AT THIS COMPUTER MODEL!
THE CHEMICAL PROFILE SUGGESTS THE COMPOUND IS A POWERFUL STIMULANT OF THE PREFRONTAL CORTEX, THE NUCLEUS ACCUMBENS--THE SO-CALLED "PLEASURE CENTER" OF THE BRAIN.
THIS COULD EVEN DWARF PSILOCYBIN!
PLEASURE CENTER...!
NOW, IT'S *JUST* A MODEL. THE TRIAL THEY'RE RUNNING ACROSS CAMPUS WILL GIVE US MUCH MORE PRACTICAL INFORMATION.
WE WERE VERY CAREFUL ABOUT HOW MUCH OF THE FUNGUS FRUIT WE MIXED IN WITH THE SOLUTION.
ABOUT THE EQUIVALENT OF A TEN-GRAM PIECE FO AN ADULT MALE HUMAN.
AND HOW QUICKLY SHOULD WE SE RESULTS ON THE E.E.G.?
WHO NEEDS THE E.E.G.?
PURRRR
WOW! LOOK AT HIM!
HEH HEH. SEEMS TO BEAR OUT THE COMPUTER MODEL, DOESN'T IT?

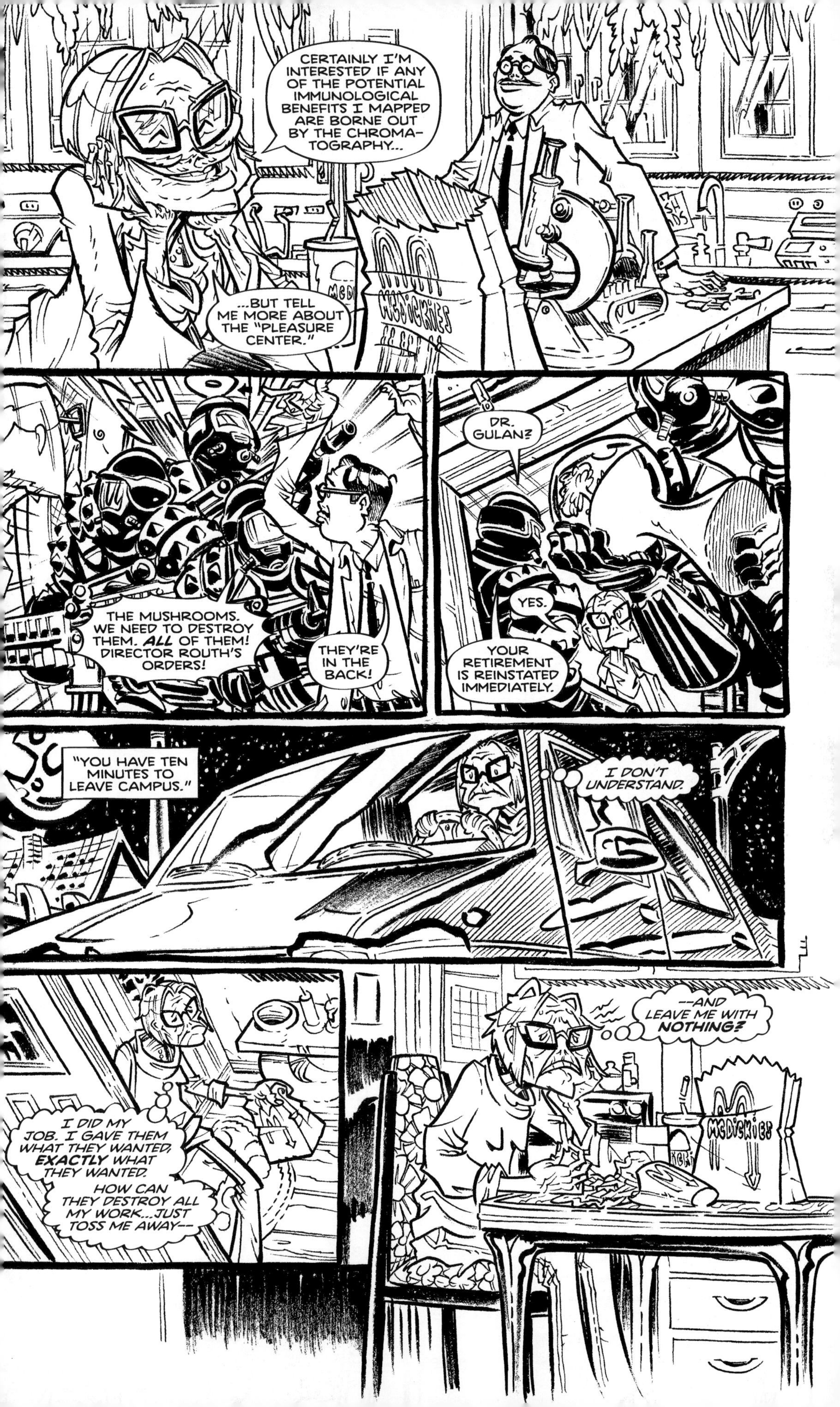
CERTAINLY I'M INTERESTED IF ANY OF THE POTENTIAL IMMUNOLOGICAL BENEFITS I MAPPED ARE BORNE OUT BY THE CHROMATOGRAPHY...
...BUT TELL ME MORE ABOUT THE "PLEASURE CENTER."
McDICKIES
THE MUSHROOMS. WE NEED TO DESTROY THEM. ALL OF THEM! DIRECTOR ROUTH'S ORDERS!
THEY'RE IN THE BACK!
DR. GULAN?
YES.
YOUR RETIREMENT IS REINSTATED IMMEDIATELY.
"YOU HAVE TEN MINUTES TO LEAVE CAMPUS."
I DON'T UNDERSTAND.
I DID MY JOB. I GAVE THEM WHAT THEY WANTED, EXACTLY WHAT THEY WANTED.
HOW CAN THEY DESTROY ALL MY WORK...JUST TOSS ME AWAY--
--AND LEAVE ME WITH NOTHING?
McDICKIES

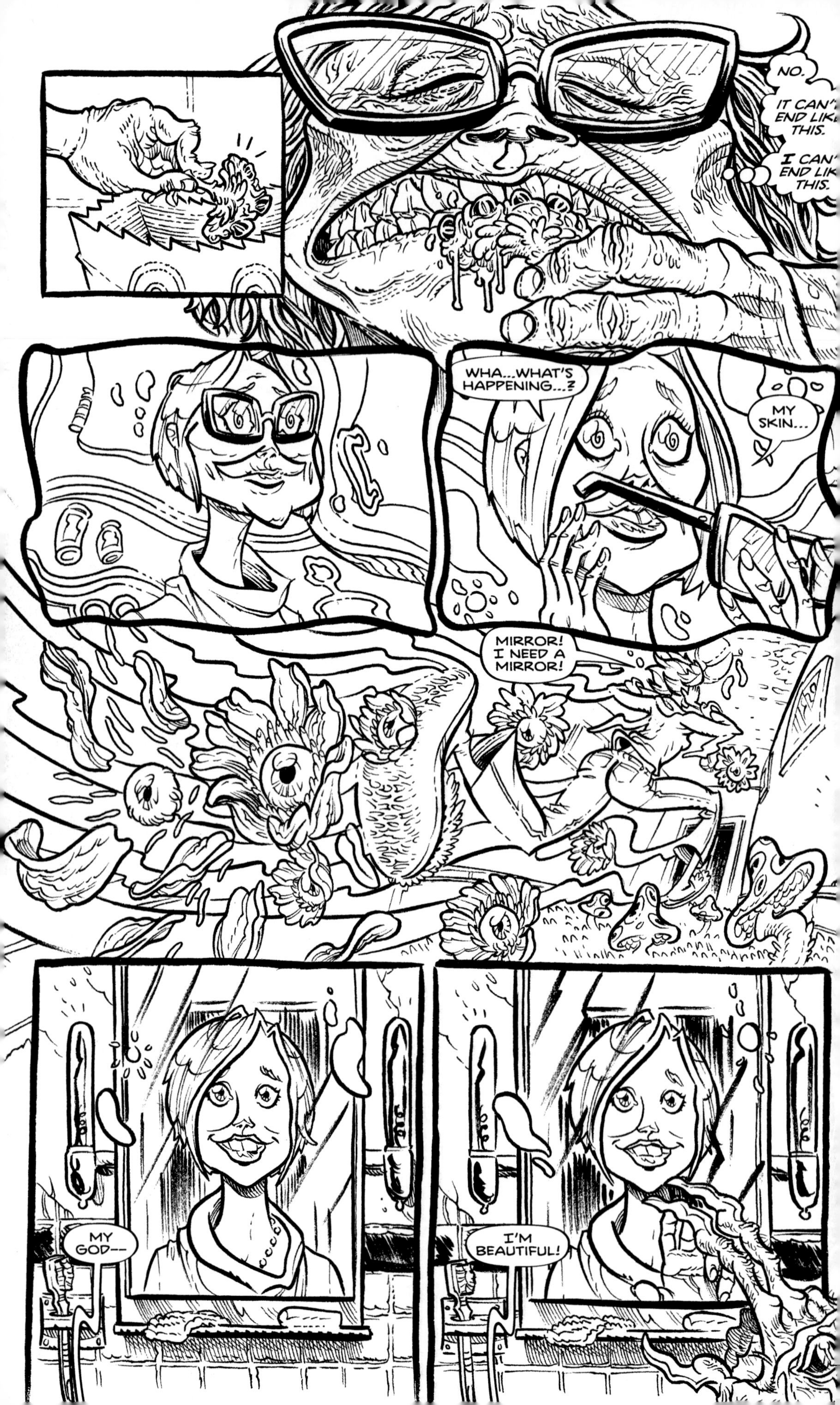
NO.
IT CAN'T END LIKE THIS.
I CAN'T END LIKE THIS.
WHA...WHAT'S HAPPENING...?
MY SKIN...
MIRROR! I NEED A MIRROR!
MY GOD--
I'M BEAUTIFUL!

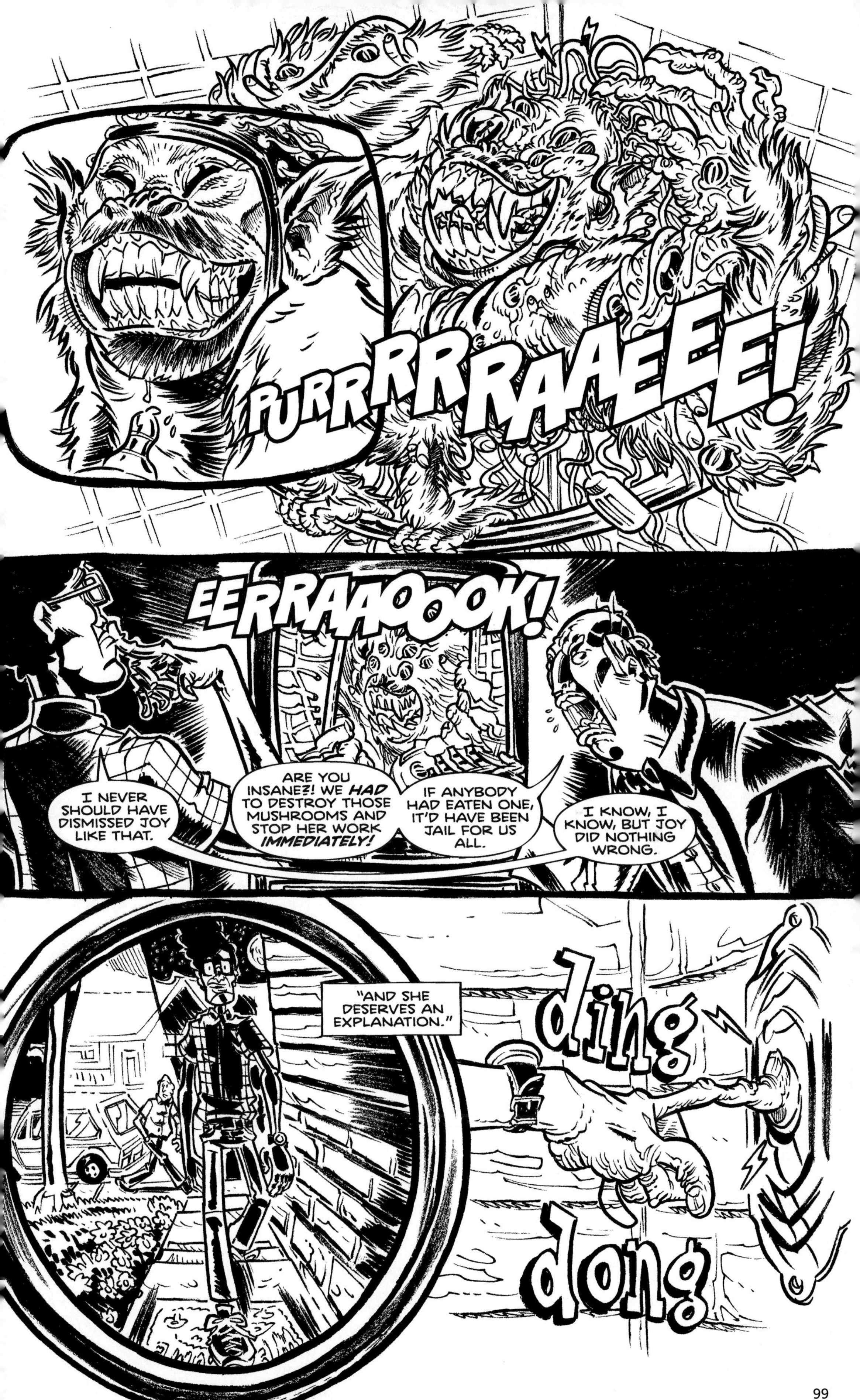
PURRRRRRAAEEEE!
EERRAAOOOOK!
I NEVER SHOULD HAVE DISMISSED JOY LIKE THAT.
ARE YOU INSANE?! WE *HAD* TO DESTROY THOSE MUSHROOMS AND STOP HER WORK *IMMEDIATELY!*
IF ANYBODY HAD EATEN ONE, IT'D HAVE BEEN JAIL FOR US ALL.
I KNOW, I KNOW, BUT JOY DID NOTHING WRONG.
"AND SHE DESERVES AN EXPLANATION."
ding
dong

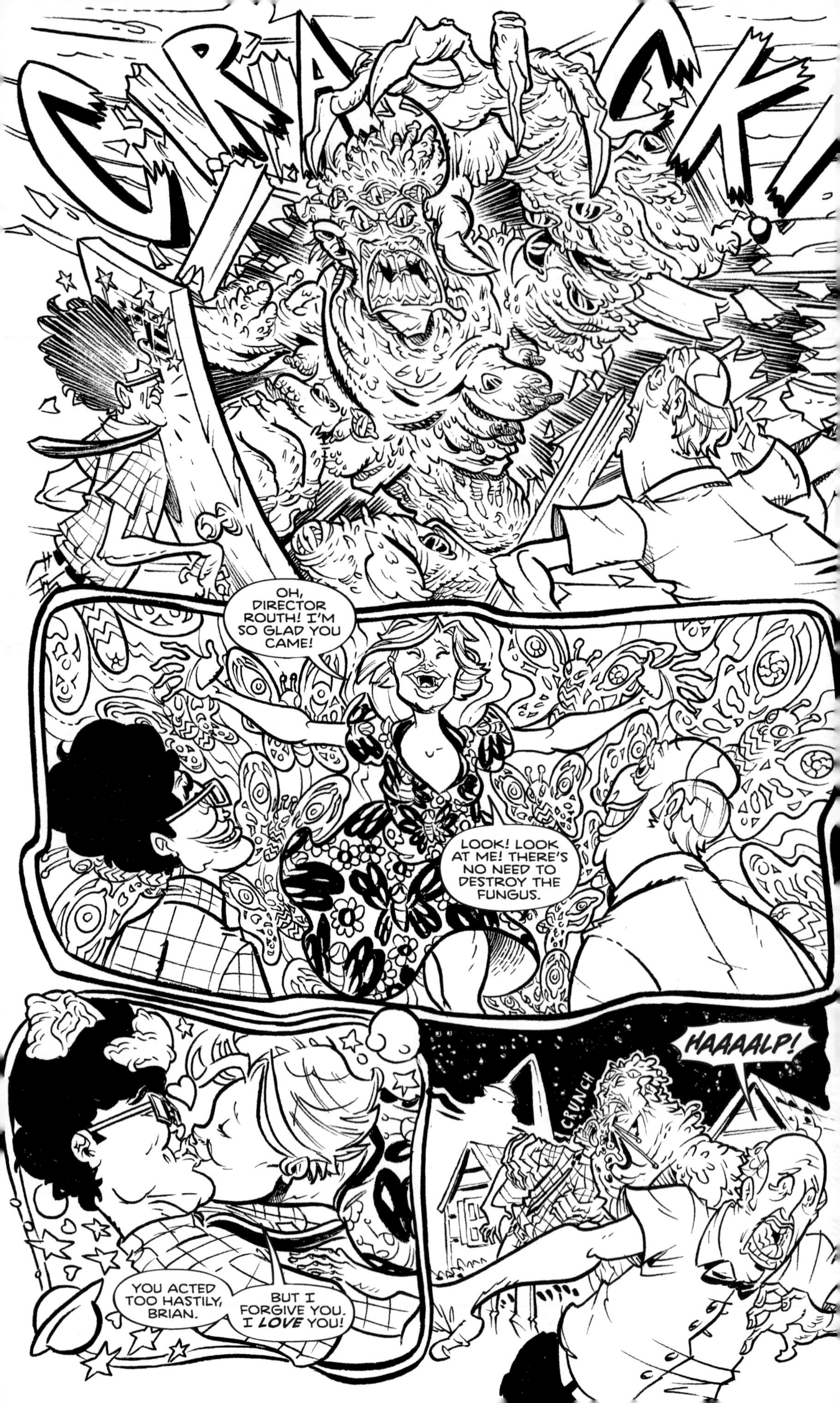
CRACK!
OH, DIRECTOR ROUTH! I'M SO GLAD YOU CAME!
LOOK! LOOK AT ME! THERE'S NO NEED TO DESTROY THE FUNGUS.
YOU ACTED TOO HASTILY, BRIAN.
BUT I FORGIVE YOU. I *LOVE* YOU!
CRUNCH
HAAAALP!

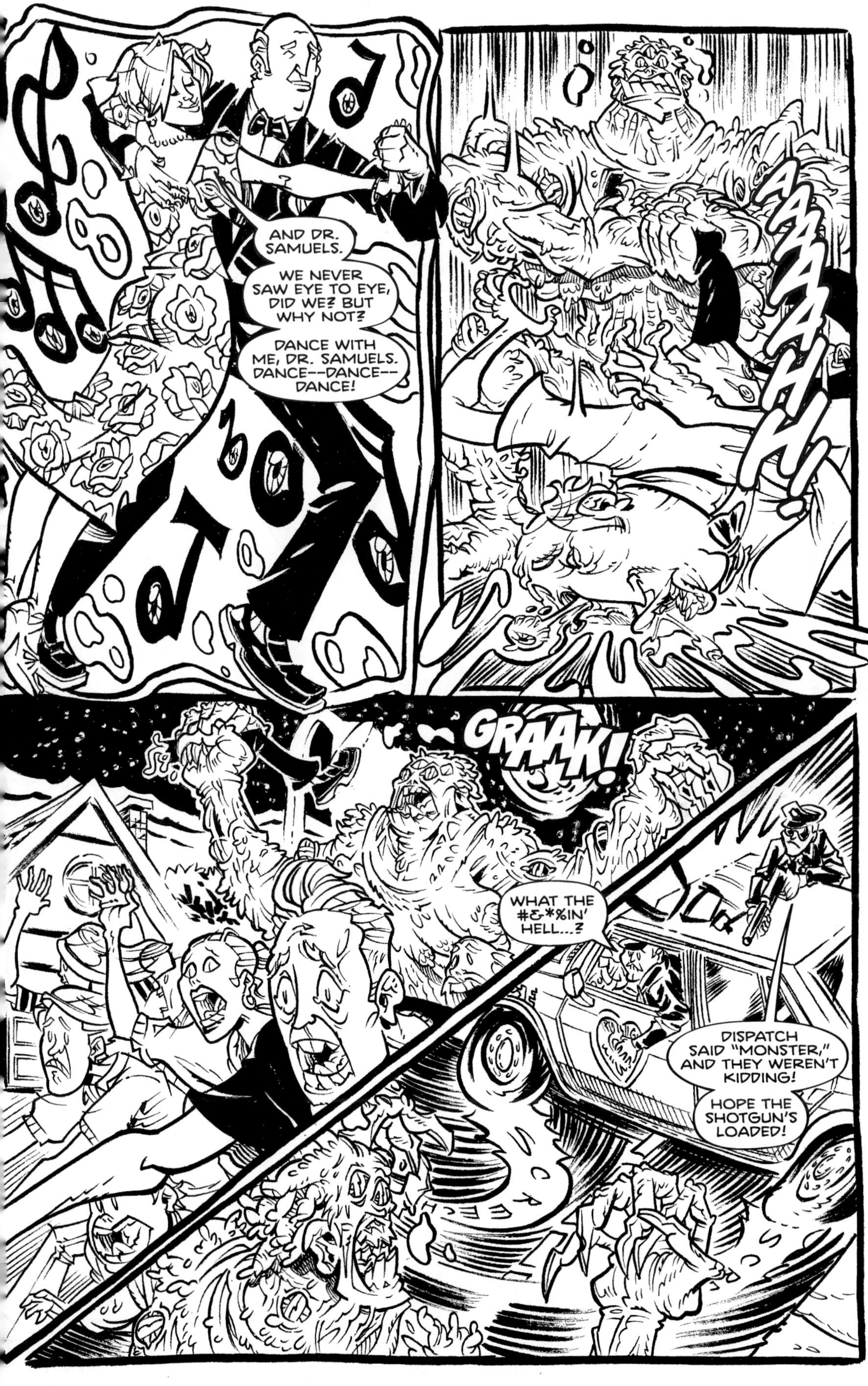
AND DR. SAMUELS.
WE NEVER SAW EYE TO EYE, DID WE? BUT WHY NOT?
DANCE WITH ME, DR. SAMUELS. DANCE--DANCE--DANCE!
AAAAHHH!
GRAAAK!
WHAT THE #&*%IN' HELL...?
DISPATCH SAID "MONSTER," AND THEY WEREN'T KIDDING!
HOPE THE SHOTGUN'S LOADED!

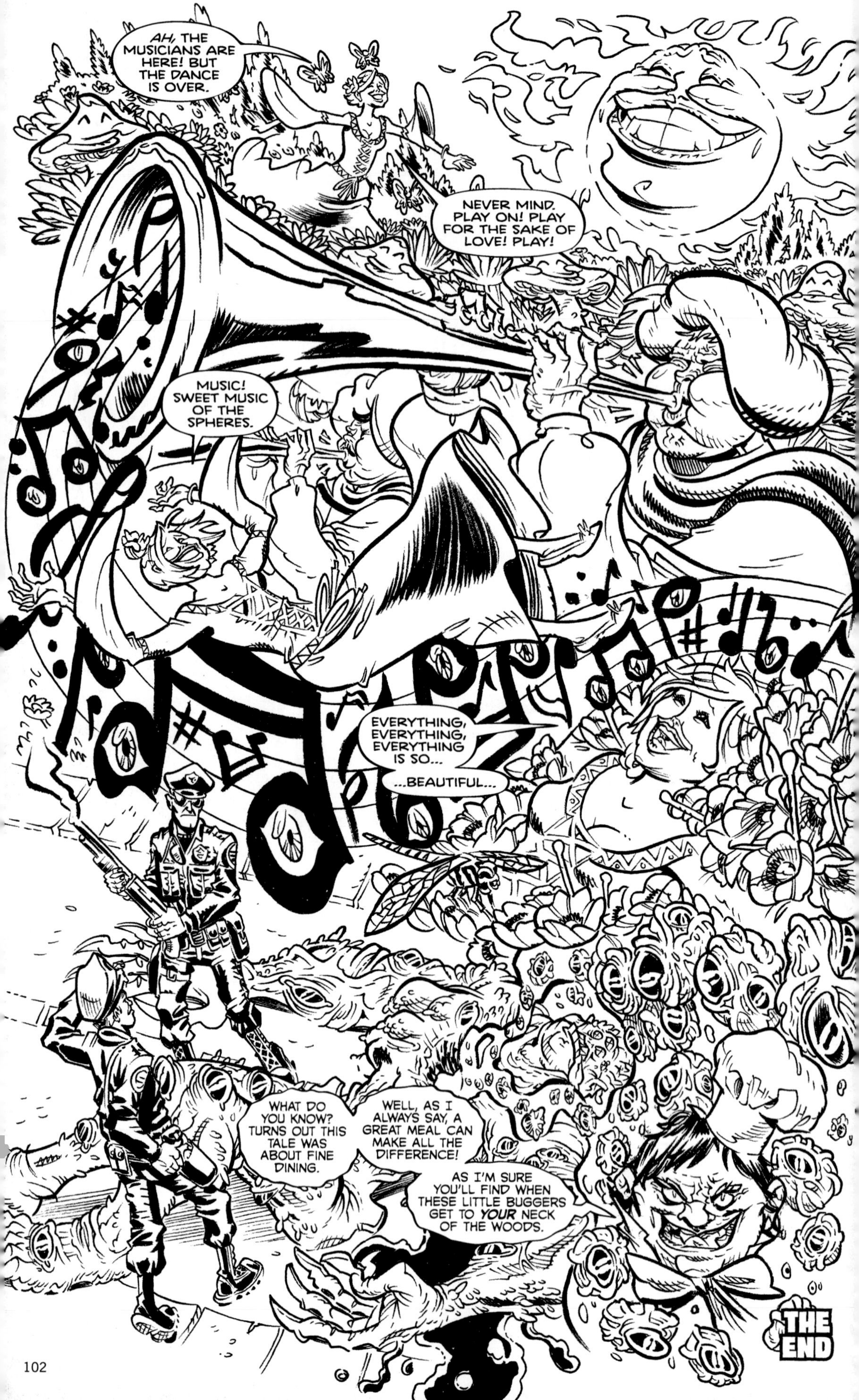
AH, THE MUSICIANS ARE HERE! BUT THE DANCE IS OVER.
NEVER MIND. PLAY ON! PLAY FOR THE SAKE OF LOVE! PLAY!
MUSIC! SWEET MUSIC OF THE SPHERES.
EVERYTHING, EVERYTHING, EVERYTHING IS SO...
...BEAUTIFUL...
WHAT DO YOU KNOW? TURNS OUT THIS TALE WAS ABOUT FINE DINING.
WELL, AS I ALWAYS SAY, A GREAT MEAL CAN MAKE ALL THE DIFFERENCE!
AS I'M SURE YOU'LL FIND WHEN THESE LITTLE BUGGERS GET TO *YOUR* NECK OF THE WOODS.
THE END

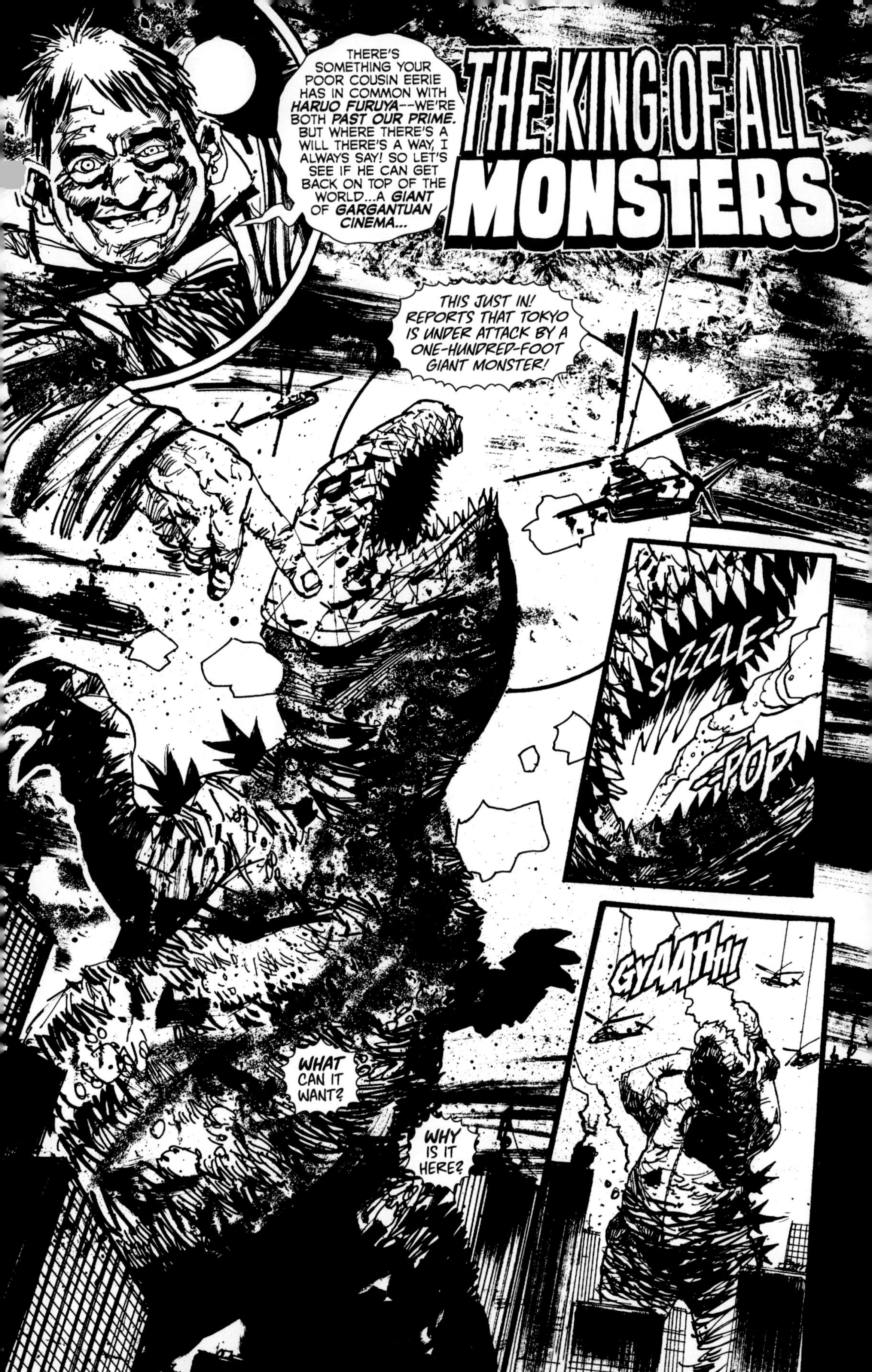
THE KING OF ALL MONSTERS
THERE'S SOMETHING YOUR POOR COUSIN EERIE HAS IN COMMON WITH HARUO FURUYA--WE'RE BOTH PAST OUR PRIME. BUT WHERE THERE'S A WILL THERE'S A WAY, I ALWAYS SAY! SO LET'S SEE IF HE CAN GET BACK ON TOP OF THE WORLD...A GIANT OF GARGANTUAN CINEMA...
THIS JUST IN! REPORTS THAT TOKYO IS UNDER ATTACK BY A ONE-HUNDRED-FOOT GIANT MONSTER!
SIZZLE--
--POP
GYAAHH!
WHAT CAN IT WANT?
WHY IS IT HERE?
Script by BRANDON MONTCLARE / Art by HENRY FLINT

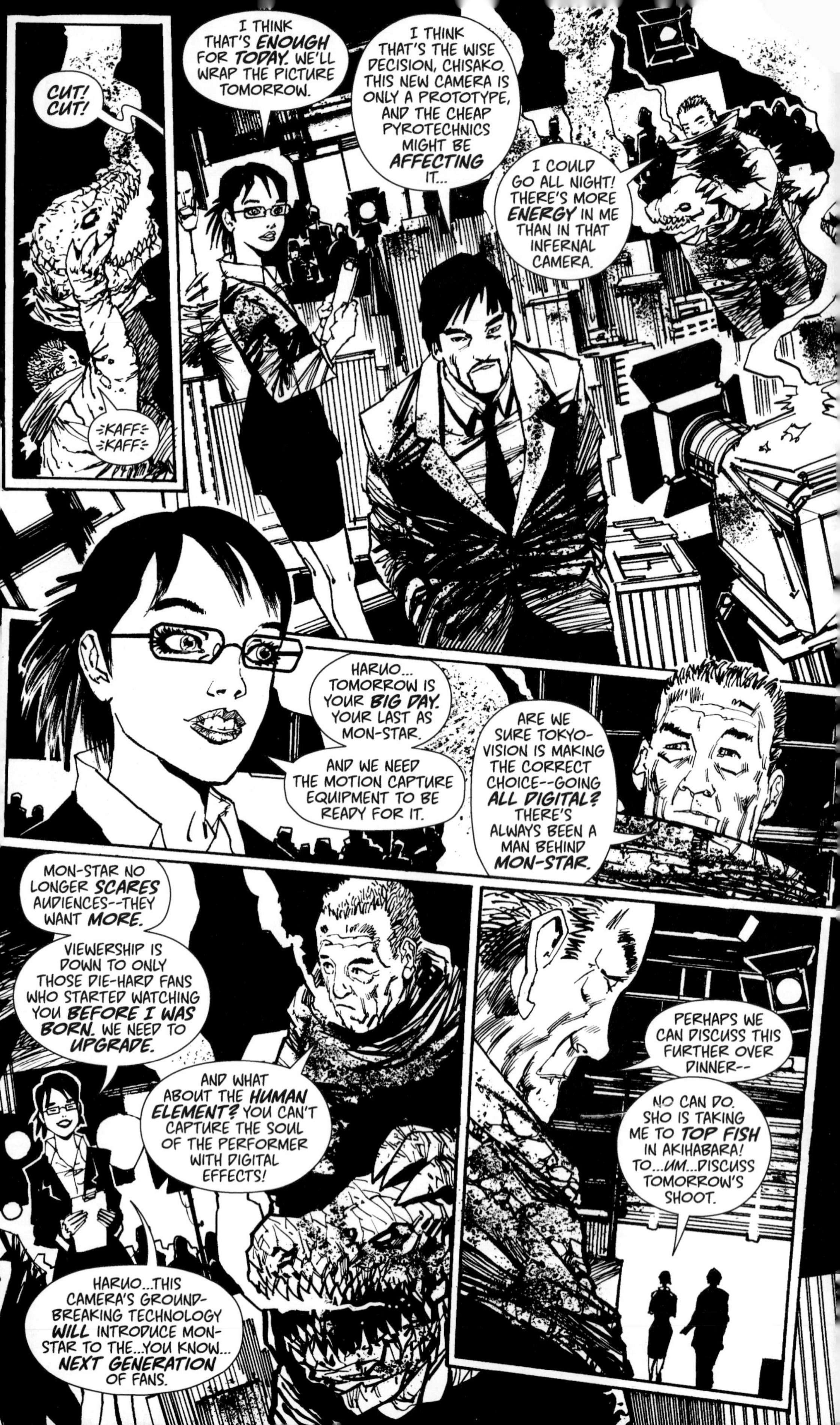
CUT! CUT!
KAFF KAFF
I THINK THAT'S ENOUGH FOR TODAY. WE'LL WRAP THE PICTURE TOMORROW.
I THINK THAT'S THE WISE DECISION, CHISAKO. THIS NEW CAMERA IS ONLY A PROTOTYPE, AND THE CHEAP PYROTECHNICS MIGHT BE AFFECTING IT...
I COULD GO ALL NIGHT! THERE'S MORE ENERGY IN ME THAN IN THAT INFERNAL CAMERA.
HARUO... TOMORROW IS YOUR BIG DAY. YOUR LAST AS MON-STAR.
AND WE NEED THE MOTION CAPTURE EQUIPMENT TO BE READY FOR IT.
ARE WE SURE TOKYO-VISION IS MAKING THE CORRECT CHOICE--GOING ALL DIGITAL? THERE'S ALWAYS BEEN A MAN BEHIND MON-STAR.
MON-STAR NO LONGER SCARES AUDIENCES--THEY WANT MORE.
VIEWERSHIP IS DOWN TO ONLY THOSE DIE-HARD FANS WHO STARTED WATCHING YOU BEFORE I WAS BORN. WE NEED TO UPGRADE.
AND WHAT ABOUT THE HUMAN ELEMENT? YOU CAN'T CAPTURE THE SOUL OF THE PERFORMER WITH DIGITAL EFFECTS!
HARUO...THIS CAMERA'S GROUND-BREAKING TECHNOLOGY WILL INTRODUCE MON-STAR TO THE...YOU KNOW... NEXT GENERATION OF FANS.
PERHAPS WE CAN DISCUSS THIS FURTHER OVER DINNER--
NO CAN DO. SHO IS TAKING ME TO TOP FISH IN AKIHABARA! TO...UM...DISCUSS TOMORROW'S SHOOT.

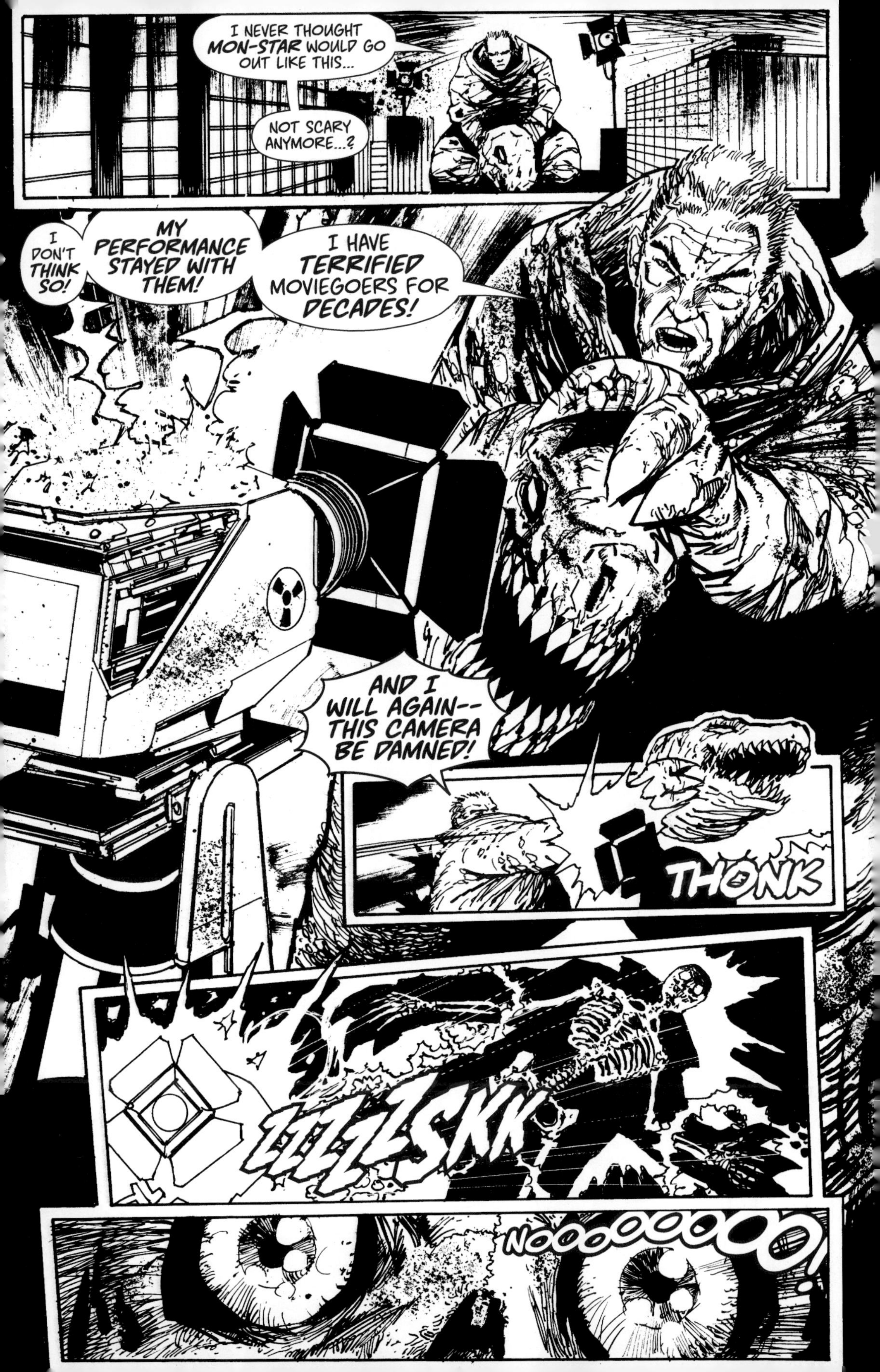
I NEVER THOUGHT MON-STAR WOULD GO OUT LIKE THIS...
NOT SCARY ANYMORE...?
I DON'T THINK SO!
MY PERFORMANCE STAYED WITH THEM!
I HAVE TERRIFIED MOVIEGOERS FOR DECADES!
AND I WILL AGAIN-- THIS CAMERA BE DAMNED!
THONK
ZZZZZSKK
NOOOOOOOOO!

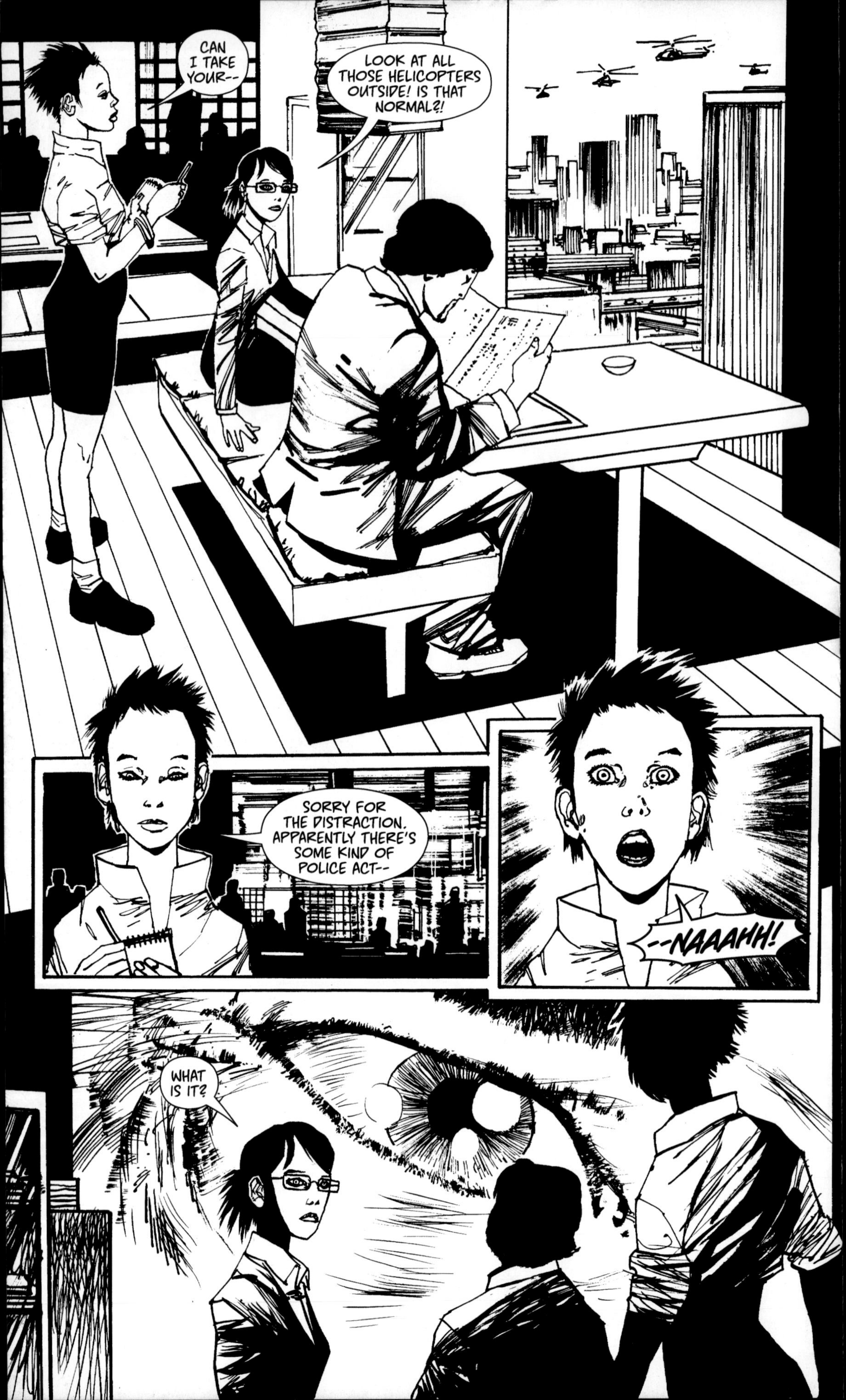
CAN I TAKE YOUR--
LOOK AT ALL THOSE HELICOPTERS OUTSIDE! IS THAT NORMAL?!
SORRY FOR THE DISTRACTION. APPARENTLY THERE'S SOME KIND OF POLICE ACT--
--NAAAHH!
WHAT IS IT?

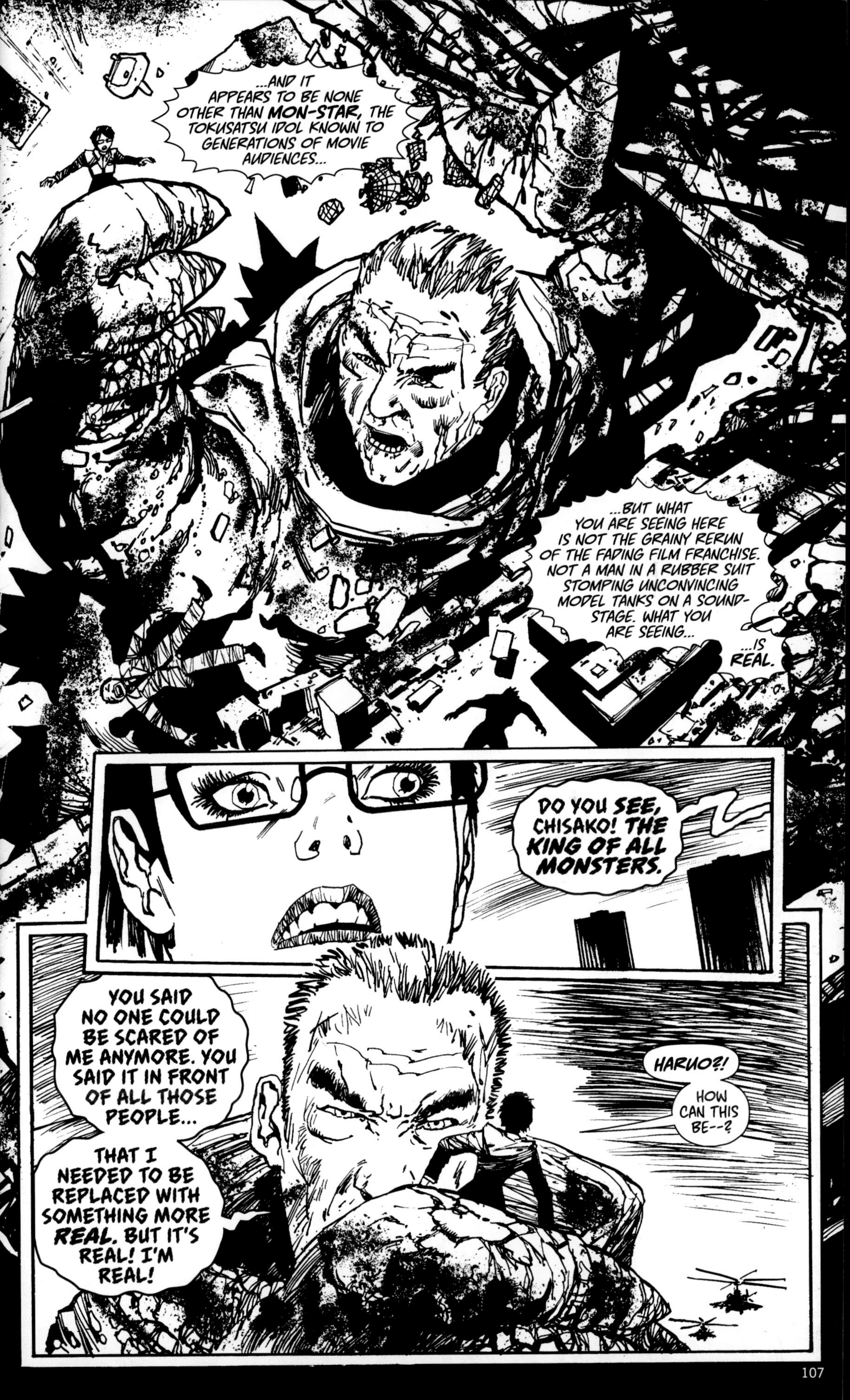

...AND IT APPEARS TO BE NONE OTHER THAN MON-STAR, THE TOKUSATSU IDOL KNOWN TO GENERATIONS OF MOVIE AUDIENCES...
...BUT WHAT YOU ARE SEEING HERE IS NOT THE GRAINY RERUN OF THE FADING FILM FRANCHISE. NOT A MAN IN A RUBBER SUIT STOMPING UNCONVINCING MODEL TANKS ON A SOUND-STAGE. WHAT YOU ARE SEEING...
...IS REAL.
DO YOU SEE, CHISAKO! THE KING OF ALL MONSTERS.
YOU SAID NO ONE COULD BE SCARED OF ME ANYMORE. YOU SAID IT IN FRONT OF ALL THOSE PEOPLE...
THAT I NEEDED TO BE REPLACED WITH SOMETHING MORE REAL. BUT IT'S REAL! I'M REAL!
HARUO?!
HOW CAN THIS BE--?

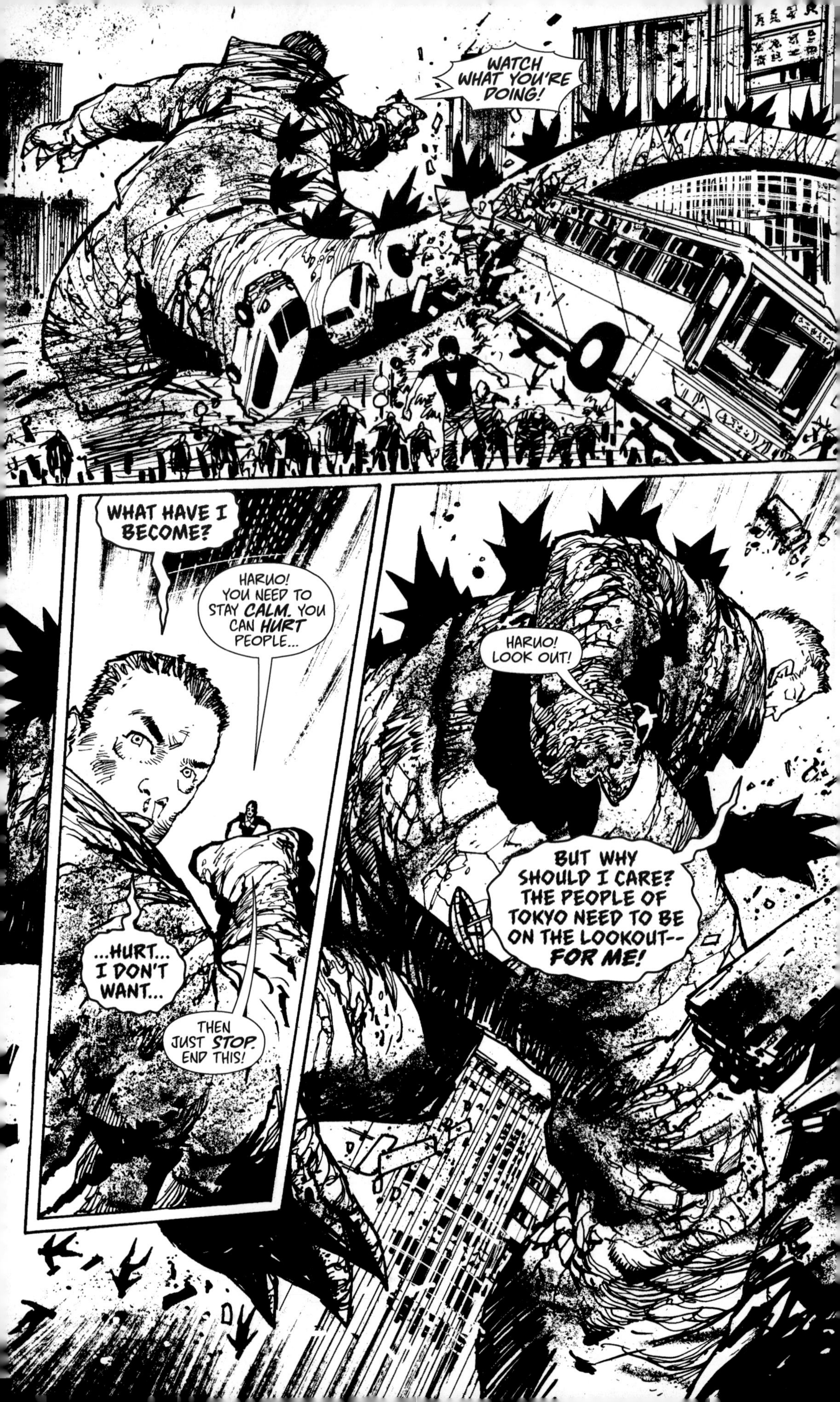
WATCH WHAT YOU'RE DOING!
WHAT HAVE I BECOME?
HARUO! YOU NEED TO STAY CALM. YOU CAN HURT PEOPLE...
...HURT... I DON'T WANT...
THEN JUST STOP. END THIS!
HARUO! LOOK OUT!
BUT WHY SHOULD I CARE? THE PEOPLE OF TOKYO NEED TO BE ON THE LOOKOUT-- FOR ME!

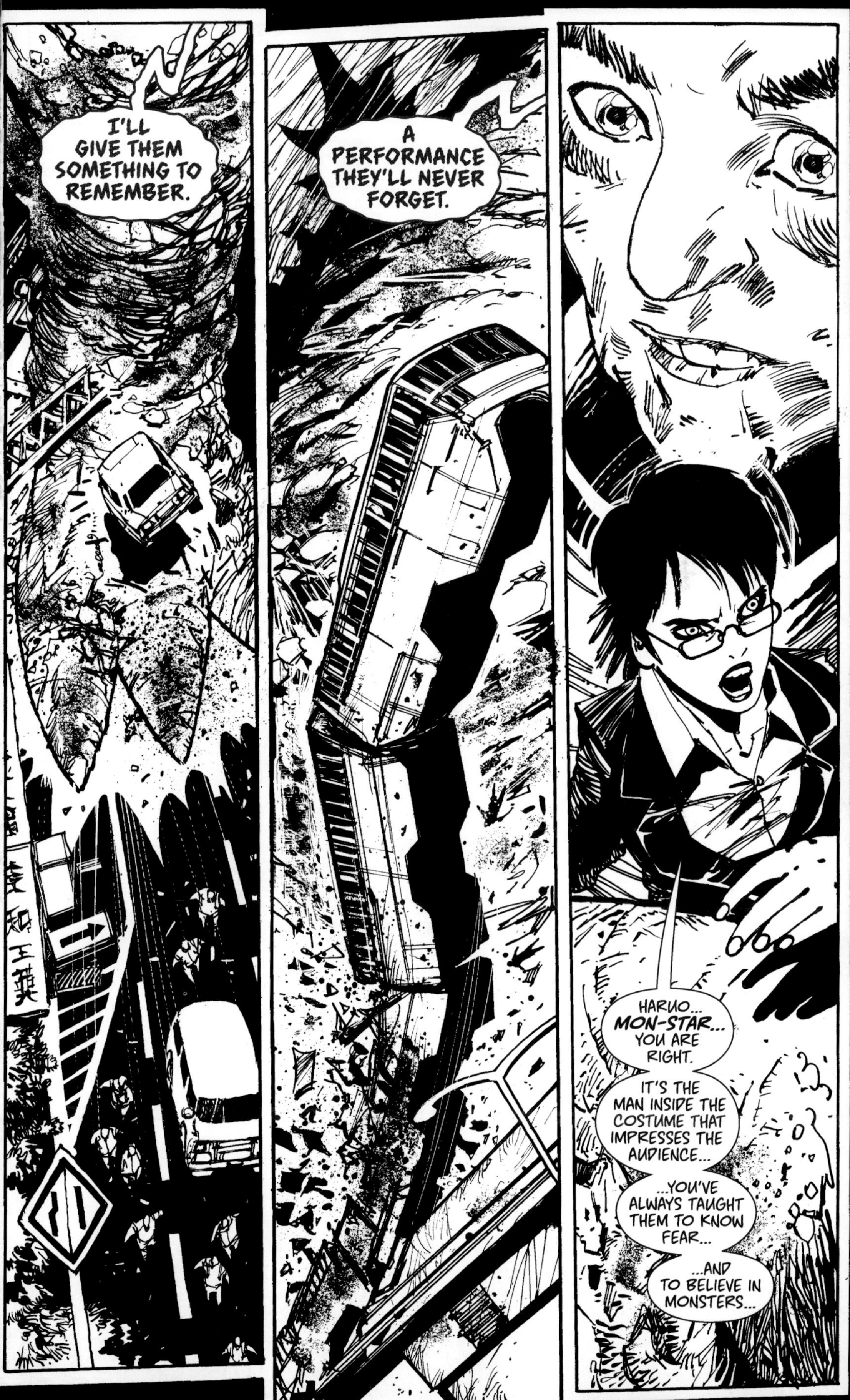
I'LL GIVE THEM SOMETHING TO REMEMBER.
A PERFORMANCE THEY'LL NEVER FORGET.
HARUO... MON-STAR... YOU ARE RIGHT.
IT'S THE MAN INSIDE THE COSTUME THAT IMPRESSES THE AUDIENCE...
...YOU'VE ALWAYS TAUGHT THEM TO KNOW FEAR...
...AND TO BELIEVE IN MONSTERS...

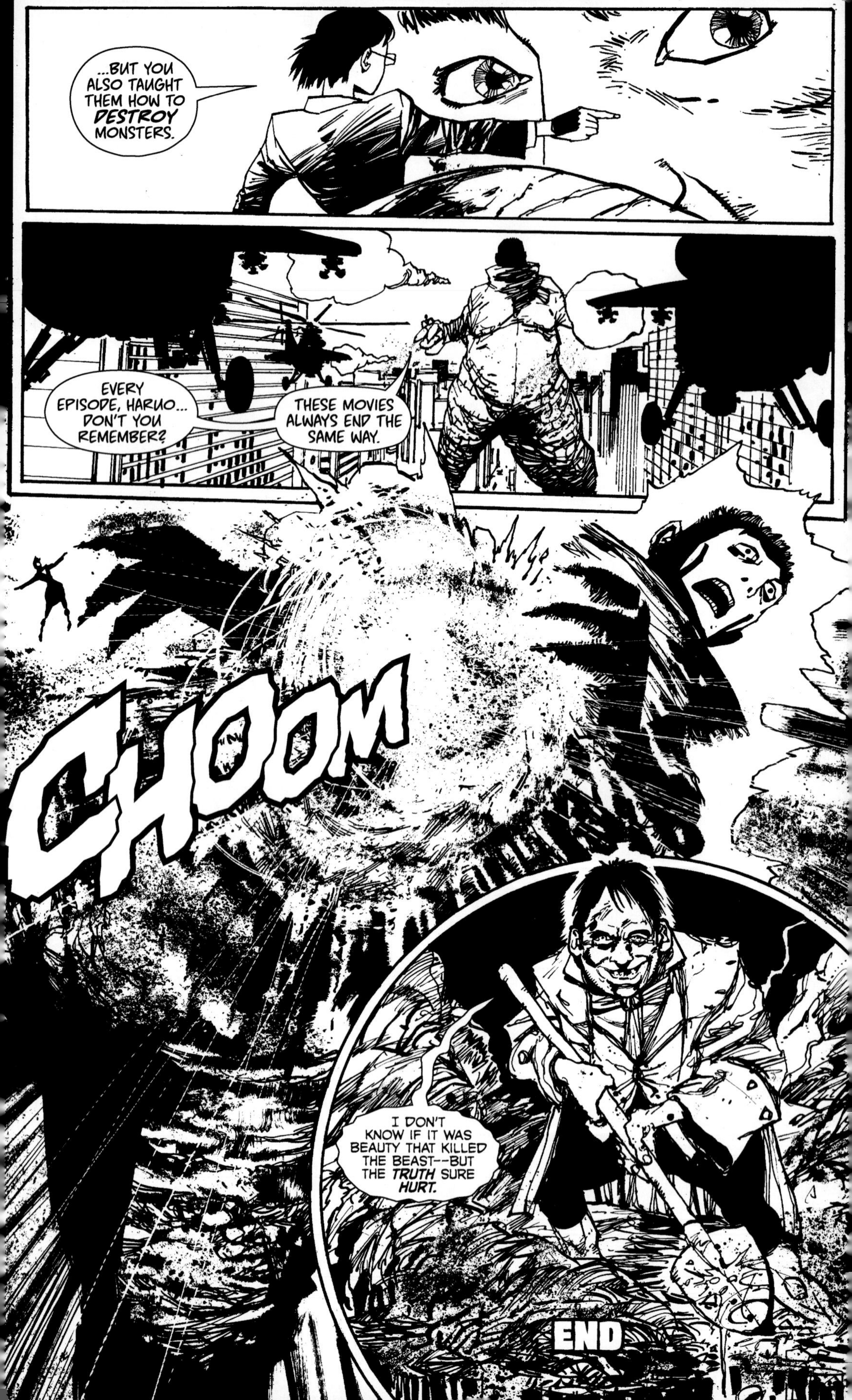
...BUT YOU ALSO TAUGHT THEM HOW TO *DESTROY* MONSTERS.
EVERY EPISODE, HARUO... DON'T YOU REMEMBER?
THESE MOVIES ALWAYS END THE SAME WAY.
CHOOM
I DON'T KNOW IF IT WAS BEAUTY THAT KILLED THE BEAST--BUT THE *TRUTH* SURE *HURT.*
END

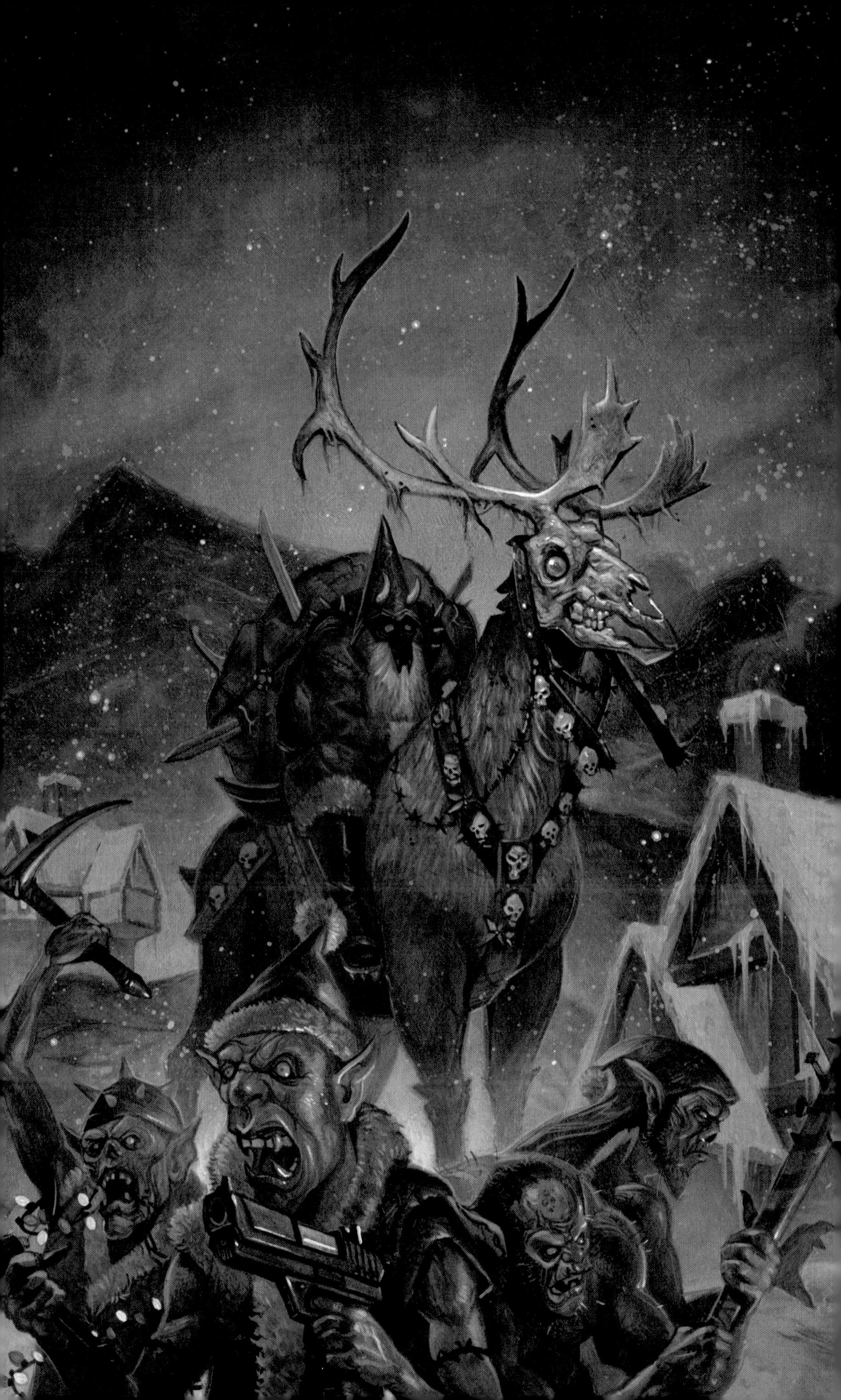

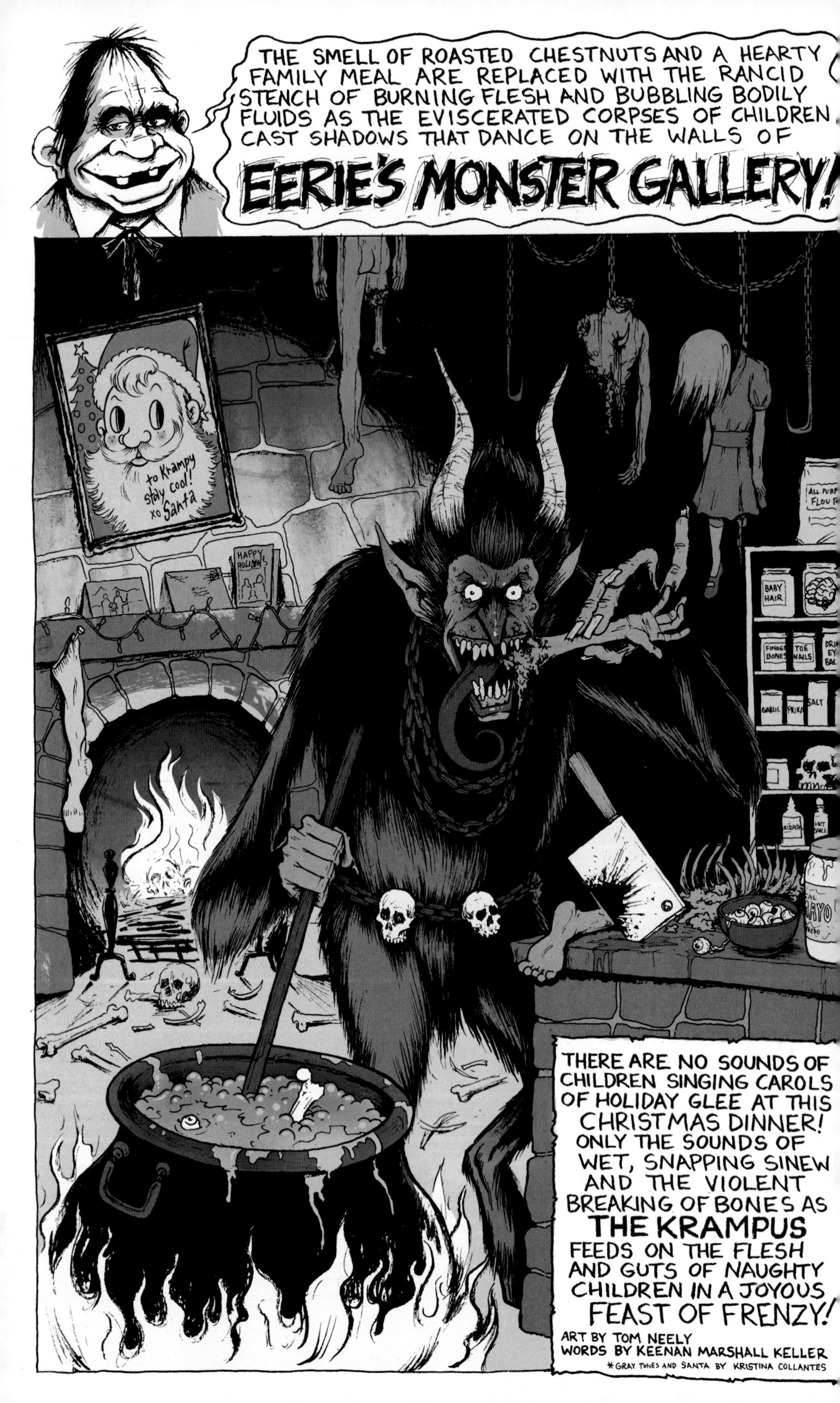
THE SMELL OF ROASTED CHESTNUTS AND A HEARTY FAMILY MEAL ARE REPLACED WITH THE RANCID STENCH OF BURNING FLESH AND BUBBLING BODILY FLUIDS AS THE EVISCERATED CORPSES OF CHILDREN CAST SHADOWS THAT DANCE ON THE WALLS OF
EERIE'S MONSTER GALLERY!
to Krampy stay cool! xo Santa
HAPPY HOLIDAYS
BABY HAIR
FINGER BONES
TOE NAILS
GARLIC
SALT
THERE ARE NO SOUNDS OF CHILDREN SINGING CAROLS OF HOLIDAY GLEE AT THIS CHRISTMAS DINNER! ONLY THE SOUNDS OF WET, SNAPPING SINEW AND THE VIOLENT BREAKING OF BONES AS THE KRAMPUS FEEDS ON THE FLESH AND GUTS OF NAUGHTY CHILDREN IN A JOYOUS FEAST OF FRENZY!
ART BY TOM NEELY
WORDS BY KEENAN MARSHALL KELLER
*GRAY TONES AND SANTA BY KRISTINA COLLANTES

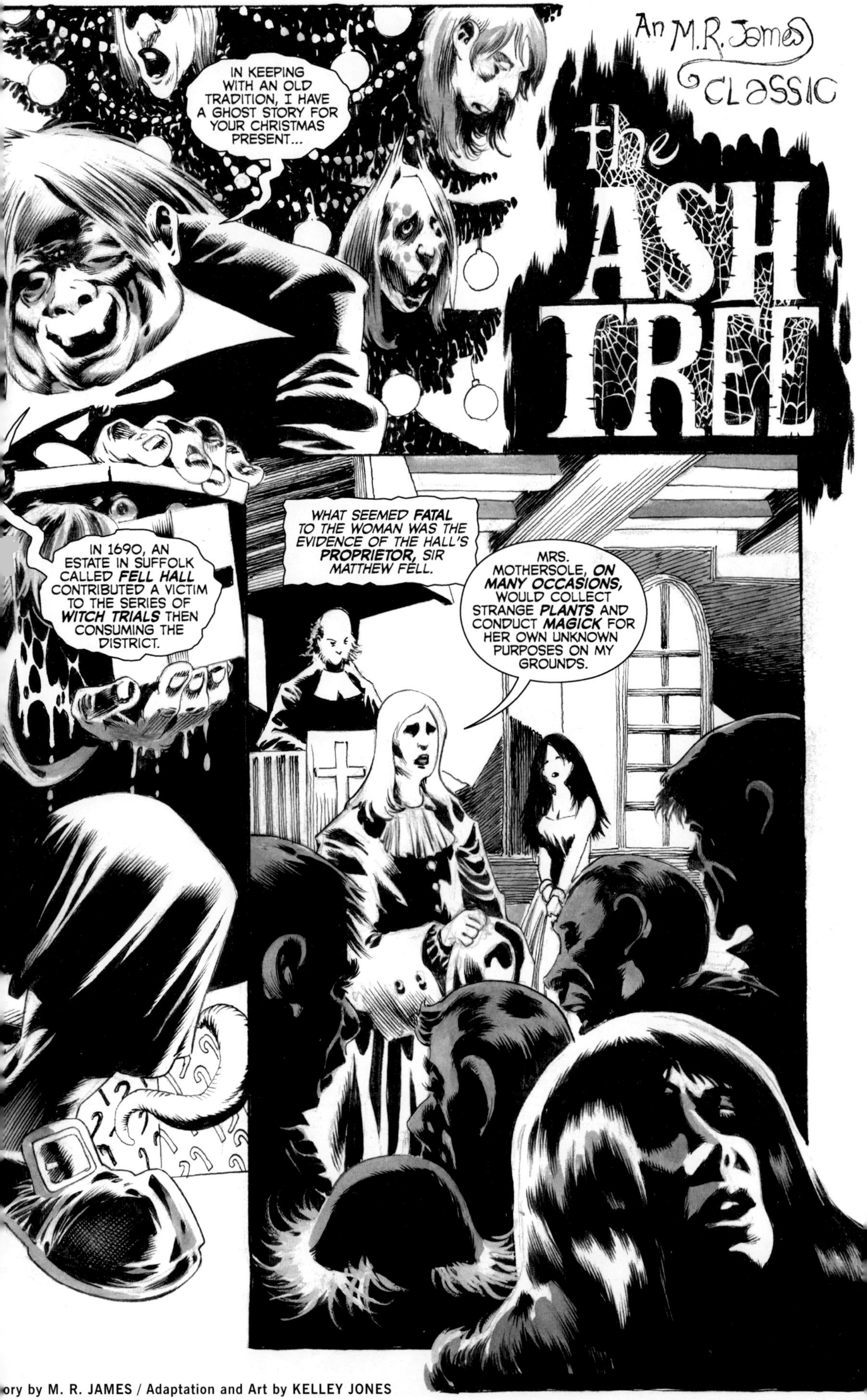

An M.R. James Classic
the ASH TREE
IN KEEPING WITH AN OLD TRADITION, I HAVE A GHOST STORY FOR YOUR CHRISTMAS PRESENT...
IN 1690, AN ESTATE IN SUFFOLK CALLED FELL HALL CONTRIBUTED A VICTIM TO THE SERIES OF WITCH TRIALS THEN CONSUMING THE DISTRICT.
WHAT SEEMED FATAL TO THE WOMAN WAS THE EVIDENCE OF THE HALL'S PROPRIETOR, SIR MATTHEW FELL.
MRS. MOTHERSOLE, ON MANY OCCASIONS, WOULD COLLECT STRANGE PLANTS AND CONDUCT MAGICK FOR HER OWN UNKNOWN PURPOSES ON MY GROUNDS.

ory by M. R. JAMES / Adaptation and Art by KELLEY JONES

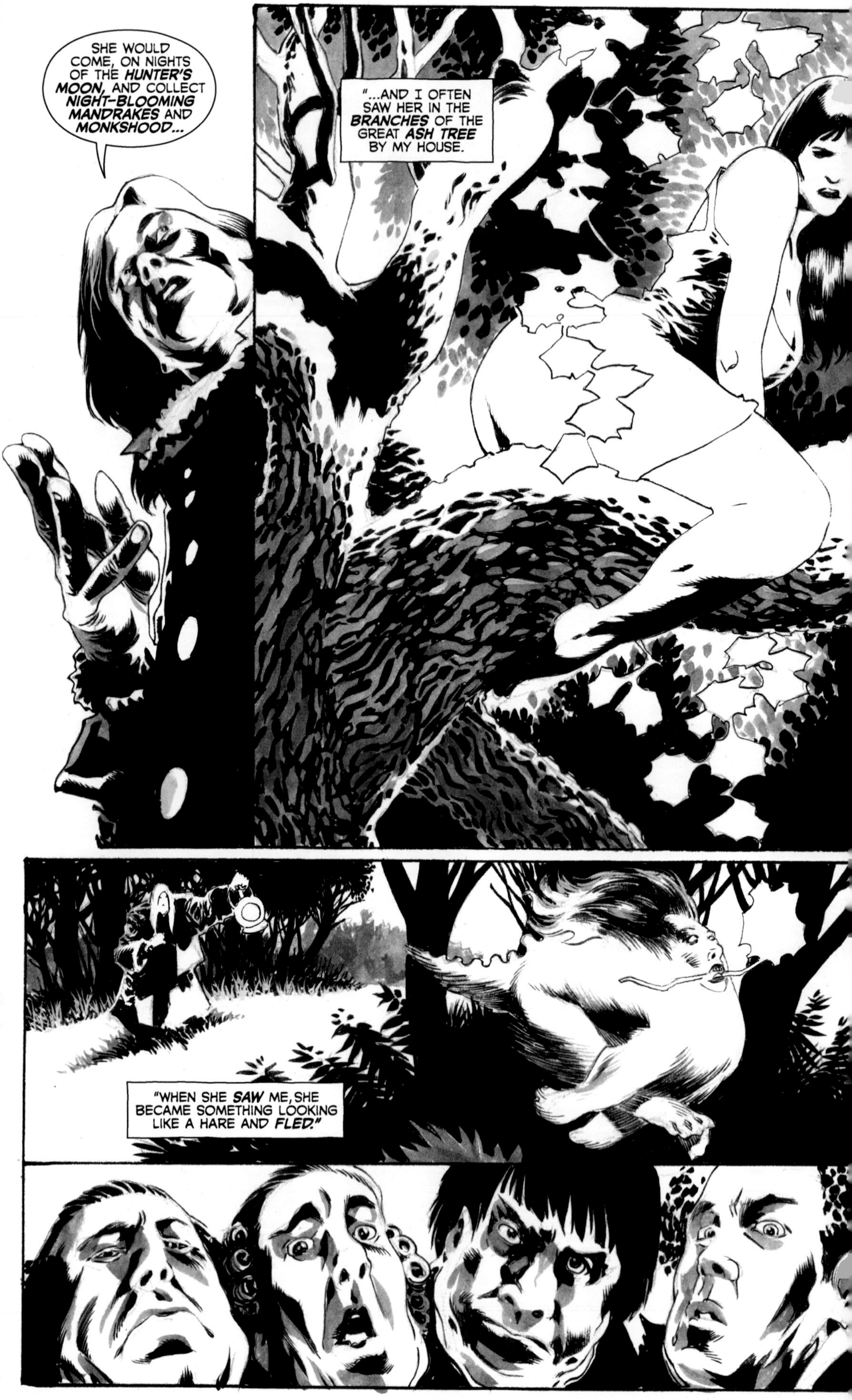
SHE WOULD COME, ON NIGHTS OF THE HUNTER'S MOON, AND COLLECT NIGHT-BLOOMING MANDRAKES AND MONKSHOOD...
"...AND I OFTEN SAW HER IN THE BRANCHES OF THE GREAT ASH TREE BY MY HOUSE.
"WHEN SHE SAW ME, SHE BECAME SOMETHING LOOKING LIKE A HARE AND FLED."

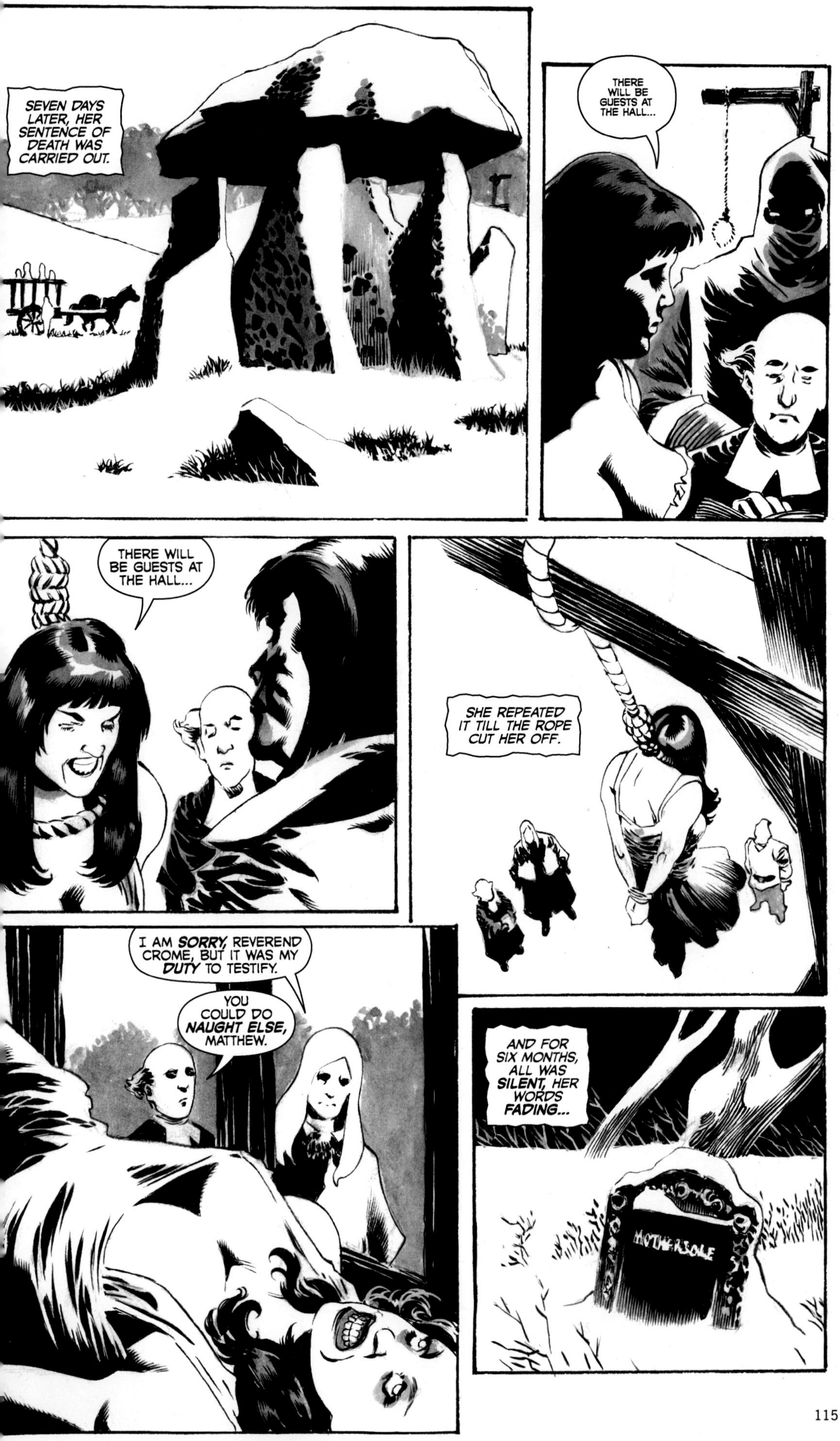

SEVEN DAYS LATER, HER SENTENCE OF DEATH WAS CARRIED OUT.
THERE WILL BE GUESTS AT THE HALL...
THERE WILL BE GUESTS AT THE HALL...
SHE REPEATED IT TILL THE ROPE CUT HER OFF.
I AM SORRY, REVEREND CROME, BUT IT WAS MY DUTY TO TESTIFY.
YOU COULD DO NAUGHT ELSE, MATTHEW.
AND FOR SIX MONTHS, ALL WAS SILENT, HER WORDS FADING...
MOTHERSOLE

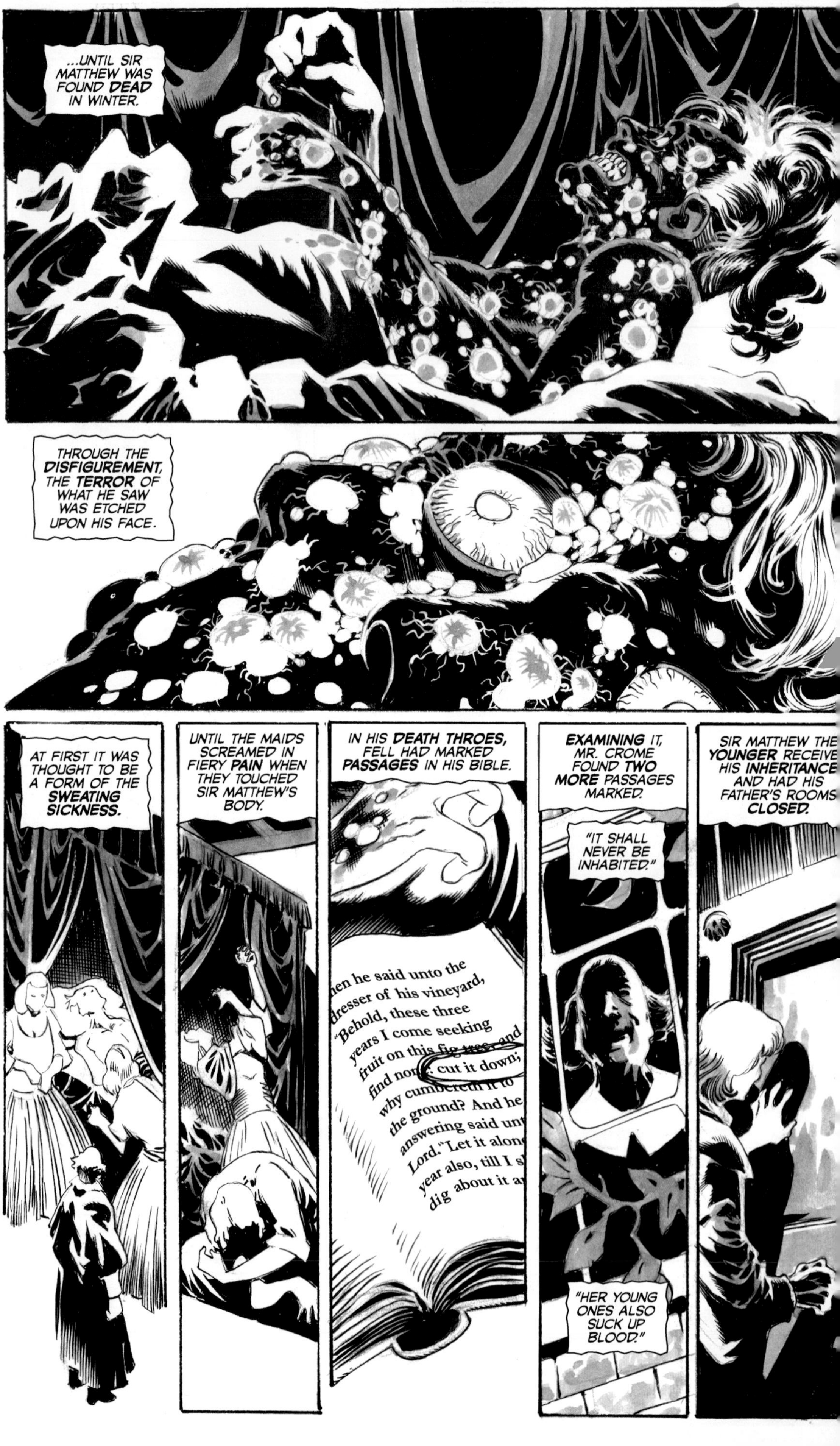

...UNTIL SIR MATTHEW WAS FOUND DEAD IN WINTER.
THROUGH THE DISFIGUREMENT, THE TERROR OF WHAT HE SAW WAS ETCHED UPON HIS FACE.
AT FIRST IT WAS THOUGHT TO BE A FORM OF THE SWEATING SICKNESS.
UNTIL THE MAIDS SCREAMED IN FIERY PAIN WHEN THEY TOUCHED SIR MATTHEW'S BODY.
IN HIS DEATH THROES, FELL HAD MARKED PASSAGES IN HIS BIBLE.
hen he said unto the
dresser of his vineyard,
"Behold, these three
years I come seeking
fruit on this fig tree, and
find none: cut it down;
why cumbereth it
the ground? And he
answering said unt
Lord."Let it alone
year also, till I s
dig about it a
EXAMINING IT, MR. CROME FOUND TWO MORE PASSAGES MARKED.
"IT SHALL NEVER BE INHABITED."
"HER YOUNG ONES ALSO SUCK UP BLOOD."
SIR MATTHEW THE YOUNGER RECEIVE HIS INHERITANCE AND HAD HIS FATHER'S ROOMS CLOSED.

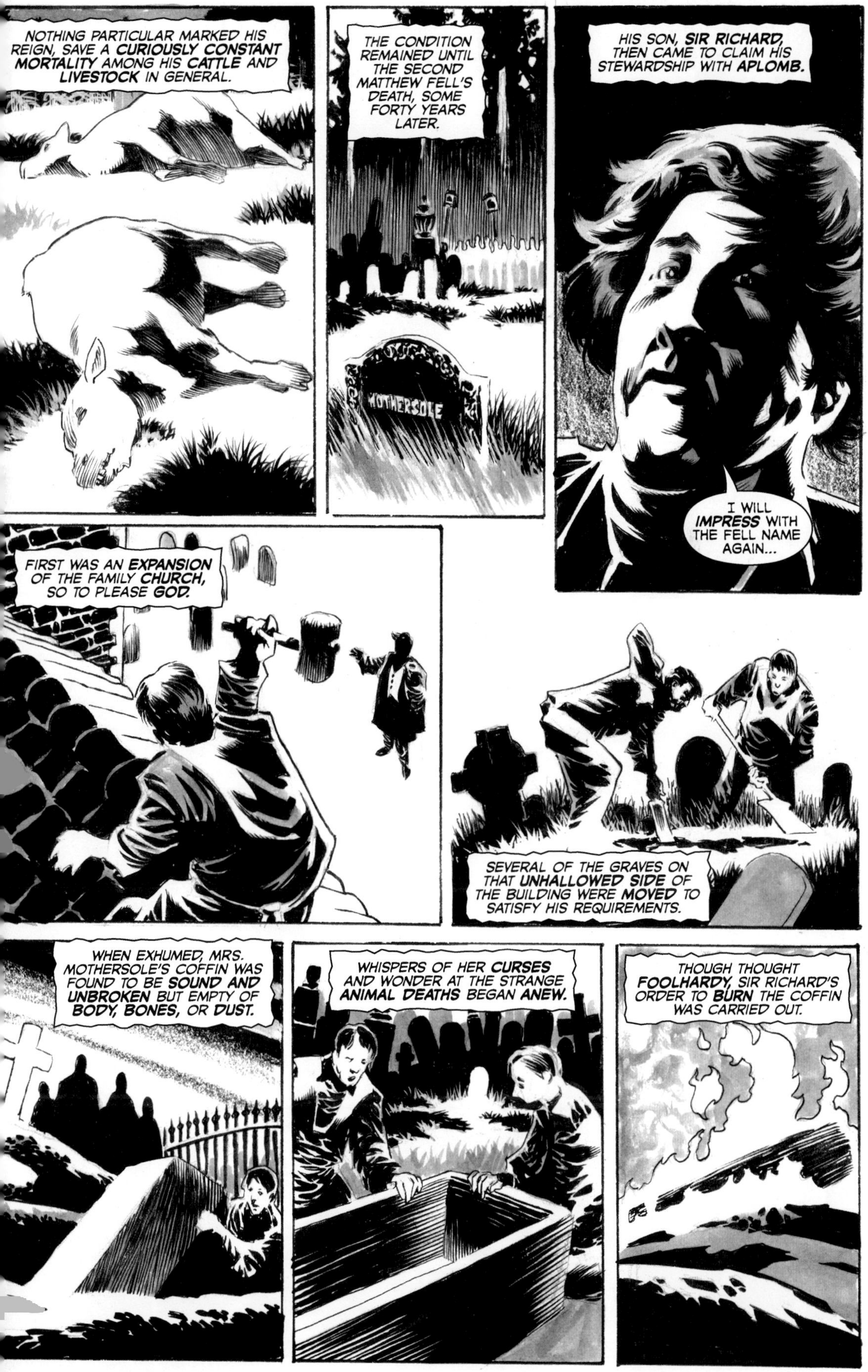

NOTHING PARTICULAR MARKED HIS REIGN, SAVE A CURIOUSLY CONSTANT MORTALITY AMONG HIS CATTLE AND LIVESTOCK IN GENERAL.
THE CONDITION REMAINED UNTIL THE SECOND MATTHEW FELL'S DEATH, SOME FORTY YEARS LATER.
MOTHERSOLE
HIS SON, SIR RICHARD, THEN CAME TO CLAIM HIS STEWARDSHIP WITH APLOMB.
I WILL IMPRESS WITH THE FELL NAME AGAIN...
FIRST WAS AN EXPANSION OF THE FAMILY CHURCH, SO TO PLEASE GOD.
SEVERAL OF THE GRAVES ON THAT UNHALLOWED SIDE OF THE BUILDING WERE MOVED TO SATISFY HIS REQUIREMENTS.
WHEN EXHUMED, MRS. MOTHERSOLE'S COFFIN WAS FOUND TO BE SOUND AND UNBROKEN BUT EMPTY OF BODY, BONES, OR DUST.
WHISPERS OF HER CURSES AND WONDER AT THE STRANGE ANIMAL DEATHS BEGAN ANEW.
THOUGH THOUGHT FOOLHARDY, SIR RICHARD'S ORDER TO BURN THE COFFIN WAS CARRIED OUT.

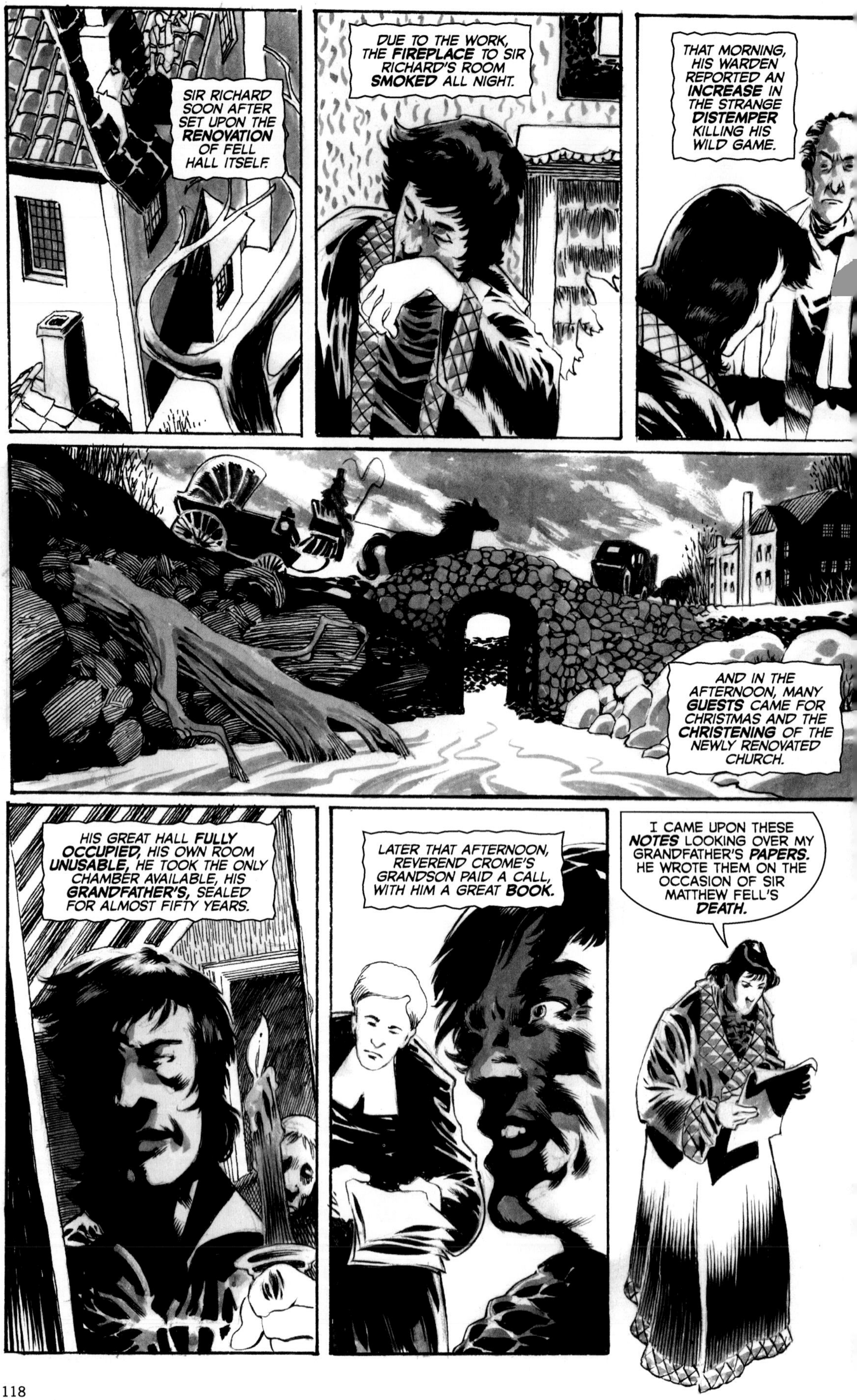
SIR RICHARD SOON AFTER SET UPON THE RENOVATION OF FELL HALL ITSELF.
DUE TO THE WORK, THE FIREPLACE TO SIR RICHARD'S ROOM SMOKED ALL NIGHT.
THAT MORNING, HIS WARDEN REPORTED AN INCREASE IN THE STRANGE DISTEMPER KILLING HIS WILD GAME.
AND IN THE AFTERNOON, MANY GUESTS CAME FOR CHRISTMAS AND THE CHRISTENING OF THE NEWLY RENOVATED CHURCH.
HIS GREAT HALL FULLY OCCUPIED, HIS OWN ROOM UNUSABLE, HE TOOK THE ONLY CHAMBER AVAILABLE, HIS GRANDFATHER'S, SEALED FOR ALMOST FIFTY YEARS.
LATER THAT AFTERNOON, REVEREND CROME'S GRANDSON PAID A CALL, WITH HIM A GREAT BOOK.
I CAME UPON THESE NOTES LOOKING OVER MY GRANDFATHER'S PAPERS. HE WROTE THEM ON THE OCCASION OF SIR MATTHEW FELL'S DEATH.

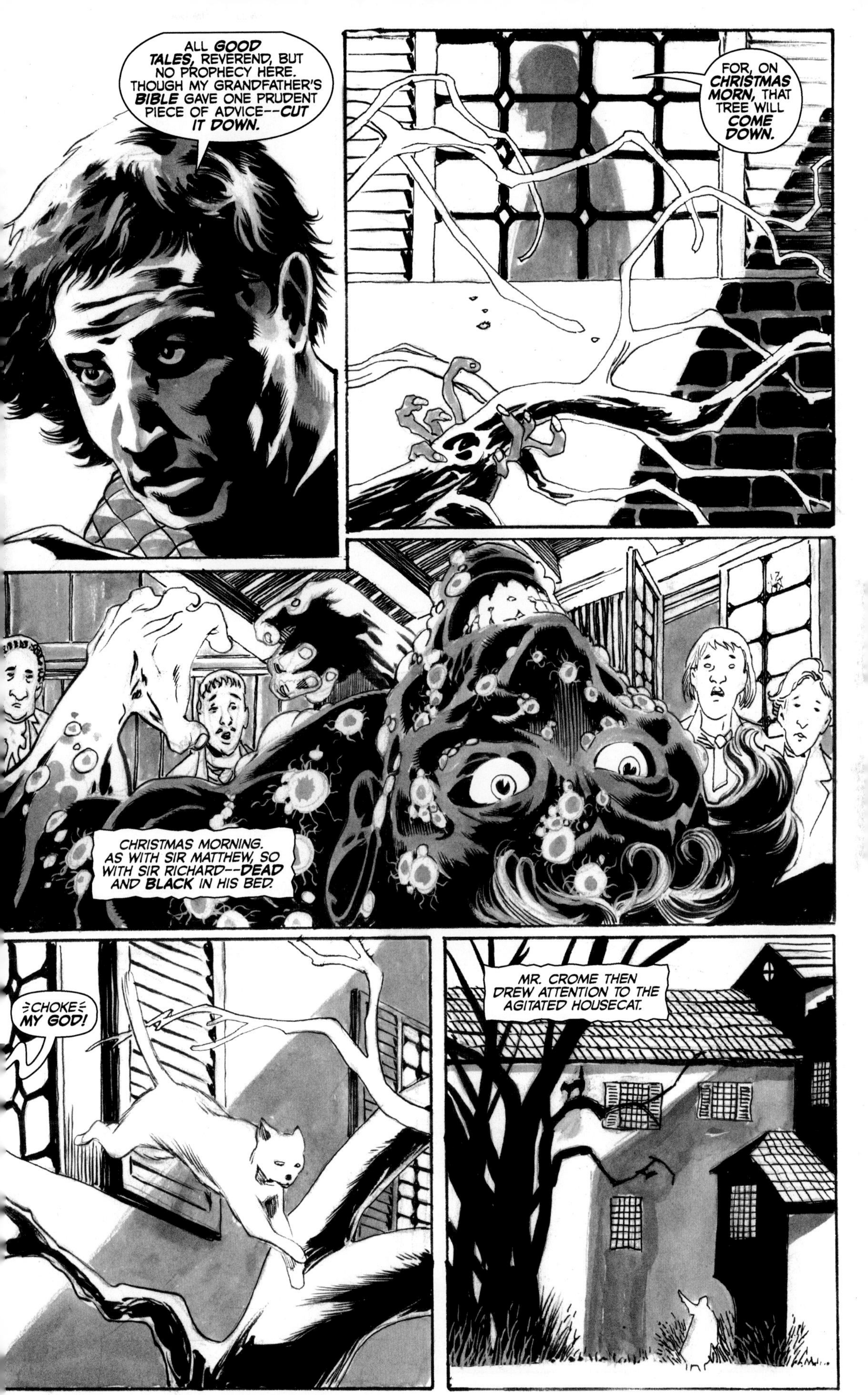
ALL GOOD TALES, REVEREND, BUT NO PROPHECY HERE. THOUGH MY GRANDFATHER'S BIBLE GAVE ONE PRUDENT PIECE OF ADVICE--CUT IT DOWN.
FOR, ON CHRISTMAS MORN, THAT TREE WILL COME DOWN.
CHRISTMAS MORNING. AS WITH SIR MATTHEW, SO WITH SIR RICHARD--DEAD AND BLACK IN HIS BED.
CHOKE MY GOD!
MR. CROME THEN DREW ATTENTION TO THE AGITATED HOUSECAT.

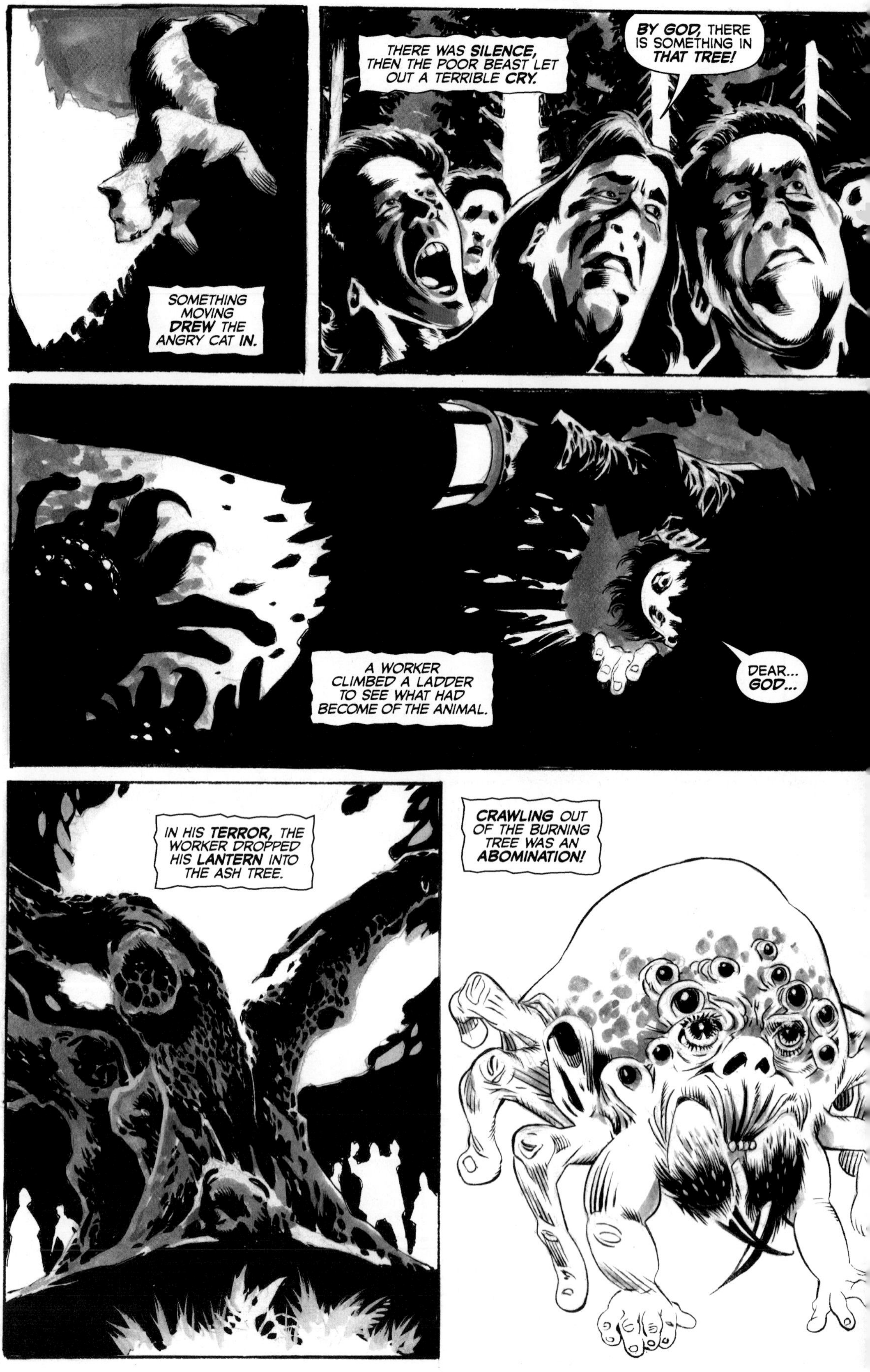
SOMETHING MOVING DREW THE ANGRY CAT IN.
THERE WAS SILENCE, THEN THE POOR BEAST LET OUT A TERRIBLE CRY.
BY GOD, THERE IS SOMETHING IN THAT TREE!
A WORKER CLIMBED A LADDER TO SEE WHAT HAD BECOME OF THE ANIMAL.
DEAR... GOD...
IN HIS TERROR, THE WORKER DROPPED HIS LANTERN INTO THE ASH TREE.
CRAWLING OUT OF THE BURNING TREE WAS AN ABOMINATION!

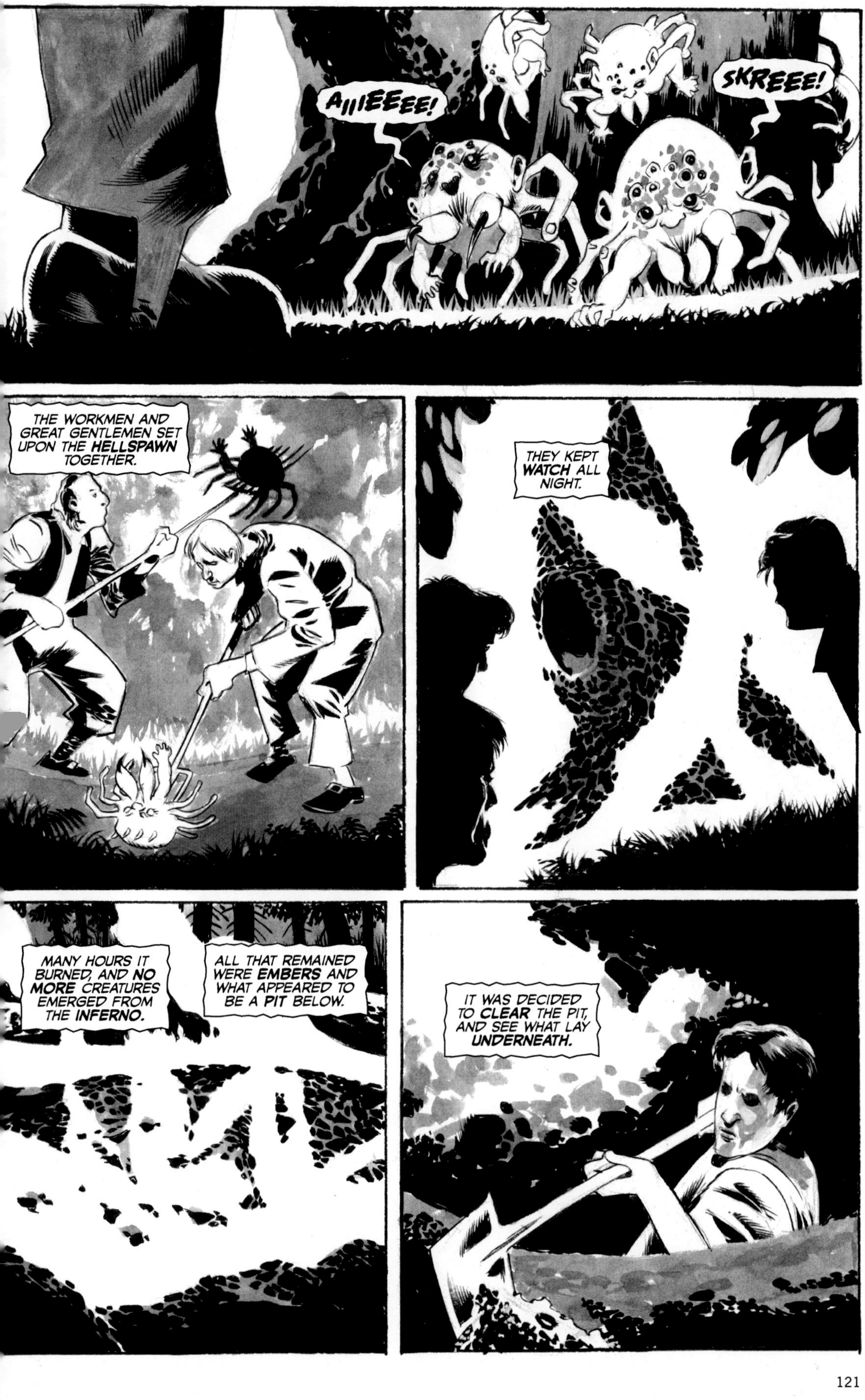

AIIIEEEEE!
SKREEE!
THE WORKMEN AND GREAT GENTLEMEN SET UPON THE HELLSPAWN TOGETHER.
THEY KEPT WATCH ALL NIGHT.
MANY HOURS IT BURNED, AND NO MORE CREATURES EMERGED FROM THE INFERNO.
ALL THAT REMAINED WERE EMBERS AND WHAT APPEARED TO BE A PIT BELOW.
IT WAS DECIDED TO CLEAR THE PIT, AND SEE WHAT LAY UNDERNEATH.

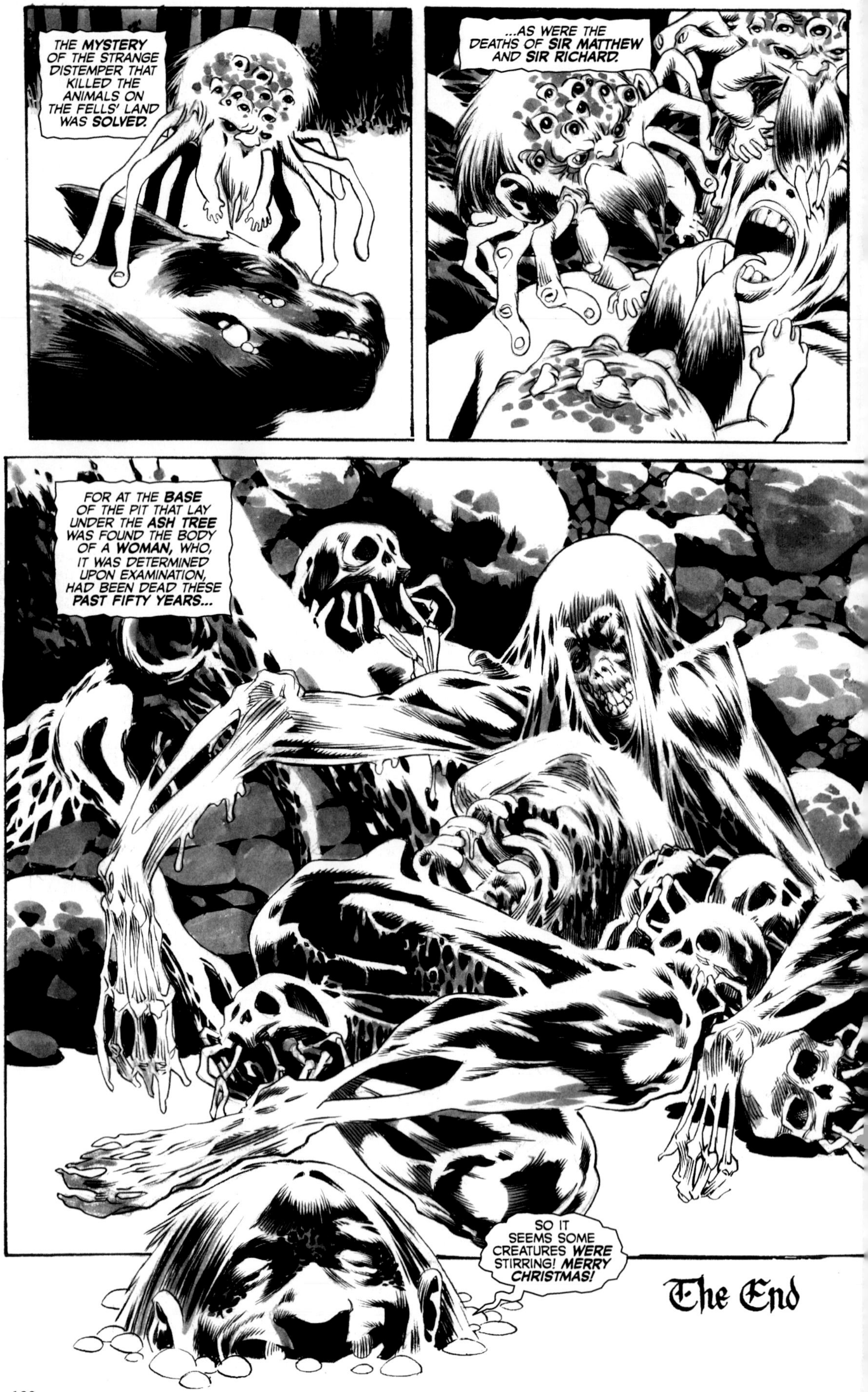
THE MYSTERY OF THE STRANGE DISTEMPER THAT KILLED THE ANIMALS ON THE FELLS' LAND WAS SOLVED.
...AS WERE THE DEATHS OF SIR MATTHEW AND SIR RICHARD.
FOR AT THE BASE OF THE PIT THAT LAY UNDER THE ASH TREE WAS FOUND THE BODY OF A WOMAN, WHO, IT WAS DETERMINED UPON EXAMINATION, HAD BEEN DEAD THESE PAST FIFTY YEARS...
SO IT SEEMS SOME CREATURES WERE STIRRING! MERRY CHRISTMAS!
The End

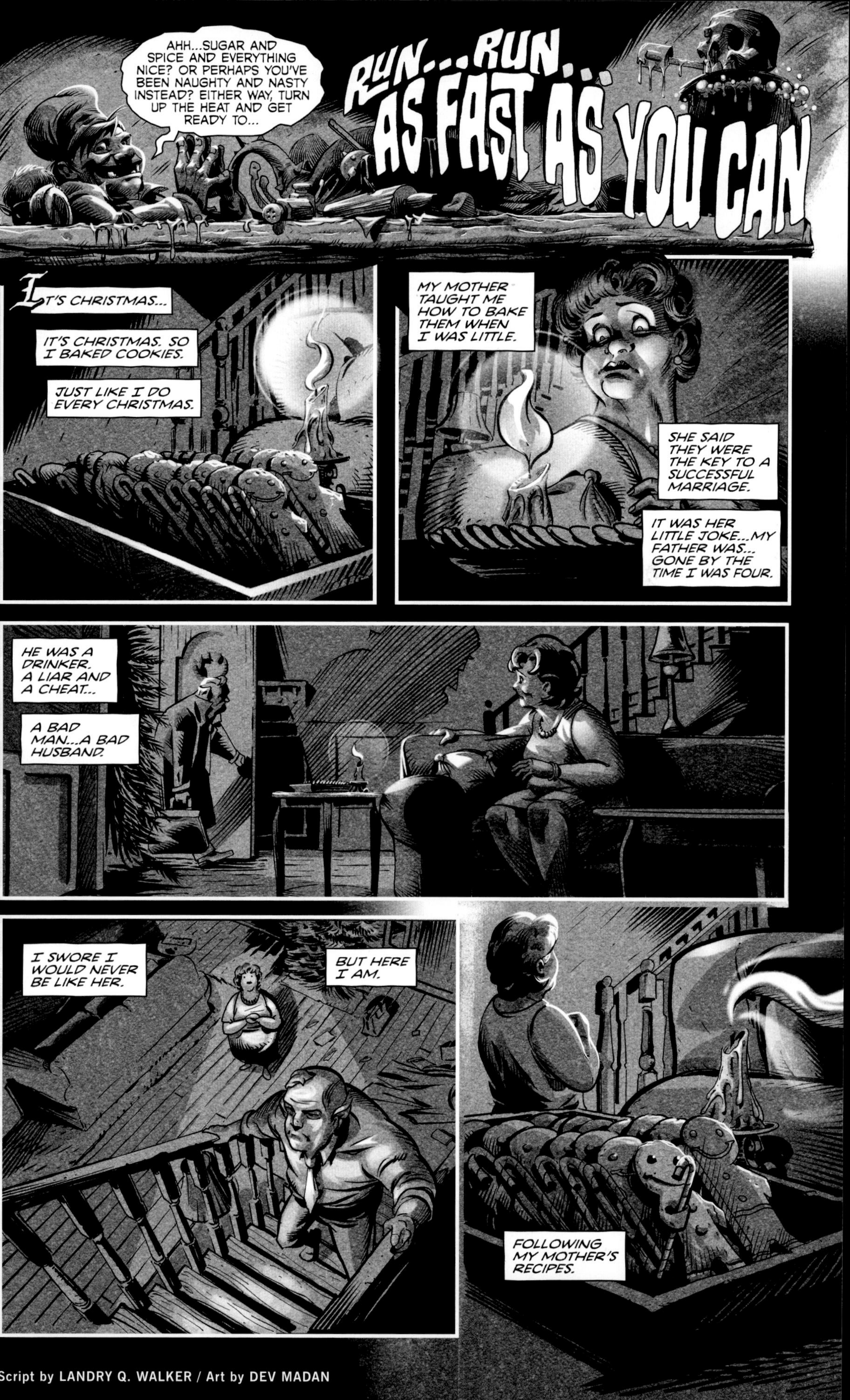
AHH...SUGAR AND SPICE AND EVERYTHING NICE? OR PERHAPS YOU'VE BEEN NAUGHTY AND NASTY INSTEAD? EITHER WAY, TURN UP THE HEAT AND GET READY TO...
RUN...RUN... AS FAST AS YOU CAN
IT'S CHRISTMAS...
IT'S CHRISTMAS. SO I BAKED COOKIES.
JUST LIKE I DO EVERY CHRISTMAS.
MY MOTHER TAUGHT ME HOW TO BAKE THEM WHEN I WAS LITTLE.
SHE SAID THEY WERE THE KEY TO A SUCCESSFUL MARRIAGE.
IT WAS HER LITTLE JOKE...MY FATHER WAS... GONE BY THE TIME I WAS FOUR.
HE WAS A DRINKER. A LIAR AND A CHEAT...
A BAD MAN...A BAD HUSBAND.
I SWORE I WOULD NEVER BE LIKE HER.
BUT HERE I AM.
FOLLOWING MY MOTHER'S RECIPES.

Script by LANDRY Q. WALKER / Art by DEV MADAN

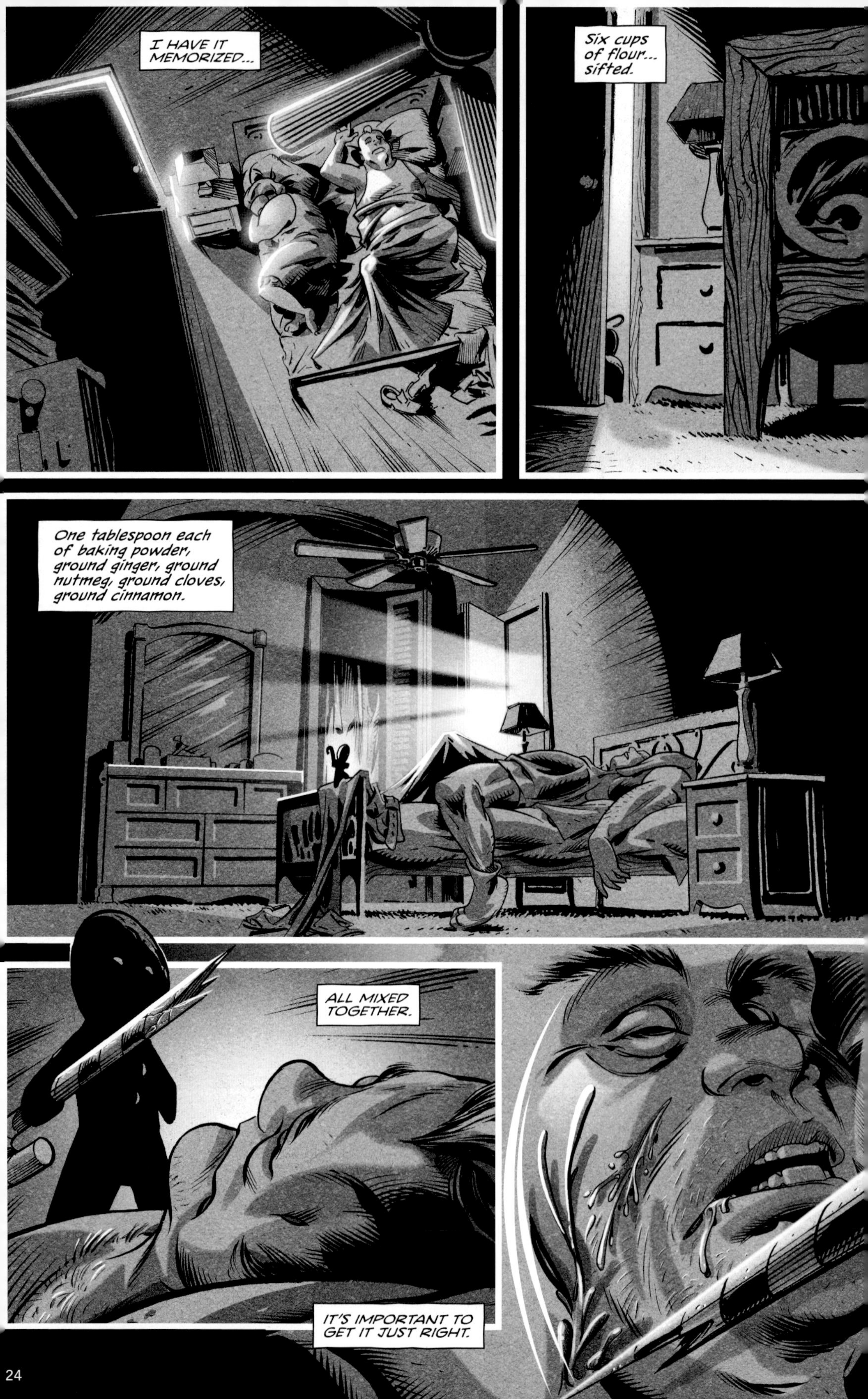
I HAVE IT MEMORIZED...
Six cups of flour... sifted.
One tablespoon each of baking powder, ground ginger, ground nutmeg, ground cloves, ground cinnamon.
ALL MIXED TOGETHER.
IT'S IMPORTANT TO GET IT JUST RIGHT.

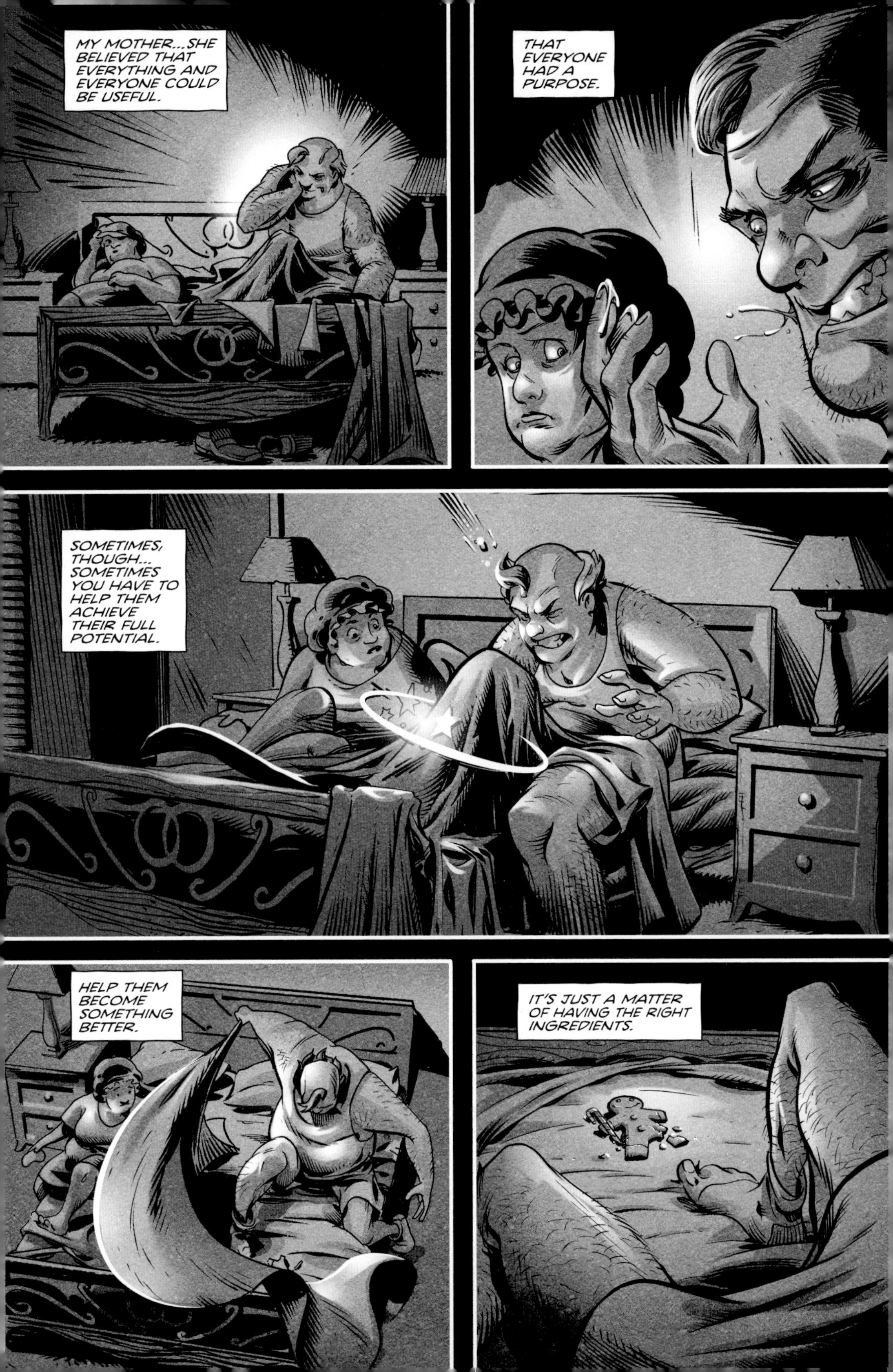
MY MOTHER...SHE BELIEVED THAT EVERYTHING AND EVERYONE COULD BE USEFUL.
THAT EVERYONE HAD A PURPOSE.
SOMETIMES, THOUGH... SOMETIMES YOU HAVE TO HELP THEM ACHIEVE THEIR FULL POTENTIAL.
HELP THEM BECOME SOMETHING BETTER.
IT'S JUST A MATTER OF HAVING THE RIGHT INGREDIENTS.

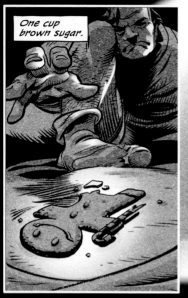

One cup brown sugar.

One egg.

A half a cup of water.

One cup molasses.

One teaspoon vanilla extract.

Mix together on a low speed.

Beat until smooth.

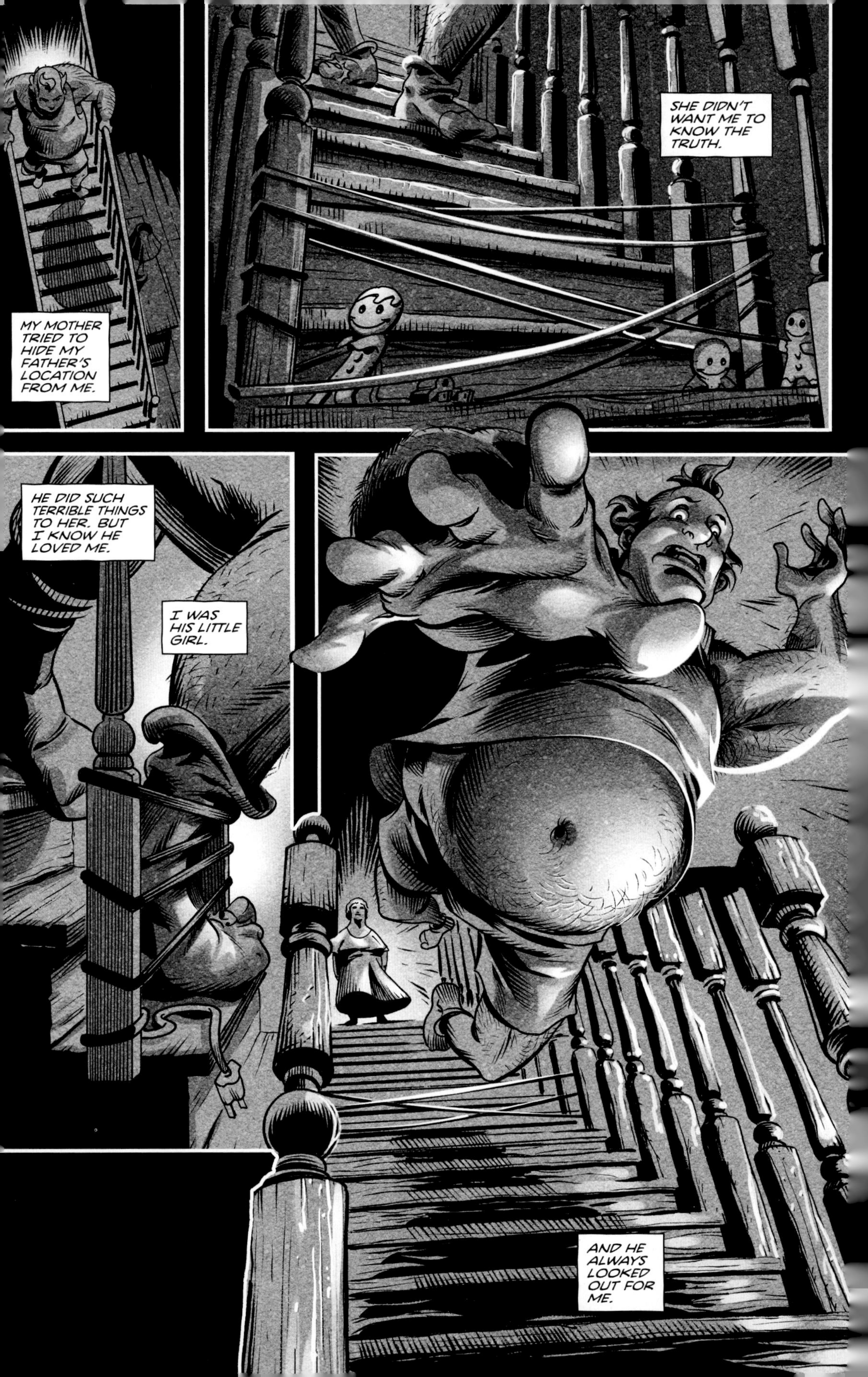
MY MOTHER TRIED TO HIDE MY FATHER'S LOCATION FROM ME.
SHE DIDN'T WANT ME TO KNOW THE TRUTH.
HE DID SUCH TERRIBLE THINGS TO HER. BUT I KNOW HE LOVED ME.
I WAS HIS LITTLE GIRL.
AND HE ALWAYS LOOKED OUT FOR ME.

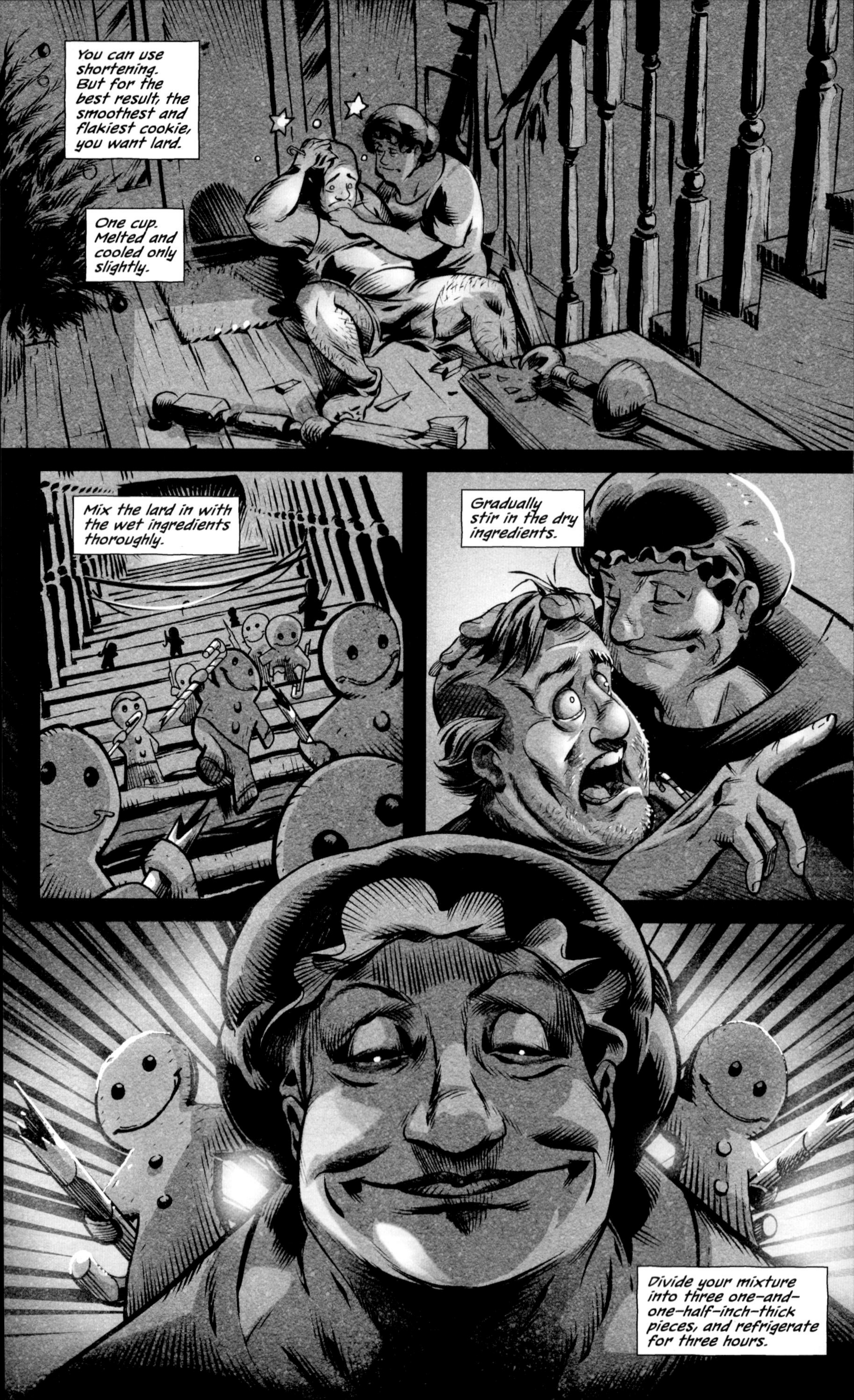
You can use shortening. But for the best result, the smoothest and flakiest cookie, you want lard.
One cup. Melted and cooled only slightly.
Mix the lard in with the wet ingredients thoroughly.
Gradually stir in the dry ingredients.
Divide your mixture into three one-and-one-half-inch-thick pieces, and refrigerate for three hours.

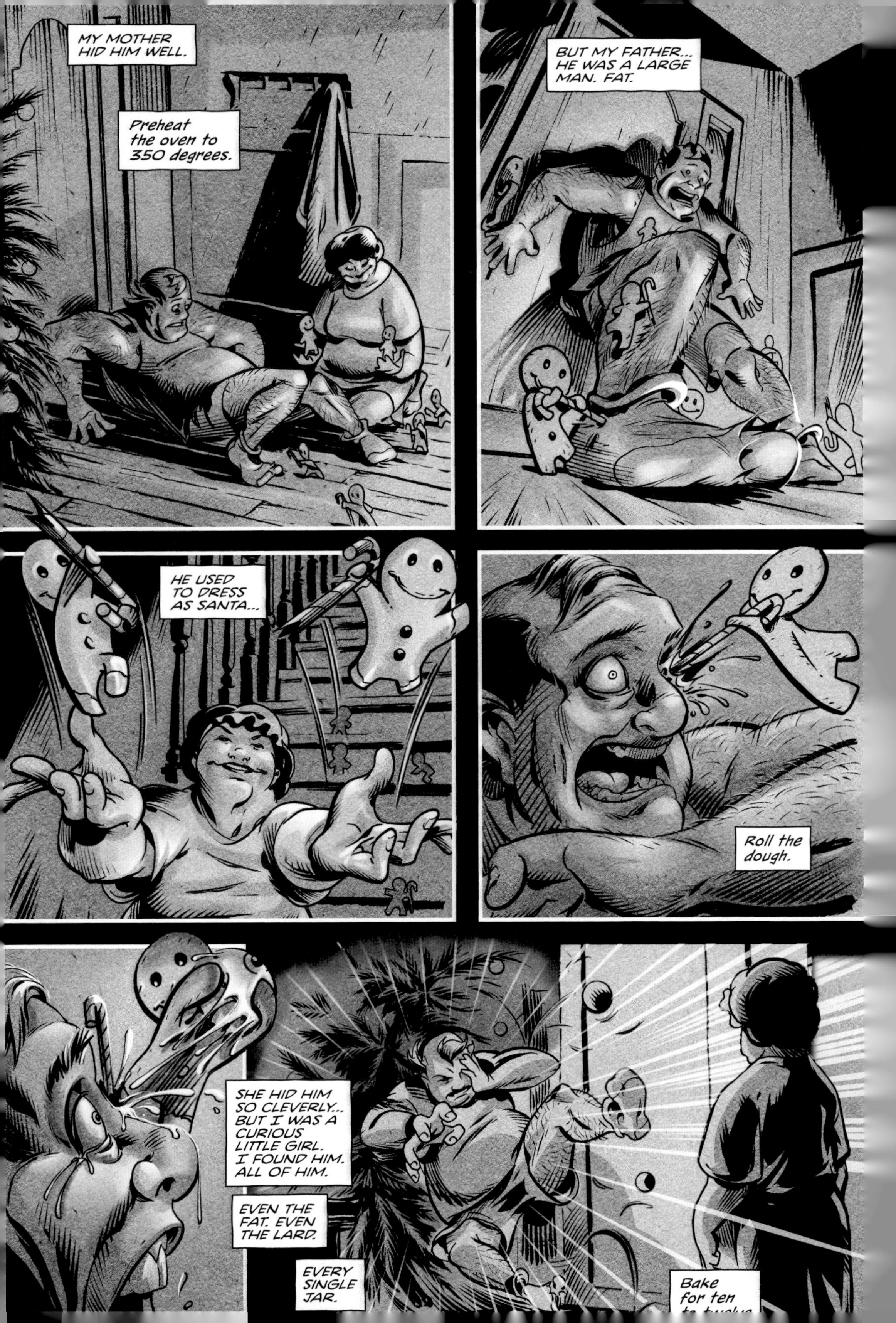
MY MOTHER HID HIM WELL.
Preheat the oven to 350 degrees.
BUT MY FATHER... HE WAS A LARGE MAN. FAT.
HE USED TO DRESS AS SANTA...
Roll the dough.
SHE HID HIM SO CLEVERLY... BUT I WAS A CURIOUS LITTLE GIRL. I FOUND HIM. ALL OF HIM.
EVEN THE FAT. EVEN THE LARD.
EVERY SINGLE JAR.
Bake for ten

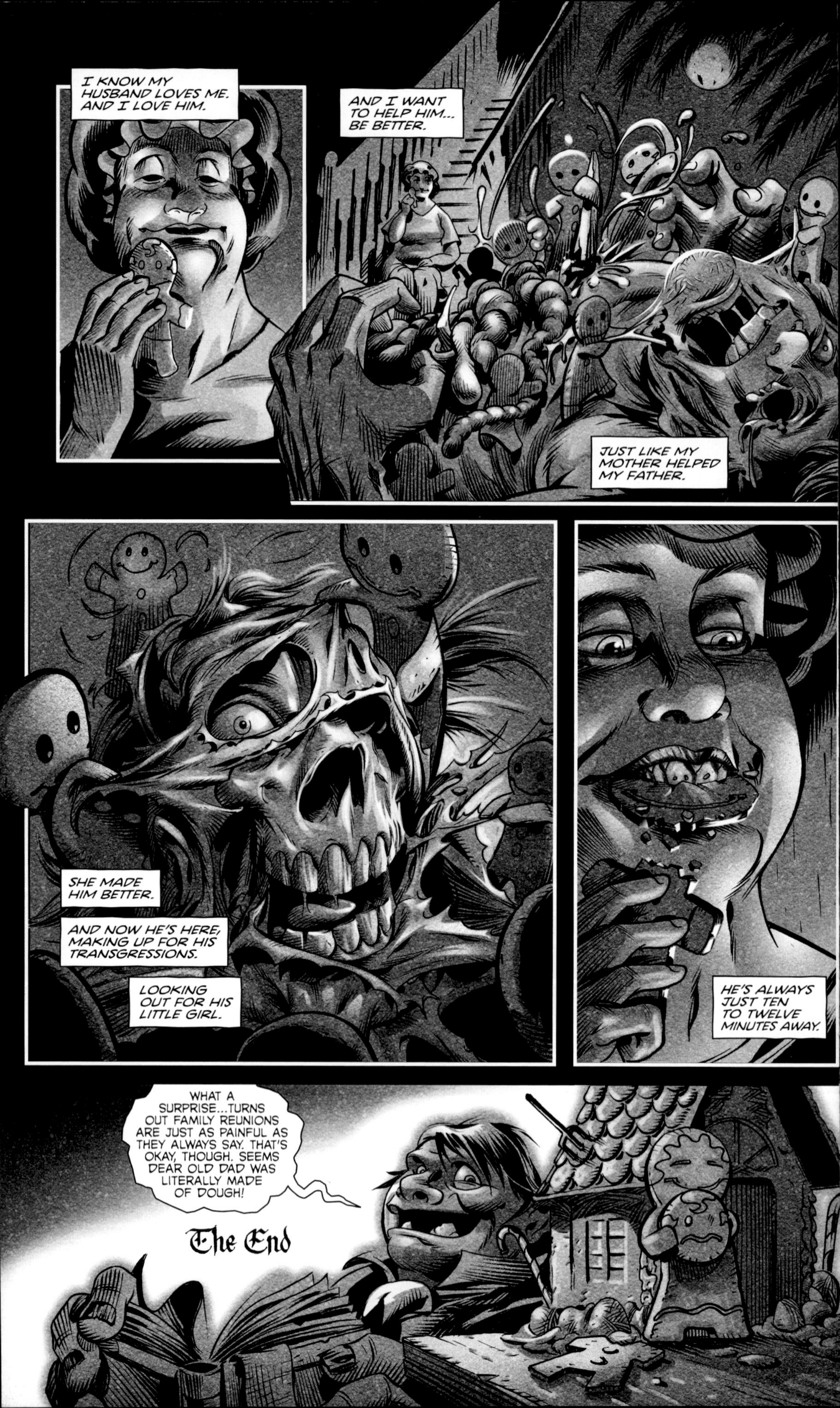
I KNOW MY HUSBAND LOVES ME. AND I LOVE HIM.
AND I WANT TO HELP HIM... BE BETTER.
JUST LIKE MY MOTHER HELPED MY FATHER.
SHE MADE HIM BETTER.
AND NOW HE'S HERE, MAKING UP FOR HIS TRANSGRESSIONS.
LOOKING OUT FOR HIS LITTLE GIRL.
HE'S ALWAYS JUST TEN TO TWELVE MINUTES AWAY.
WHAT A SURPRISE...TURNS OUT FAMILY REUNIONS ARE JUST AS PAINFUL AS THEY ALWAYS SAY. THAT'S OKAY, THOUGH. SEEMS DEAR OLD DAD WAS LITERALLY MADE OF DOUGH!
The End

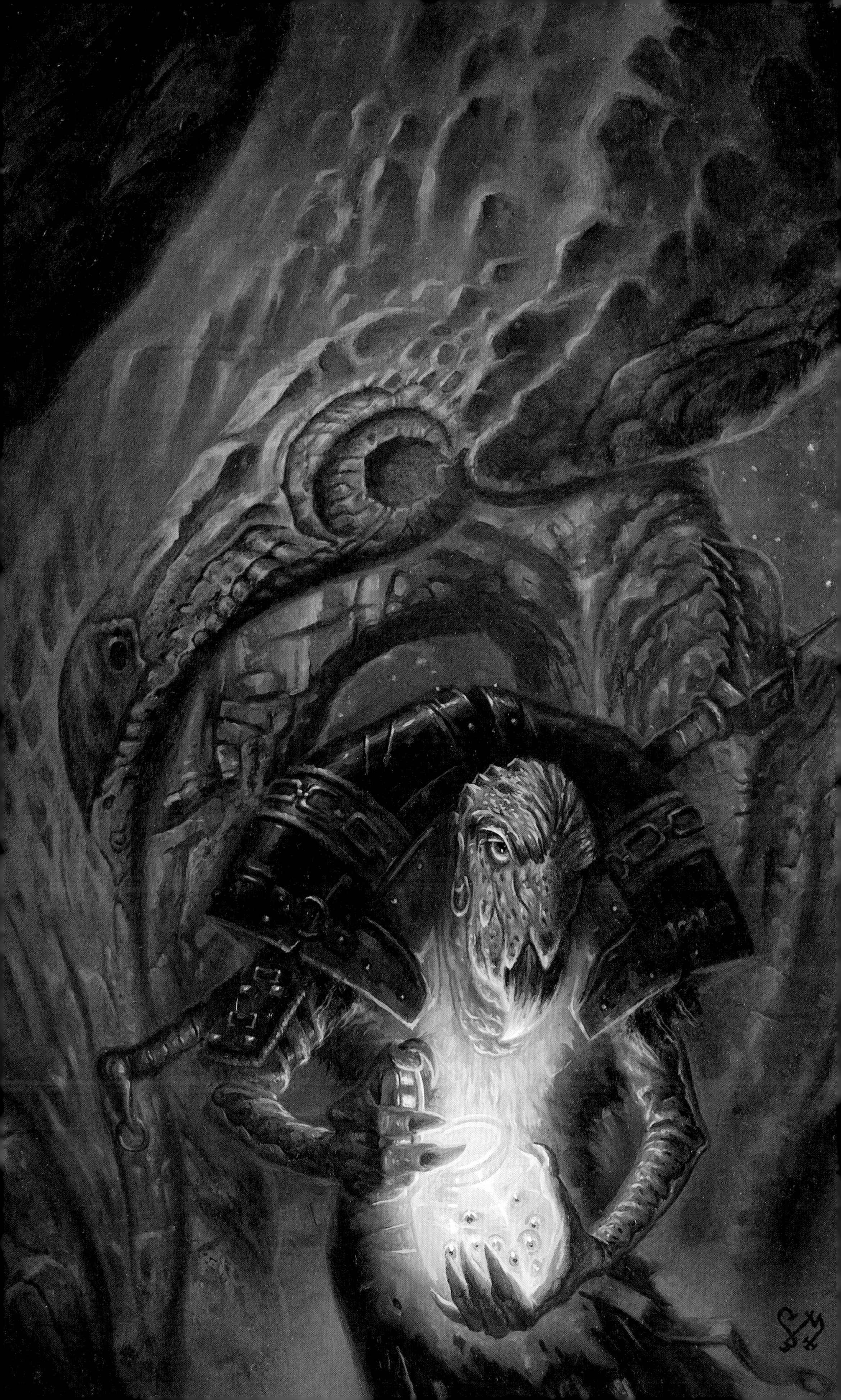

EERIE'S MONSTER GALLERY

The saying goes, *"You can catch more flies with honey than with vinegar"*... unless you thirst for what the vinegar attracts.

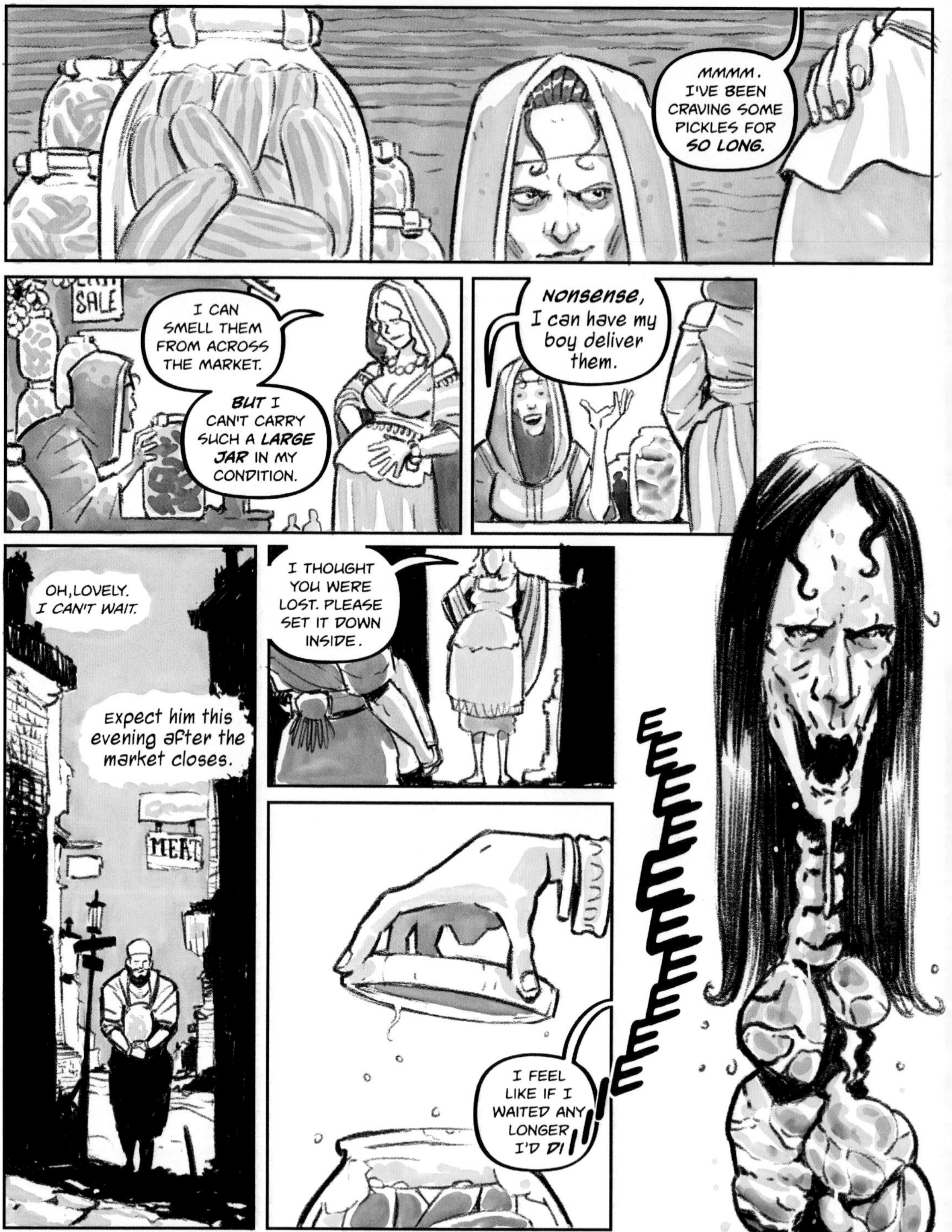
MMMM. I'VE BEEN CRAVING SOME PICKLES FOR **SO LONG.**
SALE
I CAN SMELL THEM FROM ACROSS THE MARKET.
BUT I CAN'T CARRY SUCH A **LARGE JAR** IN MY CONDITION.
Nonsense, I can have my boy deliver them.
OH, LOVELY. *I CAN'T WAIT.*
Expect him this evening after the market closes.
MEAT
I THOUGHT YOU WERE LOST. PLEASE SET IT DOWN INSIDE.
I FEEL LIKE IF I WAITED ANY LONGER I'D ***DI***

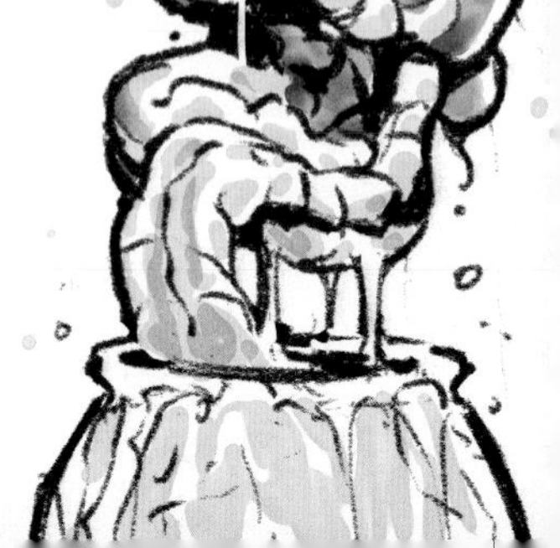

PENANGGALAN

She is forever cursed to be a bloodsucking vampire, often drinking the blood of newborns or pregnant women. After detaching her head at night and feeding, she will return and immerse her entrails in a vat of vinegar so she may shrink them for easy entry back into her body--which carries the odd vinegar odor with it.

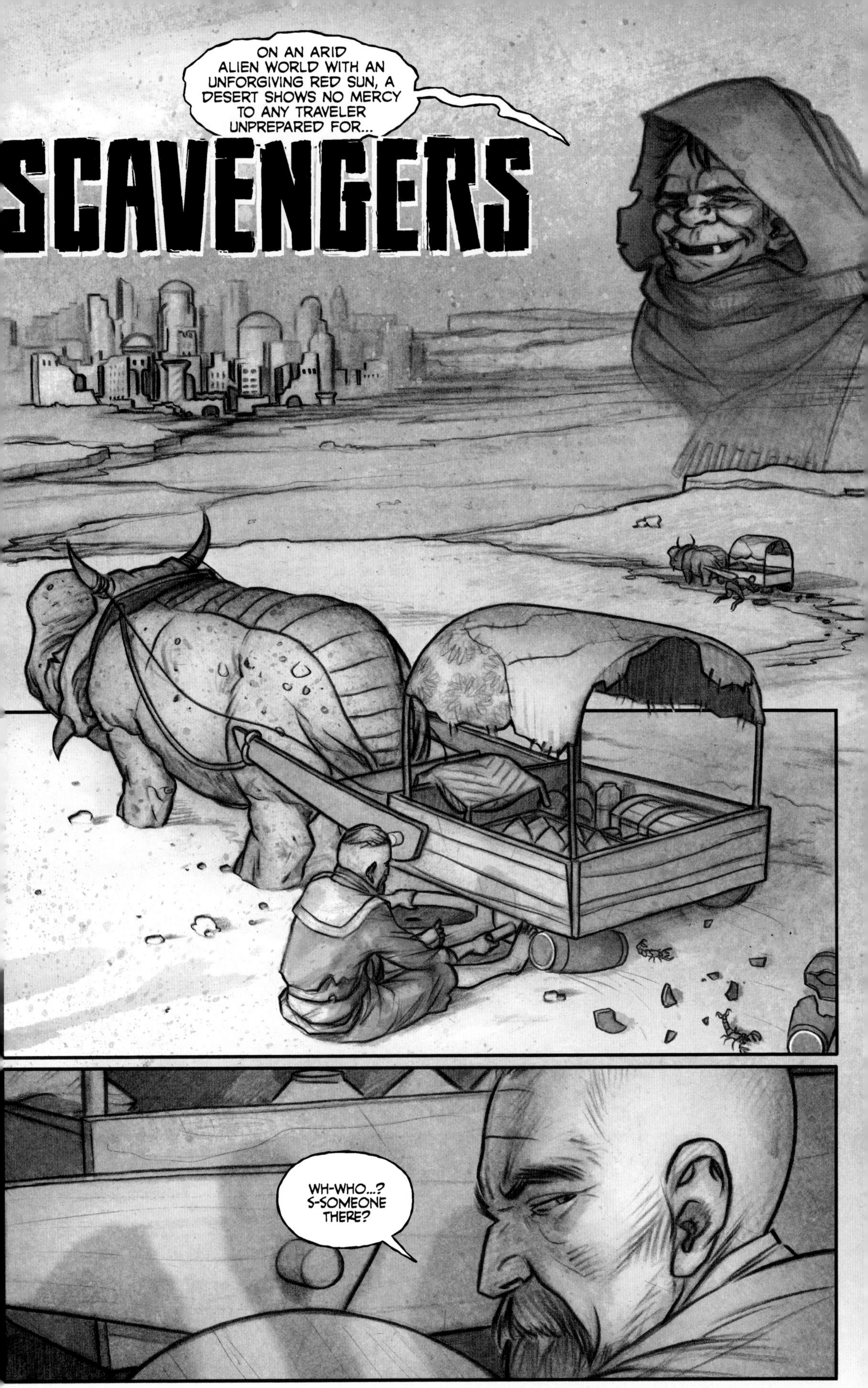
ON AN ARID ALIEN WORLD WITH AN UNFORGIVING RED SUN, A DESERT SHOWS NO MERCY TO ANY TRAVELER UNPREPARED FOR...
SCAVENGERS
WH-WHO...? S-SOMEONE THERE?

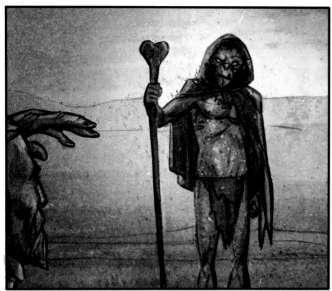

PLEASE! PLEASE HELP ME...WHEEL FELL OFF...RAN OUT OF WATER...SO WEAK...

NO...

...PLEASE!

NGG! FIX...THE WHEEL...!

OH! I SEE...

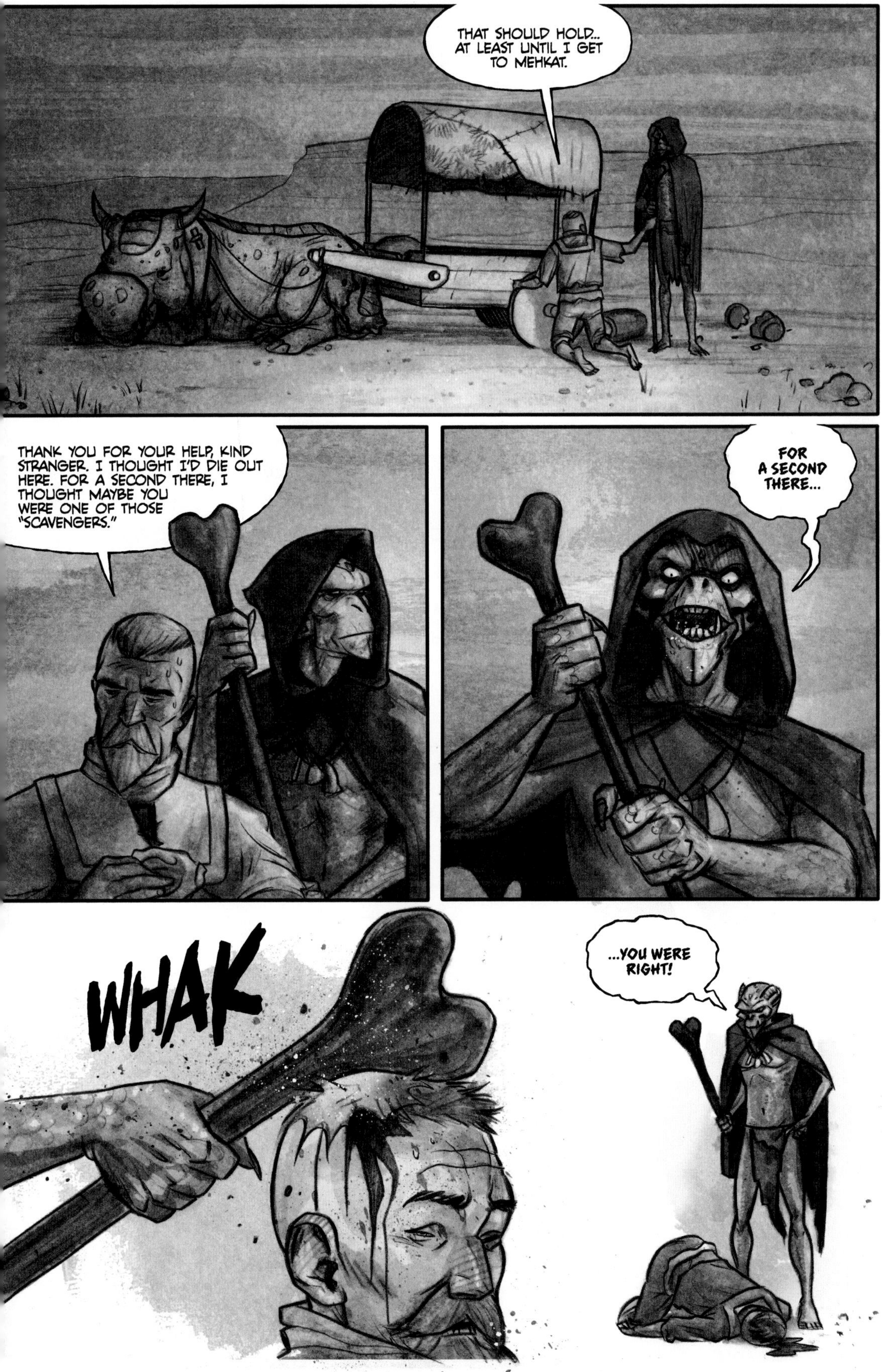

THAT SHOULD HOLD... AT LEAST UNTIL I GET TO MEHKAT.
THANK YOU FOR YOUR HELP, KIND STRANGER. I THOUGHT I'D DIE OUT HERE. FOR A SECOND THERE, I THOUGHT MAYBE YOU WERE ONE OF THOSE "SCAVENGERS."
FOR A SECOND THERE...
WHAK
...YOU WERE RIGHT!

BAH...

...NOTHING OF VALUE!

WHAT ABOUT IN HERE? GOT ANY GOLD?

HUH! JUST ROTTEN TEETH...

UHHHH...

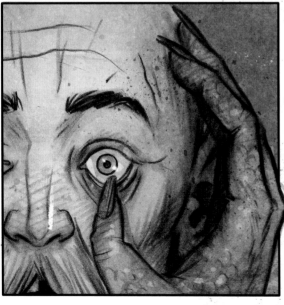

AHA! GREEN EYES... GREEN EYES ARE WORTH A HUNDRED COINS...

ARRGGH!

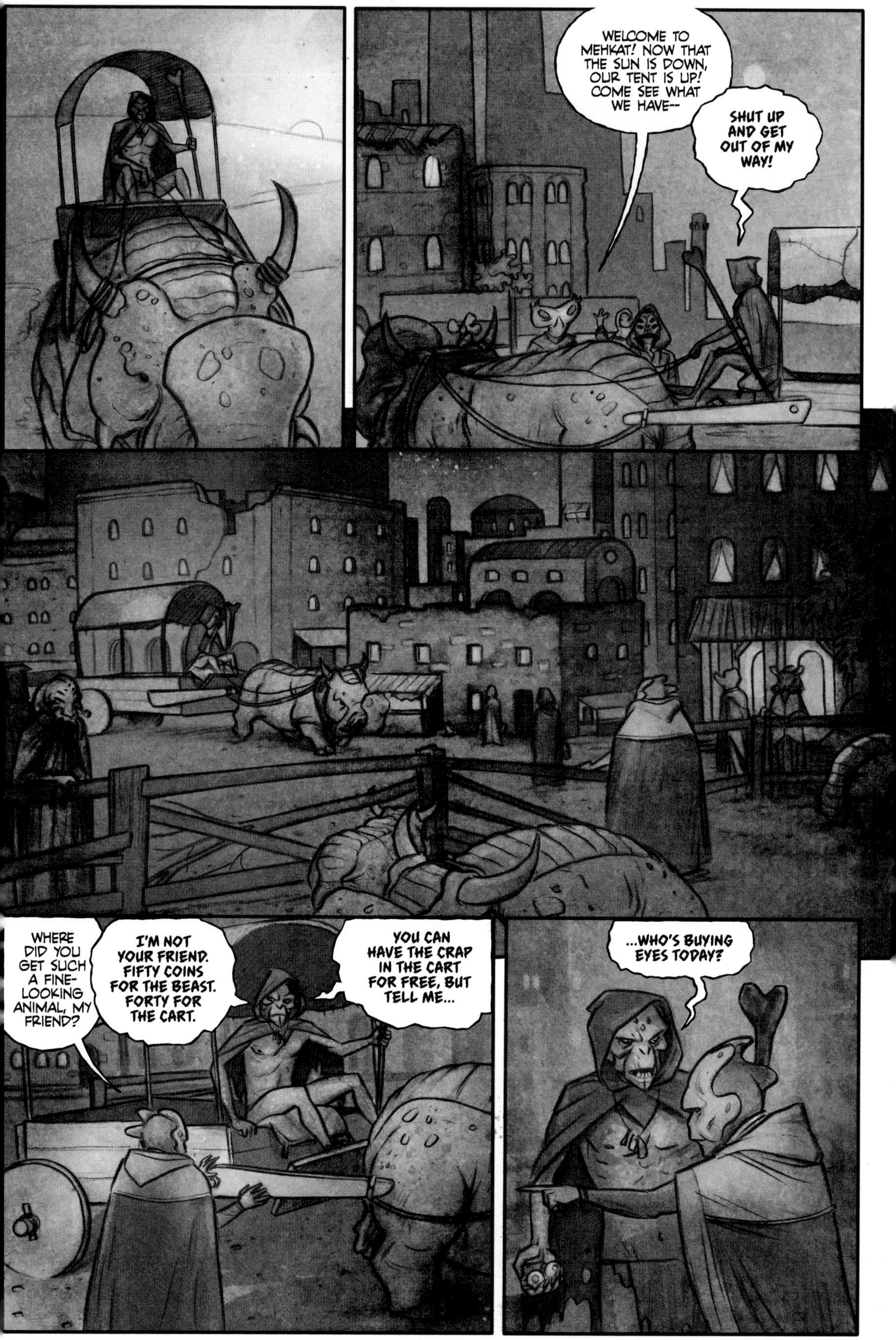
WELCOME TO MEHKAT! NOW THAT THE SUN IS DOWN, OUR TENT IS UP! COME SEE WHAT WE HAVE--
SHUT UP AND GET OUT OF MY WAY!
WHERE DID YOU GET SUCH A FINE-LOOKING ANIMAL, MY FRIEND?
I'M NOT YOUR FRIEND. FIFTY COINS FOR THE BEAST. FORTY FOR THE CART.
YOU CAN HAVE THE CRAP IN THE CART FOR FREE, BUT TELL ME...
...WHO'S BUYING EYES TODAY?

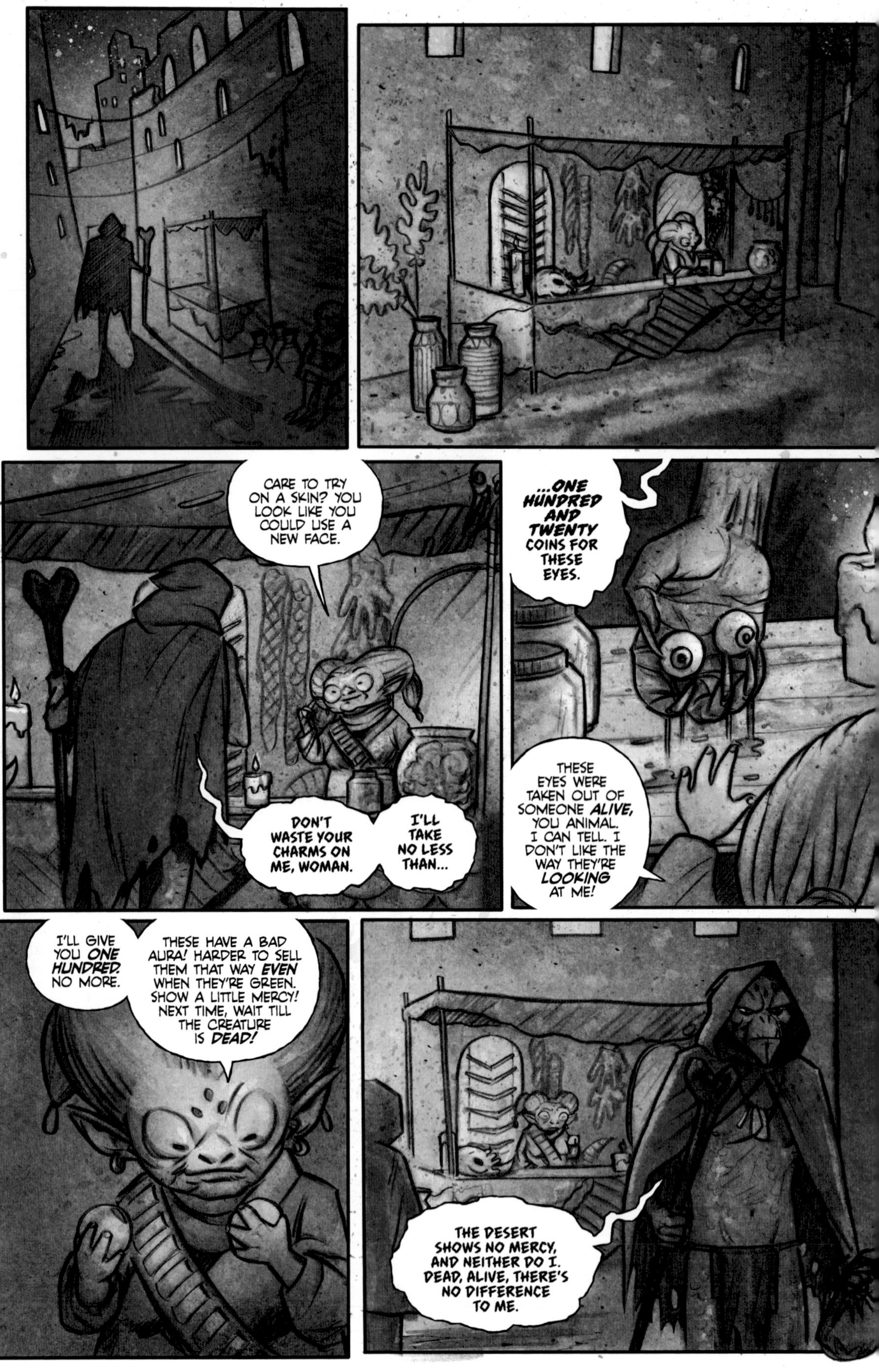
CARE TO TRY ON A SKIN? YOU LOOK LIKE YOU COULD USE A NEW FACE.
DON'T WASTE YOUR CHARMS ON ME, WOMAN.
I'LL TAKE NO LESS THAN...
...ONE HUNDRED AND TWENTY COINS FOR THESE EYES.
THESE EYES WERE TAKEN OUT OF SOMEONE ALIVE, YOU ANIMAL. I CAN TELL. I DON'T LIKE THE WAY THEY'RE LOOKING AT ME!
I'LL GIVE YOU ONE HUNDRED. NO MORE.
THESE HAVE A BAD AURA! HARDER TO SELL THEM THAT WAY EVEN WHEN THEY'RE GREEN. SHOW A LITTLE MERCY! NEXT TIME, WAIT TILL THE CREATURE IS DEAD!
THE DESERT SHOWS NO MERCY, AND NEITHER DO I. DEAD, ALIVE, THERE'S NO DIFFERENCE TO ME.

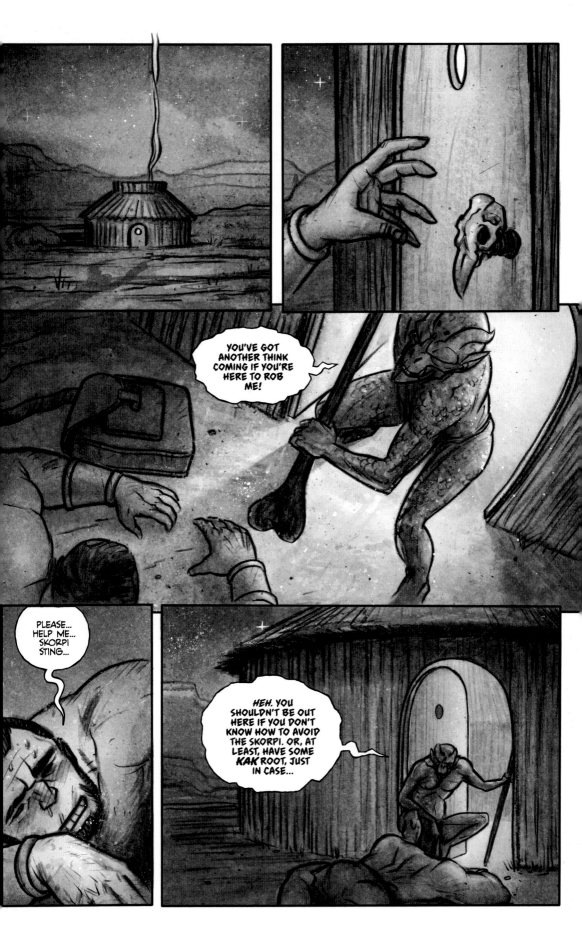

YOU'VE GOT ANOTHER THINK COMING IF YOU'RE HERE TO ROB ME!

PLEASE... HELP ME... SKORPI STING...

HEH. YOU SHOULDN'T BE OUT HERE IF YOU DON'T KNOW HOW TO AVOID THE SKORPI. OR, AT LEAST, HAVE SOME *KAK* ROOT, JUST IN CASE...

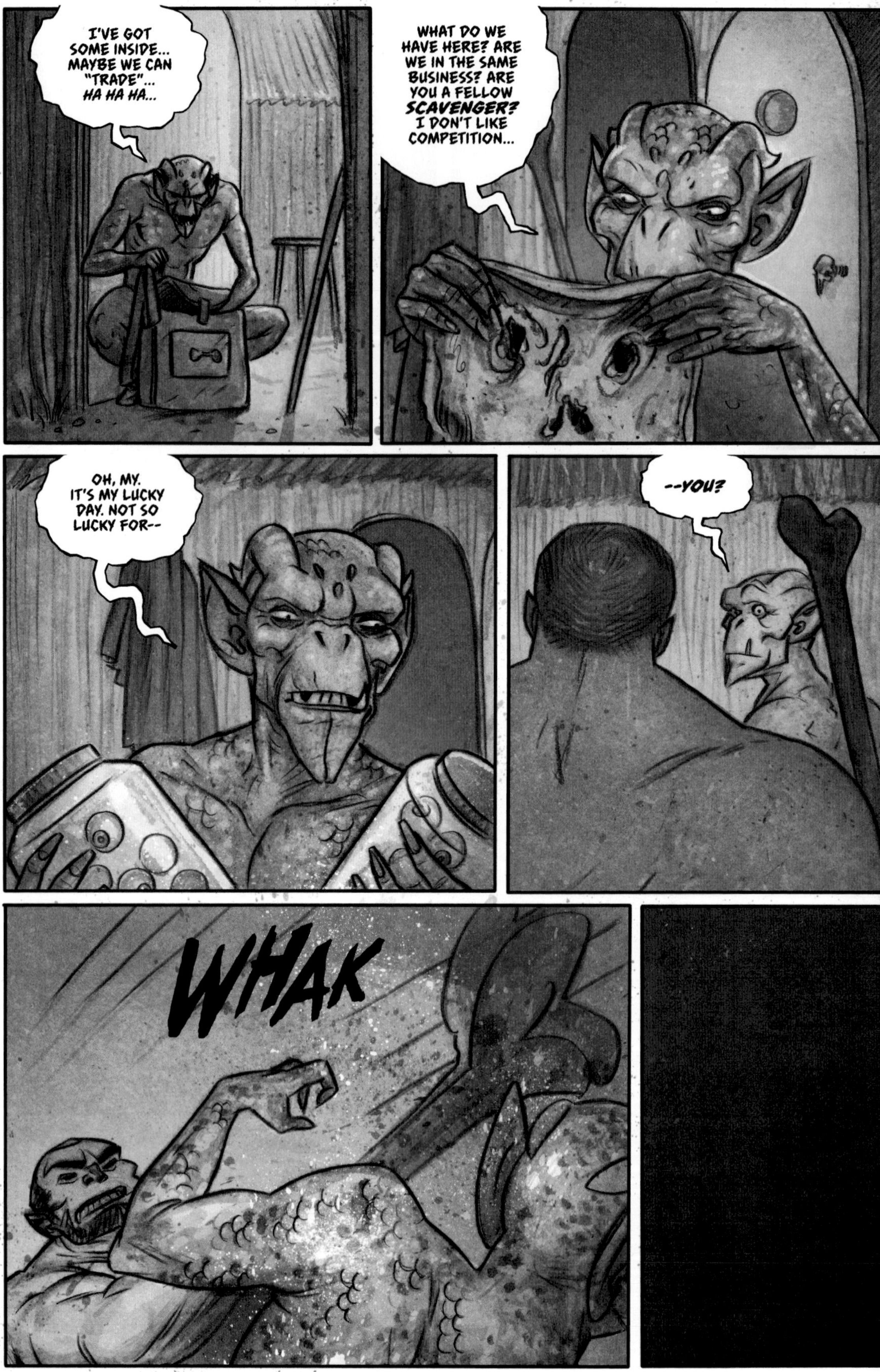

I'VE GOT SOME INSIDE... MAYBE WE CAN "TRADE"... HA HA HA...
WHAT DO WE HAVE HERE? ARE WE IN THE SAME BUSINESS? ARE YOU A FELLOW *SCAVENGER?* I DON'T LIKE COMPETITION...
OH, MY. IT'S MY LUCKY DAY. NOT SO LUCKY FOR--
--YOU?
WHAK

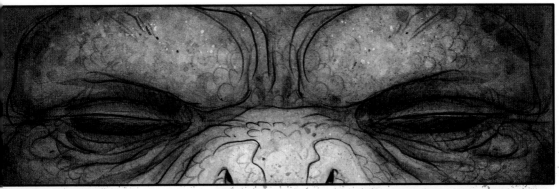

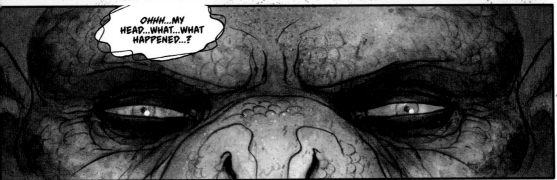

OHHH...MY HEAD...WHAT...WHAT HAPPENED...?

WHERE... WHERE AM I? MEHKAT? HOW DID I GET HERE...!

THESE EYES! FROM THAT STRANGER... WITH THE SKORPI STING...

HEH...IT MUST'VE BEEN SOME FIGHT...MY HEAD HURTS...

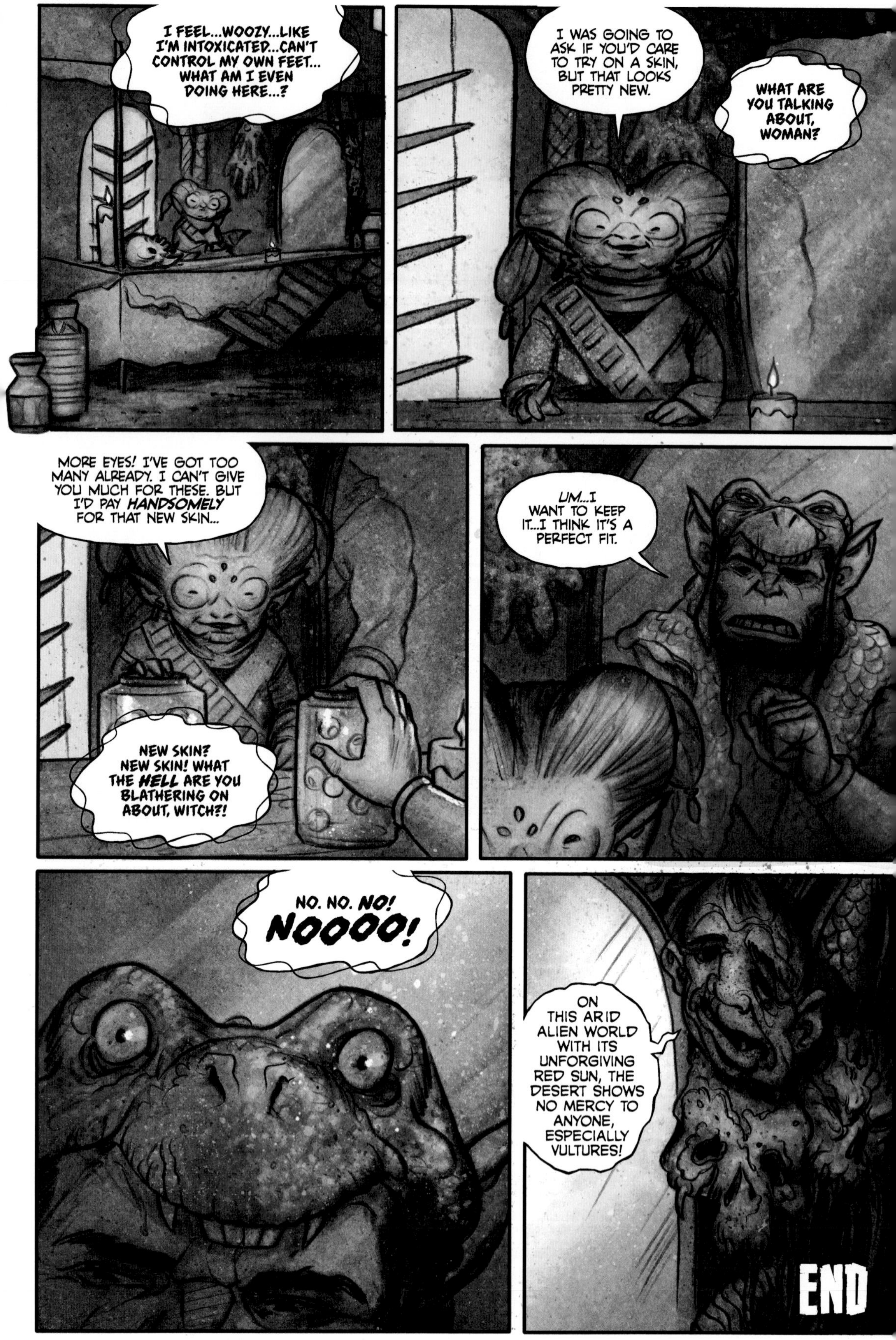
I FEEL...WOOZY...LIKE I'M INTOXICATED...CAN'T CONTROL MY OWN FEET... WHAT AM I EVEN DOING HERE...?
I WAS GOING TO ASK IF YOU'D CARE TO TRY ON A SKIN, BUT THAT LOOKS PRETTY NEW.
WHAT ARE YOU TALKING ABOUT, WOMAN?
MORE EYES! I'VE GOT TOO MANY ALREADY. I CAN'T GIVE YOU MUCH FOR THESE. BUT I'D PAY HANDSOMELY FOR THAT NEW SKIN...
NEW SKIN? NEW SKIN! WHAT THE HELL ARE YOU BLATHERING ON ABOUT, WITCH?!
UM...I WANT TO KEEP IT...I THINK IT'S A PERFECT FIT.
NO. NO. NO! NOOOO!
ON THIS ARID ALIEN WORLD WITH ITS UNFORGIVING RED SUN, THE DESERT SHOWS NO MERCY TO ANYONE, ESPECIALLY VULTURES!
END

ARE YOU READY FOR A RIP-SNORTING COMING-OF-AGE STORY FEATURING A PLUCKY FEMALE PROTAGONIST BATTLING AGAINST IMPOSSIBLE ODDS IN A SAVAGE AND ALIEN LANDSCAPE FULL OF RAVENOUS, LONG-TOOTHED BEASTIES? THEN I'VE GOT A WORLD FOR YOU. BUT BE WARNED THAT THINGS ARE NOT ALWAYS WHAT THEY SEEM TO BE...

HOW WE SURVIVED

I AM LAA LONGTOOTH FROM THE CLAN OF THE EYE AND I LIVE ON TELARIS.

IT IS THE TIME FOR MY TESTING. TO PROVE MY WORTH AS A HUNTER TO MY CLAN.

TO TRACK AND FIND A SMARGH IS EASY...

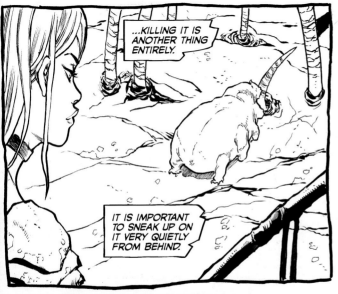

...KILLING IT IS ANOTHER THING ENTIRELY.

IT IS IMPORTANT TO SNEAK UP ON IT VERY QUIETLY FROM BEHIND.

AND YOU NEED TO PLUNGE THE SPEAR DEEP SO THAT IT PIERCES BOTH HEARTS BEFORE IT KNOWS YOU ARE THERE, OR ELSE--

Script by LARRY HAMA / Art by TIM SEELEY

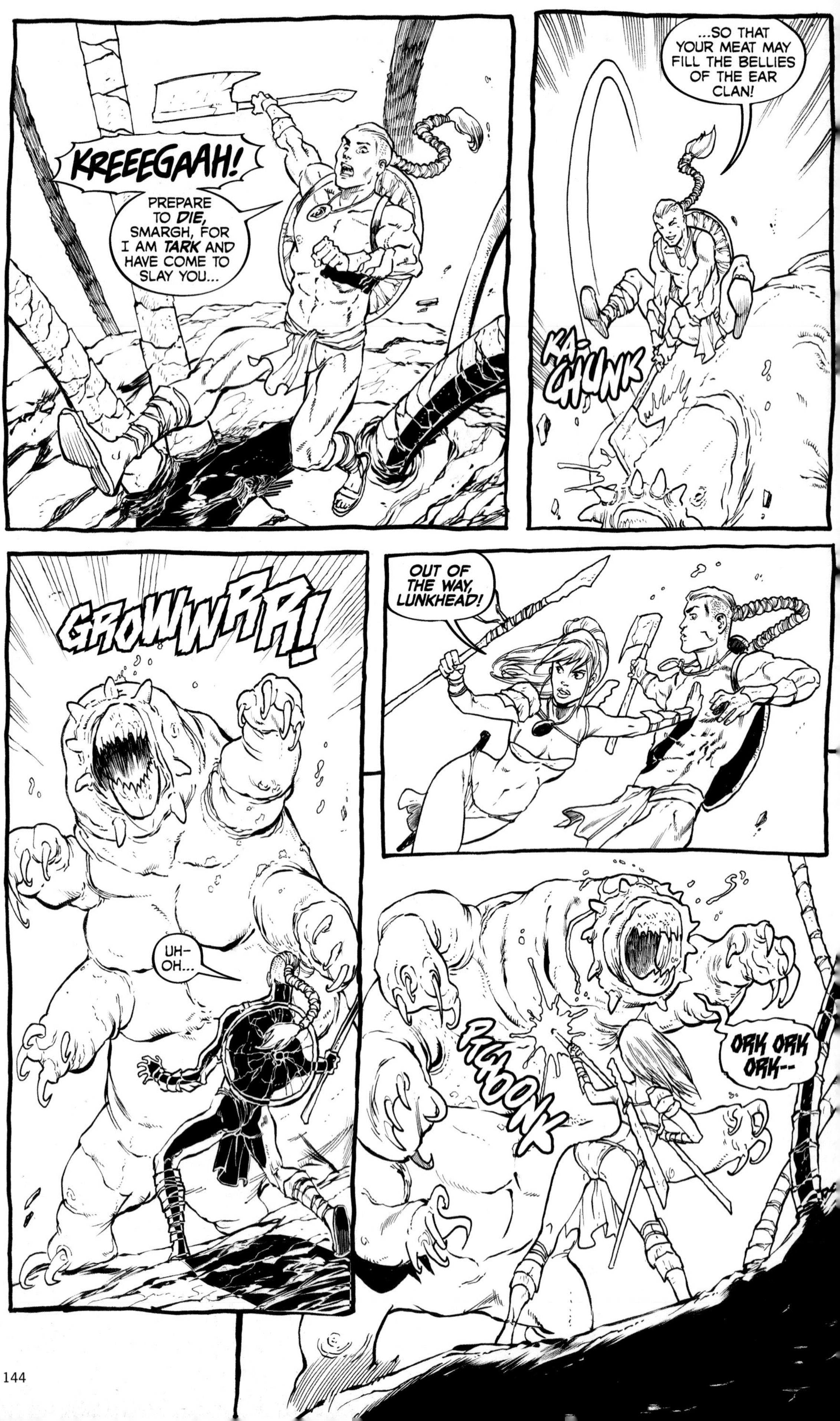
KREEEGAAH!
PREPARE TO DIE, SMARGH, FOR I AM TARK AND HAVE COME TO SLAY YOU...
...SO THAT YOUR MEAT MAY FILL THE BELLIES OF THE EAR CLAN!
KA-CHUNK
GROWWRR!
UH-OH...
OUT OF THE WAY, LUNKHEAD!
PLOONK
ORK ORK ORK--

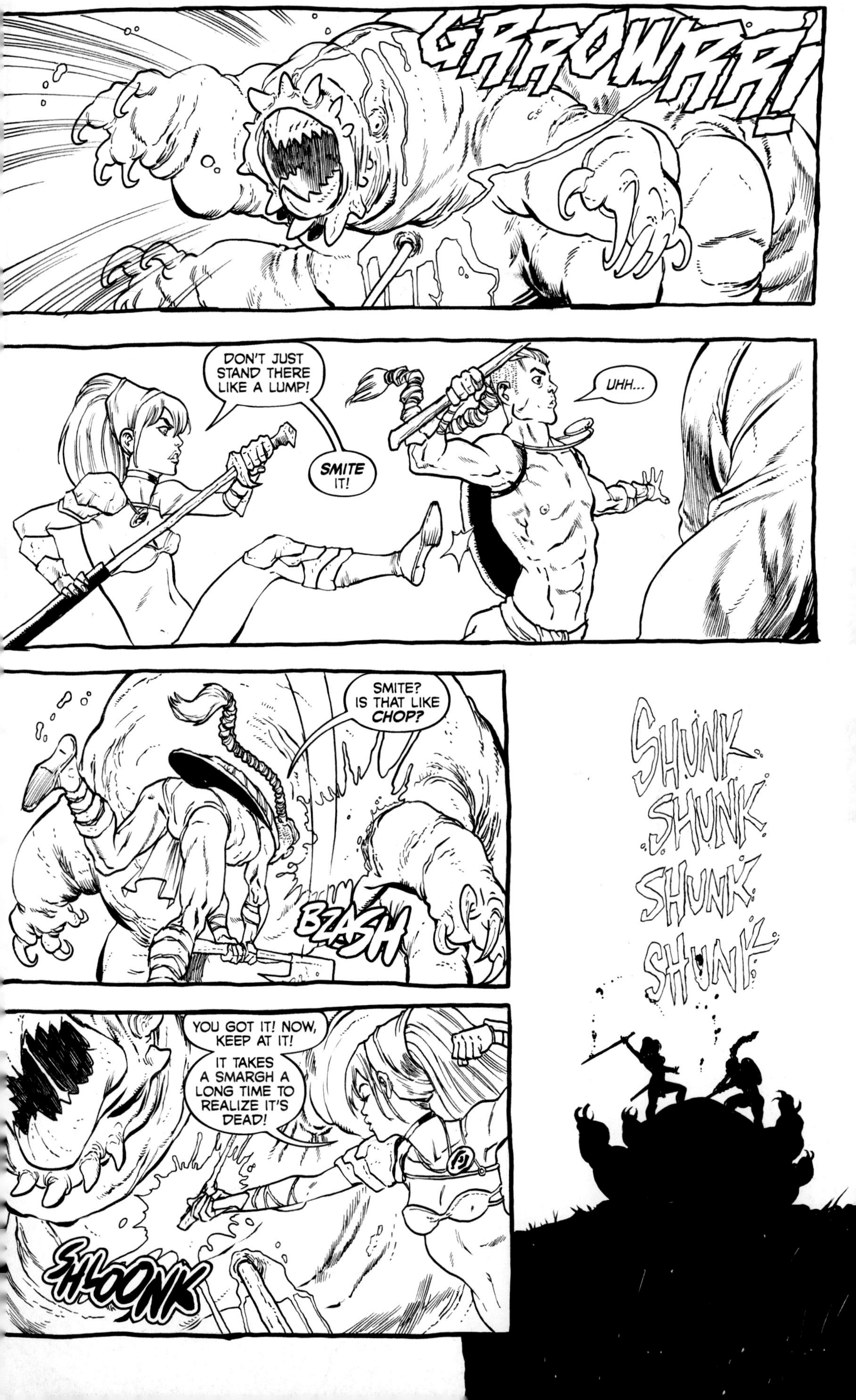
GROWRR!
DON'T JUST STAND THERE LIKE A LUMP!
SMITE IT!
UHH...
SMITE? IS THAT LIKE CHOP?
BZASH
SHUNK
SHUNK
SHUNK
SHUNK
YOU GOT IT! NOW, KEEP AT IT!
IT TAKES A SMARGH A LONG TIME TO REALIZE IT'S DEAD!
SHLOONK

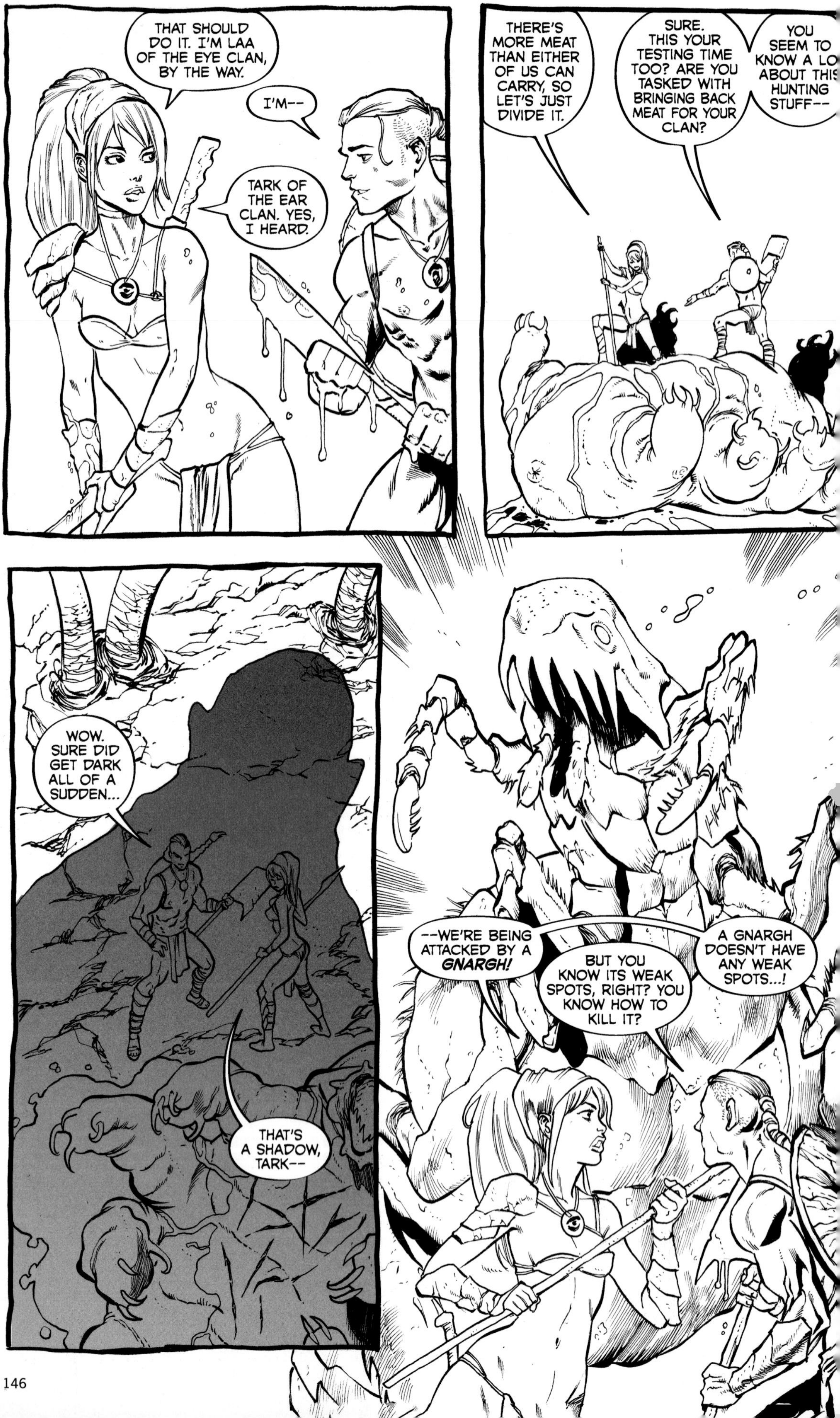
THAT SHOULD DO IT. I'M LAA OF THE EYE CLAN, BY THE WAY.
I'M--
TARK OF THE EAR CLAN. YES, I HEARD.
THERE'S MORE MEAT THAN EITHER OF US CAN CARRY, SO LET'S JUST DIVIDE IT.
SURE. THIS YOUR TESTING TIME TOO? ARE YOU TASKED WITH BRINGING BACK MEAT FOR YOUR CLAN?
YOU SEEM TO KNOW A LO ABOUT THIS HUNTING STUFF--
WOW. SURE DID GET DARK ALL OF A SUDDEN...
THAT'S A SHADOW, TARK--
--WE'RE BEING ATTACKED BY A *GNARGH!*
A GNARGH DOESN'T HAVE ANY WEAK SPOTS...!
BUT YOU KNOW ITS WEAK SPOTS, RIGHT? YOU KNOW HOW TO KILL IT?

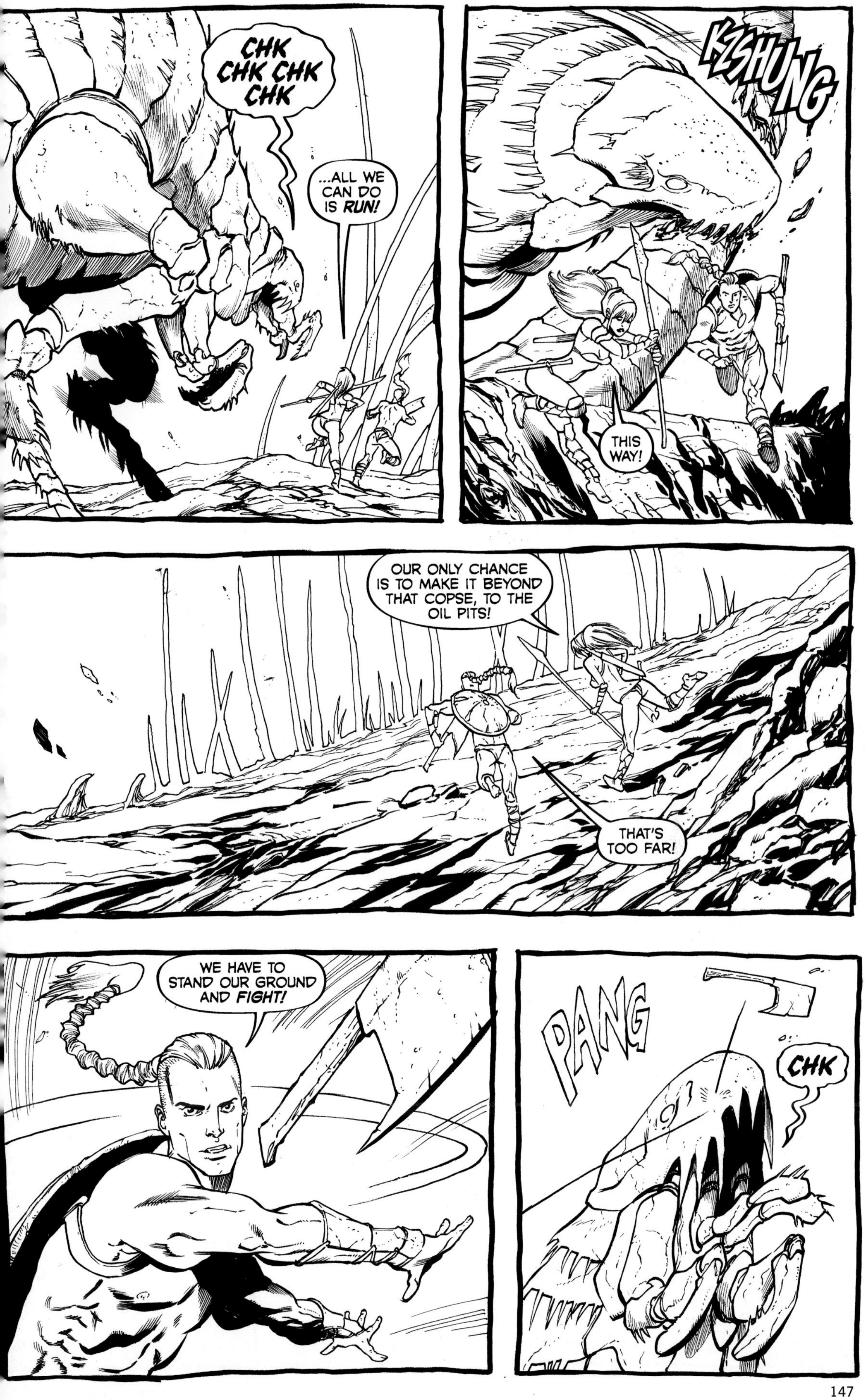
CHK CHK CHK CHK
...ALL WE CAN DO IS *RUN!*
KZSHUNG
THIS WAY!
OUR ONLY CHANCE IS TO MAKE IT BEYOND THAT COPSE, TO THE OIL PITS!
THAT'S TOO FAR!
WE HAVE TO STAND OUR GROUND AND *FIGHT!*
PANG
CHK

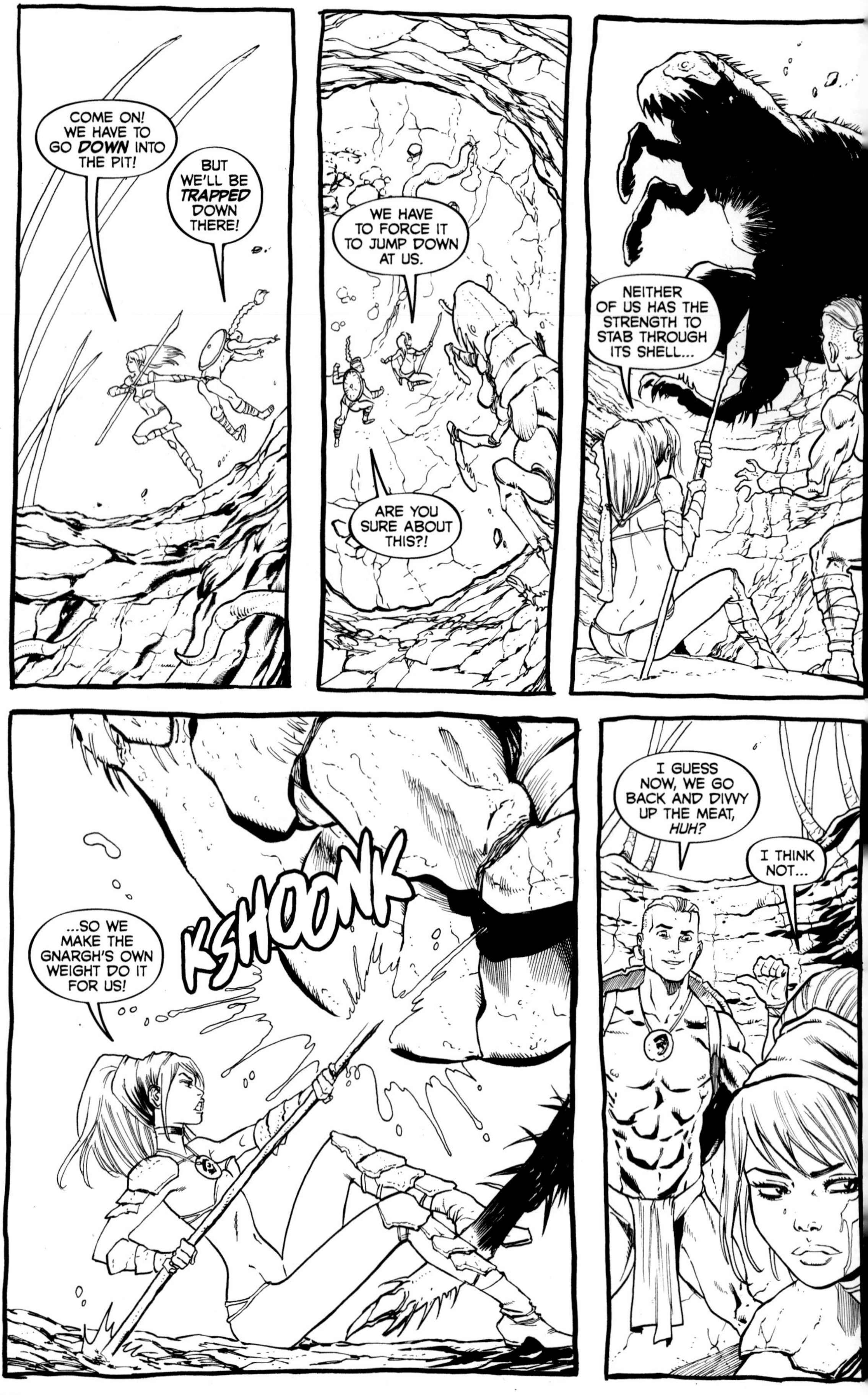

COME ON! WE HAVE TO GO DOWN INTO THE PIT!
BUT WE'LL BE TRAPPED DOWN THERE!
WE HAVE TO FORCE IT TO JUMP DOWN AT US.
ARE YOU SURE ABOUT THIS?!
NEITHER OF US HAS THE STRENGTH TO STAB THROUGH ITS SHELL...
...SO WE MAKE THE GNARGH'S OWN WEIGHT DO IT FOR US!
KSHOONK
I GUESS NOW, WE GO BACK AND DIVVY UP THE MEAT, HUH?
I THINK NOT...

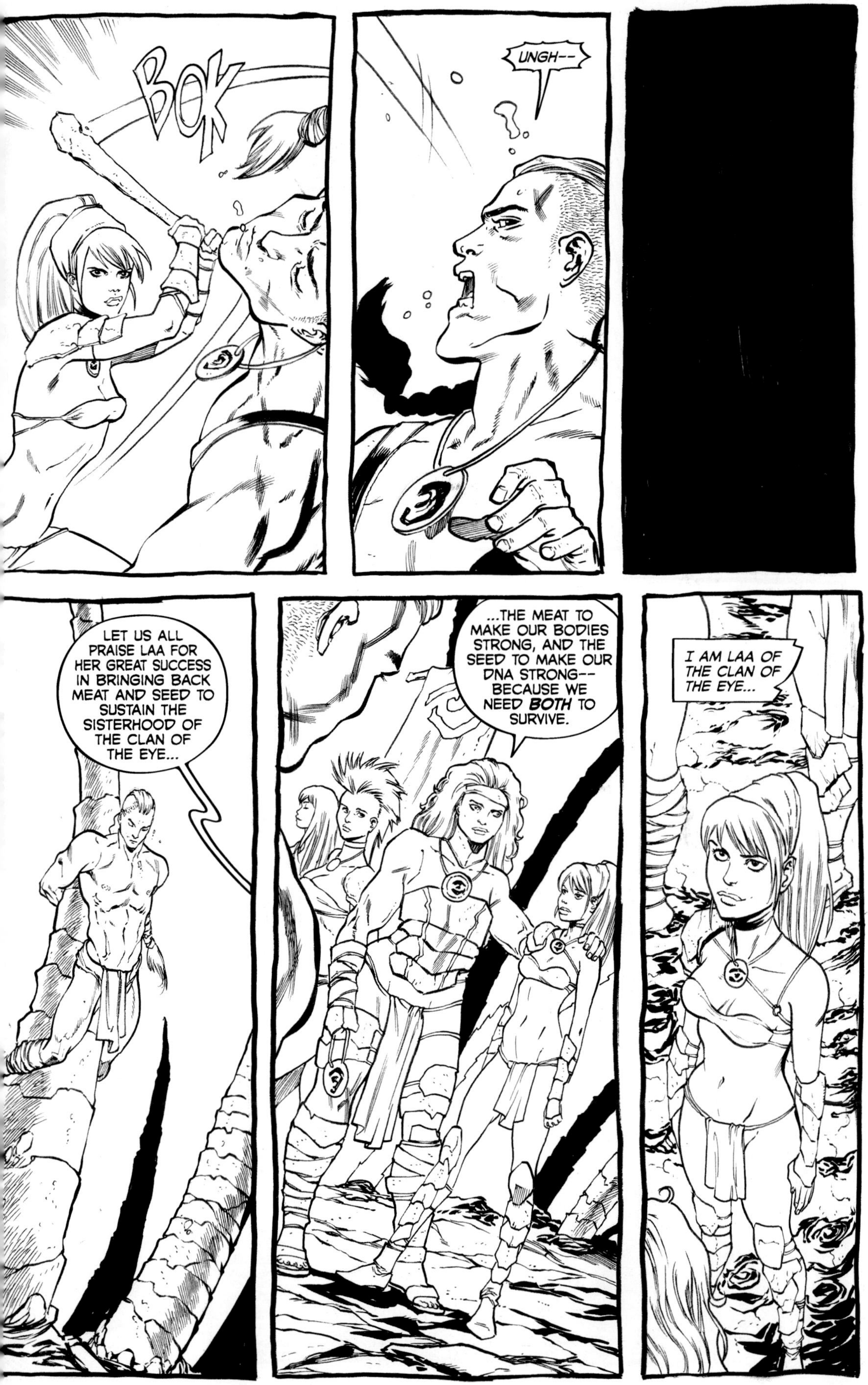
BOK
UNGH--
LET US ALL PRAISE LAA FOR HER GREAT SUCCESS IN BRINGING BACK MEAT AND SEED TO SUSTAIN THE SISTERHOOD OF THE CLAN OF THE EYE...
...THE MEAT TO MAKE OUR BODIES STRONG, AND THE SEED TO MAKE OUR DNA STRONG-- BECAUSE WE NEED BOTH TO SURVIVE.
I AM LAA OF THE CLAN OF THE EYE...

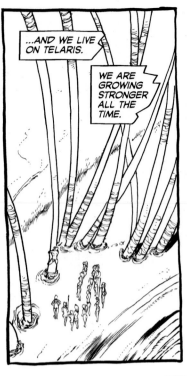

...AND WE LIVE ON TELARIS.

WE ARE GROWING STRONGER ALL THE TIME.

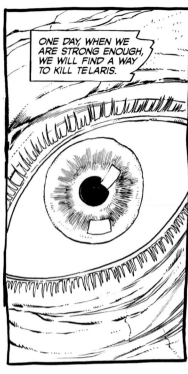

ONE DAY, WHEN WE ARE STRONG ENOUGH, WE WILL FIND A WAY TO KILL TELARIS.

THEN WE WILL KILL ALL THE OTHERS, AND WE WILL RECLAIM THE EARTH.

BUT THAT IS FOR THE FUTURE.

FOR NOW, WE WORK ON GROWING STRONG.

SORT OF MAKES YOU WONDER HOW MANY EONS IT WOULD TAKE FOR HEAD LICE TO DEVELOP TACTICAL NUKES, DOESN'T IT? ON THE OTHER HAND, IT MIGHT ONLY TAKE A FEW MUTATIONS FOR INTESTINAL BACTERIA TO START PRODUCING NERVE TOXINS. THOSE PESKY LITTLE ONE-CELLED ORGANISMS RULED THIS PLANET FOR THREE BILLION YEARS BEFORE ANYTHING WITH A CENTRAL NERVOUS SYSTEM CAME ALONG, SO IT'S HIGH TIME THEY GOT AROUND TO TAKING BACK WHAT'S THEIRS!

END

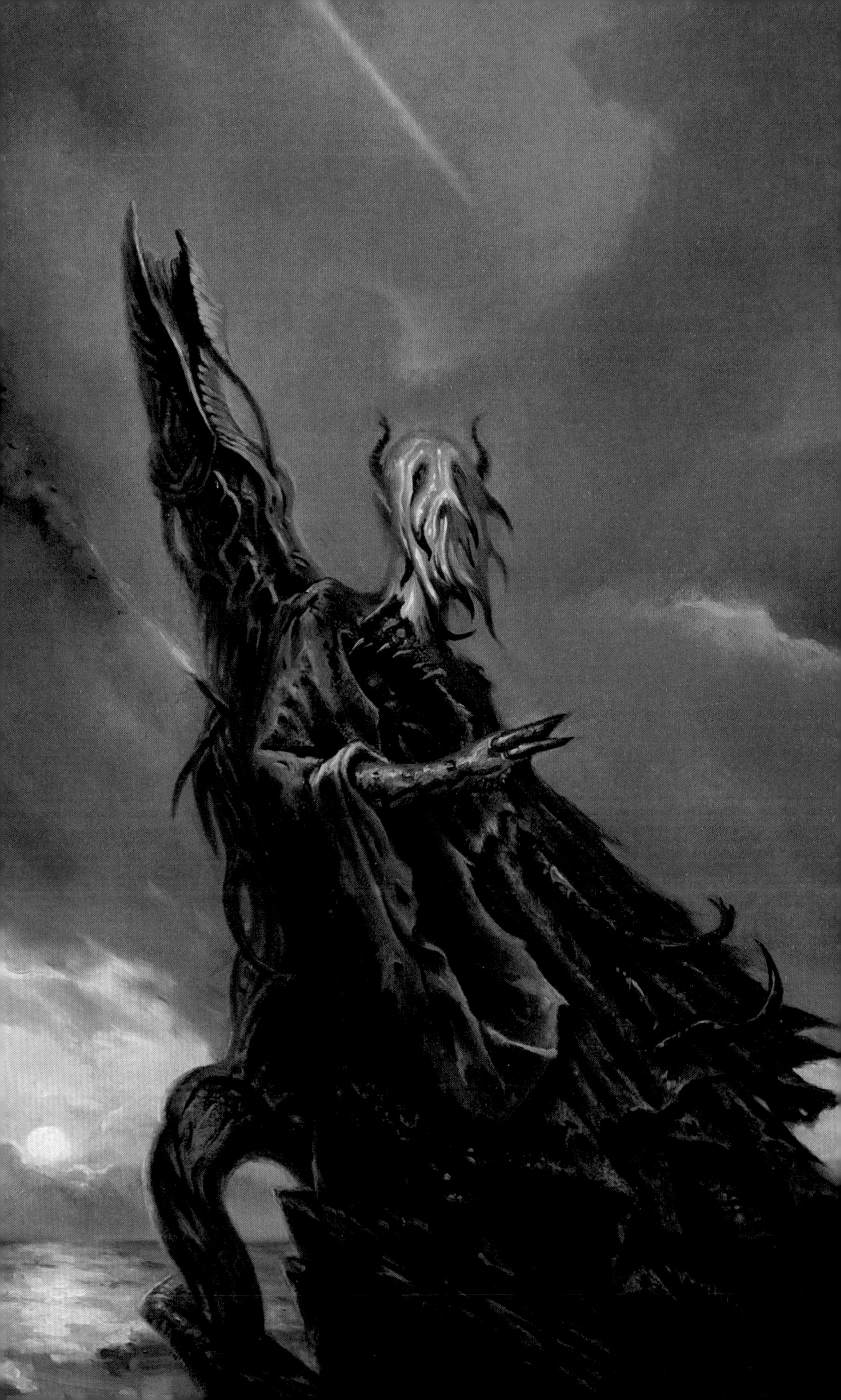

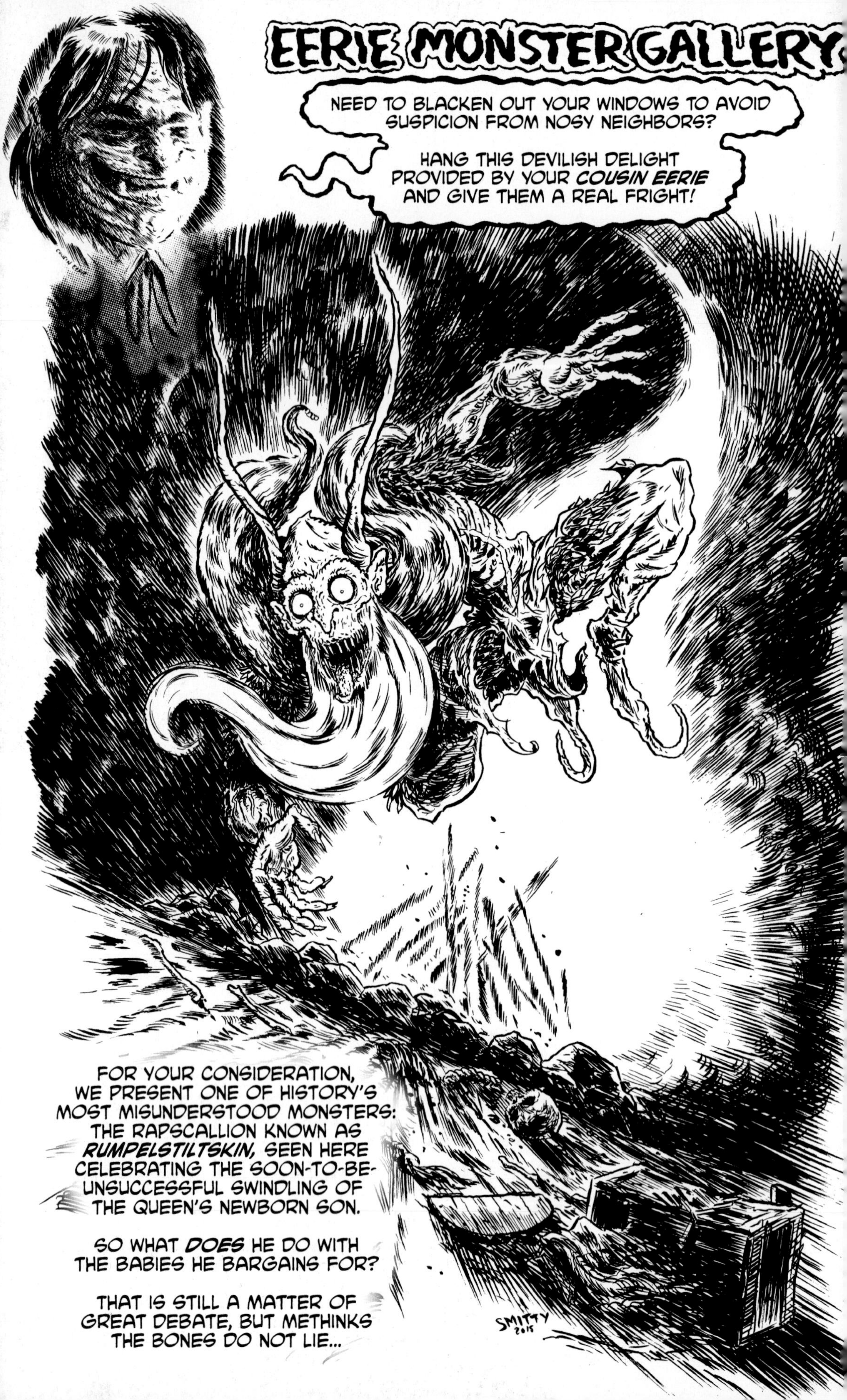
EERIE MONSTER GALLERY
NEED TO BLACKEN OUT YOUR WINDOWS TO AVOID SUSPICION FROM NOSY NEIGHBORS?
HANG THIS DEVILISH DELIGHT PROVIDED BY YOUR *COUSIN EERIE* AND GIVE THEM A REAL FRIGHT!
FOR YOUR CONSIDERATION, WE PRESENT ONE OF HISTORY'S MOST MISUNDERSTOOD MONSTERS: THE RAPSCALLION KNOWN AS *RUMPELSTILTSKIN,* SEEN HERE CELEBRATING THE SOON-TO-BE-UNSUCCESSFUL SWINDLING OF THE QUEEN'S NEWBORN SON.
SO WHAT *DOES* HE DO WITH THE BABIES HE BARGAINS FOR?
THAT IS STILL A MATTER OF GREAT DEBATE, BUT METHINKS THE BONES DO NOT LIE...
SMITTY 2015

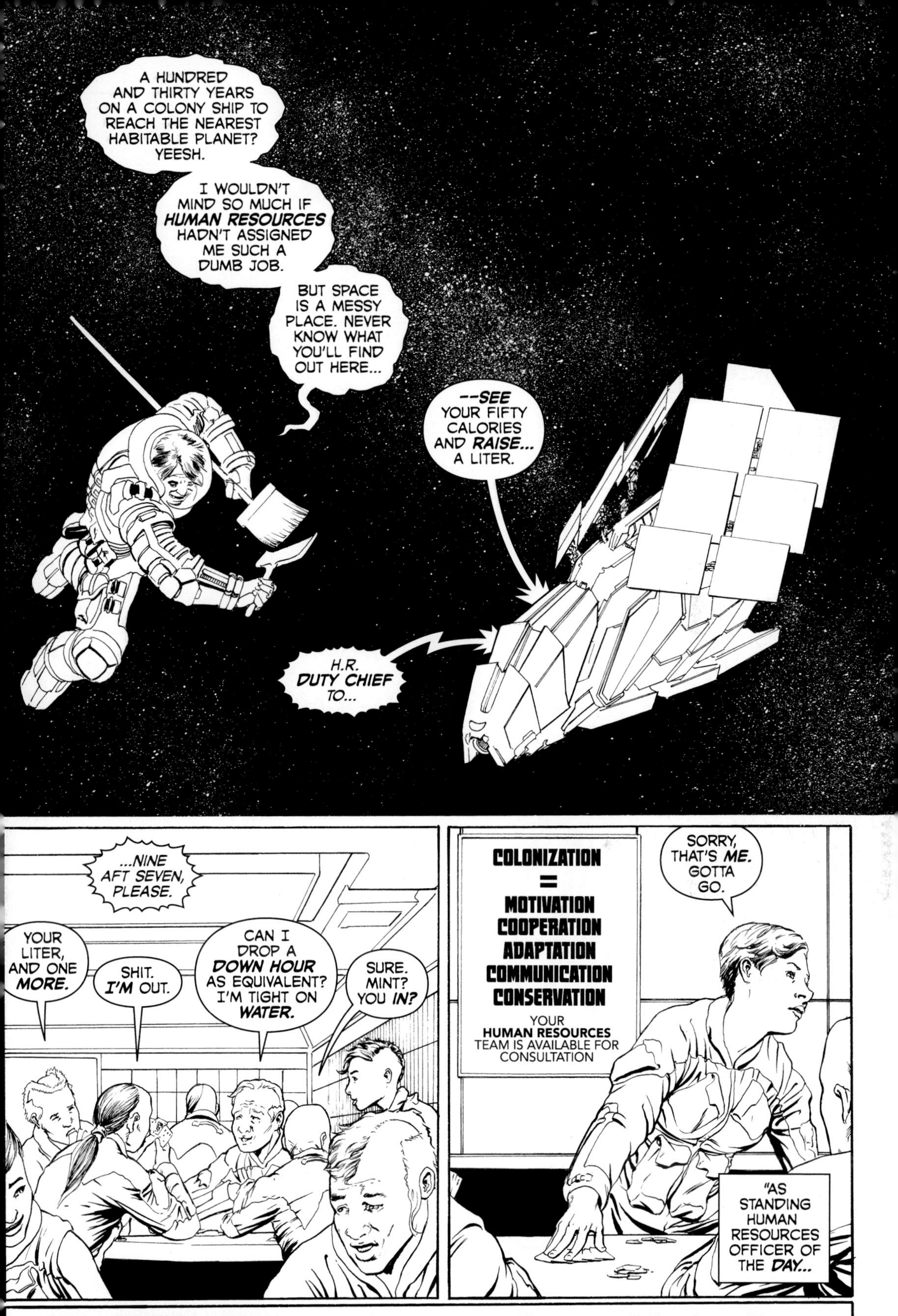
A HUNDRED AND THIRTY YEARS ON A COLONY SHIP TO REACH THE NEAREST HABITABLE PLANET? YEESH.
I WOULDN'T MIND SO MUCH IF HUMAN RESOURCES HADN'T ASSIGNED ME SUCH A DUMB JOB.
BUT SPACE IS A MESSY PLACE. NEVER KNOW WHAT YOU'LL FIND OUT HERE...
--SEE YOUR FIFTY CALORIES AND RAISE... A LITER.
H.R. DUTY CHIEF TO...
...NINE AFT SEVEN, PLEASE.
YOUR LITER, AND ONE MORE.
SHIT. I'M OUT.
CAN I DROP A DOWN HOUR AS EQUIVALENT? I'M TIGHT ON WATER.
SURE. MINT? YOU IN?
COLONIZATION = MOTIVATION COOPERATION ADAPTATION COMMUNICATION CONSERVATION
YOUR HUMAN RESOURCES TEAM IS AVAILABLE FOR CONSULTATION
SORRY, THAT'S ME. GOTTA GO.
"AS STANDING HUMAN RESOURCES OFFICER OF THE DAY...

HUMAN RESOURCES

Script by JEN VAN METER / Art by TONY PARKER

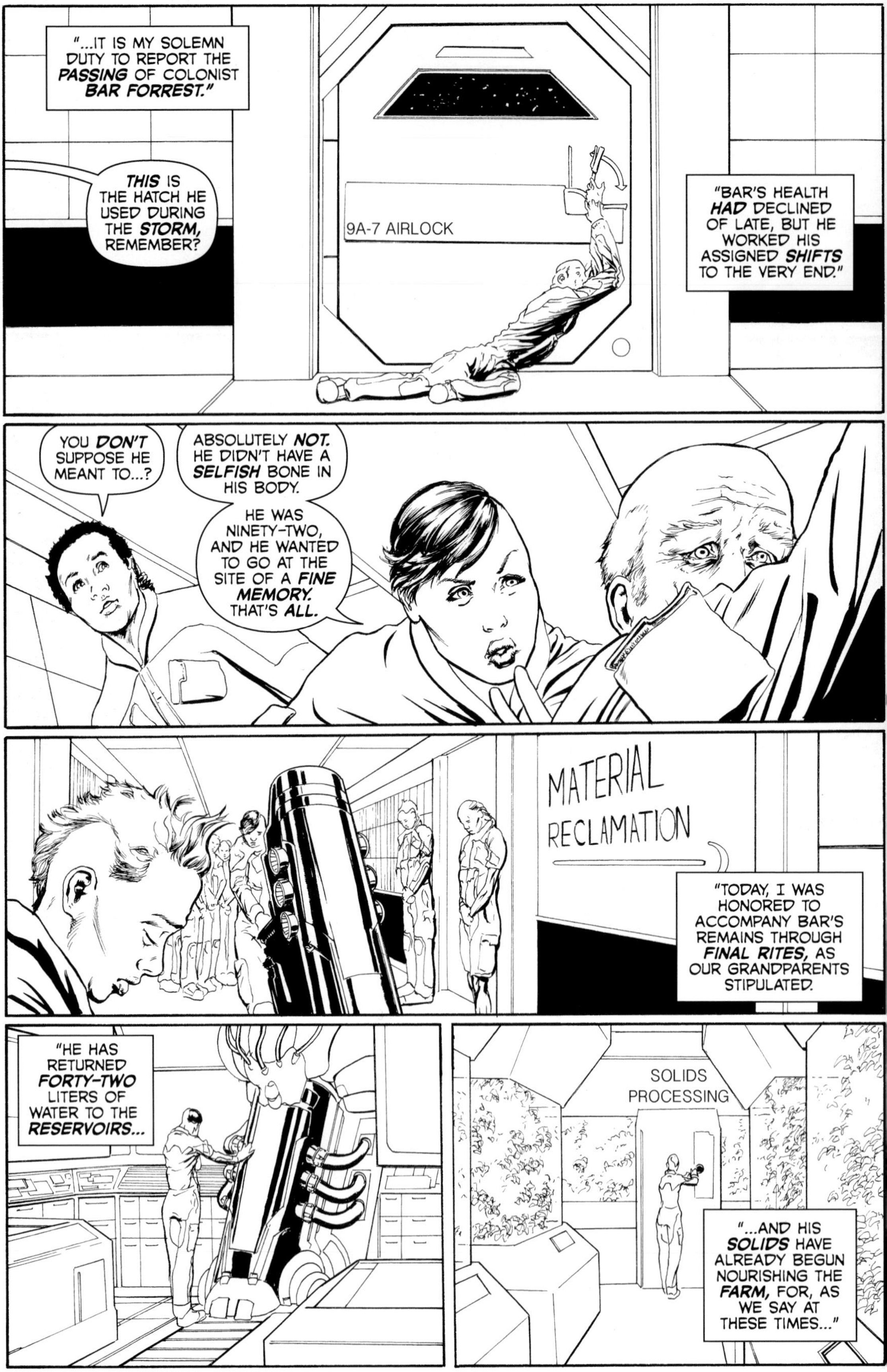
"...IT IS MY SOLEMN DUTY TO REPORT THE PASSING OF COLONIST BAR FORREST."
THIS IS THE HATCH HE USED DURING THE STORM, REMEMBER?
9A-7 AIRLOCK
"BAR'S HEALTH HAD DECLINED OF LATE, BUT HE WORKED HIS ASSIGNED SHIFTS TO THE VERY END."
YOU DON'T SUPPOSE HE MEANT TO...?
ABSOLUTELY NOT. HE DIDN'T HAVE A SELFISH BONE IN HIS BODY.
HE WAS NINETY-TWO, AND HE WANTED TO GO AT THE SITE OF A FINE MEMORY. THAT'S ALL.
MATERIAL RECLAMATION
"TODAY, I WAS HONORED TO ACCOMPANY BAR'S REMAINS THROUGH FINAL RITES, AS OUR GRANDPARENTS STIPULATED.
"HE HAS RETURNED FORTY-TWO LITERS OF WATER TO THE RESERVOIRS...
SOLIDS PROCESSING
"...AND HIS SOLIDS HAVE ALREADY BEGUN NOURISHING THE FARM, FOR, AS WE SAY AT THESE TIMES..."

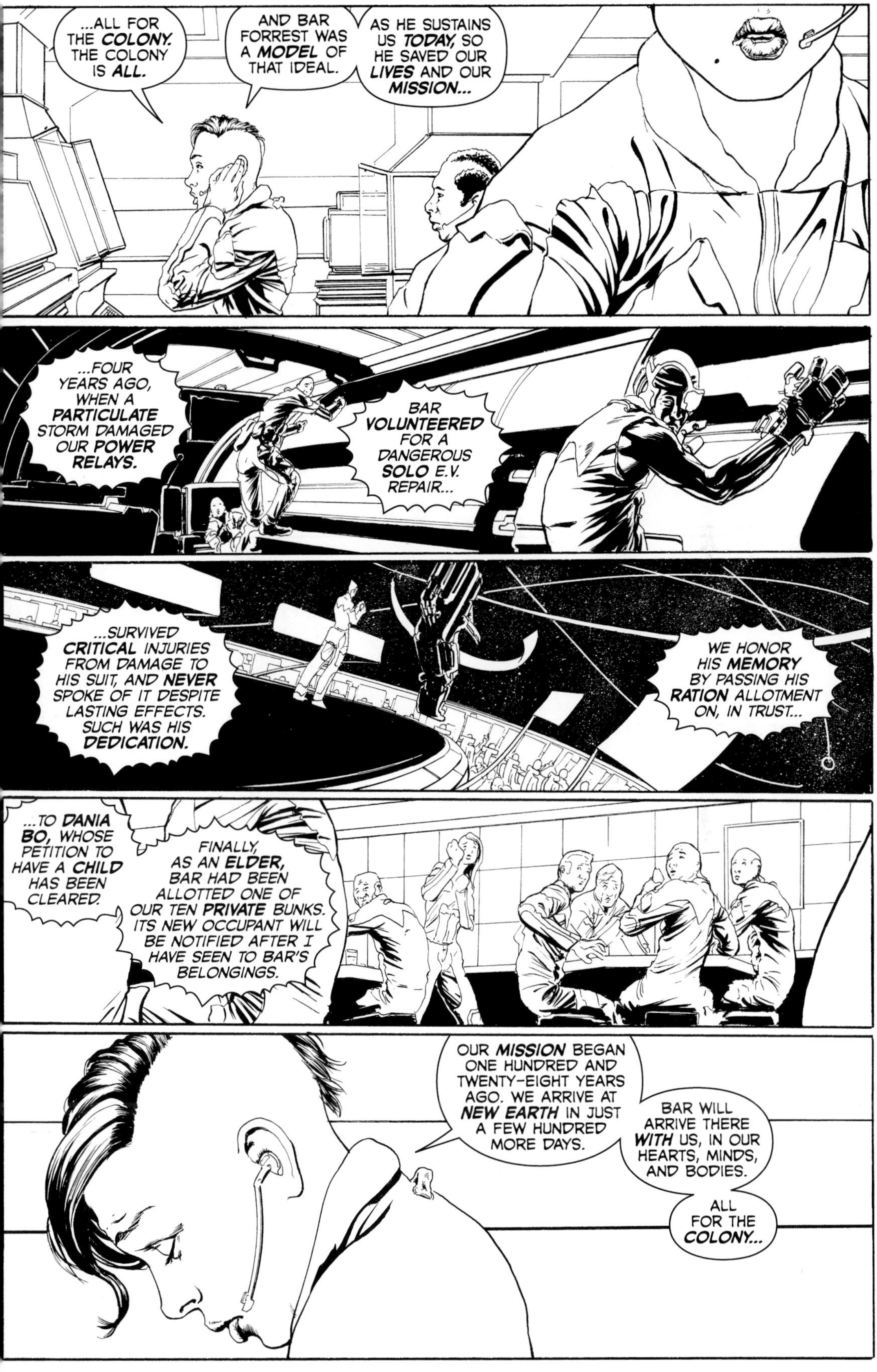
...ALL FOR THE COLONY. THE COLONY IS ALL.
AND BAR FORREST WAS A MODEL OF THAT IDEAL.
AS HE SUSTAINS US TODAY, SO HE SAVED OUR LIVES AND OUR MISSION...
...FOUR YEARS AGO, WHEN A PARTICULATE STORM DAMAGED OUR POWER RELAYS.
BAR VOLUNTEERED FOR A DANGEROUS SOLO E.V. REPAIR...
...SURVIVED CRITICAL INJURIES FROM DAMAGE TO HIS SUIT, AND NEVER SPOKE OF IT DESPITE LASTING EFFECTS. SUCH WAS HIS DEDICATION.
WE HONOR HIS MEMORY BY PASSING HIS RATION ALLOTMENT ON, IN TRUST...
...TO DANIA BO, WHOSE PETITION TO HAVE A CHILD HAS BEEN CLEARED.
FINALLY, AS AN ELDER, BAR HAD BEEN ALLOTTED ONE OF OUR TEN PRIVATE BUNKS. ITS NEW OCCUPANT WILL BE NOTIFIED AFTER I HAVE SEEN TO BAR'S BELONGINGS.
OUR MISSION BEGAN ONE HUNDRED AND TWENTY-EIGHT YEARS AGO. WE ARRIVE AT NEW EARTH IN JUST A FEW HUNDRED MORE DAYS.
BAR WILL ARRIVE THERE WITH US, IN OUR HEARTS, MINDS, AND BODIES.
ALL FOR THE COLONY...

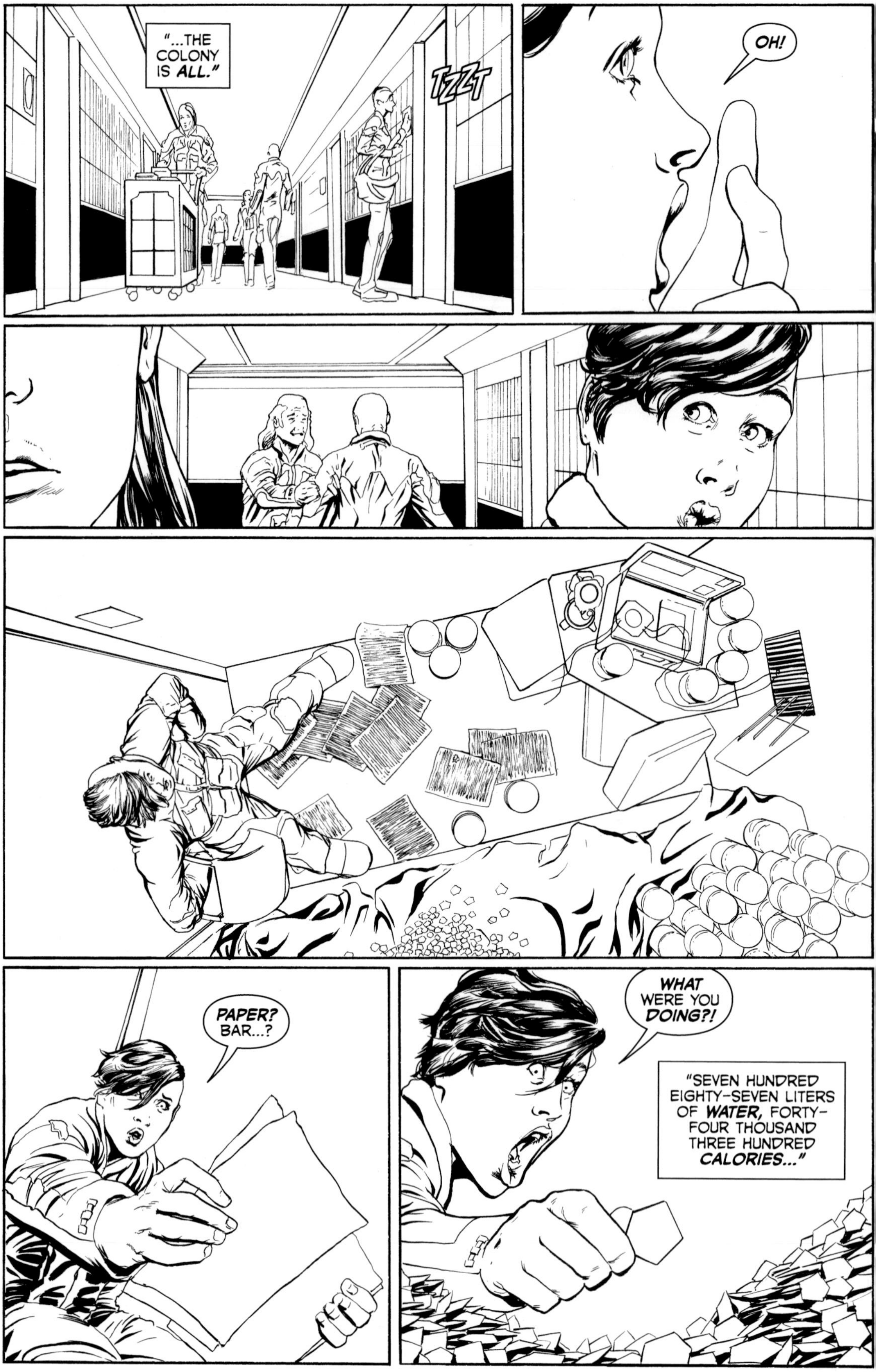
"...THE COLONY IS ALL."
TZZT
OH!
PAPER? BAR...?
WHAT WERE YOU DOING?!
"SEVEN HUNDRED EIGHTY-SEVEN LITERS OF WATER, FORTY-FOUR THOUSAND THREE HUNDRED CALORIES..."

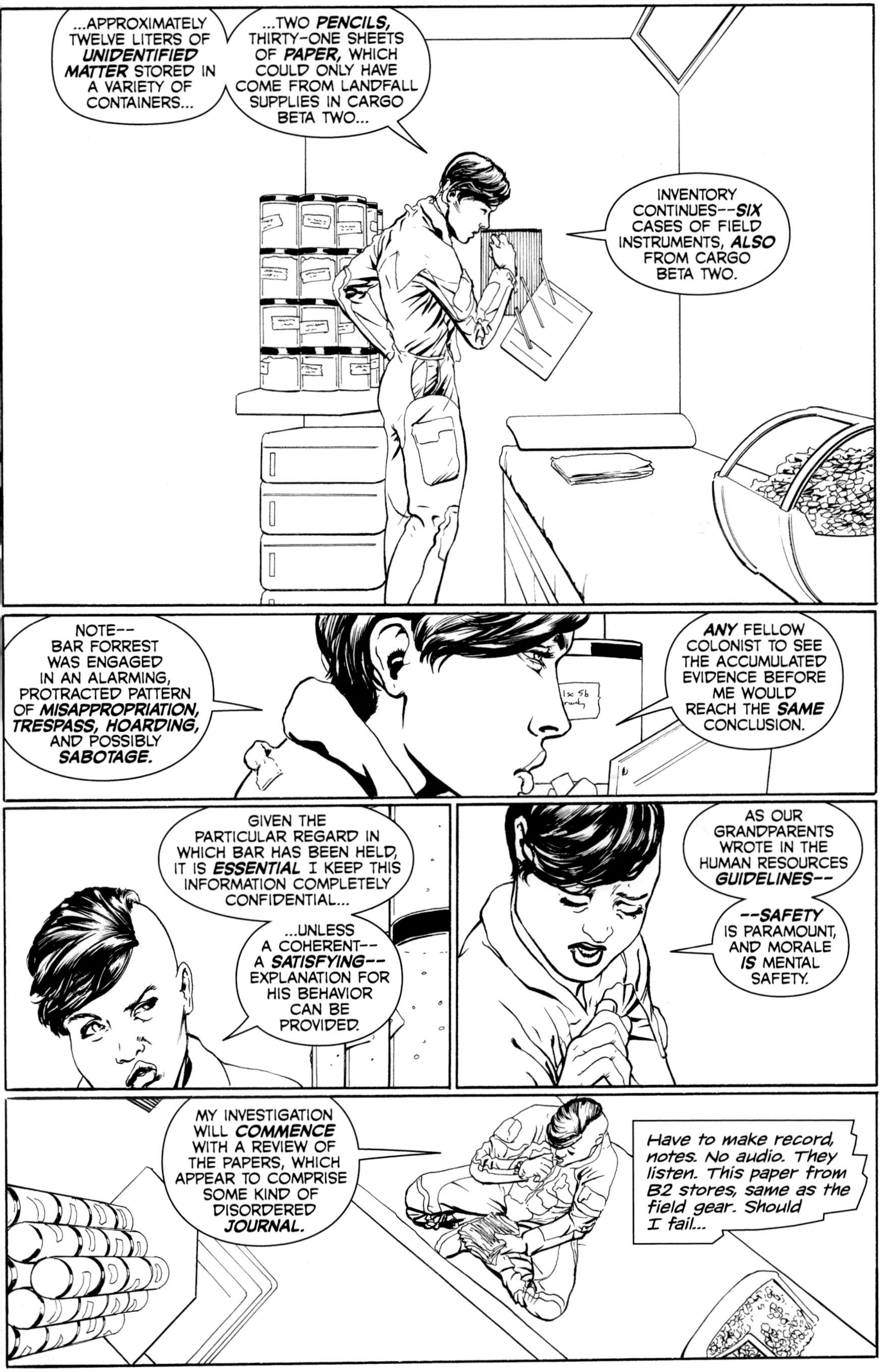
...APPROXIMATELY TWELVE LITERS OF UNIDENTIFIED MATTER STORED IN A VARIETY OF CONTAINERS...
...TWO PENCILS, THIRTY-ONE SHEETS OF PAPER, WHICH COULD ONLY HAVE COME FROM LANDFALL SUPPLIES IN CARGO BETA TWO...
INVENTORY CONTINUES--SIX CASES OF FIELD INSTRUMENTS, ALSO FROM CARGO BETA TWO.
NOTE-- BAR FORREST WAS ENGAGED IN AN ALARMING, PROTRACTED PATTERN OF MISAPPROPRIATION, TRESPASS, HOARDING, AND POSSIBLY SABOTAGE.
ANY FELLOW COLONIST TO SEE THE ACCUMULATED EVIDENCE BEFORE ME WOULD REACH THE SAME CONCLUSION.
GIVEN THE PARTICULAR REGARD IN WHICH BAR HAS BEEN HELD, IT IS ESSENTIAL I KEEP THIS INFORMATION COMPLETELY CONFIDENTIAL...
...UNLESS A COHERENT-- A SATISFYING-- EXPLANATION FOR HIS BEHAVIOR CAN BE PROVIDED.
AS OUR GRANDPARENTS WROTE IN THE HUMAN RESOURCES GUIDELINES--
--SAFETY IS PARAMOUNT, AND MORALE IS MENTAL SAFETY.
MY INVESTIGATION WILL COMMENCE WITH A REVIEW OF THE PAPERS, WHICH APPEAR TO COMPRISE SOME KIND OF DISORDERED JOURNAL.
Have to make record, notes. No audio. They listen. This paper from B2 stores, same as the field gear. Should I fail...

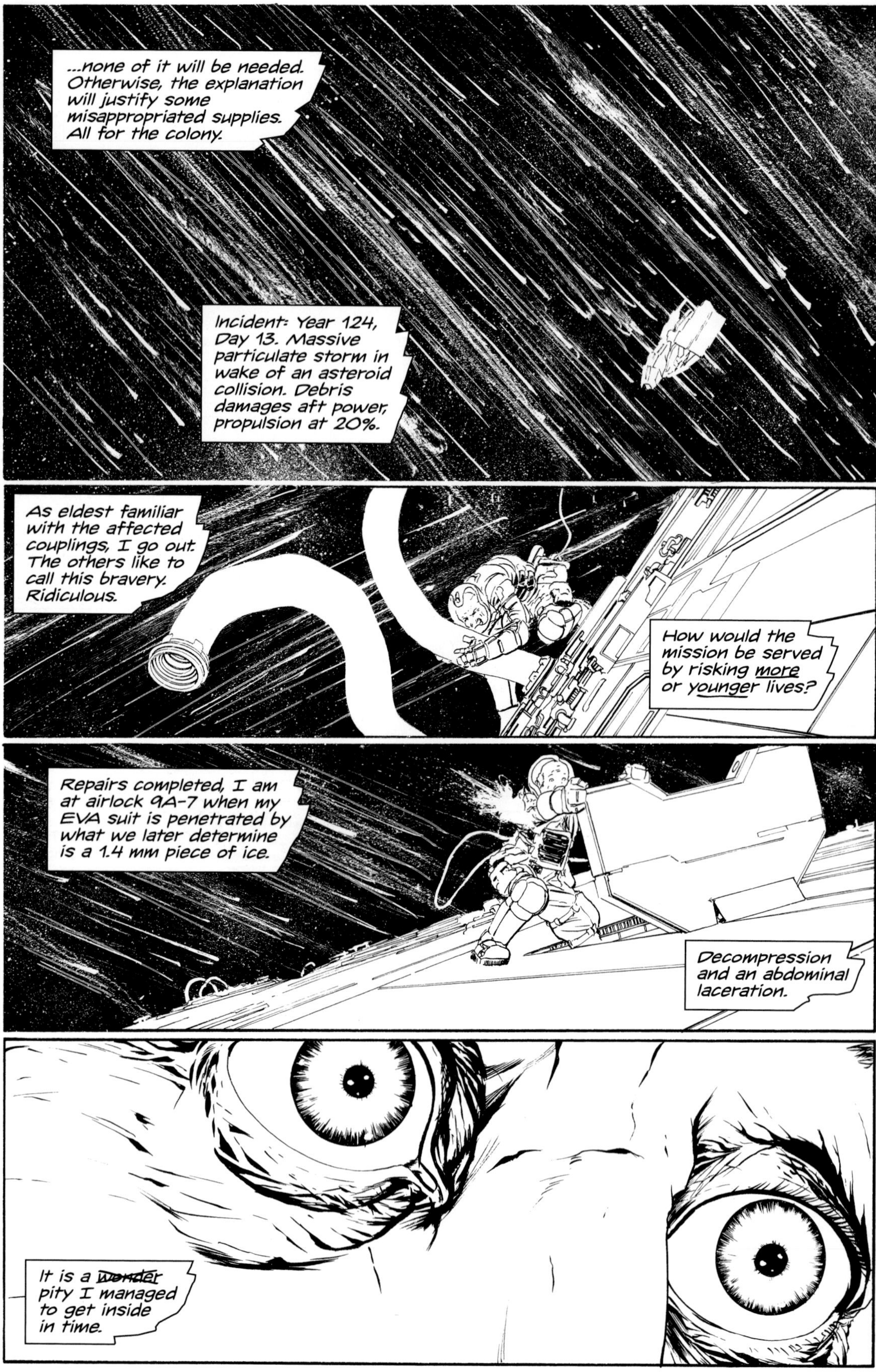
...none of it will be needed. Otherwise, the explanation will justify some misappropriated supplies. All for the colony.
Incident: Year 124, Day 13. Massive particulate storm in wake of an asteroid collision. Debris damages aft power, propulsion at 20%.
As eldest familiar with the affected couplings, I go out. The others like to call this bravery. Ridiculous.
How would the mission be served by risking more or younger lives?
Repairs completed, I am at airlock 9A-7 when my EVA suit is penetrated by what we later determine is a 1.4 mm piece of ice.
Decompression and an abdominal laceration.
It is a ~~wonder~~ pity I managed to get inside in time.

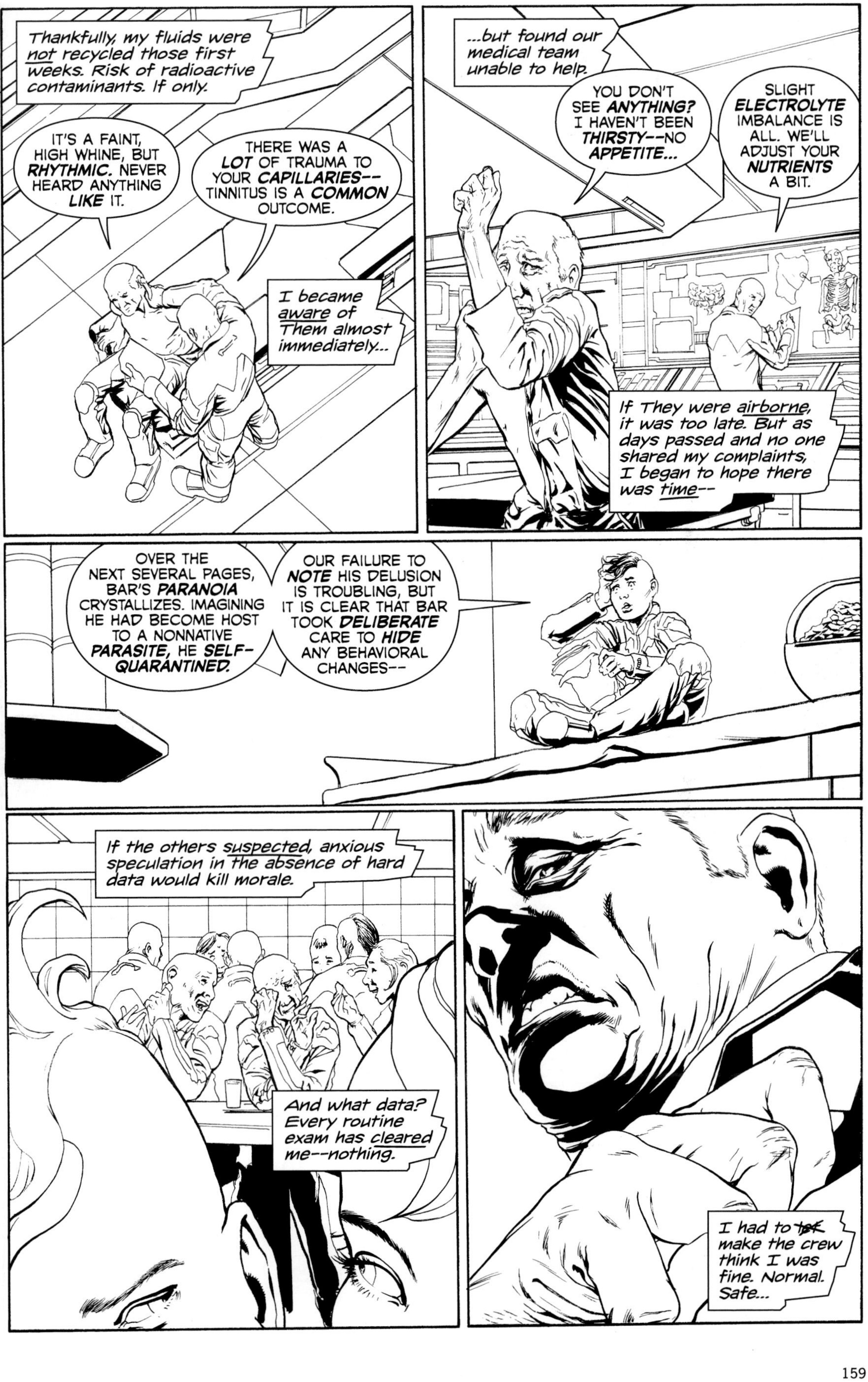

Thankfully, my fluids were not recycled those first weeks. Risk of radioactive contaminants. If only.
IT'S A FAINT, HIGH WHINE, BUT RHYTHMIC. NEVER HEARD ANYTHING LIKE IT.
THERE WAS A LOT OF TRAUMA TO YOUR CAPILLARIES--TINNITUS IS A COMMON OUTCOME.
I became aware of Them almost immediately...
...but found our medical team unable to help.
YOU DON'T SEE ANYTHING? I HAVEN'T BEEN THIRSTY--NO APPETITE...
SLIGHT ELECTROLYTE IMBALANCE IS ALL. WE'LL ADJUST YOUR NUTRIENTS A BIT.
If They were airborne, it was too late. But as days passed and no one shared my complaints, I began to hope there was time--
OVER THE NEXT SEVERAL PAGES, BAR'S PARANOIA CRYSTALLIZES. IMAGINING HE HAD BECOME HOST TO A NONNATIVE PARASITE, HE SELF-QUARANTINED.
OUR FAILURE TO NOTE HIS DELUSION IS TROUBLING, BUT IT IS CLEAR THAT BAR TOOK DELIBERATE CARE TO HIDE ANY BEHAVIORAL CHANGES--
If the others suspected, anxious speculation in the absence of hard data would kill morale.
And what data? Every routine exam has cleared me--nothing.
I had to ~~tek~~ make the crew think I was fine. Normal. Safe...

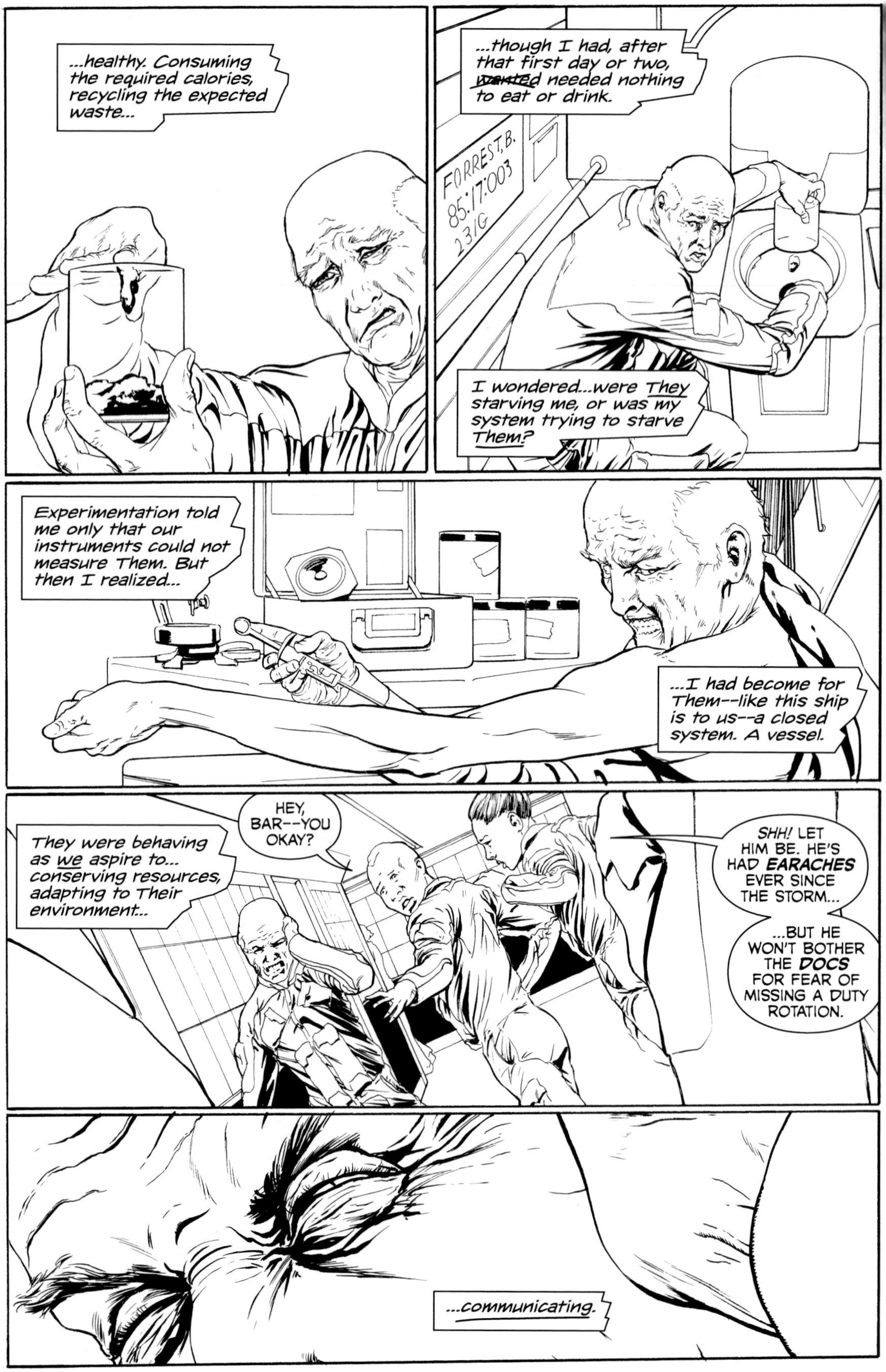
...healthy. Consuming the required calories, recycling the expected waste...
...though I had, after that first day or two, ~~wanted~~ needed nothing to eat or drink.
FORREST, B. 85:17:003 231G
I wondered...were They starving me, or was my system trying to starve Them?
Experimentation told me only that our instruments could not measure Them. But then I realized...
...I had become for Them--like this ship is to us--a closed system. A vessel.
They were behaving as we aspire to... conserving resources, adapting to Their environment...
HEY, BAR--YOU OKAY?
SHH! LET HIM BE. HE'S HAD EARACHES EVER SINCE THE STORM...
...BUT HE WON'T BOTHER THE DOCS FOR FEAR OF MISSING A DUTY ROTATION.
...communicating.

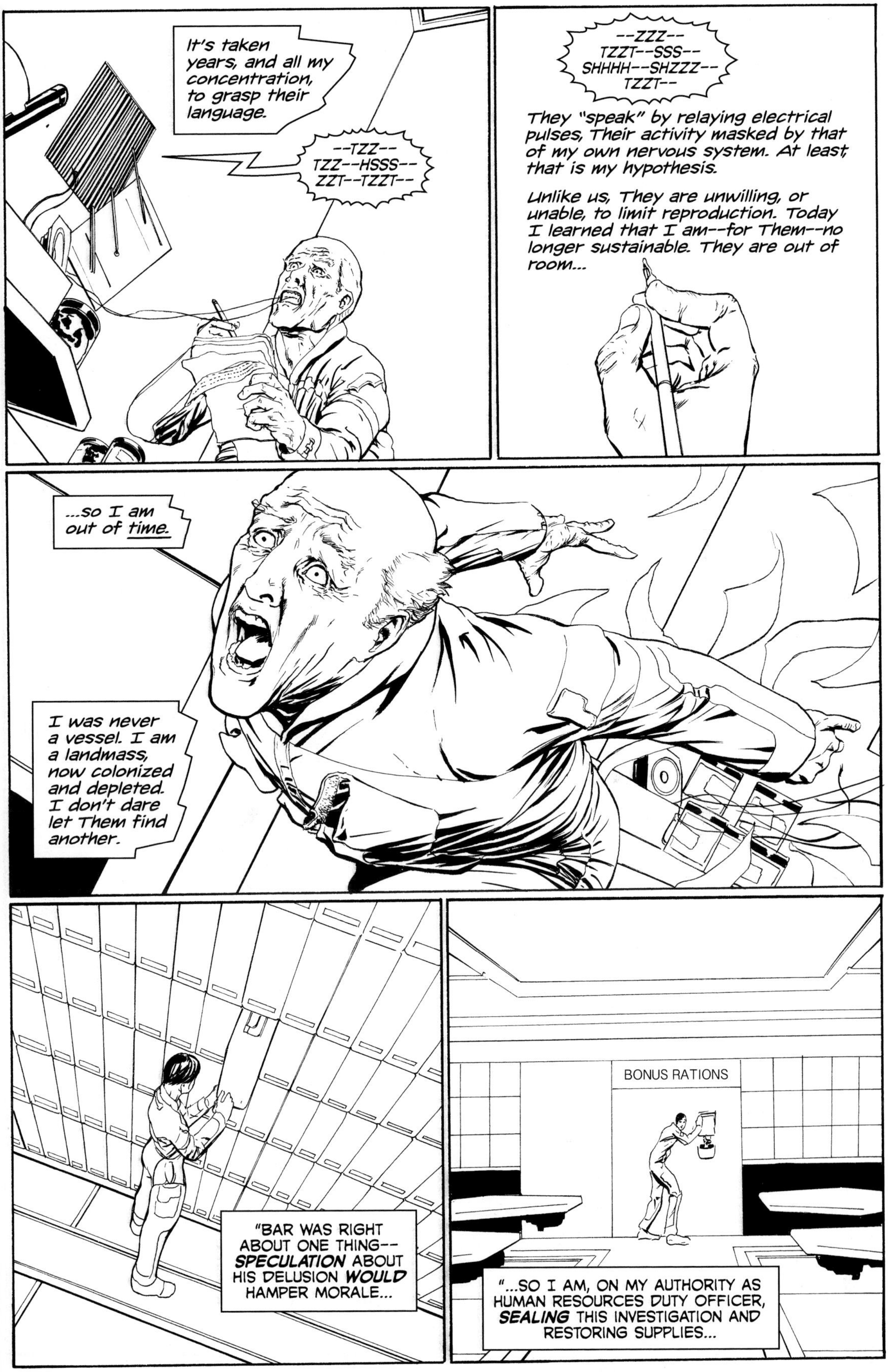
It's taken years, and all my concentration, to grasp their language.
--TZZ-- TZZ--HSSS-- ZZT--TZZT--
--ZZZ-- TZZT--SSS-- SHHHH--SHZZZ-- TZZT--
They "speak" by relaying electrical pulses, Their activity masked by that of my own nervous system. At least, that is my hypothesis.
Unlike us, They are unwilling, or unable, to limit reproduction. Today I learned that I am--for Them--no longer sustainable. They are out of room...
...so I am out of time.
I was never a vessel. I am a landmass, now colonized and depleted. I don't dare let Them find another.
"BAR WAS RIGHT ABOUT ONE THING--SPECULATION ABOUT HIS DELUSION WOULD HAMPER MORALE...
BONUS RATIONS
"...SO I AM, ON MY AUTHORITY AS HUMAN RESOURCES DUTY OFFICER, SEALING THIS INVESTIGATION AND RESTORING SUPPLIES...

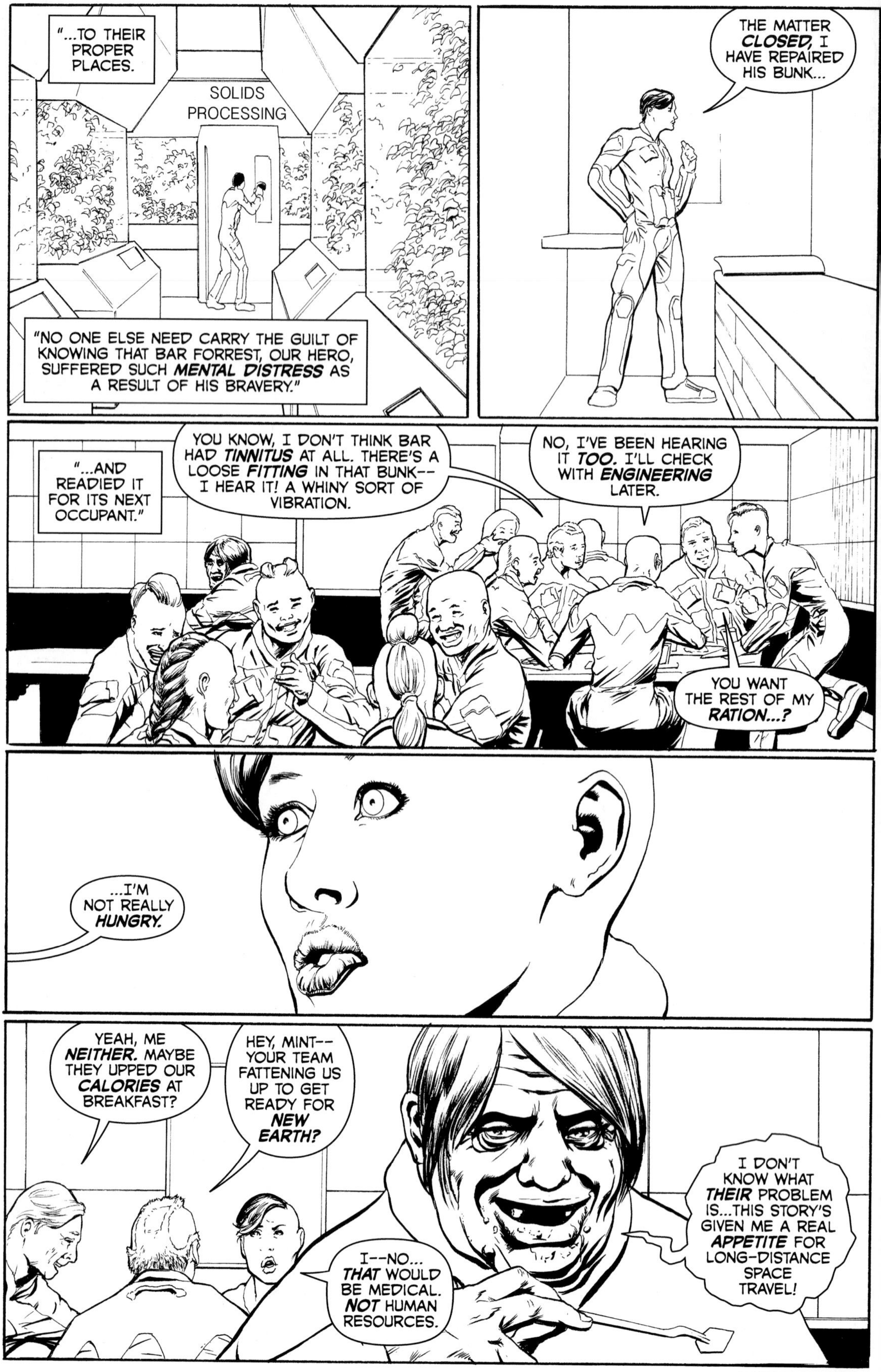
"...TO THEIR PROPER PLACES.
SOLIDS PROCESSING
"NO ONE ELSE NEED CARRY THE GUILT OF KNOWING THAT BAR FORREST, OUR HERO, SUFFERED SUCH MENTAL DISTRESS AS A RESULT OF HIS BRAVERY."
THE MATTER CLOSED, I HAVE REPAIRED HIS BUNK...
"...AND READIED IT FOR ITS NEXT OCCUPANT."
YOU KNOW, I DON'T THINK BAR HAD TINNITUS AT ALL. THERE'S A LOOSE FITTING IN THAT BUNK-- I HEAR IT! A WHINY SORT OF VIBRATION.
NO, I'VE BEEN HEARING IT TOO. I'LL CHECK WITH ENGINEERING LATER.
YOU WANT THE REST OF MY RATION...?
...I'M NOT REALLY HUNGRY.
YEAH, ME NEITHER. MAYBE THEY UPPED OUR CALORIES AT BREAKFAST?
HEY, MINT-- YOUR TEAM FATTENING US UP TO GET READY FOR NEW EARTH?
I--NO... THAT WOULD BE MEDICAL. NOT HUMAN RESOURCES.
I DON'T KNOW WHAT THEIR PROBLEM IS...THIS STORY'S GIVEN ME A REAL APPETITE FOR LONG-DISTANCE SPACE TRAVEL!

THE END

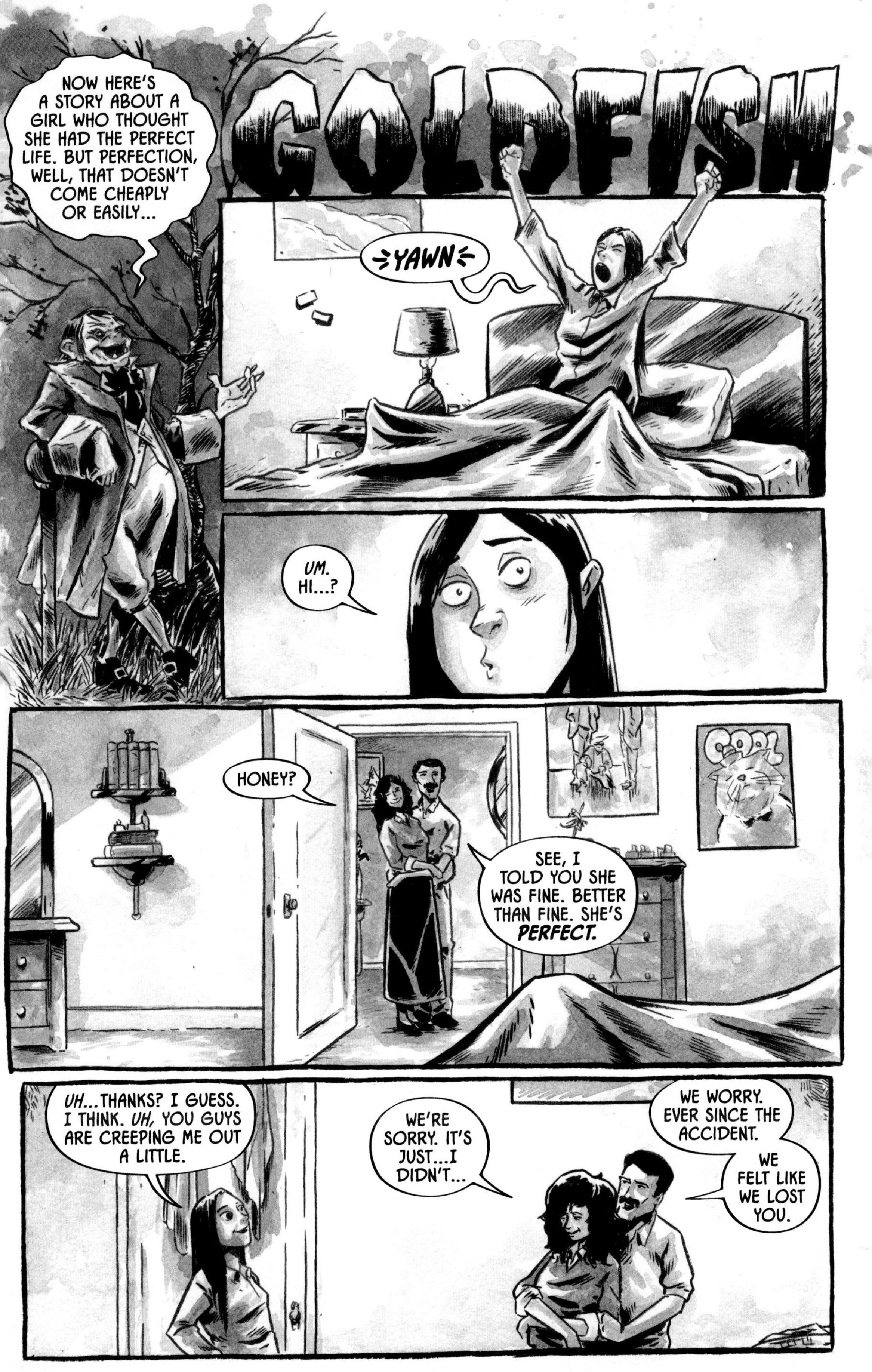
GOLDFISH
NOW HERE'S A STORY ABOUT A GIRL WHO THOUGHT SHE HAD THE PERFECT LIFE. BUT PERFECTION, WELL, THAT DOESN'T COME CHEAPLY OR EASILY...
YAWN
UM. HI...?
HONEY?
SEE, I TOLD YOU SHE WAS FINE. BETTER THAN FINE. SHE'S PERFECT.
COOL
UH...THANKS? I GUESS. I THINK. UH, YOU GUYS ARE CREEPING ME OUT A LITTLE.
WE'RE SORRY. IT'S JUST...I DIDN'T...
WE WORRY. EVER SINCE THE ACCIDENT.
WE FELT LIKE WE LOST YOU.

Script by JUSTIN JORDAN / Art by KELLY WILLIAMS

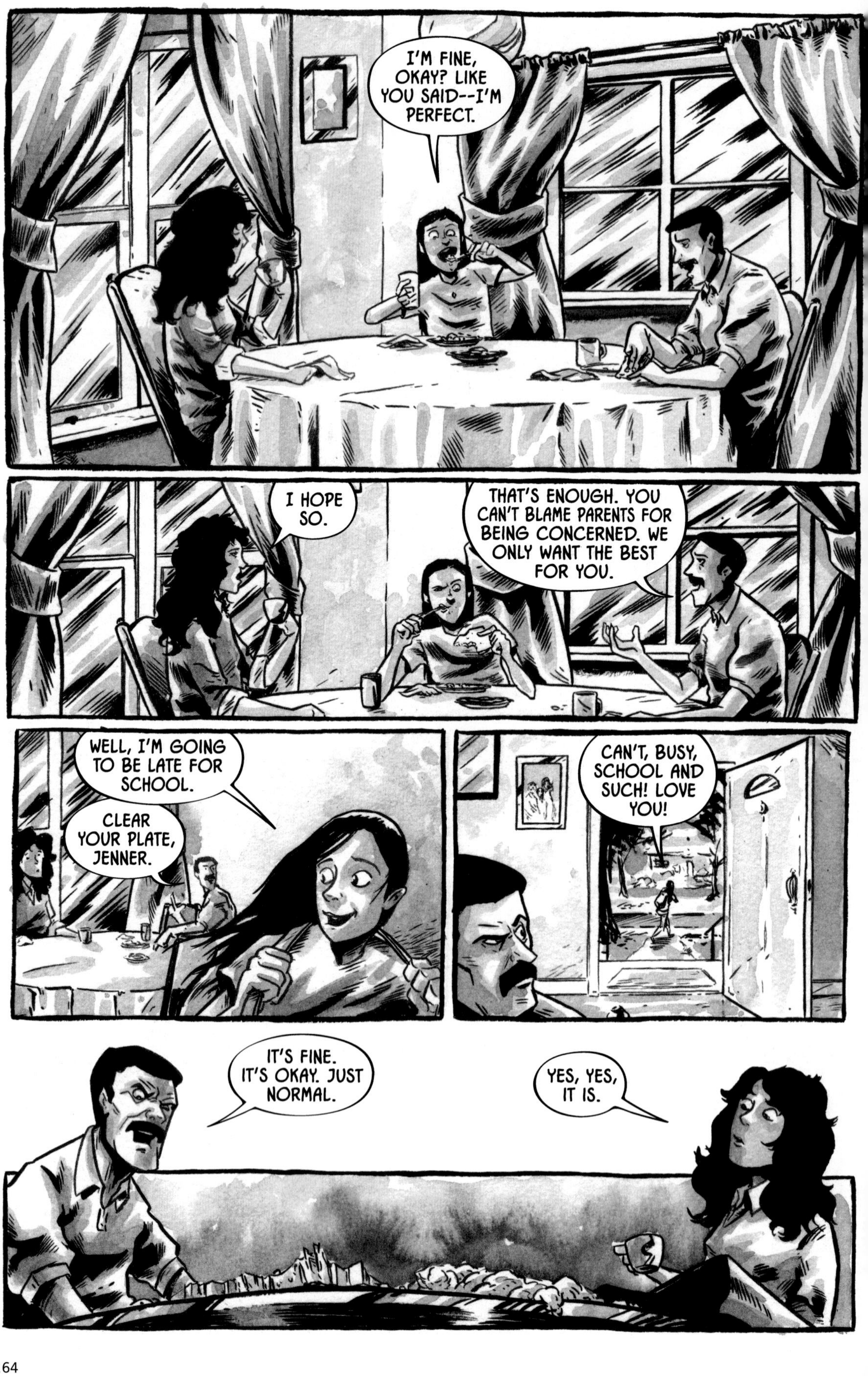

I'M FINE, OKAY? LIKE YOU SAID--I'M PERFECT.
I HOPE SO.
THAT'S ENOUGH. YOU CAN'T BLAME PARENTS FOR BEING CONCERNED. WE ONLY WANT THE BEST FOR YOU.
WELL, I'M GOING TO BE LATE FOR SCHOOL.
CLEAR YOUR PLATE, JENNER.
CAN'T, BUSY, SCHOOL AND SUCH! LOVE YOU!
IT'S FINE. IT'S OKAY. JUST NORMAL.
YES, YES, IT IS.

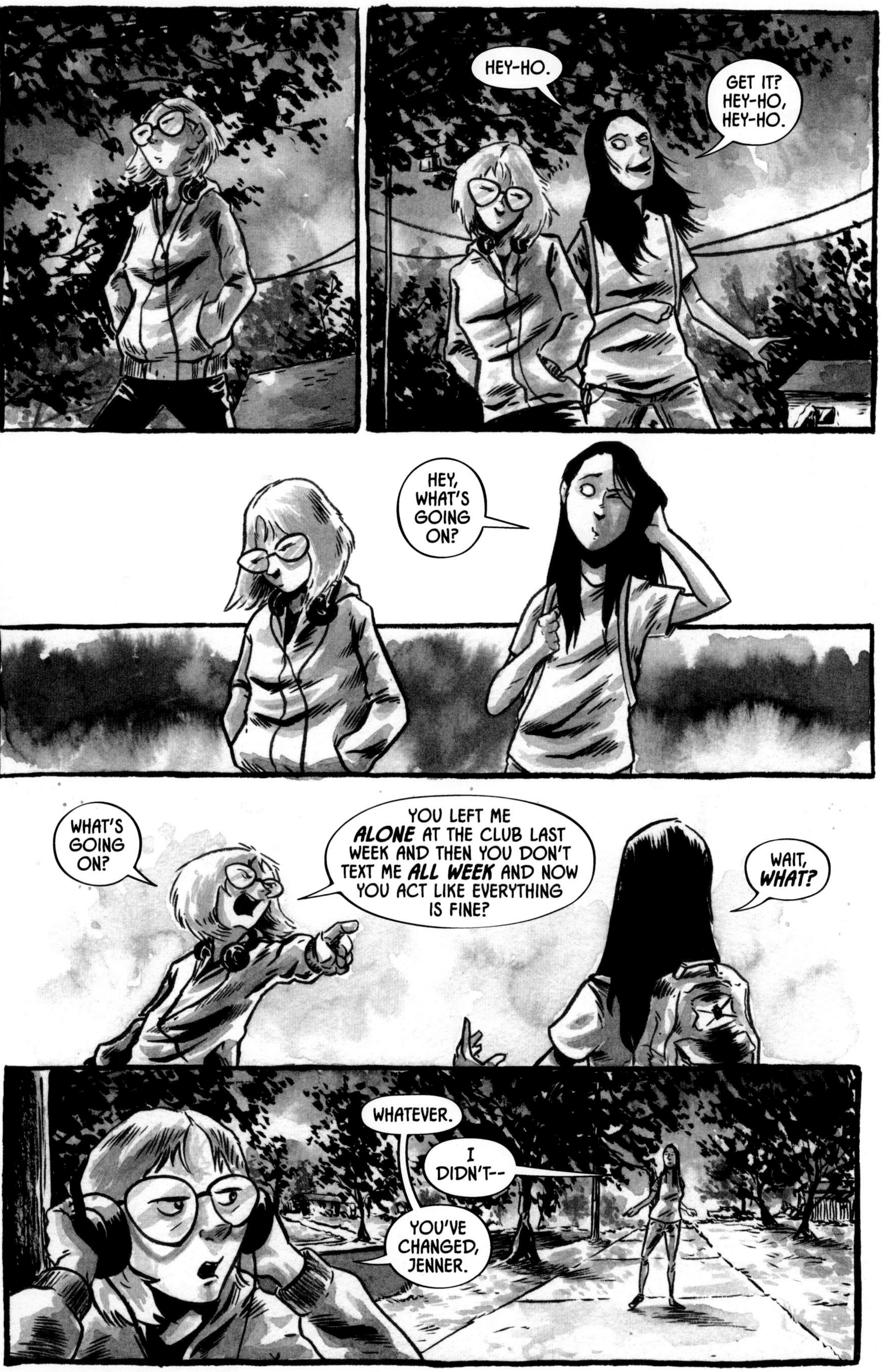
HEY-HO.
GET IT? HEY-HO, HEY-HO.
HEY, WHAT'S GOING ON?
WHAT'S GOING ON?
YOU LEFT ME **ALONE** AT THE CLUB LAST WEEK AND THEN YOU DON'T TEXT ME **ALL WEEK** AND NOW YOU ACT LIKE EVERYTHING IS FINE?
WAIT, **WHAT?**
WHATEVER.
I DIDN'T--
YOU'VE CHANGED, JENNER.

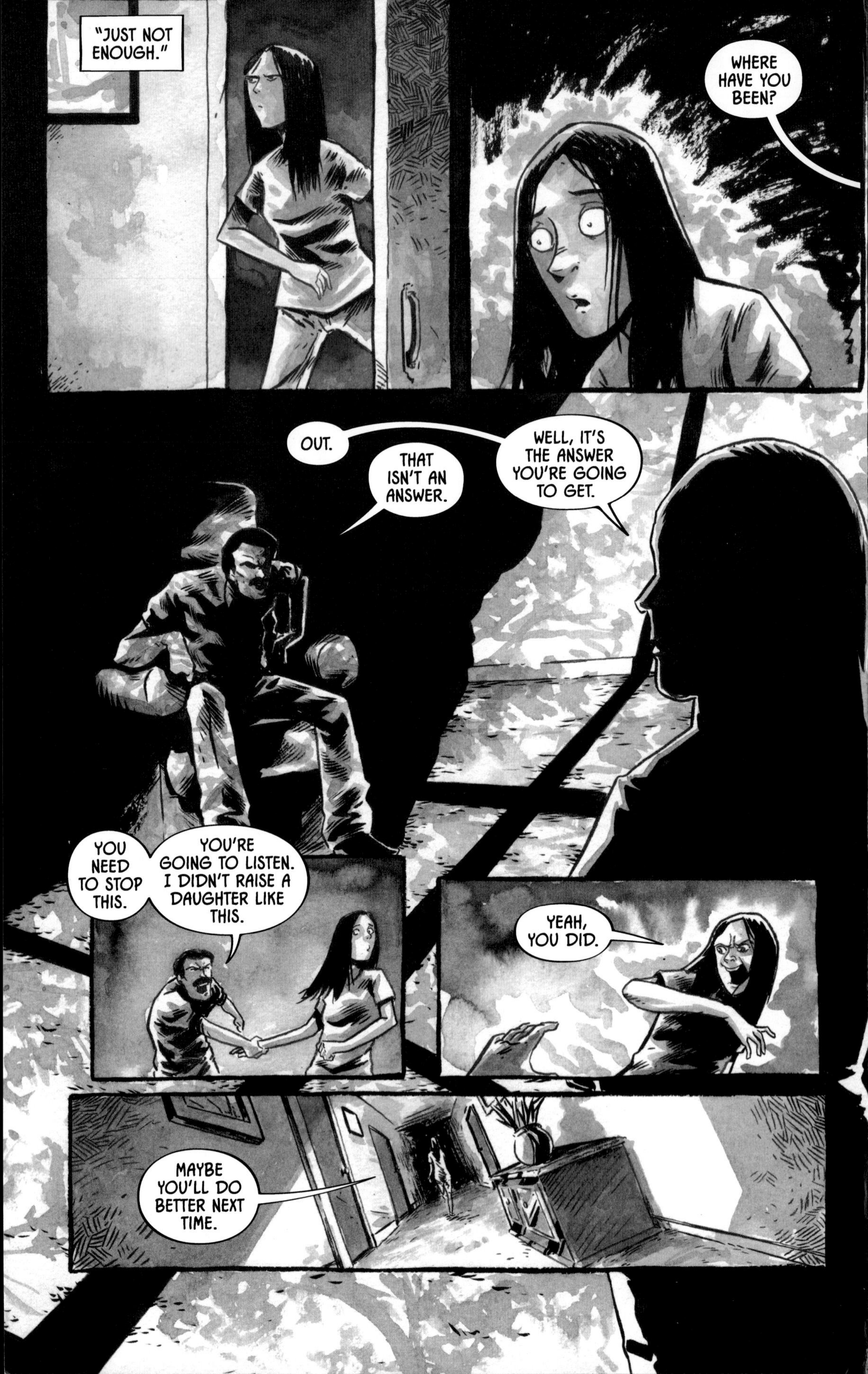
"JUST NOT ENOUGH."
WHERE HAVE YOU BEEN?
OUT.
THAT ISN'T AN ANSWER.
WELL, IT'S THE ANSWER YOU'RE GOING TO GET.
YOU NEED TO STOP THIS.
YOU'RE GOING TO LISTEN. I DIDN'T RAISE A DAUGHTER LIKE THIS.
YEAH, YOU DID.
MAYBE YOU'LL DO BETTER NEXT TIME.

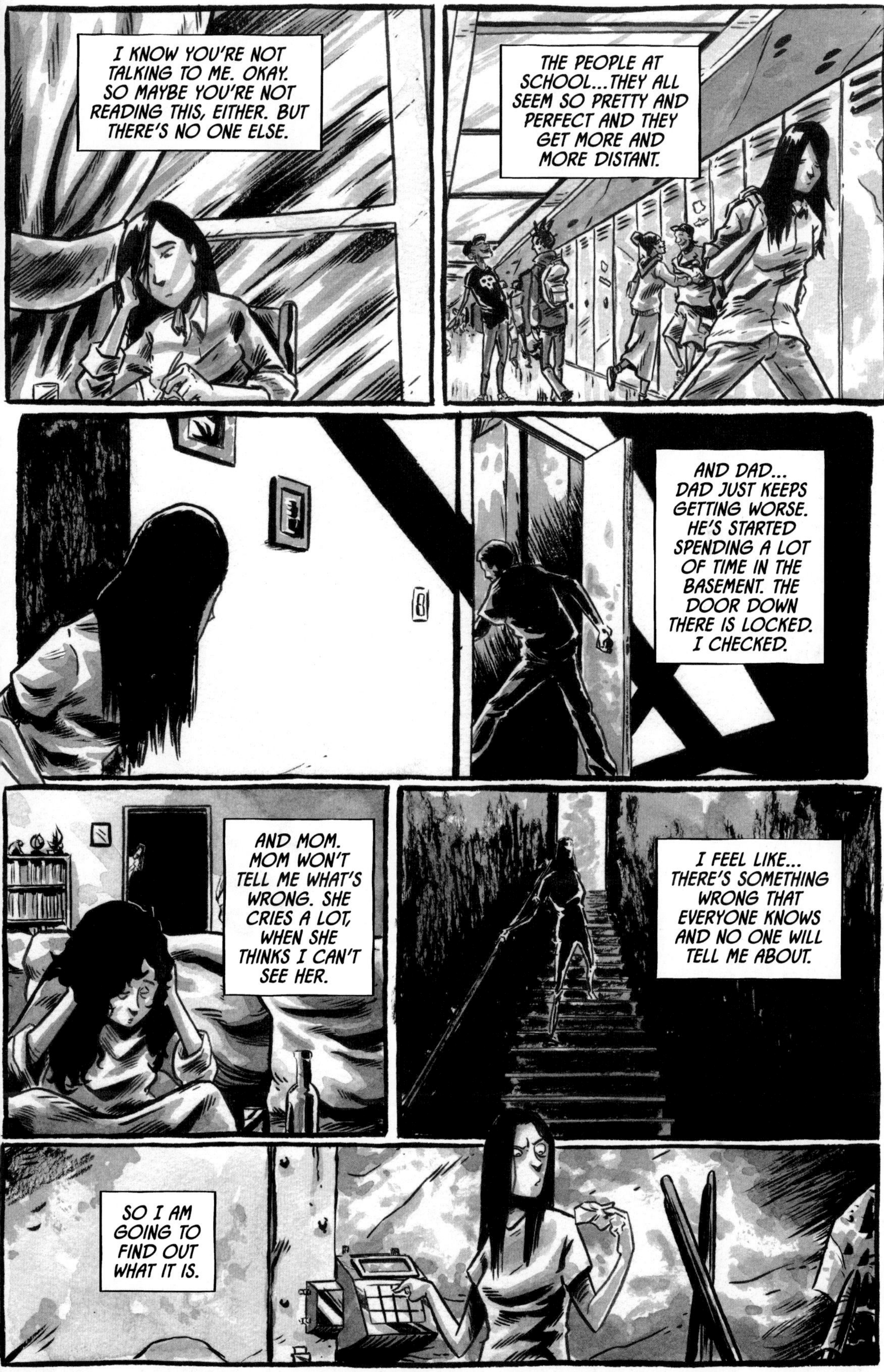
I KNOW YOU'RE NOT TALKING TO ME. OKAY. SO MAYBE YOU'RE NOT READING THIS, EITHER. BUT THERE'S NO ONE ELSE.
THE PEOPLE AT SCHOOL...THEY ALL SEEM SO PRETTY AND PERFECT AND THEY GET MORE AND MORE DISTANT.
AND DAD... DAD JUST KEEPS GETTING WORSE. HE'S STARTED SPENDING A LOT OF TIME IN THE BASEMENT. THE DOOR DOWN THERE IS LOCKED. I CHECKED.
AND MOM. MOM WON'T TELL ME WHAT'S WRONG. SHE CRIES A LOT, WHEN SHE THINKS I CAN'T SEE HER.
I FEEL LIKE... THERE'S SOMETHING WRONG THAT EVERYONE KNOWS AND NO ONE WILL TELL ME ABOUT.
SO I AM GOING TO FIND OUT WHAT IT IS.

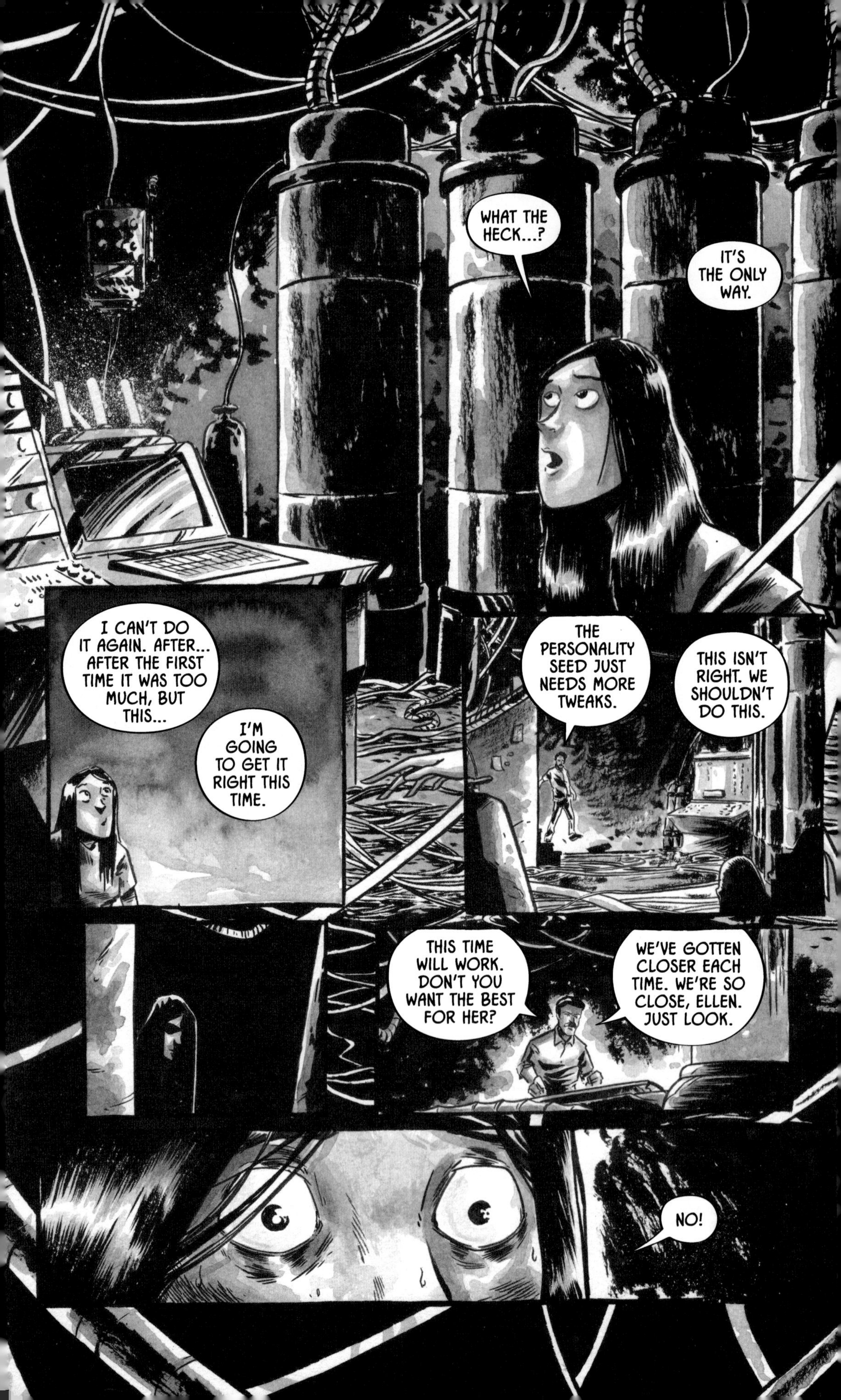
WHAT THE HECK...?
IT'S THE ONLY WAY.
I CAN'T DO IT AGAIN. AFTER... AFTER THE FIRST TIME IT WAS TOO MUCH, BUT THIS...
I'M GOING TO GET IT RIGHT THIS TIME.
THE PERSONALITY SEED JUST NEEDS MORE TWEAKS.
THIS ISN'T RIGHT. WE SHOULDN'T DO THIS.
THIS TIME WILL WORK. DON'T YOU WANT THE BEST FOR HER?
WE'VE GOTTEN CLOSER EACH TIME. WE'RE SO CLOSE, ELLEN. JUST LOOK.
NO!

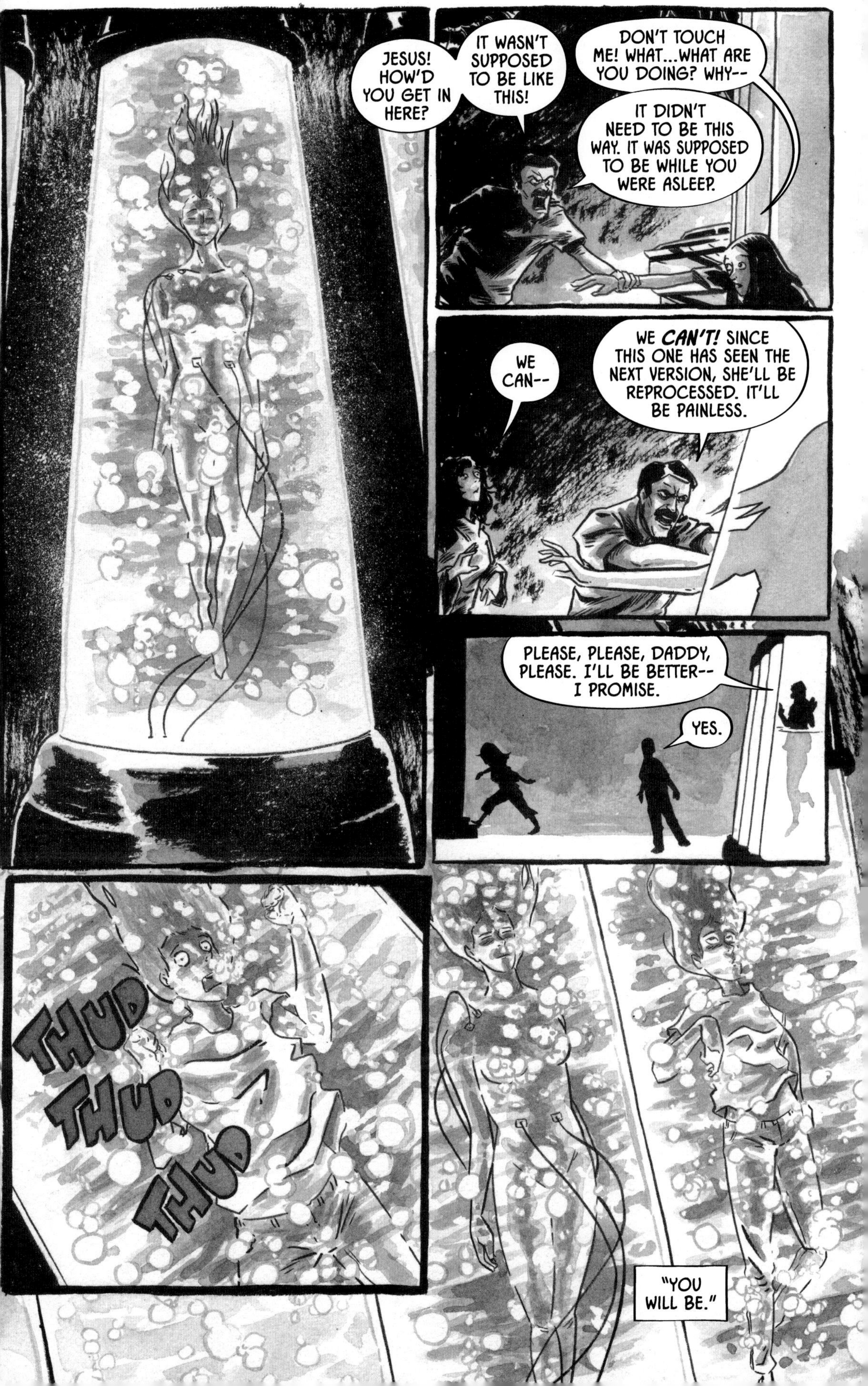

JESUS! HOW'D YOU GET IN HERE?
IT WASN'T SUPPOSED TO BE LIKE THIS!
DON'T TOUCH ME! WHAT...WHAT ARE YOU DOING? WHY--
IT DIDN'T NEED TO BE THIS WAY. IT WAS SUPPOSED TO BE WHILE YOU WERE ASLEEP.
WE CAN--
WE CAN'T! SINCE THIS ONE HAS SEEN THE NEXT VERSION, SHE'LL BE REPROCESSED. IT'LL BE PAINLESS.
PLEASE, PLEASE, DADDY, PLEASE. I'LL BE BETTER-- I PROMISE.
YES.
THUD THUD THUD
"YOU WILL BE."

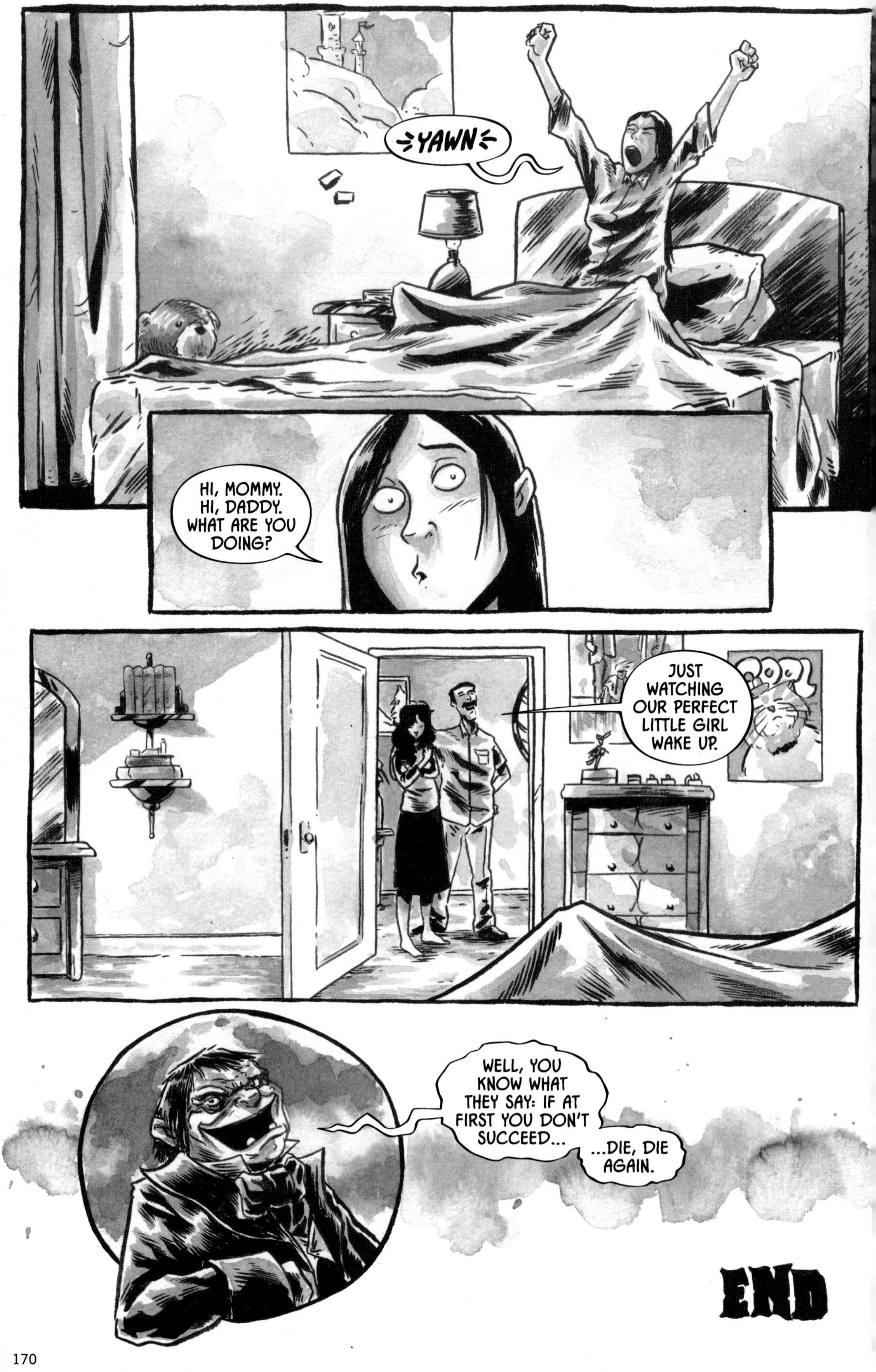
YAWN
HI, MOMMY. HI, DADDY. WHAT ARE YOU DOING?
JUST WATCHING OUR PERFECT LITTLE GIRL WAKE UP.
WELL, YOU KNOW WHAT THEY SAY: IF AT FIRST YOU DON'T SUCCEED...
...DIE, DIE AGAIN.
END

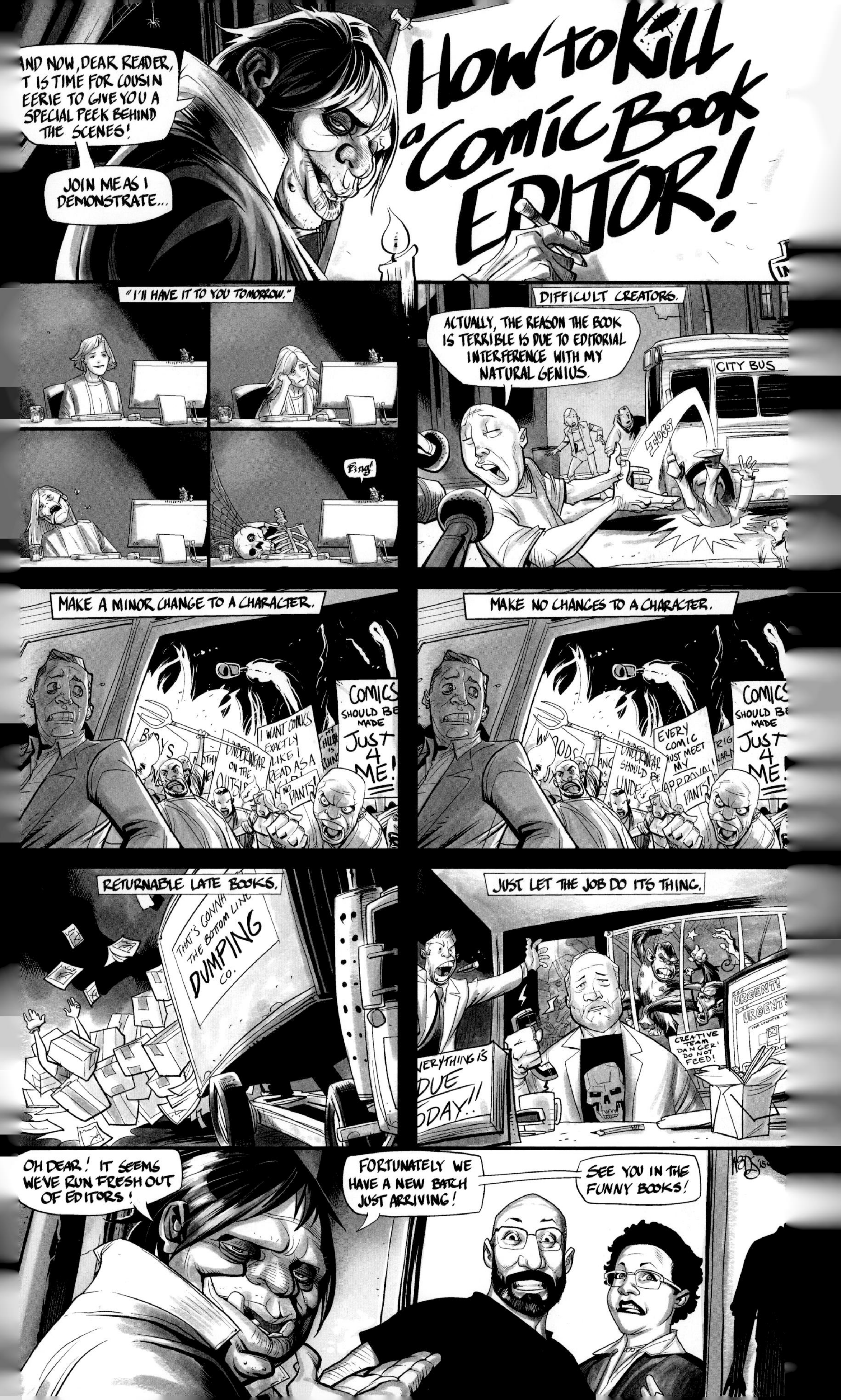

How to Kill a Comic Book EDITOR!
AND NOW, DEAR READER, IT IS TIME FOR COUSIN EERIE TO GIVE YOU A SPECIAL PEEK BEHIND THE SCENES!
JOIN ME AS I DEMONSTRATE...
"I'LL HAVE IT TO YOU TOMORROW."
Ping!
DIFFICULT CREATORS.
ACTUALLY, THE REASON THE BOOK IS TERRIBLE IS DUE TO EDITORIAL INTERFERENCE WITH MY NATURAL GENIUS.
CITY BUS
TOSS
MAKE A MINOR CHANGE TO A CHARACTER.
I WANT COMICS EXACTLY LIKE I READ AS A KID
UNDERWEAR ON THE OUTSIDE
NO PANTS!
COMICS SHOULD BE MADE JUST 4 ME!
MAKE NO CHANGES TO A CHARACTER.
EVERY COMIC MUST MEET MY APPROVAL!
UNDERWEAR SHOULD BE
PANTS!
COMICS SHOULD BE MADE JUST 4 ME!
RETURNABLE LATE BOOKS.
THE BOTTOM LINE
DUMPING CO.
JUST LET THE JOB DO ITS THING.
URGENT!
CREATIVE TEAM DANGER! DO NOT FEED!
ERYTHING IS DUE ODAY!!
OH DEAR! IT SEEMS WE'VE RUN FRESH OUT OF EDITORS!
FORTUNATELY WE HAVE A NEW BATCH JUST ARRIVING!
SEE YOU IN THE FUNNY BOOKS!

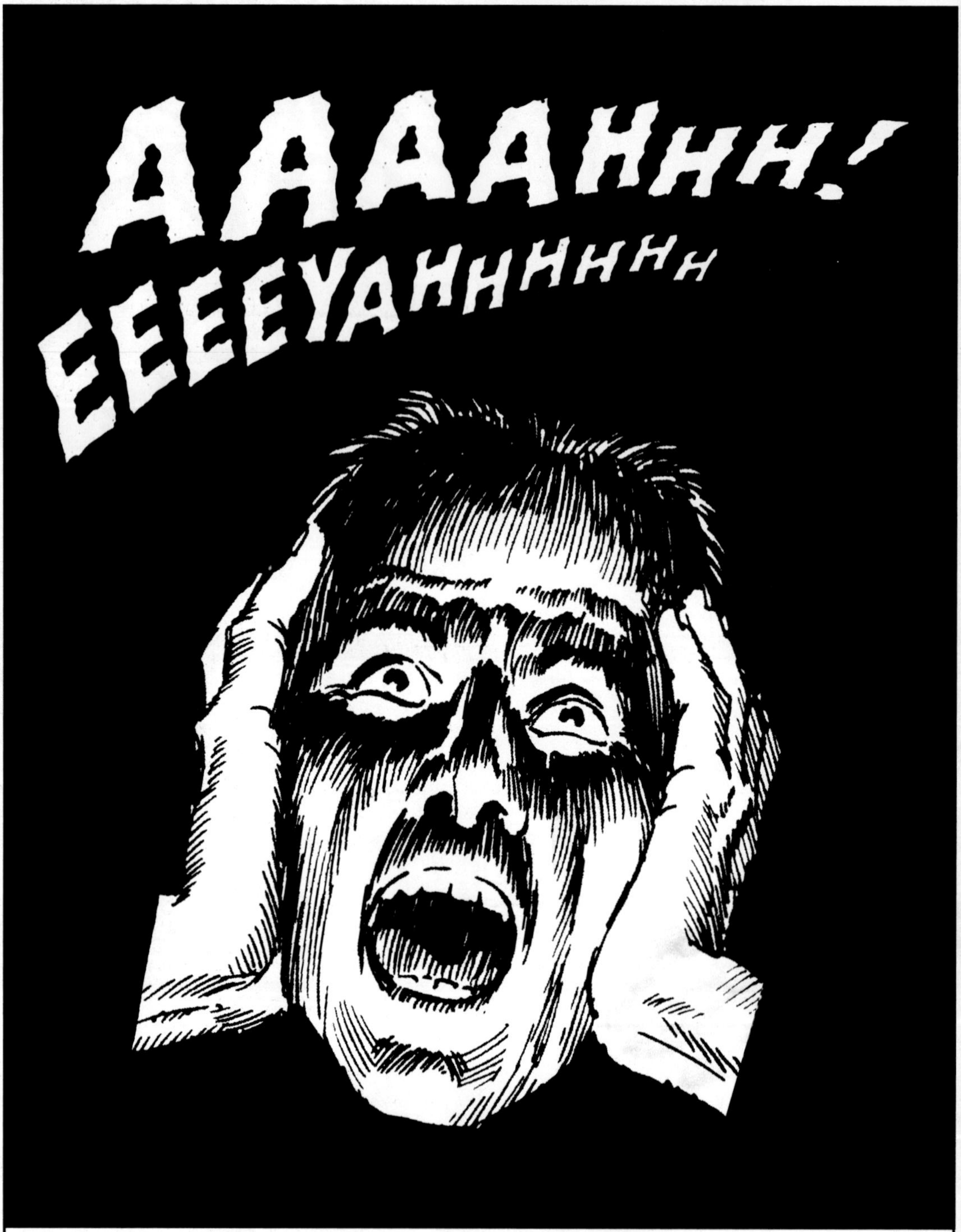
AAAAHHH!
EEEEYAHHHHHHH

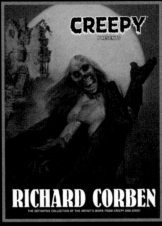

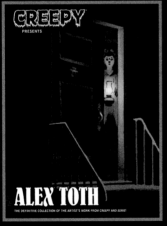
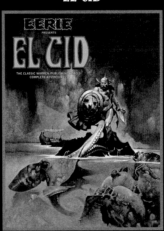

CREEPY™

ARCHIVES

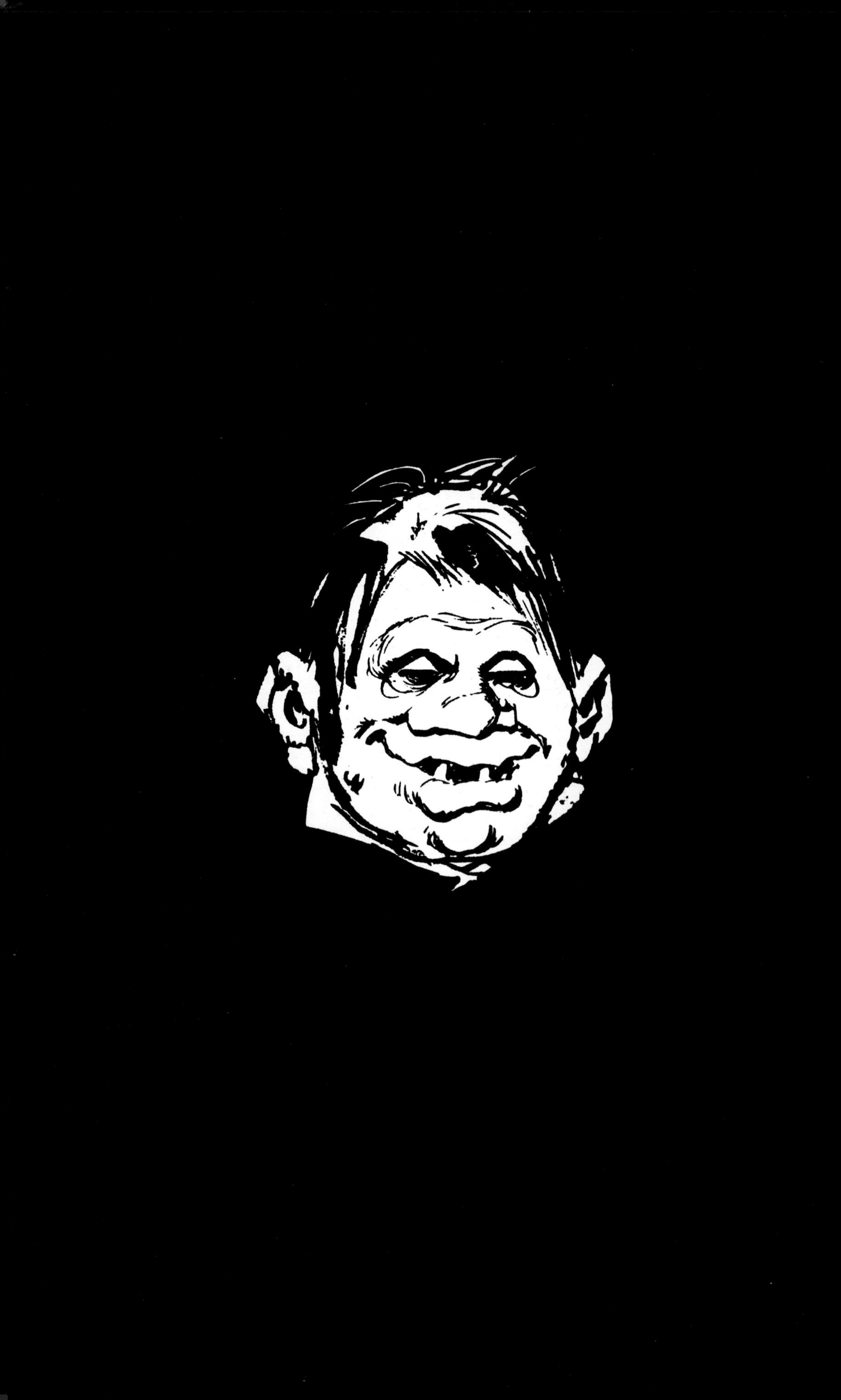

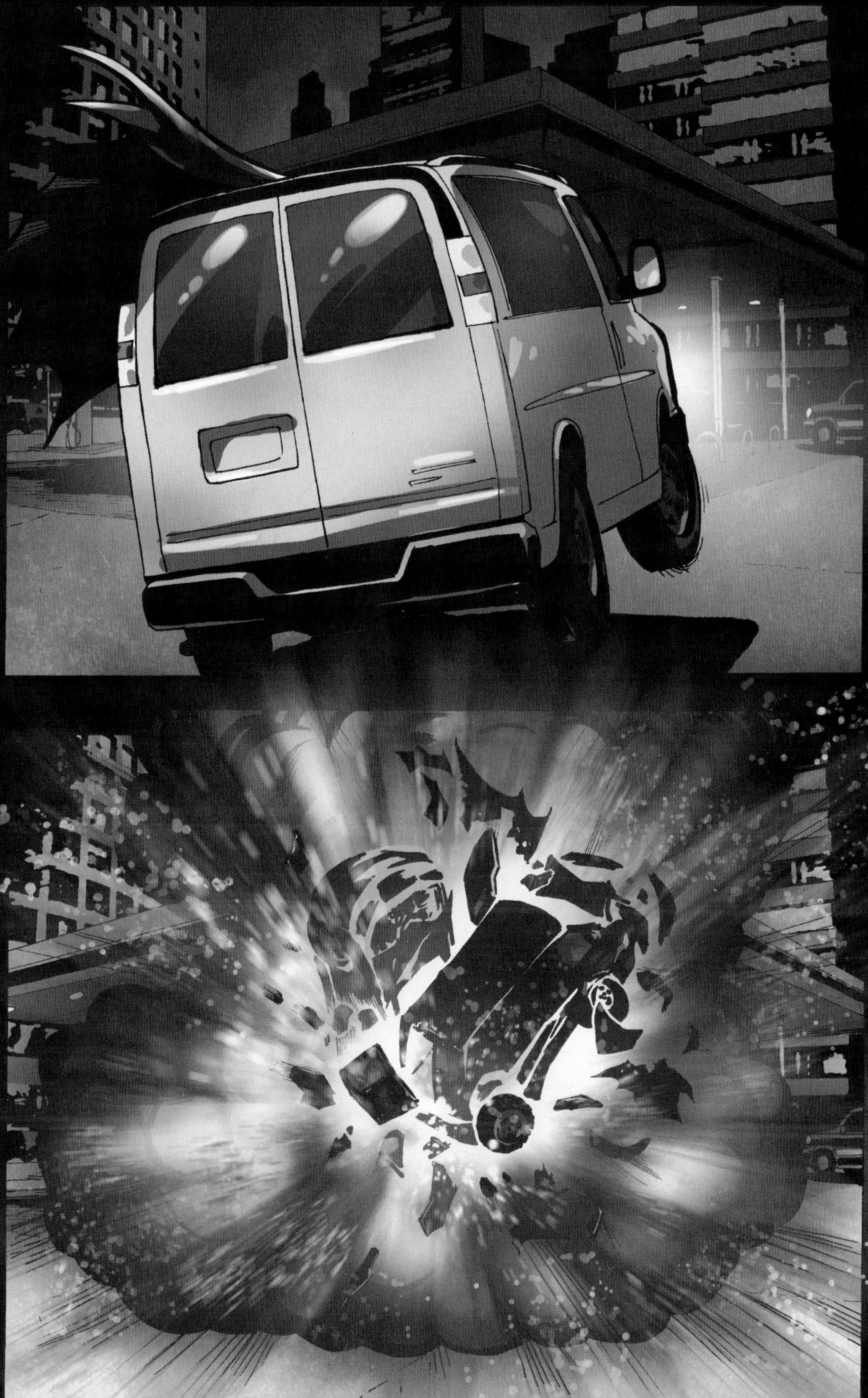

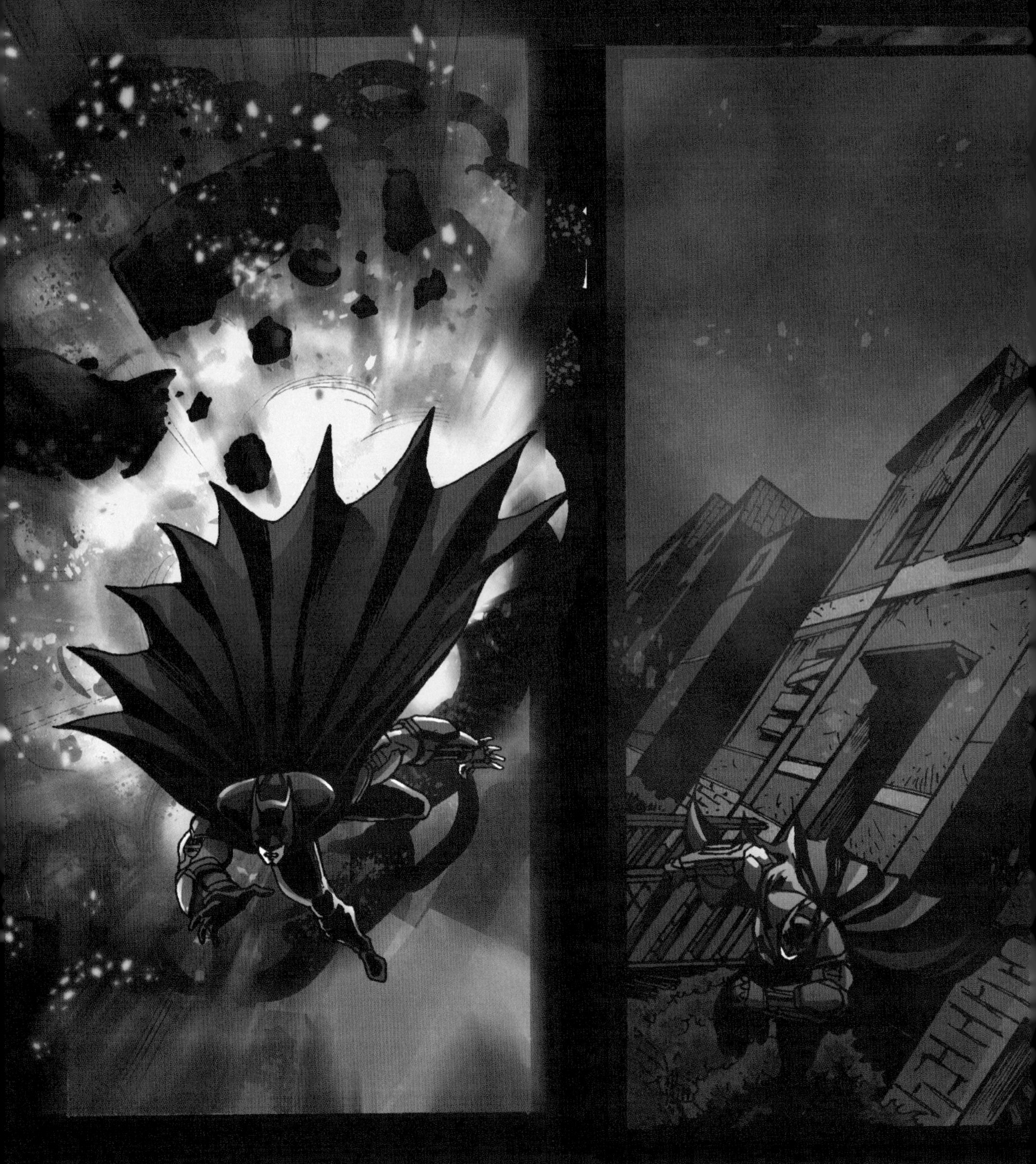

BASED ON THE BEST-SELLING VIDEO GAME

BATMAN: ARKHAM CITY

BATMAN: ARKHAM
UNHINGED VOL. 1

BATMAN: ARKHAM
UNHINGED VOL. 2

BATMAN: ARKHAM
UNHINGED VOL. 3

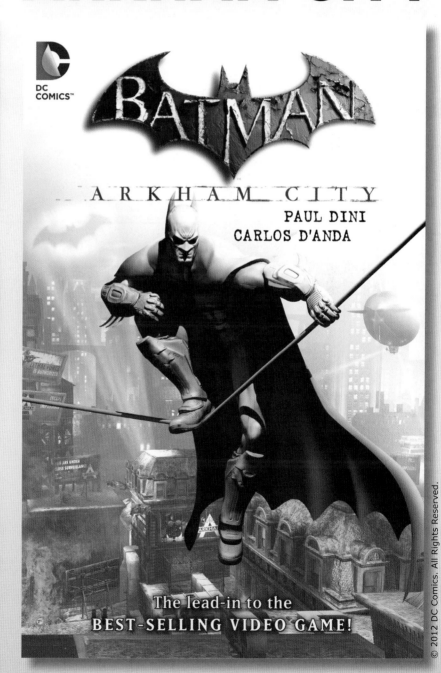

DC
COMICS™

PAUL DINI
CARLOS D'ANDA

The lead-in to the
BEST-SELLING VIDEO GAME!

"*[Writer Scott Snyder] pulls from the oldes[t] aspects of the Batman myth, combines it with sinister-comi[c] elements from the series' best period, and gives the whol[e] thing terrific forward-spin.*"—ENTERTAINMENT WEEKL[Y]

START AT THE BEGINNING!

BATMAN VOLUME 1: THE COURT OF OWLS

BATMAN VOL. 2: THE CITY OF OWLS

with SCOTT SNYDER and GREG CAPULLO

BATMAN VOL. 3: DEATH OF THE FAMILY

with SCOTT SNYDER and GREG CAPULLO

BATMAN: NIGHT OF THE OWLS

with SCOTT SNYDER and GREG CAPULLO

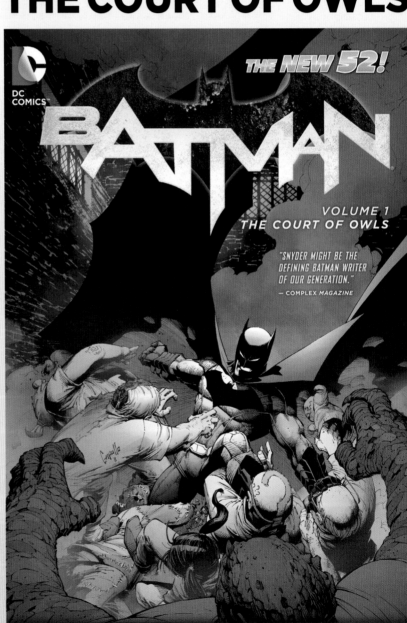

THE NEW 52!

VOLUME 1
THE COURT OF OWLS

"*SNYDER MIGHT BE THE DEFINING BATMAN WRITER OF OUR GENERATION.*"
— COMPLEX MAGAZINE

SCOTT **SNYDER**   GREG **CAPULLO**   JONATHAN **GLAPION**

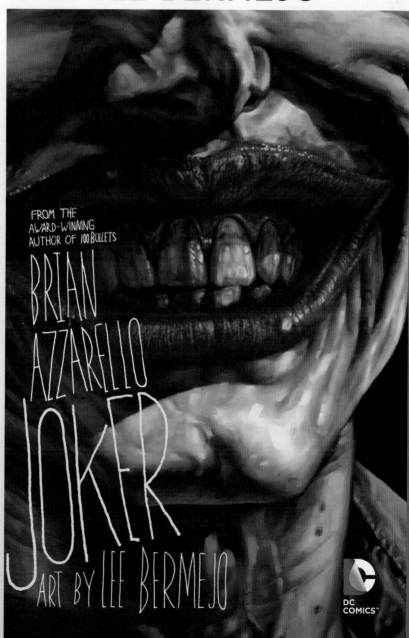

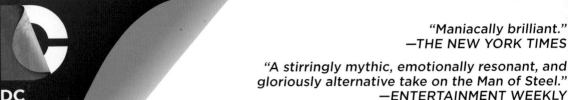

GRANT MORRISON
with FRANK QUITELY

FINAL CRISIS

with J.G. JONES, CARLOS
PACHECO & DOUG MAHNKE

BATMAN:
ARKHAM ASYLUM

with DAVE McKEAN

SEVEN SOLDIERS OF
VICTORY VOLS. 1 & 2

with J.H. WILLIAMS III &
VARIOUS ARTISTS